AMERICA, ROOSEVELT, AND WORLD WAR II

By the Same Author and Published by
New York University Press

America in the Gilded Age: Second Edition

America in the Age of the Titans:
The Progressive Era and World War I

America in the Twenties and Thirties:
The Olympian Age of Franklin Delano Roosevelt

AMERICA, ROOSEVELT, AND WORLD WAR II

Sean Dennis Cashman

NEW YORK UNIVERSITY PRESS
NEW YORK AND LONDON

Library of Congress Cataloging-in-Publication Data
Cashman, Sean Dennis.
America, Roosevelt, and World War II / Sean Dennis Cashman.
p.   cm.
Bibliography: p.
Includes index.
ISBN 0-8147-1430-7 (alk. paper)
1. World War, 1939–1945—Diplomatic history.   2. Roosevelt,
Franklin D. (Franklin Delano), 1882–1945.   3. World War, 1939–1945—
United States.   I. Title.
D753.C37   1989
940.53′2273—dc20   89-32855
CIP

New York University Press books are printed on acid-free paper,
and their binding materials are chosen for strength and durability.

Book design by Ken Venezio

For my mother,
MARGARET CASHMAN

CONTENTS

ILLUSTRATIONS

PREFACE
1939 and 1941

America, Roosevelt, and World War II is published to commemorate the fiftieth anniversaries of two tragic events of 1939 and 1941. On September 1, 1939, German troops invaded Poland in pursuit of Adolf Hitler's evil strategy of conquering Europe. On September 3, Britain and France, determined to stop him, declared war on Germany. World War II had begun. On December 7, 1941, a skillful Japanese task force launched a devastating, unprovoked, and surprise attack on the American Pacific Fleet and naval base at Pearl Harbor; the following day the United States declared war on Japan. In between came Hitler's invasion of the Soviet Union on June 22, 1941. These events reshaped the world and helped propel the United States to supreme global power as the Grand Alliance of America, Britain, and Russia determined to oust the Axis powers of Germany, Italy, and Japan; to free the nations they had subjugated; and to eliminate their fascist forms of government.

The book developed out of a series of interdisciplinary histories of the United States published by New York University Press: *America in the Gilded Age*, covering the period 1865 to 1901; *America in the Age of the Titans*, covering the Progressive Era and World War I; and *America in the Twenties and Thirties: The Olympian Age of Franklin Delano Roosevelt.* It aims at a succinct presentation of the essential facts about this brief period in which the United States assumed global preeminence.

The text is based partly on primary research and partly on a synthesis of secondary sources. It is accompanied by a selection of illustrations, consisting of photographs, cartoons, and reproductions of paintings of the dramatic events of World War II culled primarily from the Library of Congress.

Once again, Colin Jones, director of New York University Press, responded generously to the idea of a military and social history of American involvement in World War II and continuously offered constructive suggestions about composition and structure. Without the valiant help of my friend Stephen Harrison, formerly of the University of Manchester, England, my task would have been longer. He undertook comprehensive reviews of military and naval operations in the European and Asian theaters, of wartime diplomacy, and of various facets of American life on the home front from which I could draw. I appreciate his skill and greatly value his historical judgments. The book also pursues certain stories from *America in the Twenties and Thirties.* Thus, I continue to draw on work from other friends: Daniel Couzens, who provided a draft on wartime radio; and Chris Hasson, who wrote on labor.

In order to set the scene, I have incorporated some of the text from the last chapter of *America in the Twenties and Thirties* on the subjects of the twisting paths of war in Europe and Asia and on America's increasing involvement in World War II before the attack on Pearl Harbor.

The manuscript was typed partly by Eileen Grimes of the University of Manchester, England, and partly by Lee Plaut and Dorothy Kreppein of Adelphi University, Garden City, New York. In fact, the encouragement shown by my generous colleagues at Adelphi to this project was much appreciated in the crucial, final stages of composition and publication in late 1988 and early 1989. Once again, Mary Ison and Maja Felaco of the Prints and Photographs Division of the Library of Congress were helpful in the selection of illustrations. The index was devised by Robert Madison.

AMERICA, ROOSEVELT, AND WORLD WAR II

[1]

A FORTRESS ON A PAPER PAD
The Gathering Storm of War

"YESTERDAY, DECEMBER 7, 1941—a day which will live in infamy —the United States of America was suddenly and deliberately attacked by naval and air forces of the empire of Japan." Thus did President Franklin Delano Roosevelt deliver his war message to Congress on December 8, 1941. Congress responded by authorizing a declaration of war against Japan that very day.

The Japanese attack, led by waves of carrier-based Japanese dive bombers, torpedo planes, and fighters, lasted two hours and almost demolished the American fleet and the military installations at Pearl Harbor, Honolulu, Hawaii. Altogether 2,403 Americans were killed and another 1,178 wounded. This tragic event was the bitter climax to years of infamy in world affairs. One of the most crucial events in the whole of world history, not only did the attack on Pearl Harbor lead to America's formal intervention in World War II but also to America's evident dominance of the globe—by virtue of its physical and industrial resources, its economic superiority, its great military potential, and the commitment of its people to the spirit of democratic capitalism across the world.

For three days after America's declaration of war on Hitler's distant ally, Japan, the führer's advisers in Berlin argued against a declaration of war on the United States by Germany whatever the terms of its agreement with Japan. However, somewhat frustrated by setbacks in his bitter Russian campaign and infuriated by America's support of Britain in the Atlantic, Hitler announced his declaration of war on December 11, 1941.

America's entry into a war against Germany and Japan on the side of Britain, France, and Russia reinforced a common spirit of allegiance among the English-speaking peoples across the world. This communality had been growing ever since Britain and France had declared war on Germany twenty-seven months earlier on September 3, 1939—the very start of World War II. Fearful of Germany's designs against Poland, Britain's prime minister, Neville Chamberlain, had provided Poland with an Anglo-French guarantee of its integrity in early 1939. In fact, he had never consulted France. Britain had no way of keeping its bargain with Poland, nor did it provide money for military materiel. Hitler had called Chamberlain's bluff by repudiating Germany's non-aggression pact with Poland of 1934 and an early Anglo-German naval agreement of 1935.

Britain and France could not guarantee Poland without the support of Russia, the mighty nation on Poland's eastern front. Chamberlain did not truly trust the Russians; nevertheless, his government pursued protracted negotiations in Moscow in the spring and summer of 1939. To his dismay, on August 23 the foreign ministers of the Soviet Union and Germany, Vyacheslav Molotov and Joachim von Ribbentrop, signed a Russo-German pact in Moscow by which Russia would stay neutral if Germany went to war. Sensing that this was the prelude to an imminent partition of Poland, the British and Poles signed an alliance on August 25. In reality, Hitler wanted Poland's industrial resources and was determined to recover Germany's ascendancy over Poland that had been lost in 1919 at the end of World War I. After the Polish foreign minister, Józef Beck, refused to negotiate with Hitler at the behest of the fearful British cabinet, German troops crossed the frontier and invaded Poland on September 1, 1939.

Despite their previous assurances, Neville Chamberlain, his foreign secretary, Viscount Halifax, and Georges Bonnet, the French foreign minister, supported a proposal from Hitler's ally in Europe, Benito

"A day which will live in infamy." Pearl Harbor attacked. A small boat rescues a seaman from the 31,800-ton USS *West Virginia*, engulfed by smoke and flame from the yawning gap created by a Japanese bomb amidships. Two other servicemen on high await rescue. Behind lies the USS *Tennessee*. (U.S. Navy; Office of Public Relations and Office of War Information; Prints and Photographs Division, Library of Congress).

Mussolini, the fascist dictator of Italy, for a conference. However, when Chamberlain reported this to the outraged House of Commons in London on September 2, the antagonistic response there made it clear that his only possible policy would be an ultimatum delivered to Germany on September 3 and war if it expired without satisfactory assurances. This was what happened. Thus, ironically, Britain and France went to war against Germany over a state they could not defend. France and the four British dominions of Australia, New Zealand, Canada, and South Africa followed the British declaration of war against Germany with their own. Within eleven days, the Germans had subdued Poland. This was the

3

blitzkrieg—the lightning war. For centuries the cardinal features of British foreign policy had been to prevent any great European power seizing the hegemony of Europe—especially on the coastline of the English Channel. When great powers had either attempted or succeeded in gaining control of the coast opposite England in days gone by, Britain had gone to war in Europe. This had been a prime cause of antagonism between British rulers and, in succession, Philip II of Spain, Louis XIV of France, Napoleon, and Wilhelm II of Germany.

The Nazi Threat

The tragic words *appeasement* and *isolationism* hung over the infamous events of the 1930s. It seemed that whether the three little pigs built their houses of straw or hay, the big bad wolf huffed and puffed and blew them all down.

It is tempting to characterize the United States, Britain, and France as three terrified and squealing little pigs and Adolf Hitler of Germany as the big bad wolf, yet the real wolf was the ravenous nature of war itself, made more terrible by the way civilization fed its appetite with societal competitiveness and man-made munitions. However, the metaphor of unsafe houses is appropriate. In the 1930s France presumed itself secure behind the military defenses of the Maginot line; Britain counted on its naval superiority; and the United States believed a policy of isolation would serve as insulation from war. All they achieved was what poet Edna St. Vincent Millay called "a fortress on a paper pad." British and American aloofness from international cooperation was to prove futile and brought about its own tragedy.

To Italy, Germany, and Japan, the League of Nations (the international organization established at the end of World War I to prevent any such future conflagrations) was a conspiracy of nations—the possessive against the dispossessed. If the Japanese invasion of the Chinese outer province of Manchuria on September 18, 1931, was a crucial turning point between war and peace in the 1930s, the central event was the rise of Germany under the National Socialist, or Nazi, dictatorship of Adolf Hitler.

Adolf Hitler (1889–1945), a native of Austria and the feared dictator of Germany (1933–45)—as, first, chancellor from January 1933 and,

Disaster at Pearl Harbor despite the late attempts of American servicemen to limit the damage of fire to the USS *West Virginia* and the USS *Tennessee*. (Office of War Information; Library of Congress).

then, as president and chancellor, or führer (leader), from August 1934 —was the politically ambitious and willful son of an overindulgent mother. From the start he was incapable of establishing ordinary relationships. He found relief and fulfillment in military service for Germany in World War I and determined to take political power as an astute leader of the *Nationalsozialist Deutsch Arbeiterpartei* (the German Workers' party), or, for short, the Nazi party. When Hitler joined the party he found it to be small and ineffectual, largely because its aims were uncertain. He decided to create a mass movement through unrelenting propaganda, using such tools as German anti-Semitism and a gang of willing cronies—Alfred Rosenberg, Rudolf Hess, Hermann Göring, and Julius Streicher. Their abortive (beer hall) *Putsch* in Munich of November 1923, in which Hitler tried to get leaders of the *Land* government to proclaim a national revolution against the disorderly

5

Weimar Republic, ended in failure; and Hitler was imprisoned for nine months.

In prison Hitler wrote the first volume of *Mein Kampf,* which drew together earlier discredited ideas of anti-Semitism, totalitarianism, and capitalist cartels. He proclaimed that the natural unit of man was the *Volk* and that the greatest of all these *Volk*s were the German people. He believed that the state existed to serve the *Volk* and that the Weimar Republic had betrayed this trust. Thus, democratic government in Germany stood condemned. It presumed an equality in the *Volk* that did not exist. Unity could only be provided with a führer of absolute authority served by the Nazi party or movement. Yet the enemy of the *Volk* was not democracy but, rather, Marxist communism with its emphasis on class conflict and international socialism. The shadow behind Marxism was the Jewish people upon whom Hitler projected all his fears and hatred.

Upon his release from prison, Hitler reconstructed the ailing party and built it up despite opposition from a rival movement in the north and various prohibitions on his making speeches in public. The world economic slump that began in 1929 provided special opportunities for growth, partly because of widespread public dissatisfaction with the Weimar Republic and partly because of the alliances Hitler forged with magnates of industry and business. They were anxious to fund him and his party as a front for a strong, antidemocratic, right-wing government. Hitler demonstrated a devastating ability to exploit perilous conditions to his political advantage. Eventually, he was invited by the aged president, Paul von Hindenburg, to become chancellor of Germany on January 30, 1933.

The terrifying days of the Third Reich, the German empire that was intended to last for one thousand years, had begun. Hitler's rule lasted for almost the identical period as the presidency of Franklin Delano Roosevelt in the United States (1933–45). However, whereas FDR governed to achieve a balance of various capitalist and democratic

The ominous panoply of imperial power associated with the Third Reich included precise military formations, with monster banners carrying giant swastikas like great slashes in the sky. In this scene, Adolf Hitler *(center)* appears with Göring and Streicher, all giving the Nazi salute. (Library of Congress).

elements, Hitler proceeded to establish an absolute dictatorship, first by an enabling bill in the Reichstag assembly giving him full power on March 23, 1933. When von Hindenburg died on August 2, 1934, the offices of chancellor and president were merged, allowing the führer absolute control of the army and of public policy. Hitler instituted a reign of terror to maintain his control but left detailed administration to his team of managers.

The period of nazism in Germany, in which totalitarian government was achieved by a malign alliance of political dictatorship, business monopoly, and military support, has become synonymous with an underlying theme of decay in Oswald Spengler's *The Decline of the West* (1926–28), a book that is not widely read. However, the book's allusive title evokes such things as the suppression of democratic government, the use of brute force at home and abroad in pursuit of absolute control, and the debasing of the humanistic impulse in culture. Nazism employed such crimes against the human race as exploitation of labor, concentration camps, war, and genocide and made them acceptable to their perpetrators. This evil was characterized as much by banality as by barbarianism, and the appetite for savagery grew with each atrocity.

The most significant of Hitler's innermost advisers included Rudolf Hess, Joseph Goebbels, Hermann Göring, and Heinrich Himmler. Their names have become synonymous with the basest acts that can be conceived in the darkest recesses of the human soul. Rudolf Hess (1894–1987) was Hitler's deputy and minister of state until 1941. Joseph Goebbels (1897–1945) was the Nazi orator and propagandist whose effectively staged parades and mass meetings helped Hitler to power and who served him as enlightenment and propaganda minister. Hermann Göring (1893–1946) served a variety of functions at different times — as commander of the German air force from 1934, as head of the Gestapo until 1936, as minister for foreign affairs from 1937 and as Hitler's first deputy from 1938 to 1943. Heinrich Himmler (1900–1945) was chief of the SS from 1929, and chief of all police services from 1936, head of the Reich administration from 1939, and interior minister and commander of the reserve army.

The most cruel agencies of the Nazis were the Gestapo and the SS. The Gestapo, or *Geheime Staatspolizei*, was the Nazi secret police, which Hermann Göring had reorganized from the Prussian plain-clothed police in 1933. From 1934 the Gestapo was absorbed into the SS, or

An evil empire. The massed legions of the Wehrmacht appear before their adoring führer, in an overwhelming display of military discipline with seemingly endless troops extending to the horizon like flowerbeds in a nursery. (A film still from *Mein Kampf*. Columbia Pictures, 1961; Museum of Modern Art Film Stills Archive).

Schutzstaffel, by Heinrich Himmler. The *Schutzstaffel* (protective echelon) was an elite body within the Nazi party founded by Hitler in 1925 as a personal bodyguard. From 1925 until the end of the Third Reich, it was led by Himmler who organized it in two principal groups, the Allgemeine SS (General SS) and the Waffen-SS (Armed SS). In 1939 the Gestapo was merged with the SD, or *Sicherheitsdienst* (Security Service), the intelligence branch of the SS under Reinhard Heydrich. It was the SS and the Gestapo that controlled concentration camps and established secret police in every country occupied by Germany.

Hitler's overwhelming political success in seizing and maintaining power at home in his early years can be attributed to the susceptibility of Germany after World War I to Hitler's own special talents as a political opportunist of the first rank. There was no one who equaled his ability to exploit and shape events to his own ends. The power Hitler exercised was quite without precedent both in its scope and in the technical resources at his command. By the time he was defeated in 1945, Hitler had broken down the structure of the world in which he lived; and he left behind a Germany and a Europe that have remained divided ever since.

Hitler's expansionist foreign policy had two aims. The first was to unify all German-speaking peoples in Europe in the Third Reich. These included minorities, such as the Sudeten Germans in Czechoslovakia, and the Germans in Poland, and other entire nations, such as Austria. His second aim was to gain control of all of Europe. Both aims involved undermining the Treaty of Versailles of 1919 that set limits on German armaments and on Germany's quest for additional living space. Hitler's foreign policy was essentially improvised, responding to situations as much as it created them. Italy's fascist dictator, Benito Mussolini, who sought the creation of Italian blocs, began as Hitler's tutor in foreign affairs, continued as his accomplice, and declined into his lackey.

Benito Mussolini (1883–1945), "Il Duce," was the first of Europe's fascist dictators. He came to power in 1922 when his movement marched on Rome and he was invited by King Victor Emmanuel III to become prime minister—the youngest to that time in Italy. Mussolini's dramatic success owed much to his shrewd political opportunism in difficult situations pregnant with various possibilities. His government comprised Fascist and pre-Fascist members; but he governed autocratically, winning absolute power by a mix of constitutional and unconstitutional means—including fraudulent elections.

A native of Predappio, he had grown up a moody, rebellious child who was expelled from two different schools for bullying schoolmates and even for stabbing fellow pupils with a penknife. After a brief career as a schoolteacher, he traveled around Switzerland—a short, stocky youth with a jaw like a prizefighter's and piercing eyes who read the works of the great political philosophers while he was becoming immersed in revolutionary ideas, especially socialism. He was arrested and imprisoned for strike activities, first in Switzerland and then in Italy to which he returned in 1904. Financed by a publisher who wanted Italy to make war on Austria during World War I, Mussolini became editor of *Il Popolo D'Italia*, and from this position be formulated his philosophy of fascism.

Wounded in World War I, he then turned away completely from

The Nazis' obsession with the imperial style of ancient Rome is captured in this photograph of Göring, Hitler, and Himmler at a Nuremberg rally. An immense crowd watches the spectacle from a balcony decked with wreaths and flags in tribute to the mincing generals below. (Library of Congress).

socialism and, in February 1918, advocated the emergence of a dictator — "a man who is ruthless and energetic enough to make a clean sweep." In 1919 he and two hundred Republicans and anarchists and disaffected socialists and syndicalists met in an office in the Piazza San Sepolcro in Milan to form the *Fasci di Combattimento*—a group of counterrevolutionaries who were pledged by ties as close as the *fascinae* of the lictors of ancient Rome.

At rallies surrounded by supporters en masse, all wearing the black shirts that laborers of the Romagna had adopted as the uniform of anarchists, Mussolini made a superb impression as a demagogue. The disorderly government of postwar Italy was threatened by strikes, and it was in this atmosphere that the Fascists marched on Rome and King Victor Emmanuel III offered Mussolini the premiership. At first the people, already weary of warfare, of political unrest, and labor agitation, welcomed the superficial discipline and ceremonial flamboyance of

11

fascism. They accepted dictatorship on the understanding that there would be more efficiency in industry and agriculture, a better general distribution of the national wealth, and political stability. Indeed, fascism in Italy undertook major works of road building, railroad construction, and generally asserted the dignity of labor.

Mussolini dreamed of a new Roman empire. Although Italy had two colonies in East Africa, Eritrea and Somaliland, they were barren—unlike fertile Ethiopia that lay between them and had considerable underdeveloped mineral resources. Italy launched a full-scale invasion of Ethiopia in 1935 and was able to conclude its war with the decisive battle of Lake Ashangi of March 31 to April 3, 1936, after which the emperor of Ethiopia, Haile Selassie, fled the country.

The ambitions of Hitler and Mussolini posed crucial strategic, diplomatic, and ethical problems for Britain and France. The Covenant of the League of Nations pledged members to respect one another's integrity and to unite against aggressors. In practice, states were unwilling to relinquish national independence in the creation of a multilateral force—an army—for the sake of collective security.

Isolation and Insulation

What was true of President Franklin Delano Roosevelt's character and temperament in domestic policies was also true of him in foreign affairs. That FDR came from a wealthy eastern family and had visited Europe several times, that he had served as assistant secretary of the navy under President Woodrow Wilson (1913–21), and that, as Democratic candidate for the vice presidency in 1920, he had campaigned for American membership of the League of Nations (the organization conceived and promoted by Woodrow Wilson)—all these greatly influenced his foreign policy. At heart he was a committed internationalist. Nevertheless, his political experience had taught him the value of expedience and compromise. Moreover, that he had had to struggle to overcome the crippling limitations of his poliomyelitis and that he was temperamentally incapable of adhering to rigid formulas were factors that would affect the way he would lead America into the concert of nations.

On the most teasing matters of Roosevelt's secretive character, mercurial temperament, and convivial public presentation of himself and his policies, it is worth recalling remarks by two of his leading advisers. As to the secretiveness, Secretary of the Interior Harold Ickes once remarked with some exasperation, "you won't talk frankly even with people who are loyal to you. . . . You keep your cards close up against your belly. You never put them on the table." As to the presentation of policies, academic adviser Rexford G. Tugwell recalled that "[FDR] deliberately concealed the processes of his mind. He would rather have posterity believe that for him everything was plain and easy . . . than ever admit to any agony of indecision . . . any misgiving about mistakes." Events at home and abroad combined to harden FDR's tendency to indecision, while never lessening his commitment to the search for international stability.

During the 1930s, the term *isolationist* had a particular application to unilateralists or continentalists within America who wanted the United States to have complete independence of diplomatic action and to avoid entangling alliances. Above all, they wanted America to remain neutral in war. Isolationists and pacifists agreed that World War I had been a disaster, that a second world war would be even worse, and that renewed American intervention would profit only bankers, arms makers, and other industrialists. The cost would be borne by the American people who would lose their lives, their money, and their democratic institutions.

Isolationism was nurtured by the cultural and political climate of small-town America—a major component of American life. As late as 1940 the United States was still largely a nation of small towns and rural communities. Of the 131,699,275 citizens listed in the census as living in the continental United States and the 118,933 living in overseas territories and dependencies, 74.4 million (56.5 percent) were designated as urban dwellers. However, urban meant then a community of only 2,500 or more inhabitants. If we consider a community of far greater numbers to be urban, then a different picture emerges. Less than 50 percent of all Americans lived in cities with over 10,000 inhabitants; less than 40 percent lived in cities with over 25,000 inhabitants; and only 30 percent lived in cities with over 100,000. Thus in 1940, 70 million people (55 percent) lived in places with fewer than 10,000 inhabitants. In other words, small towns were a fundamental part of American life.

Another factor determining attitudes on isolation was class. Historian

Richard Polenberg declares in *One Nation Divisible* (1980) that "American society on the eve of World War II was sharply divided along class, racial, and ethnic lines." He demonstrates the truth of his assertion about class and ethnicity in a penetrating analysis. The criteria for membership of the upper, middle, and lower classes and their various subsections differed little from place to place. Between 60 and 70 percent of people belonged to the lower-middle and upper-lower categories; about 15 percent belonged to the upper-middle classes; the remaining 15 to 25 percent were in the lower-lower class. Movement across class lines was not impossible but was markedly infrequent.

Class was also, of course, largely determined by income. In 1939 factory workers earned, on average, about $1,250 a year. An advertisement quoted a man who planned to retire on $150 a month, enjoying "life-long security and freedom to do as I please." Thus a salary of $2,500 would make one well-to-do. But only 4.2 percent of working people earned that much in 1939. Annual earnings of more than $5,000 were way beyond what most people could imagine. At the base of the economic pyramid were the underemployed, the seasonally employed, and the unemployed. The severe recession of 1938 probably led to an increase in unemployment from 7.5 million people to over 11 million. Even in 1940, after the federal government had expanded yet again its programs of relief and national defense, there were still about 9 million unemployed people. Partial employment and unemployment account for some revealing statistics. In 1939, if we exclude the 2.5 million people working on public relief, 58.5 percent of men and 78.3 percent of women were working for or were seeking work that paid less than $1,000. Financial exigency and not foreign affairs was the primary interest of such people in the years of the Great Depression.

The focus of small-town life was upon the values of the community and its well-being and survival. Included in the prescription was insulation from war. Isolationists were more likely to come from small towns and the countryside in the Midwest than from the great cities of the Northeast or from the South. They were farmers, small businessmen, employees of the service industries, and manufacturers of light industrial products. Ethnically, they were drawn from the Irish-, German-, and Italian-American blocs.

In Congress, their champions included progressive Republican senators William E. Borah of Idaho, Hiram Johnson of California, Arthur

The variety of film footage on the Third Reich from various sources was the basis for an elaborate documentary montage devised in the 1950s and subsequently shown in English as *Mein Kampf: The Terrifying Decline and Fall of Hitler's Reich*. Part humanitarian propaganda, part Soviet polemic, it remains a compelling record of twelve years of military rampage that changed the world. (Columbia Pictures, 1961; Museum of Modern Art Film Stills Archive).

Capper of Kansas, and Gerald P. Nye of North Dakota; Republican senators Arthur H. Vandenberg of Michigan and Robert A. Taft of Ohio; and Republican congressman Hamilton Fish of New York; progressive Democratic senator Burton K. Wheeler of Montana; progressive senators Robert M. LaFollette, Jr., of Wisconsin and George W. Norris of Nebraska; and farmer-laborite Republican senator Henrik Shipstead of Minnesota. However, these men were pivotal voters for Roosevelt in domestic affairs. All were committed to his program of reform and to the New Deal; and their support was invaluable, especially on the more controversial legislation. FDR could not risk their antagonism in domestic affairs by provoking them on foreign policy.

Isolationist sentiment was nourished by the activities of revisionist historians and pacifists. Their histories of the origins of World War I were to have a profound impact on a whole generation and its attitude to foreign affairs. They made particular the grievances expressed in literary terms by the lost generation of war novelists, such as Ernest Hemingway, John Dos Passos, and E. E. Cummings. Historians and novelists agreed that propaganda had debased language and that in the war the state had become a servile mechanism of malign forces. Historical revisionism began as an investigation into the causes of World War I and developed into a justification of American isolationism. The leading American revisionists were Sidney Bradshaw Fay, Frederick Bausman, J. K. Turner, Harry Elmer Barnes, and C. Hartley Grattan.

Many people who shared the historians' great moral outrage already had begun to work for peace in various pacifist societies, both new and old. During the twenties and thirties, the most active were two lobbying societies based in Washington, D.C. They were the National Council for the Prevention of War (NCPW), founded in 1921 and led by its executive secretary, Frederick Libby, and the Women's International League for Peace and Freedom (WILPF), originally founded by settlement-house founder Jane Adams in 1915 and later led by its executive secretary, Dorothy Detzer.

Another crucial factor in the controversy over isolationism and interventionism was immigration. It worked for and against intervention into the war in Europe.

In 1940 11,419,000 residents, or 8.5 percent of the population, had been born abroad. There were 1,624,000 people from Italy; 1,323,000 from Russia, Lithuania, and Rumania; 1,238,000 from Germany; 993,000 from Poland; 845,000 from Denmark, Norway, and Sweden; 678,000 from Ireland; and 163,000 from Greece. There were also 23 million second-generation white immigrants, born in the United States, one or both of whose parents were immigrants; and this accounted for 17.5 percent of the population. Thus, more than one in four Americans was a first- or second-generation immigrant.

Immigrants and their children still accounted for the majority of the population in twenty large industrial cities, comprising two-thirds of the people in Cleveland, Ohio; three-quarters of the people in New York City; and three-fifths of the people in Newark, New Jersey. There were large numbers of Finns in Montana, Norwegians in North Dakota, Germans in Wisconsin, and Czechs in Iowa. Immigrants, primarily

Simeon II., Bulgariens neuer König,

den Thron seines Vaters übernommen. Bis zur Regelung der Regentschaftsfrage wird das Land vom Ministerrat geleitet. Der jetzt 6 jährige Prinz bei einem Manöver 1941

49180   Presse-Hoffmann

Nazi propaganda extolled Hitler's ideal of Aryan manhood, fair and blue-eyed, as in this affectionate publicity still of Germany's ally, Simeon II, the young king of Bulgaria who had just succeeded his father in 1941 (Presse-Hoffmann; Library of Congress).

French Canadians, constituted 40 percent of the population of Burlington, Vermont.

Among the reasons immigrants had come to America for over one hundred years was to escape the turmoil of European wars and, particularly for young men, to avoid compulsory military service. The legend of European warfare was part of their children's heritage. While this undoubtedly lent support to isolationism, it must be balanced by a contrary factor—the identification of recent immigrants with the interests of their country of origin. While German, Irish, and Italian immigrants felt divided loyalties about the possibility of American intervention on the side of Britain in a war against Italy or Germany, Slavic peoples had no hesitation in wanting the United States to support Britain in a war to free Europe, especially eastern Europe, from German domination.

Moreover, not all immigrants read, spoke, or thought in English. According to the census of 1940, English was not the mother tongue of almost 22 million people. There were not only foreign-language newspapers and magazines but also foreign-language bookstores, movie houses, and theaters. About two hundred radio stations broadcast foreign-language programs, providing, in the largest cities, almost a continuous series of programs in German, Polish, Yiddish, and other languages. They appealed primarily to older immigrants who could return to an aural world of once-familiar music, stories, and jokes. In the North End of Boston, 85 percent of Italian immigrants listened regularly to such broadcasts—more than listened to programs in English.

Foreign languages were still widely used and helped foster ethnic identities. In 1940, 237 foreign-language periodicals were being published in New York; 96 in Chicago; 38 in Pittsburgh; 25 in Los Angeles; and 22 in Detroit. Richard Polenberg estimates that over 1,000 newspapers and periodicals with an aggregate circulation of almost 7 million were printed wholly or partly in a foreign language. Thus, they could focus on events in Europe.

In convincing the American public that their foreign policy of unilateralism was to be preferred to that of Roosevelt and his secretary of state, Cordell Hull, isolationists were most fortunate that the descent of Europe and Asia into another war could be represented in the syndicated press as the inevitable outcome of a conflict of imperialist rivalries from which the United States would do best to remain aloof. However, as the tragic sequence of events unfolded abroad, the ravages of the Great Depression and a series of domestic crises at home proved of consuming interest to the American people.

The Senate investigation of the munitions industry, led by Republican senator Gerald P. Nye of North Dakota, and the ensuing four Neutrality Acts of 1935, 1936, 1937, and 1939 represented the high tide of American isolationism in the 1930s. American demands for the regulation of arms traffic had intensified after the collapse of a disarmament conference at Geneva in 1933. On April 12, 1934, the Senate approved Nye's motion calling for a seven-man Senate investigation into the munitions industry. Nye himself was subsequently elected chairman of the committee. The time was ripe. In March 1934 H. C. Engelbrecht and F. C. Hanighen had had their sensational article "Arms and the Men" published in *Fortune* magazine. They had shown that the only financial profits made out of World War I had been by the munitions manufacturers. Soon afterward, Walter Millis added fuel to the fire of economic interpretation of the causes of World War I with his *The Road to War* (1935), the best-seller known as the isolationists' bible.

The Nye committee held public hearings from September 1934 until February 1936 and during eighteen months heard evidence from almost two hundred witnesses and produced a final report of 13,750 pages in thirty-nine volumes. Nye believed he knew what had brought America into the war; and he overstated his findings, telling the Senate on January 15, 1935, how he had discovered the existence of a vicious partnership between the federal government and the munitions industry. What Nye considered the most significant part of his investigation was uncovered when the committee examined the files relating to loans by American banks to European governments in World War I—prior to American intervention in 1917.

The influence of the Nye committee and various revisionist histories of World War I on the first three Neutrality Acts was clear enough. These acts were designed specifically to prevent the "mistakes" of President Woodrow Wilson being repeated by Roosevelt. Assuming that the United States had been drawn into World War I to protect its foreign loans, Congress forbade war loans. Assuming that the export of arms in 1915 and 1916 had been another cause of intervention, Congress prohibited the export of arms. Because a third cause of intervention had been, supposedly, trade with the Allies, the act of 1937 insisted that, if belligerents bought American goods, they paid for them with cash and carried them away on their own vessels. This was known as the provision of cash-and-carry. In the belief that the loss of American lives through submarine warfare had contributed to American involvement, Congress forbade Americans to travel on belligerents' ships.

War in China

The progression to world war accelerated with the full-scale Japanese invasion of China in 1937. Moreover, the three dispossessed powers of the Axis were moving closer together. On October 25, 1936, the Berlin-Rome Axis was formed. On November 6, 1937, Italy and Germany signed an Anti-Comintern Pact; and on December 12, Italy left the

League of Nations. Japan already had signed an Anti-Comintern Pact with Germany in December 1936. Japan was deficient in crucial raw materials, especially oil, and the place to obtain them was in Southeast Asia. When fighting broke out between Japanese and Chinese troops near Beijing on July 7, 1937, the prime minister, Prince Konoye Fumimaro, gave in to the demands of his war minister, Hajime Sugiyama, to dispatch reinforcements, thus escalating an incident into war. China appealed to the League at a conference opened in Brussels to discuss the Sino-Japanese War. Japan and Germany were absent, and their position was explained by Italy. None of the states was willing to take action, and the conference was a failure.

With the outbreak of war in Asia as well as Africa and Europe, Roosevelt decided to explore the possibility of public support for a discriminatory foreign policy in place of the official neutrality legislation that he believed helped aggressor nations. On October 5, 1937, Roosevelt delivered his famous "Quarantine Speech" in Chicago, in which he proposed that the peace-loving nations should contain warlike states before aggression could not be checked: "When an epidemic of physical disease starts to spread the community approves and joins in a quarantine of the patients in order to protect the health of the community against the spread of the disease." The reaction to the speech was almost entirely hostile.

Historian Charles A. Beard, a consistent isolationist and persistent critic of FDR, observed in the *New Republic* of 2 February 1938 that any conflict between the spirit and the letter of the Neutrality Acts was all of Franklin D. Roosevelt's making. He believed that what the president sought was discretion to perform unneutral acts. The Neutrality Acts did not intend that the United States should treat all belliger-

Benito Mussolini, "Il Duce," of Italy, the first of Europe's fascist dictators to rise and fall, captured in the full flood of ecstatic arrogance at the prospect of military glory. While Italians of all classes welcomed the early fascist message of disciplinary method over disorder, they felt increasing unease with Mussolini's *braggadocio* in foreign affairs as the dictator declined from tutor to Hitler to his lackey. Mussolini's intervention in World War II was unpopular from the start. His most damning epitaph after his assassination by radical partisans was, ironically, also the most laudatory: "He made the trains run on time." (Library of Congress).

ents equally but, rather, to ensure its abstention from war. Roosevelt's proposed revision would produce "An Act for Allowing the President of the United States to Enter a War that Begins Abroad." Beard's various articles in this period betrayed his distrust of the solidarity of Americans behind isolationism, despite continuous assertions to the contrary.

Kissing Hitler

In January 1938 Roosevelt, deeply concerned by the tide of the events in Europe, proposed to Prime Minister Neville Chamberlain that there should be an international conference to discuss territorial possessions and access to raw materials. Chamberlain would have none of it. He had decided to come to terms with the dictators.

When the Austrian chancellor, Kurt von Schuschnigg, refused Hitler's offer of a union of Austria with Germany, Hitler and his army entered Austria at Braunar, his birthplace, on March 12, 1938, and on March 13 took Vienna. Winston Churchill warned the House of Commons from the back benches that Europe was being "confronted with a programme *[sic]* of aggression, nicely calculated and timed, unfolding stage by stage."

In response to the growing threat of war, American isolationists conceded that the United States required a larger navy for the defense of the Western Hemisphere, and Congress voted for the Vinson Naval Act of 1938 that was to expand the navy at a cost of $1 billion. Moreover, FDR was able to rally public opinion behind statements about the territorial integrity of nations in the Western hemisphere. In August 1938, he told an audience at Queen's University, Kingston, Ontario, that the American people "will not stand idly by if domination of Canadian soil is threatened by any other empire."

Prime Minister Neville Chamberlain had decided on a policy of appeasement. He believed he could not rely on treaties and pacts for security, and thus he asked himself what the alternative was to appeasement of Hitler's demands for the unification of all German-speaking people. The alternative was not the League nor an alliance with France, which presumed itself secure behind the Maginot line. In *The Gathering Storm*, the first of six volumes of Winston Churchill's history of World War II, a printer's error had the French Army described not as the prop but as "the poop of the French nation." Churchill and his publisher decided that this delicious misprint was "too near the truth" to be corrected.

Chamberlain believed that Hitler, and to a lesser extent Mussolini, had to be treated as rational statesmen. English historian A. J. P. Taylor subsequently has said (1965):

The opponents of appeasement . . . often failed to distinguish between "stopping" Hitler and defeating him in a great war. Hitler could be stopped only in areas directly accessible to Anglo-French forces. . . . Austria was the last occasion when direct opposition was possible. Great Britain and France could not have stopped a German invasion of Czechoslovakia. . . . Similarly, they could not stop the German invasion of Poland. They could only begin a general war which brought no aid to the Poles. There were thus two different questions. At first: shall we go to the aid of this country or that? Later: shall we start a general war for the overthrow of Germany as a Great Power? In practice . . . the two questions were always mixed up.

Thus, while Britain and France could defend areas close to them and restrict such a conflict, they could not do so in central Europe, which could only be defended by full-scale military invasion and, hence, a major war.

In the *Herald Tribune* of 16 October 1937, columnist Walter Lippmann inquired "Is it War or Peace in Europe?" and dismissed the sophistry of appeasement:

We are living in a world in which great militarized nations are bent on conquest. The democracies are potentially stronger than the dictatorships but they are softer, more self-indulgent, and more confused. They are unwilling to face the fact that in dealing with governments that are willing to fight, there is no form of influence which really counts, unless it is backed by a willingness to fight.

Hitler's next target was Czechoslovakia. His tactic was to claim the right to defend the 3 million Sudeten Germans who were citizens of Czechoslovakia and whose security normally was guaranteed by the League of Nations—to whom they could protest against any injustice. Hitler now made claims on their behalf that were acceded to by the president of Czechoslovakia, Edvard Beneš, on September 4, 1938. However, on September 12, when Hitler spoke to the Nazi party rally in Nuremberg, he said that the concessions were insufficient. His speech was broadcast live to America by CBS and was translated by Kurt Heiman. Historian William Manchester (1973) comments how "millions of Americans, hearing Hitler for the first time over shortwave, were shaken by the depth of his hatred; on his lips the Teutonic language sounded cruel, dripping with venom."

At this point the French tried to persuade Britain that Hitler's real aim was not the Sudeten Germans but the domination of Europe itself. Both Britain and France believed that Hitler would only attack Czechoslovakia if he were certain there would be no Anglo-French opposition. Chamberlain flew to Munich on September 15 and met Hitler at Berchtesgaden, where he offered the separation of the Sudeten Germans from the rest of Czechoslovakia. Chamberlain believed that Hitler only wanted the unification of all German peoples and was now satisfied. France therefore asked if Chamberlain would guarantee what was left of Czechoslovakia. Chamberlain and three members of his cabinet did so, although they had refused to guarantee the whole state. On September 21, Britain and France told the Czech president that Czechoslovakia could either capitulate to Hitler or fight alone.

The editors of the *New Republic* commented in the issue of 28 September 1938, that "The decision of the British and French governments to sacrifice Czechoslovakia to the Nazi Moloch seems like the ultimate in cowardice and faithfulness [sic] which it is impossible to justify while retaining a shred of self respect." In the view of the editors Chamberlain's strategy of appeasement sent ominous warnings to the United States about the perils for any modern nation losing confidence and self-esteem. They feared contamination. "We do need to take care that we are not overcome internally by the dry rot of incompetence, decrepitude, insincerity and lack of social energy that seems to be leaving the older democratic countries a prey to those who scorn and betray them!"

Believing the affair settled, Chamberlain flew once again to Germany to meet Hitler at Godesberg on the Rhine on September 22. Hitler now wanted immediate occupation rather than a negotiated transfer of power. Nevertheless, he promised to wait until October 1, 1938, before marching on Czechoslovakia. In London the atmosphere was entirely changed. On September 26 the British Foreign Office issued the following statement: "If German attack is made upon Czechoslovakia . . . France will be bound to come to her assistance, and Great Britain and Russia will certainly stand by France." Preparations were made for war. That very day Roosevelt made the same proposal of a general conference to Hitler that he had previously made to Chamberlain. Nothing came of it. Chamberlain knew nothing could be done to assist Czechoslovakia but nevertheless agreed to a proposal from Mussolini for a four-power conference in Munich. On September 29 Chamberlain met Hitler there, and the two of them accepted a plan submitted by Mussolini that had actually been prepared by the German Foreign Office. Czechoslovakia was obliged to agree.

On September 30, 1938, Chamberlain and Hitler met for the last time, and Hitler signed an agreement the prime minister had prepared. "We regard the agreement signed last night and the Anglo-German Naval Agreement as symbolic of the desire of our two peoples never to go to war with one another again." The same evening Chamberlain told cheering crowds in London, "I believe it is peace for our time." This notorious apogee of appeasement, using words from the Book of Common Prayer, was approved by the overwhelming majority of the press, by public opinion, and by the Conservative party. Yet this triumph of appeasement was the nadir of diplomacy. As A. J. P. Taylor (1965) states, "appeasement had been designed by Chamberlain as the impartial redress of justified grievances. It became a capitulation, a surrender to fear."

From Hitler's point of view, there was a crucial military consideration to the seizure of Czechoslovakia. The annexation involved handing over to Hitler the powerful fortifications that protected Bohemia and Slovakia, and hence eastern Europe, from invasion by Germany. It was this single achievement more than any other that ensured German dominance of central Europe. A yet more sinister advantage was that Czechoslovakia was comparatively rich in U^{235}—the uranium essential for nuclear fission.

In his foreign policy, Hitler combined complete opportunism in means and timing with unwavering pursuit of the objectives he himself had laid down earlier in *Mein Kampf*. He had shown astonishing skill in judging the mood of the democracies and exploiting their weaknesses— all this in spite of the fact that he had scarcely ever set foot outside Austria and Germany and spoke no foreign language.

The leading members of the League of Nations had abandoned the strategy of collective security and common action in the face of aggression. Winston Churchill's comment was "Britain and France had to choose between war and dishonour. They chose dishonour. They will have war."

Winston Spencer Churchill (1874–1965), later British prime minister (1940–45 and 1951–55) and knight, was soon to become the savior of his country. The son of the charismatic but ill-fated Tory politician Lord Randolph Churchill, he was a direct descendant of John Churchill, first duke of Marlborough and hero of British campaigns against Louis XIV in the war of the Spanish succession. His mother was Jenny Jerome, the beautiful daughter of New York financier Leonard W. Jerome. After a dismal school record at Harrow, Churchill was alternately a journalist and a soldier in Cuba, India, and South Africa at the turn of the century. He soon rose in the ranks of Liberal members of parliament to become a prominent cabinet member (1908–15) in a Liberal government favoring social reform during a period of considerable controversy under successive prime ministers H. H. Asquith and David Lloyd George. Churchill's strategy in World War I was highly controversial, especially his role in the Dardanelles and Gallipoli campaigns.

Between the wars Churchill's career fell into the doldrums with periods in and out of office, and his sojourn as chancellor of the exchequer (1924–29) under Stanley Baldwin was not successful. His rift with Baldwin and the mixed fortunes of the Tory party led to his exclusion from office from 1929 to 1939; yet, it was these years in the wilderness that extended his political career. They provided a respite from office and allowed him ample opportunity to write—he was as skilled an author as he was an orator and painter. His years out of office allowed him, despite a reputation for instability, indiscipline, and poor judgment, to sharpen his political wits and to analyze and describe the steps by which Adolf Hitler sought the mastery of Europe.

Despite supine British governments, Churchill consistently paraded the need to take German rearmament and German ambitions seriously and to prevent the German Luftwaffe from attaining parity with the Royal Air Force. He developed a following of gifted experts, notably Oxford physics professor Frederick A. Lindermann (later Lord Cherwell), who helped him create a private intelligence center at Chartwell (his home) that was superior to the government's. Churchill used his membership in the secret committee on air defense research in the House of Commons to discuss vital problems of strategy and to clarify

Perhaps the most significant cinematic complement to the great novels of the lost generation in protest against war was *Grand Illusion* (1937), in which French director Jean Renoir used a wintry German prison-of-war camp in World War I as a microcosm for European society. The old ruling class of atrophied aristocracy extinguishes itself in national animosities, while entrepreneurs and mechanics begin to take control. The German commandant, Erich von Stroheim *(right)*, whose war-ravaged chin is held in place by metal, must kill the French captain, Pierre Fresnay, who covers up for escaped prisoners, even though they are emotionally drawn together by culture and temperament. (Museum of Modern Art Film Stills Archive).

his own understanding of them. Yet his warnings against Hitler were ignored as if they had been voiced by Cassandra.

In short, Churchill's entire career to the late 1930s was a preparation for his supreme years of leadership in World War II. He was an intense patriot with a nostalgic belief in the greatness of Britain, and he thrived on challenge in military stalemate and political quagmire.

Light Thickens

Hitler's diplomatic success at Munich encouraged him to intensify the persecution of Jews. The Nuremberg Laws of 1935 already had divested Jews of their political and civil rights. On November 9, 1938, a new, and even more terrible, wave of persecution began as Nazi gangs attacked Jews and their businesses and synagogues. The streets of German cities were strewn with broken glass, giving the name of *Kristallnacht* to this outrage to humanity. The pretext was the assassination of a German diplomat in Paris. In the winter months hundreds of victims were killed, and thousands of Jewish men were transported to concentration camps. While the American press deplored the violence, only the *New Republic*, in its issue of 23 November 1938, urged a revision of the immigration laws to allow the entry of persecuted Jews into the United States. Subsequently, in 1939, Senator Robert Wagner of New York introduced a bill to allow the entry of 200,000 German refugee children above the official quota. However, lacking the support of FDR, the refugee bill expired in committee. As Freda Kirchwey said in the 24 May 1943 issue of the *Nation*, "we had it in our power to rescue this doomed people and we did not lift a hand to do it."

In 1938 and 1939, FDR took action to strengthen the defense of the Western Hemisphere. In April 1938 he created a Standing Liaison Committee to strengthen military missions to Latin America. The committee also established firm control over commercial airlines. In November the Joint Army and Navy Board discussed contingency arrangements in case of attack. In 1939 the five so-called Rainbow Plans defined strategy for defending the United States by safeguarding the hemisphere as a whole. Moreover, in December 1938 the American republics attending the Pan-American conference in Lima, Peru, had unanimously adopted the Declaration of Lima, which condemned religious and racial prejudice and alien political activity in the Western Hemisphere. Fear of Nazi infiltration preceded World War II. On January 4, 1939, George C. Stoney of the *New Republic* advised readers of the dangers, in an article entitled "How the Dictators Woo Argentina."

In *The Great Dictator* (1940), Charlie Chaplin lampooned Hitler as the tyrant Hynkel ruling the country of Bacteria under the sign of the double cross. Here the little corporal *(center)*, under the tutelage of Henry Daniell's Garbitch *(right)*, tries not to be outfaced by Jack Oakie's expansive and scowling Napoloni (Mussolini). (United Artists; Museum of Modern Art Film Stills Archive).

The Dark Valley of 1939

Roosevelt's annual message to Congress on January 4, 1939, was largely devoted to foreign affairs: "All about us rage undeclared wars—military and economic." Therefore, he recommended, the United States, without getting involved, should revise its neutrality legislation: "We have learned that when we deliberately try to legislate neutrality, our neutrality laws may operate unevenly and unfairly—may actually give aid to the aggressor and deny it to the victim. The instinct of self-preservation should warn us that we ought not to let that happen any more." Congress continued to oppose any change that indicated the United States would distinguish between aggressor and victim and thereby incur hostility.

Yet Gallup public opinion polls showed that 65 percent of Americans favored an economic boycott of Germany, and 57 percent wanted a revision of the neutrality laws. Fifty-one percent expected a war in Europe, and 58 percent expected that the United States would become involved. Yet, although 90 percent said they would fight if America were invaded, only 10 percent said they would do so regardless of invasion.

Events at home put these opinions to the test. On January 23, 1939, a Douglas bomber crashed in California, killing the pilot and injuring an observer from a French mission sent to inspect American airplanes for purchase. The accident led to widespread debate about the propriety of a French air-force captain being on board an American test flight. The incident prompted FDR to explain his policies to members of the Senate Military Affairs Committee on January 31. He justified the sale of airplanes to France on the grounds that it was necessary to guard the Rhine frontier from German attack and, by so doing, prevent Hitler imperiling the peace and safety of the United States. "Do you mean that our frontier is on the Rhine?" asked one senator. "No, not that. But practically speaking, if the Rhine frontiers are threatened, the rest of the world is, too." Despite their agreement to remain silent, isolationist senators leaked FDR's explanation to the press, claiming that he had drawn a "truly alarming" picture of world affairs by declaring that America's frontier lay on the Rhine.

Despite such setbacks, FDR and Secretary of State Cordell Hull continued to put pressure on Congress to repeal, or at least revise, the neutrality laws. A series of proposed revisions followed, such as giving the president discretion as to how, where, and when the neutrality laws should be applied and placing an embargo on arms and ammunition but not upon implements of war. However, all such revisions failed, partly because Democrats personally hostile to Roosevelt voted with the isolationists.

On July 18, 1939, Roosevelt and Hull invited congressional leaders to discuss European affairs with him at the White House. Roosevelt predicted war and said he believed France and Britain had only an even chance of survival. He hoped Congress would agree even now to a revision of the neutrality laws in favor of Britain and France. However, the most prepossessing senator there, William E. Borah of Idaho, declared, "There's not going to be any war this year. All this hysteria is manufactured and artificial." Brushing aside Hull's references to State Department telegrams, he went on, "I have sources of information in Europe that I regard as more reliable than those of the State Department." He meant newspaper articles. The vice president, John Nance Garner, is supposed to have advised Roosevelt, "You haven't got the votes and that's all there is to it."

The prospect of war moved closer. The newly diminished state of Czechoslovakia was divided by ethnic dispute between the Czechs and the Slovaks. On March 15, 1939, Slovakia became independent. Hungary claimed the Ukraine district of lower Carpathia. Thus, the new president, Hacha, allowed Czechia (or Bohemia) to become a German protectorate. The Sudeten territories had not been Hitler's "last territorial demand in Europe" after all. It was at this point that Britain and France, concerned that Hitler would invade either Rumania or Poland, drew more closely together.

War Begins

When Chamberlain heard a series of unfounded rumors of German troop maneuvers against Poland, on March 31 he drafted an Anglo-French guarantee of Polish integrity. If Polish independence were threatened, "His Majesty's Government and the French Government would at once lend them all the support in their power." Chamberlain had not consulted France. The Polish foreign minister, Józef Beck, accepted the offer "between two flicks of the ash off his cigarette" but, proud to the last, insisted, instead, on an alliance between equals and Chamberlain agreed to this. An alliance in peacetime between Britain and an east European nation was unprecedented and Britain could not keep its side of the bargain. Chamberlain wanted a ceremonial gesture to warn Hitler although he was actually sympathetic to Germany's claims to revise the Versailles settlement concerning Danzig (later, Gdansk).

Anglo-French overtures to Russia, a putative ally in case of war with Germany, were conducted in three stages: from April 15 to May 14; from May 27 to July 23; and from August 12 to 21. They failed— despite the overwhelming support of British public opinion. This was partly because the British government wanted to conjure a vague Russian menace like a genie in a bottle to be uncorked, poured out, and replaced at will but without any willingness to allow Russia to take any military initiative in eastern Europe. It failed partly because neither Britain nor France (nor Poland) was willing to allow Poland to become a route for Russian armies moving westward and thus risking a partition of Poland. There was also bad faith on either side. The British foreign secretary, Edward, Viscount Halifax, was invited to Moscow but declined. Then Neville Chamberlain denied in the House of Commons that any invitation had actually been extended in the first place. The British government wanted to scare Hitler—not to make practical use of Russian military might. In this way it hoped to induce him into some ill-defined economic division of Europe and Africa into spheres of influence on the mistaken assumption that Germany's grievances were economic. For this the British were prepared to abandon Poland. Their sophistry and trimming would only have the effect of convincing Hitler they would not resist him and strengthening his resolve to raise his price ever higher during a crisis.

Some American commentators interpreted British responses not as incompetent but, rather, as politically astute and downright malicious as well as successful. In the *New Republic* of 8 March and 12 April 1939, Frederick L. Schumann surveyed a host of British betrayals since 1914 including the Hoare-Laval plan to sell out Ethiopia, British connivance at the various aggrandisements of Germany and Japan, and what seemed like determination of the British upper class "to sit by" while Russia and Germany fought another world war. "This is not a program of 'muddling through.' It is a program suffused with elements of genius. If its assumptions are correct, nothing could better serve the interests of the British ruling classes nor better befuddle the British masses who have been 'sold' in the name of isolationism, pacifism, liberalism (etc.)."

In fact, Anglo-French monopoly of treaty making in Europe was at end. Nothing could have illustrated this better than the bombshell news of the Nazi-Soviet pact signed by the German foreign minister, Joachim von Ribbentrop, and the Soviet commissar for foreign affairs, Vyacheslav Molotov, in Moscow on August 23. Hitler's motive was straightforward —to protect his eastern flank in case of war. Russia would stay neutral if Germany went to war. This seemed a preface to a partition of Poland.

However, if what Hitler and Stalin believed was that Britain and France would look the other way and that Poland could be partitioned

One of Britain's most successful attempts to woo the United States came with the state visit of the king and queen in 1939. Here, in a ride with an elegantly attired Eleanor Roosevelt, Queen Elizabeth (later, the queen mother) displays her easy ability to exude charm before the crowd. Both women contributed to public morale in their respective countries during the war on account of numerous appearances and speeches, both heartfelt and professional. (Library of Congress).

without a major war, there was some evidence to support their thinking. Georges Bonnet, the French foreign minister, wanted to repudiate the Anglo-French guarantee of Poland and revive the defunct military talks with Russia. His colleagues demurred, did nothing, and thus the chance of settling the destiny of the French was left to others who seized the occasion. However, there was more to the Nazi-Soviet pact than the fate of Poland.

Ever since the Russian Revolution in 1917 Russian governments had preached a gospel of continuous socialist revolutions across the world, thereby arousing ingrained fears in the leading capitalist countries. On

A German tank plows its way down a street in Poland at the beginning of the war, as citizens cower in doorways in disbelief. (Office of Emergency Management; Library of Congress).

their side Soviet attitudes toward western Europe were largely shaped by a traditional Russian concept of capitalist encirclement. Soviet leaders believed that certain capitalist countries wanted to eliminate the world's first socialist state. They had tangible evidence to support this interpretation—armed intervention by Britain, France, Japan, and the United States on the side of counterrevolutionaries in the period 1918–20. In the days of deepening international crises before the outbreak of World War II Stalin and other Soviet leaders believed that the end would be an agreement between Britain, France, and Germany at the expense of the Soviet Union. Thus Russia tried to divide the capitalist world and prevent the major powers' ganging up on the Soviet Union. In August 1939 Stalin decided to choose an alliance with Hitler, fully realizing that, whatever the length of his understanding with Hitler, this very agreement made war between Britain and Germany likely. Christopher Seton-Watson opines in "The Cold War: Its Origins" in *Since 1945*, a collection of essays edited by James Henderson in 1966, how

Stalin "counted on being able to sit back and watch the two halves of the capitalist world tearing themselves to pieces."

Whereas the French government accommodated itself to the Nazi-Soviet Pact with comatose complacency, the British government and, in particular, the House of Commons, regarded it as an affront to British pride. This gave some impetus to the passing of an Emergency Powers Act through all its stages on August 24 and the signing of the Anglo-Polish treaty of mutual assistance on August 25. A clause by which Danzig was guaranteed as well as Poland was kept secret so that Hitler would not be provoked.

The Anglo-Polish alliance lacked teeth. When the Poles asked for £60 million ($300 million) of financial assistance to purchase military supplies, the British offered only £8 million worth of credits to be used in Britain and then denied the Poles sorely needed supplies of bombs and rifles. Nevertheless, Chamberlain convinced himself that he had stood up to Hitler whose splutterings about Germans in Danzig needing protection had died away. Yet, in the past Hitler had succeeded by riding out the agony of suspense he had inflicted upon his victims. Joseph Kennedy, the American ambassador to Britain, told Cordell Hull that Chamberlain "says the futility of it all is the thing that is frightful; after all they cannot save the Poles." Hitler renewed his demands on Poland. Despite Britain's public assurances, Viscount Halifax urged Poland to negotiate with Hitler. Beck refused to do so and German troops crossed the frontier at 4:45 A.M. on September 1, 1939; at 6:00 A.M. German planes bombed the capital, Warsaw. The Polish cabinet appealed to its ally. The response was frigid. The British government declared that it would be possible to find a peaceful solution if only Germany would end hostilities. However, the outrage expressed in the House of Commons obliged Chamberlain to issue the ultimatum calling for the withdrawal of German troops by September 3 and the British declaration of war on Germany when it expired without any assurances.

Unless you regard Hitler as hellbent on a world war, it is not easy to see why, by ignoring the British ultimatum, he decided on war rather than on another round of negotiations. Despite his braggadocio, or because of it, he had carried Germany to domination of central Europe by an astute mix of disingenuous bluff and masterly timing—and all at the expense of lesser powers. It is possible that he thought Britain was about to desert Poland as it had Czechoslovakia and that it would welcome another chance to keep the peace at Munich. It is also possible that Hitler stumbled into war rather than be discredited in the opinion of his generals whom he had ordered to prepare for an invasion of Poland by September 1, 1939.

Despite later rhetoric about the war's being a crusade by the great democracies to eliminate fascism, the only powers to declare war on Germany were France, Britain, and the Dominions of Australia, New Zealand, Canada, and South Africa. All other countries that were drawn into the war waited until Germany, Italy, or Japan attacked them — and these included the United States and the Soviet Union. In all likelihood the English-speaking people of Britain and the Dominions were surprised at the noble enterprise that events had conferred upon them. A. J. P. Taylor also reminds us in his *English History 1914–1945* (1965) that

the government made nothing of the national mood. They remained a government of National pretence. . . . [Chamberlain] and his fellows were at a loss to explain why they were at war or what they were fighting for. Their policy was in ruins. They had wanted to settle with Hitler on reasonable terms or, failing that, to shift the brunt of the fighting on to Soviet Russia. Now they were pledged to the defence of Poland — a pledge which they could not fulfill. Hitler offered peace when Poland had been conquered. The government, after some hesitation, turned down the offer formally in both houses of parliament. But what now? Did the British government seek to overthrow fascism throughout Europe?, to destroy Germany as a Great Power?, or merely to substitute Goering or some other Nazi for Hitler as dictator of Germany? They did not know, and the British people were more or less told that they should not ask such questions. It was hardly surprising that in return the bulk of people came to feel that the war was little concern of theirs.

Responding to the Nazi invasion of Poland and the British declaration of war on Germany, FDR said in his radio "fireside chat" of September 3, "This nation will remain a neutral nation." However, going further than Woodrow Wilson in 1914, he added, "But I cannot ask that every American remain neutral in thought as well."

On September 3, 1939, the day Britain declared war on Germany, Chamberlain appointed Churchill to one of his previous posts as first lord of the Admiralty. The signal went to the fleet: "Winston is back." Unfortunately, Churchill's valiant efforts failed to galvanize the torpor of Britain's War, Naval, and Foreign-Office departments.

The Winter's War

In October 1939 Russian troops occupied eastern Poland. Russia, eager to secure the Baltic, also occupied Latvia, Estonia, and Lithuania. Russia also demanded that Finland should cede, or at least lease, parts of its territory considered essential to Russian security. Whatever were Stalin's long-term goals, his immediate objective was to guard the southern approach to Leningrad. In exchange for certain strategic lands, he offered Finland a considerable stretch of Russian lands to the north that were rich in timber. This was to no avail. Ready to accede to several demands, Finland refused a thirty-year lease on the port of Hanko as a Russian naval base and also refused to give up its territory across the isthmus of Karelia by Leningrad. On a pretext that Finns had fired across the frontier, Russian armies invaded Finland on November 30 and established an exiled Communist, Otto Kuusinen, as head of the Democratic Republic of Finland. Kuusinen then acceded to specific Russian demands. Buoyed up by what its leaders felt to be the tide of world opinion, Finland protested the Russian invasion to the League on December 2, 1939. On December 14, the League expelled Russia— the only time it had expelled a member that had broken the covenant. On March 12, 1940, Finland sued for peace and accepted Russian terms.

American public support for Finland was based partly on the widely reported fact that Finland, alone among nations, had paid its debts to America. It mattered not that these had been incurred after, and not during, World War I and that the amount was trivial in comparison with those of America's allies in the Great War. The Roosevelt administration was strongly pro-Finnish but dared not act. This particular tragedy of the winter's war was most bitter to Roosevelt and the secretary of state, Hull. FDR knew that supporting Finland would have encouraged the isolationists to rally support for new defeats of his foreign policies; Hull believed that any action against Russia would drive Stalin more firmly than ever into a permanent alliance with Hitler. In any case, neither Russia nor Finland had formally declared war. Therefore, Roosevelt did not invoke the Neutrality Act of 1939. Meanwhile, Congress passed a bill proposed by Senator Prentiss Brown of Michigan to provide funds for a loan to Finland from the Reconstruction Finance Corporation

Tremulous anxiety breaks out of the otherwise stunned expressions of the hapless citizens of Warsaw at the time of the German entry into the capital of Poland. Of all beleagured cities, Warsaw was to bear possibly the heaviest brunt of all the suffering and degradation during the terrible course of the war. (Office of War Information; Library of Congress).

—the first turning point toward American intervention. Unfortunately, two years later, Finland sided with Hitler in his war against Russia.

"Battle of Washington"

Never again would American isolationists hold the dominant position that had been theirs in 1939. But, although they were gradually forced to retreat, they consistently deployed considerable influence against every proposal to involve the United States in World War II.

The cash-and-carry provisions of the 1937 Neutrality Act had expired, and the munitions embargo was still in effect. Roosevelt called

Congress into special session on September 21 so that the embargo could be replaced by a provision allowing belligerents to purchase munitions and raw materials on a cash-and-carry basis. The administration argued that such a measure would strengthen American neutrality rather than aid Britain and France; however, its fundamental purpose was not in doubt. Germany had increased its own manufacturing capacity and, in seizing Czechoslovakia, had taken over its great munitions works; thus, Germany already possessed military supplies on a scale that neither Britain nor France could match. Divisions within public opinion allowed Congress to revise the legislation it could not yet repeal. On October 27, 1939, the Senate by 63 votes to 30 and, on November 3, the House by 243 votes to 181, agreed to a revision in the Neutrality Acts permitting the sale of goods to belligerents on the basis of cash-and-carry, provided Congress approved.

The inactive "Phony War" of the winter of 1939–40 lulled Britain and France into a false sense of security. They believed they now had time to make their own arms and thus reduced their orders from the United States. Moreover, since the Johnson Act of 1934 had barred countries that defaulted on their loans from borrowing more American money, Britain and France decided to conserve their dollar and gold reserves by restricting their purchase of American goods to food, raw materials, aircraft, and machine tools. FDR insisted that Britain and France set up a special purchasing mission in the United States that was to operate through the Federal Reserve Board. By exercising such controls, FDR hoped to avoid the Allies' interests clashing with America's own military needs.

In fact, in early 1940 FDR had to fight a "battle of Washington" with his own administration over aid to Britain and France. Secretary of War Henry Woodring opposed Allied purchases of war materiel and aircraft that interfered with American needs and flatly refused Allied access to secret information necessary to fly the planes they had ordered. FDR became so exasperated that in March he told the War Department that its opposition must end, that leaks to the isolationist press must stop, and that he would transfer any truculent officers to Guam.

However, America was not even prepared for its own national defense, let alone to defend the democracies affectively. In May 1940 the War Department reported that the army could field only 80,000 men and had equipment for fewer than 500,000 combat troops. As to aircraft and qualified crews, America had but 160 pursuit planes, 52 heavy bombers, and only 260 fully trained pilots. This was partly why Air Corps Chief of Staff General Henry ("Hap") Arnold was reluctant to sell aircraft to Britain and France. At their current rate of loss, 100 planes would last only three days, while substantively reducing the number of American planes for self-defense and thus delaying the training of American pilots.

During the 1930s, Congress had been miserly about defense appropriations; however, in May 1940 it could not provide enough. Members of Congress voted $1.5 billion more for defense—$320 million above what Roosevelt had requested—and then voted another $1.7 billion to expand the regular army from 280,000 to 375,000 men and allowed the president to summon the National Guard for active service.

In the autumn of 1939, Kennedy and Bullitt, America's ambassadors to Britain and France, both consistently predicted that, unless the Allies were given more immediate material aid, they would fall victim to a German assault from the air. At this time FDR expected Germany and Russia to divide Europe between them and then extend their control to Asia Minor and thence the European colonies in Africa and Asia. As a result, the United States would be imperiled. Thus, in his State of the Union message on January 5, 1940, he expressed his anxiety in a significant distinction, explaining that "there is a vast difference between keeping out of war and pretending that war is none of our business. We do not have to go to war with other nations, but at least we can strive with other nations to encourage the kind of peace that will lighten the troubles of the world, and by so doing help our own nation as well." For both domestic and international consumption, FDR was anxious to assert that America must play a decisive part in shaping postwar peace: "For it becomes clearer and clearer that the future world will be a shabby and dangerous place to live in—yes, even for Americans to live in—if it is ruled by force in the hands of a few." Moreover, he warned, "I hope we shall have fewer ostriches in our midst. It is not good for the ultimate health of ostriches to bury their heads in the sand."

The degree of sympathy for Europe and support for American intervention varied throughout the United States and depended partly on ethnic origins. New York City was more interventionist than any other part; Texas was more anti-German; the South showed itself most ready to fight; and the West Coast was more concerned with Japan than Germany. The upper classes were most interventionist: in 1940 more than 66 percent of America's business and intellectual elite wanted increased supplies to be sent to Britain; almost half the people in *Who's Who in America* wanted an immediate declaration of war. Almost everybody favored increasing military and naval strength. Yet opinion polls indicated an unwillingness to accept the inevitable. In late 1939, after the outbreak of war in Europe, 40 percent thought the United States would become involved. In 1940, after the fall of Western Europe, when the likelihood was greater, only 7.7 percent thought so. But one pattern was consistent in these months. To the Gallup question "Do you think the United States should keep out of war or do everything possible to help England, even at the risk of getting into war ourselves?" the public showed increasing acceptance of involvement during 1940. Those willing to take the risk by helping England were 36 percent in May, 50 percent in November, and 60 percent in December.

Proponents of intervention did not simply keep their own counsel; they mobilized their forces. The Committee to Defend America by Aiding the Allies was organized in May 1940 by William Allen White. The committee's aim was to rouse public opinion first to support all aid to Britain short of war and later outright intervention. The "White Committee" included industrialists, financiers, college presidents and faculty, professional men and women, and people from the world of entertainment.

Initial British Strategy

Initial British strategy in the war was to build up military resources slowly for a major offensive against Germany at a later date when Germany was on the verge of economic collapse; meanwhile, the government would give the country the impression of continuous fighting by some diversionary attacks on Italy, first in Africa, later in Europe. The British government believed time was on its side. It was mistaken. It was assumed that a naval blockade of crucial resources such as oil would immobilize Germany's economy. In fact, Germany was not short of raw materials. During World War I it had learnt to make synthetic rubber and other materials. Moreover, Germany acquired various reserve supplies from Russia during the crucial period of its alliance. Meanwhile, it was Britain that was running into difficulties. Its attempted blockade sprung leaks in Italy, Russia, and elsewhere. It had failed to ensure adequate reserves of crucial war materiel.

Perhaps the worst hazard the British faced in the first months of war was loss of merchant shipping to German U-boats. In September the aircraft carrier *Courageous* was sunk; in October the battleship *Royal Oak* was sunk within the defenses of Scapa Flow (a stretch of water around the Orkney Islands off Scotland). In all, Britain lost 229 ships, 800,000 tons of merchant shipping in the first nine months. To compensate, Britain acquired ships from neutrals, brought retired ships back into commission, and began to build new ships. The German pocket battleship *Graf Spee* alone sank eight cargo ships in the South Atlantic until she was detected in December 1939, and pursued to Montevideo, Uruguay, where she was scuttled on the orders of Hitler himself. The British shortage was in carrying capacity and the system of convoy, successful in anticipating attack by U-boats, meant that ships made fewer voyages and took longer to complete them.

The British government sent an expeditionary force of four divisions to France led by Lord Gort who, it is said, was chosen by Secretary of War Leslie Hore-Belisha because Hore-Belisha was on bad terms with him. The first British casualty fell defending the Maginot line on December 13, 1939. When Hore-Belisha said, quite rightly, that British defenses of the unfortified French frontier with Belgium were inadequate, his generals complained and Chamberlain fired him.

Churchill, supported by the French, persuaded the British government to "mine the leads"—the long strip of Norwegian territorial waters that German ships used in the winter, when the Baltic was frozen, to carry iron ore from Sweden. His plan, and that of the French, was aided by the Anglo-French response to the Russo-Finnish War: assembling an expeditionary force of 100,000 men. To reach Finland the expeditionary force would first have to cross Norway and Sweden. En route it could seize Narvik, the Norwegian port from which iron ore was despatched to Germany, and could then proceed to wreck the Swedish iron mines. The proposal seemed to suit everyone: the British government, which wanted action; the French government, which wanted to distance its country from the war; the British and French peoples, who wanted to support gallant Finland; and Churchill, who wanted to divert French

.

The cadavers of Poles executed by German forces await burial, a residue of the atrocity that was to become so common in the war and that would lead to the measuring of human bodies in terms more appropriate to those for real estate. (Inter-Allied Information Center, probably 1942; Library of Congress).

opposition to the Soviet Union against Germany. It was supposed that the supply of iron ore to Germany would be brought to an abrupt end and German industry would be crippled. Yet for Britain and France to challenge Russia and risk a second war while they were at war with Russia's new ally, Germany, was absurd. In January 1940 both Norway and Sweden refused to allow Anglo-French forces to cross through their lands.

It was while Britain and France dithered but took no action that Finland acceded to the Russian demands on March 12, 1940. Chamberlain, seconded by Churchill, tried to silence British outrage at his failure to protect Finland by getting the cabinet to approve the long-delayed plan to mine the Norwegian leads. This was planned for April 8, 1940. Unfortunately, Hitler also struck. That very night the Germans entered Denmark without encountering any opposition and also occupied every significant port in Norway, including Oslo and Narvik. Incensed by the German advantage in what they regarded as their waters, the North sea, the British responded to Norway's pleas for aid.

It seemed that, unlike Austria, Czechoslovakia, and Poland, Norway was within the range and compass of British ability.

However, the Narvik campaign was a catastrophe. The British units were raw; Churchill, the cabinet, and the chiefs of staff were divided as to which should be the precise target — Narvik, Trondheim, Namsos, or Aandalsnes; and the admiralty and the war office issued contradictory orders. Moreover, Germany held most of Norway's air fields. Britain's army and navy could not maneuver whilst in range of the German air force. Nevertheless, Narvik was taken and occupied briefly — from May 28 to June 8, 1940. There were certain immediate gains, including the transfer of the king of Norway to Britain with a million tons of shipping and the German loss of three cruisers and ten destroyers. However, the British public recognized the general disaster and understood something of the technical reasons — inadequacies of preparation, men, and air power. Chamberlain was blamed. Churchill, who was far more responsible for the failure, gained in public esteem. The British people — and, after them, English-speaking peoples across the world — were assessing their politicians on the entire record of their careers and their spirit rather than on a specific contribution at a particular time. Chamberlain had long been a compromiser and an appeaser: Churchill had been the eloquent lone voice in the wilderness who had argued against appeasement. Although the government survived what was essentially a vote of no confidence in the House of Commons by 281 votes for to 200 against, Chamberlain's days as prime minister were clearly numbered.

[2]

TO BE OR NOT TO BE?
American Intervention in World War II

A T LAST Winston Churchill became British prime minister, swept to power by an incipient revolt of backbenchers in the House of Commons. The alternative would have been the foreign secretary, Edward, Viscount Halifax, who had connived at Chamberlain's strategy of appeasement without incurring any opprobrium. In fact, all political leaders would have accepted him and he was actually favored by Chamberlain and King George VI.

It seemed that Churchill would have to concede the position he desperately wanted. He was still outside any inner circle of power and he had declared repeatedly that, in this terrible emergency, he would serve with or under anyone. He was counseled by his friends and advisers, the press baron Lord Beaverbrook and Bendan Bracken, just to stay silent if he were asked to serve under Halifax. When he met Chamberlain, Halifax, and the Conservative chief whip, he did, indeed, stay silent for two whole minutes when he was asked whether he would serve under Halifax. Thus the appeasers at last faced the unpalatable truth. If Churchill stayed outside a future coalition government, they

45

would all be swept away in a tide of public indignation. When Halifax modestly remarked how it would be difficult for a peer of the realm to be prime minister, especially "in such a war as this," his prospects died with his ebbing phrase. It transpired that the Labour party was not averse to Churchill after all and, once Germany invaded Belgium and Holland, the Labour party declared unequivocally it would only serve "under a new Prime Minister."

Chamberlain resigned and Churchill was summoned to Buckingham Palace. However, in the House of Commons he was cheered only by Labour. In a speech combining words from Garibaldi and Clemenceau he declared, "I have nothing to offer but blood, toil, tears and sweat. You ask, What is our policy? I will say: It is to wage war by sea, land, and air, with all our might and with all the strength that God can give us. . . . You ask, What is our aim? I can answer in one word: Victory —victory at all costs, victory in spite of all terror; victory, however long and hard the road may be." This was precisely what Churchill's detractors dreaded. Churchill himself hardly saw what was involved. Victory would entail Russian domination of central and eastern Europe and the ascent of the United States to globalism at the expense of the old British Empire Churchill cherished so much. Perhaps his decision to make Halifax British ambassador to Washington (1941–46) was a portent of placing Britain in pawn to the United States.

Fall of Western Europe

Until this time, every move Hitler had made had been successful. Even his anxiety over British and French entry into the war had been dispelled by the rapid success of the war in Poland. As a result, he was convinced he could push further ahead still faster with his plans for the conquest of Europe. Hitler took personal control of all war strategy, and he believed that his success in Poland would lead to peace negotiations with Britain. In fact, bad weather allowed his reluctant generals to postpone a planned western offensive. The next outstanding military successes were the result of the skills of Germany's leading militarists. there was little that any of them, beyond factory workers, could do, to taries of war and the navy. They replaced the two most isolationist

The lull before the storm. A calm Fourth of July for Hartford, Wisconsin, in 1941. A solitary youth saunters along a sun-drenched street decorated with an American flag and a giant advertising ice-cream cone. (Photo by John Vachon for the Farm Security Administration; Library of Congress).

Manstein planned the attack against France through the Ardennes (from May 10, 1940), instead of through the Low Countries.

The German invasion of Holland and Belgium of spring 1940 was prompted in part because these neutral countries would provide Britain and France with an easy route to the Ruhr, the center of German industry. By driving his troops through the end of the Maginot line Hitler could, at one stroke, break through French defenses, cut Holland and Belgium off from Allied support, and thereby win his war in the West. The Allies' supreme commander, Gamelin, decided to move his troops into Belgium, partly to shorten the Allied front, partly to stir the Dutch and Belgian armies, and in part to compensate for the Allies' numerical inferiority. However, Holland capitulated on May 15 and Queen Wilhelmina escaped to England. In Belgium Allied troops at first held their own against the Germans. Once the Germans penetrated their lines at Sedan on May 14 and took Amiens, they were able to reach the coast and thus cut the Allies off from their escape route.

The Germans continued to advance across French territory while the French planned offensives on paper. Just before Belgium capitulated in the early hours of May 28, operation Dynamo began—the evacuation of British troops from Dunkirk. Hitler's interference here was to cost him dearly later. He held back General Heinz Guderian's tanks south of Dunkirk, enabling Britain to organize the evacuation of its army. The British army, with 330,000 men trapped in Europe, evacuated the beaches of Dunkirk with such heroism that propaganda almost succeeded in transfiguring this unmitigated disaster into a symbolic victory. Italy then declared war on Britain and France on June 10, 1940. The French government of Paul Reynaud survived by two days the German occupation of Paris on June 14. Eventually, the total evacuation of troops during the Battle of France reached 558,032 of whom 368,491 were British and the remainder French, Poles, Belgian, and Dutch, all of whom escaped to the moated fortress of the island kingdom.

Hitler insisted on accepting the French surrender at exactly the same spot in the forest of Compiègne where Germany had surrendered twenty-two years earlier. Fascism was the philosophy of Reynaud's successor, Marshal Henri Philippe Pétain, the eighty-four-year-old hero of Verdun in World War I who was determined to use the defeat of France to rid his country of the ideologies of the left. Pétain reached an armistice with Germany on June 22, and he established a fascist government—first at Bordeaux and then at the resort of Vichy in southern France—that arranged terms of collaboration on October 24. On July 3, 1940, the British government ordered the scuttling of the French fleet at Mers-el-Kebir (Oran) (with considerable loss of life) to prevent its falling into German hands. The fall of France was devastating not only for Britain and the rest of Europe but also for the United States, where it was taken as a clear signal that, unless Britain were given substantive material aid, it could not stand alone against the Nazis, far less turn the tide of the German advance and shield America from the greatest military threat ever. Robert Sherwood, in *Roosevelt and Hopkins* (1950), has said that during the early war Roosevelt was at a loss to know what to do. This was "a period of terrible stultifying vacuum."

To Be or Not to Be? Part of the propaganda on behalf of the beleaguered European Allies so dreaded by Charles Lindbergh and America First came from the great Hollywood studios in a series of films extolling the values of freedom and democracy. Hamlet's most famous line was not only the title for a war comedy set against the Nazi invasion of Poland but also the rhetorical question that guided America's hesitation over intervention in World War II.

The film focuses on the valiant efforts of a troop of actors, led by Jack Benny (as unlikely a gloomy Dane as any since Sarah Bernhardt), to escape to England. With Jack Benny and Carol Lombard *(center)* in her last film are Shemp Howard, shedding his Three Stooges persona to disguise himself as Hitler, and Robert Stack *(fourth from right)*. While Ernst Lubitsch's comedy initially received bad reviews because the film seemed in bad taste, it is now considered a minor classic, especially for its throwaway delivery of lines that always hit their target. (United Artists; Museum of Modern Art Film Stills Archive).

Battle of Britain

Despite increased taxation, the British people were in a somewhat
exultant mood as they waited for an imminent German attack. Their
mood of defiance prompted Churchill to declare to the House of Commons on June 18, 1940, in one of the most memorable expressions of
the war, "Let us therefore brace ourselves to our duties, and so bear
ourselves that, if the British Empire and its Commonwealth last for a
thousand years, men will say: 'This was their finest hour.' " The general
public rallied to his call although few grasped that their ultimate fate
would lie with the skill and tenacity of the British air force and that
there was little that any of them, beyond factory workers, could do, to
contribute to the final victory.

The battle of Britain of the summer of 1940 began with German
attacks on convoys of merchant ships. On August 13 the second part of
the battle commenced with a full-scale German attack on England with
bomber aircraft protected by fighters. Provided with five hundred new
fighters, Air Marshal Hugh Dowding concentrated on the destruction of
the bombers. Hence the Germans set out to destroy the fighter bases in
the county of Kent, and they nearly succeeded. However, on September
7 the Germans began to bomb London, which resulted in massive loss
of life and the dislocation of society, but the Kent airfields were saved.
The German Luftwaffe made its last effort on September 15 and then
conceded air superiority to the British by withdrawing. Hitler postponed
his immediate invasion of Britain on September 17. However, the
Germans bombed London every night from September 7 to November 2
and then turned to other industrial cities and western ports. The last
severe air raid of the so-called blitz came on Birmingham on May 16,
1941. Thereafter, the Luftwaffe prepared to cooperate with the German
army for the invasion of Russia, which began on June 22, 1941. The

Their faces betraying horror and anxiety, a Belgian mother and her three
children walk through the ruins of their home town after invading German
forces have passed through and demolished obstacles in their way with brutal
rapture. The plight of the innocent is made more poignant in the photograph by
the contrast of moving figures and tall tree with the billowing smoke that tells
us the devastation is recent. (Office of War Information; Library of Congress).

conflict then turned to the battle of the seas. The German attempt to destroy the convoys carrying American supplies reached its first climax between March and July 1941 in the battle of the Atlantic. That April, 700,000 tons of shipping were sunk.

Increasing Involvement

In response to Germany's conquest of Europe and Japan's conquest of Southeast Asia, American foreign policy from the summer of 1940 to the winter of 1941 developed in five stages. Three of the stages—the destroyers-bases deal, lend-lease, and the war at sea—led to the Atlantic Charter signed by Roosevelt and Churchill. The other two—economic restrictions on Japan and intransigent opposition to Japan's territorial claims—led to Pearl Harbor and the full intervention of the United States in the war.

After Italy's declaration of war and the conquest of Holland, Belgium, and France, it was possible for Roosevelt to arouse the American people to the needs of national defense. Roosevelt said at Charlottesville, Virginia, on June 10, 1940, "We will extend to the opponents of force the material resources of this nation and, at the same time, we will harness and speed up the use of those resources in order that we ourselves in the Americas may have equipment and training equal to the task of any emergency and every defense." The next month representatives of the American republics at the Havana conference in Cuba agreed to take action to prevent any change in the status of the European colonies in the Western Hemisphere and to consider aggression against any one of them as aggression against them all. This solidarity lasted until Pearl Harbor, when Chile refused, temporarily, and Argentina, permanently, to sever their relations with the Axis powers. Some countries offered the United States military bases, while others replaced German military advisers with Americans. The United States increased its purchase of raw materials within the hemisphere and sold its products at restricted prices to the other countries that had been deprived of European goods.

In an attempt to widen his base of support, on June 19, 1940, Roosevelt appointed two prominent Republicans who had opposed the New Deal, Henry L. Stimson and Frank Knox, as, respectively, secre-

The savage beauty of this dramatic photograph of St. Paul's Cathedral illuminated in the London night sky by the terrifying fireworks of the German blitz on the British capital in 1940 has made it an icon of the darkest days of the war against Hitler. (Library of Congress).

taries of war and the navy. They replaced the two most isolationist members of the cabinet, Harry Woodring and Charles Edison. Knox, the Republican vice presidential candidate in 1936, favored considerable military expansion, an army of one million men, the strongest air force in the world, and the immediate shipment of late-model planes to Britain. Stimson wanted the repeal of all neutrality legislation and the introduction of military conscription. In fact, in this period Harry L. Hopkins exercised more influence on Roosevelt than either Cordell Hull or Sumner Welles. Called "Lord Root of the Matter" by Churchill, Hopkins had the same sort of position with Roosevelt that Colonel Edward House had enjoyed with Woodrow Wilson. Unlike House, Hopkins did not pretend to know his chief's mind when he did not; and, since his sole aim was to serve, he did not quarrel with the president.

Hitler expected Britain to surrender. When that did not happen, he turned his attention increasingly to a planned invasion of the Soviet Union, which had occupied eastern Poland and Bessarabia. Hitler wanted to counter further Soviet advances by getting Hungary and Rumania to come to terms with him. He urged Mussolini to abandon a proposed Italian invasion of Greece. Nevertheless, Mussolini, chagrined at Germany's successes, did invade Greece. Mussolini's lack of success there made it necessary for German forces to come to the rescue of Italians in the Balkans and North Africa, which was an unwelcome diversion and a distraction of German forces. Hitler's plans were further disrupted by a coup d'état in Yugoslavia in March 1941 that overthrew the government that had made an agreement with the Third Reich. Hitler decided to retaliate by invading Yugoslavia.

On July 21, 1940, Winston Churchill made a specific plea to Roosevelt for a transference of destroyers from America in exchange for leases of British naval bases. Although Roosevelt had announced in June all aid short of war, he delayed action until the transfer could be presented as an act of defense and accomplished without reference to Congress. The eventual agreement, which was incorporated in letters exchanged among Cordell Hull, Philip Kerr (Lord Lothian), the British ambassador, on September 2, 1940, gave British bases in Newfoundland and Bermuda to the United States as an outright gift, In addition, the agreement granted to the United States ninety-nine-year leases on other bases in the Bahamas, Jamaica, St. Lucia, Trinidad, British Guiana, and Antigua in exchange for fifty old American destroyers, which were built in World War I, were now out of commission, and not needed while the British navy controlled the Atlantic. Only nine destroyers entered British service before 1941. The gesture was one of sympathy, rather than support, and was granted by Roosevelt in a calculated and careful maneuver. The fact that the destroyers would otherwise have been sold as scrap metal for about $5,000 apiece allowed FDR to comment that, for a total of $250,000, the United States had taken "the most important action in the reinforcement of our national defense that has been taken since the Louisiana Purchase."

Moreover, after the destroyers-bases deal, the United States was not neutral in any real sense of the term. It seemed Roosevelt and Hull believed that total aid short of war would be the best way of avoiding attack or intervention. Joseph Kennedy, former ambassador to the court of Saint James, declared that talk about Britain fighting for democracy was "bunk." John Foster Dulles, a prominent lawyer and later secretary of state, said, "Only hysteria entertains the idea that Germany, Italy or Japan contemplates war upon us."

Election of 1940

The dispute over intervention was exacerbated by the presidential campaign of 1940. The dark horse of the Republicans' campaign was Indiana utility tycoon Wendell Willkie, who was president of the Commonwealth and Southern Corporation and had fought the Tennessee Valley Authority and thus could present himself as a hapless business victim of the encroaching power of the state. Willkie was a liberal and an internationalist. Historian Ralph F. de Bedts comments in *Recent American History* (1973) that

it is easy to see why Willkie impressed so many Republicans weary of the typical candidate of that party. He was known and respected on Wall Street, yet a man of liberal persuasion who had no intention of swapping the New Deal in a desperate attempt to return to the era of [William] McKinley. He concurred in most of the New Deal's programs, insisting only that they had been inefficient in operation and could be carried out without as much bureaucracy and regimentation. He was a strong internationalist who belied his midwestern origins by speaking out unhesitatingly for increased aid to Britain. An exuberant and refreshing personality, Willkie's candor and boyish grin were an attractive alternative to the usual run of Republican party politicians.

The international crisis was the most crucial factor in prompting FDR to decide on his candidacy in May 1940. Ironically, he was supported by a group of leading politicians that included both the proponents and opponents of intervention. Although Roosevelt chose Chicago as the site of the Democratic National Convention—because he could rely on the local political boss, Ed Kelly, to "pack the galleries"—he would not openly campaign for his nomination, seeking instead the fiction of a spontaneous draft. Kelly had his superintendent of sewers rouse delegates for FDR through loudspeakers around the hall. After a dutiful show of reluctance and deference, Roosevelt was nominated by 946 votes on the first ballot. In place of John Nance Garner, FDR chose Secretary of Agriculture Henry A. Wallace as his running mate because

Wallace was a committed New Dealer who could carry the Corn Belt. The choice was accepted (although reluctantly in some quarters) by the delegates.

In the election FDR received 27,307,819 votes (54.8 percent) to Willkie's 22,321,018 (44.8 percent) and 449 votes in the electoral college to Willkie's 82. (Socialist candidate Norman Thomas, who was a prominent isolationist, polled 99,557 votes.) Roosevelt had won all but ten states, eight in the Midwest and Maine and Vermont in the Northeast. Roosevelt won his victory in the cities; and it was his decisive pluralities in New York City, Chicago, Cleveland, and Milwaukee that gave him the pivotal states of New York, Illinois, Ohio, and Wisconsin. He attracted the ethnic groups, such as Norwegians, Poles, and Jews, who had most at stake on his policy of intervention in the war.

Because Willkie had been a committed internationalist until the eleventh hour, his campaign convinced isolationists they had been deprived of a genuine choice in the election. Thus Senator Gerald P. Nye told an America First meeting in Kansas City on June 19, 1941, "I shall be surprised if history does not show that beginning at the Republican convention in Philadelphia a conspiracy was carried out to deny the American people a chance to express themselves." Against the wishes of Willkie the Republican National Committee had made anti-intervention broadcasts that declared to mothers "Don't blame Franklin D. Roosevelt because he sent your son to war—blame yourself because you sent Franklin D. Roosevelt back to the White House." Accepting the counsel of his advisers, immediately before the election on October 30, 1940, FDR consented to promise, "Your boys are not going to be sent into any foreign wars." Most significant, under pressure from his advisers, FDR had dropped the crucial qualifying phrase "except in case of attack."

In the early 1940s, isolation was increasingly synonymous with the America First Committee. America First was founded on September 4, 1940, by two students at Yale, Kingman Brewster, Jr., and R. Douglas

Their lives, if not their homes, secure from the terrors of Hitler's nightly blitz on London, citizens sleep as best they can in the Elephant and Castle underground station. (A British official photo released in America by the Office of War Information; Library of Congress).

Stuart, Jr. Stuart, the son of the Quaker Oats magnate, arranged for considerable financial backing from Chicago businessmen, led by Robert E. Wood, chairman of Sears Roebuck. The strength of America First lay in its exceptional organization of 450 chapters across the country, with a total membership of between 800,000 and 850,000 that drew on support from the rank and file of the National Council for the Prevention of War and the Women's International League for Peace and Freedom. Members included conservative opponents of FDR, college students opposed to the draft, and a few Communists. The big guns were Herbert Hoover, Joseph P. Kennedy, Hugh S. Johnson, and Henry Ford.

It was America First's association with star aviator Charles Augustus Lindbergh, Jr., that ensured intense and thorough press coverage of its activities. Lindbergh had become known internationally for his solo fight across the Atlantic in May 1927. Lindbergh's visits to Germany in 1930, 1937, and 1938 had been widely reported in the press. During those visits, he had inspected German air power and had reported his findings back to the American military attaché in Berlin, Major Truman Smith. Lindbergh did not accept the general contemporary pro-British and anti-German interpretation of European affairs. His sympathies for Britain and France had been blunted by what he regarded as their inability to accommodate themselves to the new phenomenon of German air power. He thought American intervention in the war would be a disaster for the American economy and that American democracy might not survive it.

Knowing Lindbergh's views, the members of America First wanted him to become the organization's principal speaker. He was, quite simply, one of the most popular men in America. However, Lindbergh's popularity was as effervescent as a film star's. Furthermore, Lindbergh was a political novice who failed to realize that his generalizations divided where they were meant to unite. Thus, at Des Moines, Iowa, on September 11, 1941, he told an audience of eight thousand that the interventionists' "ever-increasing effort to force the United States into

The morning after the night before. Firemen in the city of London on Cannon Street, close to St. Paul's Cathedral, attempt to quench the flames of a burning building following a German air raid. (British Press Service; Library of Congress).

the conflict" had been "so successful that, today, our country stands on the verge of war." Further, he identified the "war agitators":

The three most important groups who have been pressing this country toward war are the British, the Jewish, and the Roosevelt Administration. Behind these groups, but of lesser importance, are a number of capitalists, anglophiles, and intellectuals, who believe that their future and the future of mankind, depend upon the domination of the British Empire. Add to these the communistic groups who were opposed to intervention until a few weeks ago, and I believe I have named the major war agitators in this country.

He concluded that these particular groups were trying to involve the United States by advocating increased military preparedness for defense and creating "a series of incidents which would force us into the actual conflict." His designation of the British, the Jews, and the Roosevelt administration as "war agitators" was wide open to the interpretation that he and America First suffered from anglophobia, anti-Semitism, and selfish conservatism. The Des Moines speech was bitterly attacked by the press, deeply resented by Lindbergh's nominal allies, and, worst of all, praised by the very elements from which America First wished to dissociate itself.

House Resolution 1776: Lend-Lease

Roosevelt realized that because Britain had exhausted its cash reserves, it could not continue to pay for heavy purchases of materials in the United States — and without these materials it could not continue the war. While on a Caribbean cruise recovering from his campaign, Roosevelt received a letter from Winston Churchill explaining the British plight and pleading with him to find a way of providing the necessary additional aid. Britain had less than $2 billion with which to pay orders costing $5 billion. Stimulated by Churchill, by Lord Lothian, and the White committee, Roosevelt proposed lend-lease. Roosevelt explained lend-lease at a press conference in Washington, D.C., on December 16, 1940. He introduced it with a parable suggested by Harold Ickes:

Suppose my neighbor's house catches fire, and I have a length of garden hose. If he can take my garden hose and connect it up with his hydrant, I may help him put out the fire. Now what do I do? I don't say to him before that operation,

Victims injured in a night raid during the blitz on London when their air-raid shelter was hit by a bomb are carried into an ambulance by police. As part of their propaganda for the United States, British officials released this photograph under the heavily ironic title *Nazi "Military Objectives."* (Library of Congress).

"Neighbor, my garden hose cost me fifteen dollars; you have to pay me fifteen dollars for it." What is the transaction that goes on? I don't want fifteen dollars —I want my garden hose back after the fire is over. All right if it goes through the fire all right, intact, without damage to it, he gives it back to me and thanks me very much for the use of it.

Roosevelt proposed loans of tanks, planes, and ships to Britain without detailed suggestions as to how Britain might repay "in kind" after the war. The argument was sophistical; the appeal was unsophisticated. Furthermore, Roosevelt renewed the proposal in his fireside chat of December 29, 1940, when he told the country it was necessary for America to expand its industrial production, for "we must be the great arsenal of democracy." Mail to the White House was 100 to 1 in favor,

61

while polls of public opinion showed that 80 percent who had heard the talk directly or read about it approved, while only 12 percent were opposed to FDR's arguments. FDR repeated the argument in his State of the Union address of January 6, 1941, and went further, claiming that victory over the Axis powers would mean "a world [based] upon four essential human freedoms: freedom of speech and religion and freedom from want and fear."

Fortuitously numbered House Resolution 1776, the lend-lease bill gave the president power to lend, lease, sell or barter arms, food, or any "defense article," to foreign nations "whose defense the president deems vital to the defense of the United States." Of course, one reason for freeing lend-lease entirely from the question of loans was to avoid the sort of controversy attached to Wall Street loans to the Allies in World War I. On March 11, 1941, the Senate approved the bill by 60 votes to 31, and the House did so by 317 votes to 71. Once the president had signed the act, Congress voted an appropriation of $7 billion to implement its terms.

The conception was bold, the accomplishment a bare minimum. In *Rise to Globalism* (1971) historian Stephen E. Ambrose describes Roosevelt's reluctance to provide strong central control and assesses the conflicting interests of the officials involved: "American officials used the new system as a wedge to get American firms into the British Commonwealth market and to force the British to sell their holdings on the American continents, and the Army resisted sending arms needed in the United States to Britain, so that the total amount of goods shipped, in comparison with the need, was small." British imports from the United States increased by only 3 percent in 1941, and the increase was principally in foodstuffs and steel. Most of the American arms obtained were still bought with cash in 1941, and Britain lost most of its remaining dollars. Naturally, Britain could not turn lend-lease goods into exports, but exports not made from lend-lease materials were cut down so as to avoid an outcry from American manufacturers.

Senator Arthur Vandenberg of Michigan wrote in his diary after the passing of House Resolution 1776 that he thought this was the suicide of the Republic: "We have torn up 150 years of traditional foreign policy. We have tossed Washington's Farewell Address into the discard. We have thrown ourselves squarely into the power politics and power

Hollywood pulled out all the stops to show beleaguered Britain ennobled by suffering in its tale of *Mrs. Miniver*, a valiant housewife coping with the perils of the blitz. While a generation of American filmgoers was deeply touched by the situations and Greer Garson's performance was awarded an Oscar, the actress's overlong speech of thanks at the ceremony, rich in breathy pauses and poor in depth of feeling, somewhat dissipated the goodwill the film had nurtured. (Museum of Modern Art Film Stills Archive).

wars of Europe, Asia and Africa. We have taken the first step upon a course from which we can never hereafter retreat."

War in the Atlantic

Lend-lease was no use unless American supplies reached Britain. In February and March 1941, German submarines sank or seized twenty-two ships. Despite the opposition of about half the Senate to the idea of American convoys supporting British freighters across half the Atlantic,

Roosevelt announced that America's security zone would be extended one thousand miles into the Atlantic beginning April 11, 1941. The air force was used to patrol the North Atlantic as far as Iceland in order to warn British ships of the presence of German submarines. A majority of the cabinet favored a declaration of war on Germany. Henry Stimson was concerned that Roosevelt had not followed his victory with the Lend-Lease Act with more positive policy but had continued to move with great caution. In this concern he was supported by Secretary of the Navy Frank Knox, Attorney General Robert H. Jackson, and Secretary of the Interior Harold L. Ickes. Stimson writes in his diary entry for April 25, 1941, how Roosevelt introduced a program for patrolling the western Atlantic and then added defensively, "Well, it's a step forward." Stimson answered back, "Well, I hope you will keep on walking, Mr. President. Keep on walking." Clare Booth Luce said Roosevelt's symbolic gesture was not—like Churchill's defiant one—two fingers raised in a *v* shape but, rather, a moistened finger held to test the wind.

In fact, FDR did not believe in war as social therapy—that is, as a means of strengthening national fiber. In his account of FDR's foreign policy, Robert Dallek (1979) develops this point to explain why the president moved the United States to war so cautiously.

Roosevelt appreciated that he could command a national majority on escorting, on occupation of Atlantic islands, and possibly on direct involvement in the war. But these actions did not promise a broad, stable consensus for fighting which a major provocation abroad could give. In his view, if a substantial minority in the country felt that he, rather than a meaningful threat to national security, compelled involvement in the conflict, it would be difficult to assure wartime unity in the United States, especially in the face of any temporary defeat. In short, if he were to avoid painful wartime divisions, the nation would have to enter the fighting with a minimum of doubt and dissent, and the way to achieve this was not through educational talks to the public or strong Executive action, but through developments abroad which aroused the country to fight.

Nevertheless, despite FDR's caution, British military staffs already had had secret conversations in Washington, D.C., with the American Combined Chiefs of Staff from January 29 to March 27, 1941. Britain and the United States were not yet formal allies. However, they were already "associated powers" with a common goal.

Elsewhere, other weaker countries were seeking support from strong allies. By early 1941 Hungary, Bulgaria, and Rumania had been conquered by Germany. Italy had failed to subdue Yugoslavia and Greece; but, once Germany had launched an offensive on these countries on April 6, 1941, they too were made subject to the Axis powers within three weeks.

In May 1941 the American freighter *Robin Moor* was sunk by Germans in the southern Atlantic. Roosevelt declared an "unlimited national emergency," froze all German and Italian assets in the United States, and closed their consulates. According to public opinion polls, in June popular support for convoys was 52 percent; and 75 percent of Americans approved the use of convoys if it seemed that Britain would not win the war without the security of supplies the United States provided.

To make the Atlantic patrols more effective, Roosevelt and his advisers decided to secure territories on the edge of the zone. On April 9, 1941, the State Department concluded an agreement in Washington, D.C., with the exiled Danish minister to occupy the Danish possession of Greenland. In June and July the administration negotiated with Iceland to replace British and Canadian troops stationed there with an American force that landed on July 7. The American patrol ships were given secret orders to extend their duties beyond patrolling rather than allow any hostile force to deflect them from their course.

On May 10, 1941, Hitler's deputy, Rudolf Hess, created an international sensation by flying secretly to Scotland with peace proposals of his own. It is thought he did so partly to restore his own flagging prestige, but, in any case, it was to no avail. He was immediately treated as a prisoner of war, held prisoner throughout the remaining years of the war, and, subsequently, after a trial at Nuremberg for war crimes, kept in solitary confinement at Spandau prison in Berlin. The Russians were deaf to pleas for any remission during his last years of illness; and he died, a prisoner still, in 1987.

On June 22, 1941, Hitler repudiated the Nazi-Soviet Pact and invaded Russia. On June 26, 1941, the United States announced that the neutrality laws would not be invoked against Russia because American security was not endangered. But on July 26 Roosevelt sent Hopkins to Moscow to ascertain Stalin's needs, and on August 2 Roosevelt promised Russia aid against aggression. On November 7, 1941, lend-lease was applied to Russia as well as Britain.

Stalin was, ultimately, the most successful of all the leaders of the

Grand Alliance. Recognizing that Hitler would soon attack the Soviet Union he decided to exercise total control of Russian defense. In May 1941 Stalin appointed himself chair of the Council of People's Commissars and thus de facto head of the government. (This was the first time Stalin had held government office since 1923. In between he had been general secretary of the Communist party—a post that he also held until his death.) Hitler's initial success in attacking Russia exposed numerous weaknesses in Stalin's defense measures. (Nikita Khrushchev was to claim later that Stalin was so stunned by Germany's initial success that he was shocked into inactivity. Yet, he rallied to assume supreme control as commander in chief.)

In an attempt to discuss the objectives of Britain and the still technically neutral America in the war, Roosevelt met Churchill at sea in Placentia Bay off Argentia, Newfoundland, from August 9 to August 12, 1941. Their meeting had been planned by Harry Hopkins. Intending a complement to Woodrow Wilson's Fourteen Points, the two leaders declared in the Atlantic Charter that their countries sought no new territory in the course of the war; that territorial changes would only be made with reference to the populations involved; that all peoples had the right to choose the form of their government; that all nations had equal right of access to raw materials and trade throughout the world; and that after the war aggressor nations would be forced to disarm until a permanent system of international security was established. In short, the future peace should, as FDR's earlier promise had suggested, give all peoples freedom from want and freedom from fear and freedom of speech and religion. Roosevelt's recollection of how the United States had treated Woodrow Wilson's scheme for the League of Nations led him to have explicit references to systems of international security deleted. More significantly, the experience of working together drew the two leaders closer. Roosevelt appreciated the tenacity and charm of Churchill, and Churchill liked Roosevelt's subtlety and sense of timing.

In response to Churchill's desire that America should declare war, FDR explained that a request to Congress for a declaration of war would simply produce a political debate lasting three months. Instead, according to Churchill's report of August 19, 1941, to his own cabinet, FDR had "said that he would wage war, but not declare it, and that he would become more and more provocative. . . . Everything was to be done to force an 'incident' . . . which would justify him in opening hostilities."

American public opinion was overwhelmingly favorable to the principles of the Atlantic Charter, provided it did not lead to outright intervention in the war. Moreover, isolationist sentiment in Congress was
still strong. The occupation of Iceland by 4,000 marines on July 7,
1941, opened debate about the appropriate size and disposition of
American forces. The Selective Service Act of 1940 had allowed for
900,000 draftees for one year's service in the Western Hemisphere.
Military strategists agreed this number was inadequate. However, Congress was reluctant to take the initiative in the unpopular measure of
increasing and extending the draft. FDR agreed with congressional
leaders on July 14 that he would take the responsibility in his strong
recommendation to Congress on July 21, in which he warned against
the "tragic error" of allowing the "disintegration" of the comparatively
modest army. The Senate voted for an extension of selective military
service to eighteen months—rather than for the duration of the emergency, as FDR had asked—with 45 in favor and 21 senators not voting
at all. On August 12 the House agreed by a majority of one: 203 votes
in favor to 202 against. That narrow victory was essentially due to the
work of Chief of Staff General George C. Marshall from behind the
scenes.

On September 4 the United States and Germany began an undeclared
naval war after an incident in which the commander of a German
submarine U-652 off Iceland sent torpedoes at what he thought was a
British destroyer. It was an American ship, the *Greer*. Describing the
attacks on the *Greer* and other ships as "acts of international lawlessness" intended by Germany to destroy freedom of the seas, Roosevelt
said in a radio address of September 11, 1941, that American vessels
and planes "will no longer wait until Axis submarines lurking under the
water, or Axis raiders on the surface of the sea, strike their deadly blow
—first."

Had FDR said that the U-boat had fired in self-defense—which was
what had really happened—and had he admitted that Hitler did not
intend to attack American ships in the Atlantic—which was what
Churchill told his colleagues—he would have had to wait for the
imminent collapse of Britain and Russia before getting nationwide support for declared military intervention. Yet here was cause for future
unease of a different sort—the manipulation of an incident by a president, acting on the basis that the end justifies the means. Historian

A series of pictures found on a German officer killed on the Russian front recorded the grisly stages of execution of five Russian civilians outside the town of Velizh in the region by Smolensk in September 1941. Moscow Radio made powerful use of this damning evidence of German war tactics when the pictures were discovered in February 1942. (Office of Emergency Management; Library of Congress).

Robert Dallek (1979) observes, somewhat ruefully, "Yet for all the need to mislead the country in its own interest, the President's deviousness also injured the national well-being over the long run. His action in the *Greer* incident created a precedent for manipulation of public opinion which would be repeated by later Presidents in less justifiable circumstances."

In October another destroyer, the *Reuben James*, was sunk off Iceland with the loss of one hundred American lives. However, when Roosevelt signed a revision of the neutrality laws on November 17, 1941, permitting the arming of American marine ships and allowing them to carry cargoes to belligerents' ports, he was giving assent to an act that was passed by narrow margins in both houses — 50 to 37 in the Senate and

212 to 194 in the House—that reflected the still prevalent division of opinion.

Oil and Troubled Waters

Roosevelt's attempt to exert diplomatic pressure upon foreign governments as he thought appropriate in these years was somewhat undermined by the separate resolve and conflicting power aims of two major oil companies, Standard Oil of New Jersey (or Exxon from 1972 onward) and Texaco.

In 1941 Standard Oil of New Jersey was investigated by the Department of Justice which then brought two antitrust suits against the company. The first suit was for conspiring to control oil transportation through pipelines; the second was on account of its restrictive agreement with I. G. Farben. Walter Teagle, chairman of Standard Oil, encountered considerable press censure when Thurman Arnold launched a vicious and overstated attack on the company, accusing it of retarding research into synthetic rubber and providing Nazi Germany with valuable industrial secrets. In fact, America had learned much from German research. Nevertheless, the newspaper *PM* was typical in its charge that "the plain fact is that Adolf Hitler has used and is using American citizens and American laws to advance the Nazi cause in this hemisphere." Moreover, it was true that, by their restrictive agreement with Farben, Teagle and the new chief executive, Bill Farish, had broken antitrust laws. Indeed, their agreement with Farben was foolhardy. Despite Teagle's impassioned appeal to FDR, Roosevelt would not do anything to help him; and the company's other directors preferred to settle with the Department of Justice. In exchange for the company's promise to release its patents and pay a fine of $50,000, the department reduced its charges.

When the members of a Senate committee investigating defense heard some of Arnold's charges, they were outraged. The timing could hardly have been more unfortunate. Just as Japan was over-running Malaya with its valuable rubber plantations, Arnold disclosed how Standard Oil of New Jersey had delayed research into synthetic rubber. Asked if the charges were treasonable, Senator Harry Truman of Missouri, who headed the committee, answered, "Why, yes, what else is it?" Although the charges died away, the company's sales suffered on account of public odium; and both Teagle and Farish were broken men. Farish died suddenly, and Teagle resigned prematurely.

Another scandal disgraced Texaco. Texaco's chief was Norwegian immigrant Torkild Rieber, who first arrived in the United States as a skipper's mate aboard a tanker with oil from Port Arthur. He joined Texaco when the oil company bought the tanker. Rieber was imaginative and daring. He had a 260-mile pipeline constructed across the Andes Mountains to transport oil from Colombia to the sea, and he joined forces with Standard Oil of California, later Socal, to penetrate Saudi Arabia. His outlook was international, in keeping with his nautical background, but, like Teagle and Sir Henry Deterding, head of Shell, he had no instinct for the world of conventional domestic politics. This allowed him to flout neutrality during the Spanish Civil War of 1936–39. Despite the neutrality laws, Rieber had Texaco tankers divert oil designated for Belgium to General Francisco Franco, leader of the military revolt in Spain. Although FDR was infuriated and had his attorney general, Homer S. Cummings, warn Rieber that he would be indicted for conspiracy if there were any further violations, Rieber continued to supply Franco with oil, this time through Italy. Altogether, Texaco provided Franco with $6 million worth of oil, to be paid at the end of the war—another factor in Franco's ultimate victory over the constitutionally elected left-wing government. Thereafter, Rieber used his Spanish contacts to secure deals with the Nazis, whom he agreed to supply with oil from Colombia. He continued such shipments after the start of World War II and evaded the British embargo by dispatching his tankers to neutral ports. Since he could not get payment in money out of Germany, he settled instead for three tankers from Hamburg, another deal that drew him closer to the Third Reich.

When Rieber met Göring in Berlin, Göring insisted that, as part of the Hamburg-tankers-for-Texaco-oil deal, he must apprise FDR of Göring's peace plan to end the war by ensuring Britain's surrender. Rieber did so in January 1940. Not only did Roosevelt ignore the plan, but he also asked Rieber to withdraw from his connections with Nazi Germany. However, Rieber became more deeply implicated than ever. In June 1940 he had Texaco pay for the reception in New York City of Dr. Gerhardt Westrick, a German lawyer who represented several American companies, including Texaco and ITT. Rieber also paid Westrick's

The Russians began to repel the German invasion of 1941 along a front of fifteen hundred miles as soon as winter came to their aid that year. These soldiers from the Red Army pursue German stragglers, who have become separated from their retreating units, and hunt them down in the streets of Rostov-on-Don in November 1941. (Office of Emergency Management; Library of Congress).

salary and provided him with an office in the Chrysler Building and a house in Scarsdale. Westrick's real reason for being in America was to try and dissuade American businessmen from supplying Britain with weapons. He argued that Britain was almost done for and that, therefore, German-American relations would supersede the old Anglo-American unofficial alliance. All of this was done under the pretence of purely commercial advice. At the same time, Rieber's agent in Germany, Niko Beusmann, ensured that Texaco obtained the three tankers.

However, Beusmann went further. He was a skilled German spy and used his position with Texaco to obtain various reports about America from Texaco's headquarters in New York City. These reports included a review by Texaco economists of how fast the American aircraft industry was expanding as it aimed to produce 50,000 planes. The Rieber-Westrick-Beusmann connection, in which Rieber was partly the dupe, was broken by Canadian millionaire William Stephenson, head of British intelligence services in New York City. Stephenson guessed Westrick's real intentions and got the *New York Herald Tribune* to reveal the story. Westrick was abruptly declared persona non grata by the federal government. He left the United States aboard a Japanese ship and, on his return to Germany, took charge of the ITT companies. Rieber was disgraced, and, when the value of Texaco shares fell suddenly, he was compelled to resign. Texaco's official history omits any mention of the incident. However, it was precisely at this time that Texaco began to sponsor weekly radio broadcasts of Saturday matinee performances from the Metropolitan Opera in New York City. The broadcasts were not interrupted by any commercial breaks, but the underlying intention was clear. By attaching itself to one of America's cherished institutions, and probably the one with the longest continuous tradition in the performing arts, Texaco was out to prove its impeccable credentials as a bulwark of American society and art. The broadcasts have continued ever since.

War in the Pacific

In the Pacific, the United States was on a collision course with Japan; and it was this that led to its formal entry into World War II.

In December 1938 the Japanese prime minister, Prince Konoye, had announced Japan's ambitious foreign policy for a "Greater East Asia Coprosperity Sphere." From 1938 the State Department issued protests against Japanese interference with American rights in China and the bombing of Chinese civilians. Moreover, Secretary of State Cordell Hull had gone further than the letter of the neutrality laws and had asked American bankers not to extend credits to Japan. He also asked American manufacturers not to sell airplanes and airplane parts to any nation that might attack civilians. American disapproval of Japan's foreign policy culminated in the announcement of July 1939 that the commercial treaty of 1911 would be terminated at the end of the year. The actual sale of goods did not come to an end immediately in January 1941; but within months such exports as gasoline, steel, and scrap iron were made subject to government license.

Japan took full advantage of the fall of France to extend its imperial ambitions to northern Indochina, a French colony comprising the three states of Laos, Cambodia, and Vietnam. Unable to resist Japanese demands for airfields, Vichy France consented to Japanese occupation of Indochina in September 1940. That month Japan concluded the Axis agreement with Germany and Italy, by which the three powers were obliged to come to one another's aid if any one of them were attacked. Japan thereby extracted from the others acceptance of its own sphere of influence in Southeast Asia and the Pacific. Germany hoped the Tripartite Pact would deter the United States from entering the European war; Japan hoped the pact would dissuade it from entering the Sino-Japanese War.

Senator Robert A. Taft of Ohio, who succeeded Vandenberg as Republican spokesman on foreign policy, commenting on opposition within the White House to the Japanese invasion of Vietnam, said no American mother was prepared to let her son be killed in a war "for some place with an unpronounceable name in Indochina." Ironically, those who advocated strict neutrality toward Europe did not advance the same arguments toward Southeast Asia. For example, Senator Burton K. Wheeler of Montana criticized Roosevelt's European policy for its tendency to intervention but supported the stronger line on Japan.

In April 1941, when the Japanese foreign minister, Matsuoka Yosuka, visited Berlin, Germany and Japan discussed plans for a projected war on two fronts against America. Joachim von Ribbentrop, the German foreign minister, urged Matsuoka to commit Japan to an immediate assault on the British protectorate Singapore. He then concluded a neutrality pact with Stalin to last five years. But, after the German invasion of Russia on June 22, 1941, Matsuoka cynically suggested to the Japanese cabinet that they order an attack on Russia from the east, whereupon Prime Minister Konoye forced him to resign. Although some members of the cabinet agreed with Matsuoka that Japan could take advantage of Russia's misfortune, others believed that Hitler's war on the Russian front would extend his forces and thus reduce the threat to Britain, which would, with American aid, then be free to strengthen its own position in the Pacific.

By July 1941 Japan had completed occupation of southern as well as northern Indochina. The United States looked askance at a situation in which the oil, tin, rubber, bauxite, and other resources of Southeast Asia were controlled by a hostile power; and on July 24, 1941, Roosevelt froze all Japanese credits in the United States. When Britain and the

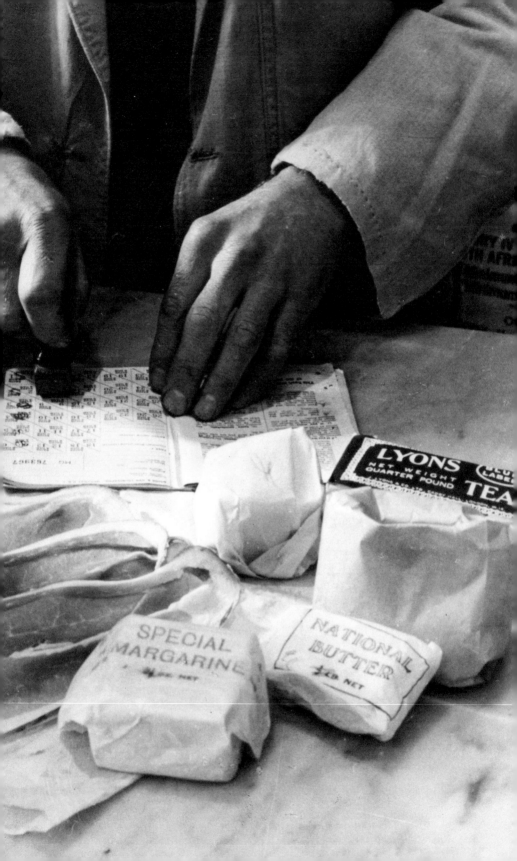

Dutch colonial governor in Djakarta in the Dutch East Indies took similar action, Japan's sources of petroleum dried up. The American ambassador in Tokyo, Joseph Drew, warned Secretary of State Hull that if America humbled Konoye by its action he would fall and be replaced by a more belligerent prime minister.

Konoye suggested a meeting at sea between himself and Roosevelt at the end of August 1941. Hull advised the president against discussions without prior agreement on the basic principles underlying any prospective negotiations. This proved impossible; and in September, an imperial conference of cabinet ministers and chiefs of staff met in Tokyo to consider preparations for war, should talks between Japan and the United States fail.

The Japanese were convinced that the United States—especially after the Atlantic Charter—would recognize that Japan needed access to raw materials and markets. Japan could afford to stay out of Southeast Asia with economic guarantees. But Manchukuo and control of China were minimum necessities, the one with essential raw materials and the other a potential market as well as a threat to Japanese security. It was obvious that the United States would not allow Japan to become a great power. Japan had to choose war while it was able to do so. Without war, economic collapse was inevitable and thus, even if Japan lost a war with the United States, there would still be nothing to regret. With the failure of the Japanese ambassador in Washington, Admiral Nomura Kichisaburo, to secure terms with the United States, Prince Konoye was, indeed, humbled as American ambassador Joseph Drew had predicted. He was

Britain could only continue the war against Hitler by stringent economies at home, including food rationing. Churchill, interested in seeing what the ordinary people ate, asked to see a family's allowance. He was encouraged by its size only to discover this was not a "good meal" nor even supplies for a day, but, rather, supplies for a whole week. Meanwhile, the king and queen ate spam (luncheon meat) off the royal plates at Windsor Castle.

Scientific advisers to the British ministry of health devised an economical diet but this was not based on ample supplies of red meat that many, including Churchill, regarded as essential to a good diet. Moreover, the ministry of agriculture was, at first, determined to produce ever more meat. Later, it conceded that cereals for direct consumption by people were ten times more effective than cereals for livestock. (Library of Congress).

succeeded as prime minister on October 16, by the war minister, General Tojo Hideki.

Tojo Hideki (1884–1948), the general who was minister of war (1938–44) and prime minister of Japan (1941–44) for much of World War II, rose rapidly after becoming chief of staff of the Kwantung Army in Manchuria. His name was to become synonymous with totalitarian government in Japan, with unswerving allegiance to the doctrine of military supremacy, and a policy of no compromise beyond victory in war.

Because the Washington ambassador was not a trained diplomat, Tojo sent Kurusu Saburo, a veteran diplomat and once ambassador to Berlin, to assist him in November 1941. He brought an offer of conciliation: Japan would withdraw from Indochina and halt its advance in Southeast Asia if the United States agreed to Japanese control of China. The American reply on November 26 was equally candid: if Japan withdrew its troops from both China and Indochina, America would resume liberal trade with Japan. In this period Winston Churchill, perhaps out of consummate political strategy, appeared content to let the United States negotiate with Japan in a matter affecting not only Britain but also Australia, New Zealand, Malaya, and Hong Kong, as well as Guam, the Philippines, and Hawaii. The last Japanese offer, with a final deadline set at November 29, contained nothing new. Hull originally decided to propose a three-month truce during which limited withdrawal of troops from Indochina would be complemented by limited economic offers from the United States but when he learned on November 26 of large Japanese convoys moving down the South China coast, he submitted stiff terms leaving no room for compromise. Both envoys disliked General Tojo and deplored his policies but they hesitated to transmit those demands to their government.

When American intelligence services reported the movements of Japanese troops with their naval escort ever southward and concluded that the Japanese would, indeed, launch some form of surprise attack, they dismissed both Guam and the Philippines as possible targets. They did so because, while Guam and the Philippines were clearly valuable to the Japanese as strategic outposts, any attack upon them was bound to draw an immediate American response. The consensus of American military opinion was that the Japanese would attack colonies of Britain or its European allies such as British Malaya or the Dutch East Indies.

Opinion in the American federal government concentrated on what should be an appropriate response, especially given the ambivalence of public opinion. FDR and his advisors rejected the idea that the United States should declare war on Japan following its suspected attack on Malaya or the Indies. They believed that it would be difficult to unite the country behind a declaration of war based on their concerns for European colonies. They were inclined to think that the United States would drift into an undeclared naval war against Japan in the Pacific much as it was doing against Germany in the Atlantic. Nevertheless, Roosevelt had his advisors prepare a message for Emperor Hirohito urging a peaceful solution. For various reasons, it was not sent until December 6.

Meanwhile, the Japanese answer to Cordell Hull's earlier note of November 29 was delivered to the Japanese embassy in Washington on December 6. Because the Americans had cracked the secret code they knew its contents before it was officially delivered on December 7. It comprised a lengthy and tedious rejection of Hull's request. Nomura and Kurusu were to await final instructions on December 7 and present a fully completed note to Hull at 1:00 P.M. Meanwhile, after various conferences with military and naval chiefs, General George C. Marshall sent a war message to his field commanders. Instead of arriving at 1:00 P.M. Nomura and Kurusu arrived at 2:00 P.M. By that time Pearl Harbor had been devastated. This mistiming made the Japanese attack seem even more treacherous.

The Japanese force that bombed Pearl Harbor left the protected Kurile Islands on November 25 and positioned itself north of Hawaii. The care with which the attack was completed was a result of months of adroit reconnaisance and careful preparation. The principal attack was at 7:55 A.M. just as many crews were about to attend their Sunday services aboard deck. Although in this devastating attack eight battleships were either sunk or badly damaged, several were raised, repaired, and returned to action. Nevertheless, the Pacific Fleet had suffered a cruel blow. It would be many months before it could be deployed again. In comparison, the Japanese suffered only miniscule losses—twenty-seven planes, five midget submarines, and one fleet submarine.

Ironically, the Japanese had had the opportunity to cause far more lasting damage and had overlooked it. Their bombing had completely missed the actual docks and repair yards in Pearl Harbor. The damaged battleships were a temporary loss: the repair facilities would have been irreplaceable. Yet they were left practically unscathed and were to be the prime source for rebuilding the Pacific fleet. Moreover, submarines, torpedo shops, and submarine-repair facilities were also overlooked. Yet, these provided the basis for immediate attacks upon Japan's navy and shipping. Their survival was evidence of a serious tactical omission in Japan's surprise attack.

The surprise, size, and success of the attack, coming as it did in a domestic atmosphere pregnant with tension and suspicion led to vociferous questions about this unprecedented debacle in the history of America's army and navy.

An immediate question concerned America's widely touted insight into the Japanese code. Yet interception by "Magic" was neither infallible nor complete. Diplomatic messages did not carry military information. Moreover, messages in code always included false information in order to tantalize and confuse enemy code breakers. In addition, the information came from a wide horizon of sources right across the mighty Pacific Ocean. Intelligence services received information from Indochina, the Aleutians, the Dutch East Indies, and even Siberia. The actual volume of information was so great that it could not be transmitted complete to commanders in the field, as this would have severely overtaxed communications facilities. The American communications systems were already complex and somewhat riven by bureaucratic rivalries. Naval intelligence considered its functions and responsibilities to be different from those of the army. Various units differed greatly in terms of the speed and competence with which they decoded information. All these factors made it difficult to receive, interpret, and decide upon intelligence information. As Roberta Wohlstetter explains in her *Pearl Harbor: Warning and Decision* (1962), "it is only fair to remark . . . that no single person or agency ever had at any given moment all the signals existing in this vast information network." Despite the comprehensive picture of Japanese activities gleaned by American intelligence—and perhaps because ot it—it was especially difficult for the United States to evaluate exactly its significance.

Tragically, some information was wasted. The day of the attack a minesweeper sighted the periscope of a midget submarine outside Pearl Harbor and patrol craft sank it, but information about this did not reach navy command posts until after the bombing had started. Other suspi-

The battleship USS *California* settles into the mud of Pearl Harbor, Hawaii, following the Japanese surprise attack on December 7, 1941.· (U.S. Navy, Office of Public Relations and Office of War Information; Prints and Photographs Division, Library of Congress).

cious sightings in the air were also reported but to no avail. A civilian pilot who noted Japanese war planes during his morning flight was laughed at when he reported the sighting. Signals on experimental radar screens were rationalized as coming from American bomber reserves.

The tide of accusations led to a congressional committee that interviewed the witnesses and published a report in thirty-nine volumes. The report criticized both the War and Navy departments and their field officers. It transpired that Hull had given the two departments responsibility for intelligence well before the attack. The committee reprimanded Admiral R. Stark, chief of naval operations, and General Leonard T. Gerow, chief of army operations, for failing to send reports to their commanders in the field and for lack of coordination. The commanders in Hawaii, Admiral Husband E. Kimmel and General Walter C. Short, were found remiss in failing to maintain appropriate reconnaissance, to achieve due liaison between the various services, and to "appreciate the significance of intelligence and other information available to them." Historians have subsequently found lack of action by almost all of the officers involved but also a chaotic jumble of bureaucracy that contributed to the debacle.

The American press had realized that war between Japan and the United States was an imminent possibility, but all public opinion polls disclosed that only half of the American people realized, expected, or accepted this fact. Public opinion was also evenly divided about sending troops abroad, whether to the Pacific or European theaters of war. The most bitter lesson learned in the wake of Pearl Harbor was that if America were going to get drawn into others' wars, it would be better to do so on its own terms. Never again would the United States seek to isolate itself from world affairs.

What all parties agreed was that the Japanese attack brought the United States together as a nation as nothing else had previously. Senator Arthur H. Vandenberg of Michigan, then a leading spokesman on isolation, admitted, "That day ended isolationism for any realist." Entry into World War II marked the beginning of a diplomatic revolution in American foreign policy.

Hitler was, by various accounts, pleased by the attack, partly because he had come to believe he should not postpone making war on the United States and, like Japan, because he realized the advantages of immediate action—in his case, by German submarines. When Japan invoked the tripartite pact, both Hitler and Mussolini declared war on the United States on December 11, 1941. Most jubilant of all was Winston Churchill: "Now at this very moment I knew the United States was in the war, up to the neck and in to the death. So we had won after all! . . . Hitler's fate was sealed. Mussolini's fate was sealed. As for the Japanese, they would be ground to powder. . . . No doubt it would take a long time. . . . But there was no more doubt about the end."

[3]

ETERNAL FATHER, STRONG TO SAVE
The War in Europe and North Africa

WORLD WAR II was the first war truly to involve the entire globe. This overwhelming fact and the length of the war and intensity of fighting among soldiers, sailors, and air crews and the gross suffering of millions of civilians drew the United States into entirely new experiences. Safe for so long, the American people suffered a greater sense of outrage over the surprise of Pearl Harbor than they did in any subsequent setback. The industrial and economic strength of the United States held out promise of ultimate victory over the Axis powers. Britain had sustained the war until the United States was drawn in, and, with that, Britain's special contribution was over.

During the war FDR was, of course, commander in chief of the armed forces of the United States; Admiral Harold R. Stark was chief of naval operations until March 1942, when he was replaced by Admiral Ernest J. King, commander in chief of the United States Fleet; General George C. Marshall was chief of staff of the United States Army. Subordinate to Marshall, but enjoying largely autonomous status, was General Henry H. Arnold, commanding general, United States Army Air Forces (USAAF). (FDR's executive order of March 1942 granted "dominion status within the Army" to the USAAF.) King and Marshall served under the civilian authority of, and as military advisers to, Secretary of War Henry L. Stimson and Secretary of the Navy Frank Knox and, subsequently, in 1944 upon the death of Knox to James V. Forrestal. Appointed by the president, Stimson, Knox, and Forrestal were members of FDR's cabinet, responsible for the administration of their respective departments. However, they were virtually excluded from meetings where vital military decisions were made, since FDR chose to deal directly with his service chiefs on matters of strategy. As before, Harry Hopkins remained FDR's most trusted go-between.

Years later the journalist Walter Lippmann assessed Harry Hopkins for his "Today and Tomorrow" column of January 31, 1946. He recalled how, "When Hopkins was there, decisions went well and toward good results. When he was absent, things went all to pieces," for he had an ability of

cutting aside the details and coming to the crux of the matter, of finding swiftly the real issue which had to be decided, the sticking point at which pride, vested interests, timidity, confusion, were causing trouble. He would bring it nakedly into the open, ruthlessly, almost cynically, with no palaver, often with deliberate tactlessness meant to shock men into seeing the reality. These are not the qualities which make a conventionally successful politician. But in the grim business of war, among men who carry the tremendous burden of decision, they were just the qualities which the times called for.

King, Marshall, and Arnold comprised the Joint Chiefs of Staff (JCS). With their British counterparts, they made up the Combined Chiefs of Staff (CCS), a group that had its own staff planners and committees. The CCS was responsible for devising broad policies and plans for the strategic conduct of the war, allocating resources (both in men and materiel), and deciding priorities in war production and the conduct of operations. The final decision on their findings and proposals always lay with FDR and Churchill. The CCS was born because both sides knew it was essential to have unity of command in each theater of war. While the political leaders decided on a strategy, the CCS carried it out. While the leaders could meet only during a conference, the combined committee met regularly in Washington, D.C.

In mid-1942, the JCS and the CCS were joined by Admiral William D. Leahy—appointed by FDR as his own personal representative and

Morocco bound. An absorbed FDR dines from an army mess kit on the field in French Morocco as he discusses tactics with *(from left to right)* General Mark W. Clark, Harry Hopkins *(with back to camera)*, and Major General George J. Patton, Jr., commander of American forces in French Morocco. (Office of War Information; Library of Congress).

chief of staff. As presiding chairman at JCS meetings, Leahy served as FDR's mouthpiece and ears. He kept his colleagues informed as to FDR's opinions and at almost daily meetings with the president paraphrased the arguments set forth by the JCS. In World War II, King and Marshall were the supreme architects of American strategy. However, they were aware that they would be overruled by the president should their proposals run counter to his priorities. Thus, they shaped their strategy to fit what they perceived to be his grand design.

As chairman of the Combined Chiefs of Staff, George C. Marshall (1880–1959) was the principal Allied strategist in the war. Marshall had graduated from the Virginia Military Institute in 1901 and was

83

commissioned in the army in 1902. During the course of his duties with the American Expeditionary Force in 1917–19, he served as chief of operations, First Army; as chief of staff, Eighth Army Corps; and helped plan the Saint-Mihiel and Meuse-Argonne offensives in 1918. Having also served as assistant commandant of the Infantry School at Fort Benning, Georgia (1927–32), he subsequently rose to chief of staff (1939–45) at the rank of general. After World War II, he served under Truman as secretary of state (1947–49), giving his name to the Marshall Plan—the European recovery program of economic aid to postwar Europe. Before becoming secretary of defense (1950–51), he formulated the so-called Truman Doctrine of March 1947.

With the exception of the central Pacific, which was an American preserve, the Allies fought as one team on all fronts. Britain assumed decisive responsibility for the Middle East and Far East, apart from China. The United States assumed chief responsibility for the Pacific theater, which also included Australia and China. The invasion of, and battle for, western Europe was a combined operation. However, because the supreme Allied commander was an American, the American JCS became the executive agents of the CCS.

However, despite the growth, efficiency, and influence of both the JCS and the CCS, the ultimate decision on strategy lay with FDR. The war changed Roosevelt and brought out a new vigor and sense of purpose in him. It allowed him to escape the sterile circumstances and politics of the depression and gave him the opportunity to reassert his special genius for apparently random initiatives that could be arranged so as to make up a cohesive strategy at home and abroad. As in his running of domestic administration, he remained a great delegator of tasks, allocating responsibility to a variety of agencies and individuals. In this way he served to enhance his authority, since he alone provided the coordinating link among the subordinate agencies. He also managed to protect himself against any stigma of failure when things went wrong and thus defused the anger of the American people. Whereas Churchill distrusted military leaders in politics, Roosevelt, according to Warren F. Kimball, editor of the Churchill-Roosevelt correspondence (1984), "perceived his top officers as men whose vision of the world paralleled

General George C. Marshall, chairman of the Combined Chiefs of Staff, was the principal Allied strategist in World War II. (Library of Congress).

his own." Time and time again FDR took his dispatches on controversial issues of politics and strategy from drafts prepared by the JCS or General Marshall or Admiral Leahy.

Another crucial factor in the Anglo-American victory was the unique relationship between Roosevelt and Churchill as wartime leaders. Both had strong personalities; both worked within a framework of constitutional democratic government; and both expressed themselves freely, knowing that what they promised they could deliver. Moreover, their political and personal strength had been forged in adversity. Neither Roosevelt nor Churchill had had greatness thrust upon him. Each had put himself at the helm in troubled waters, and both relished the excitement of their positions.

Nevertheless, despite Churchill's great personal standing and the prestige Britain enjoyed for having stood briefly alone against Hitler, this was no partnership of equals. The United States was clearly the dominant partner, having massive resources for the future. However, the Americans had to fit into a war already in progress. Thus Britain, by its solitary war of June 1940 to December 1941, had staked out its claim to remain a great power. Inasmuch as he could, Churchill tried continuously to move Anglo-American policy in directions that would buttress his preferred strategy of the balance of power.

Diplomacy and Strategy Toward Europe

The first wartime meeting between Churchill, FDR, and their military advisers was the Arcadia conference, held in Washington, D.C., from December 22, 1941, until January 14, 1942. The various Anglo-American conferences and operations all bore code names, partly for convenience and partly for security. Churchill's undoubted literary gifts can be discerned in the choice of names. At Arcadia, FDR dispelled Churchill's fears on two key issues. He agreed with Churchill that the war against Germany must and would take precedence over the war against Japan. Such an agreement had already been reached by the heads of the American army, navy, and army air force and their British counterparts during a secret ABC-1 meeting on March 27, 1941.

Although defeat of Germany was the prime aim of the Allies, what

Hitler's most imaginative and charismatic general, Field Marshal Erwin Rommel, the "desert fox," inspecting the crack troops of the German Afrika Korps in North Africa before numerically superior Allied forces defeated them at the battle of El Alamein. (Presse-Hoffmann; Library of Congress).

this meant was giving priority to the war in the European theater despite the fact that America's more immediate interests were in the Pacific. It did not mean that within Europe the Allies would concentrate on an all-out offensive against Germany. Indeed, their strategy—attacking the Axis powers first in North Africa and then in Italy—was circuitous to say the least. In the case of Italy, it was also time-consuming, costly in terms of men and materiel, and not especially effective in pursuit of the principal aim of eliminating Hitler first.

FDR also assured Churchill that, despite the American armed forces' own demand for supplies, lend-lease deliveries to the Allies would not be reduced, whatever the danger from German ships. As to supplies, the American services refused to produce an order of battle or even to define their needs precisely. However, Britain had to justify every claim to materiel, unlike Russia, which was given every demand up to the limit of available supplies and carrying capacity. The total American expenditure on lend-lease was $43.61 billion, of which Britain and the empire received $30.07 billion. Britain contributed £1.89 billion to

87

reciprocal aid, of which the United States received £1.20 billion, or $5.66 billion—between one-fifth and one-quarter of what was provided by the Lend-Lease Act.

While British representatives could commit their government, American representatives could only make an informal arrangement that they hoped to make good by smuggling it past Congress and the American forces. English historian A. J. P. Taylor opines in *English History 1914–1945* (1965):

> There was never any true pooling of resources. Lend-lease remained the legal base for aid, and in American eyes, this had always been an act of charity towards a poor relation. The British tried to change the atmosphere by themselves behaving in a spirit of unreserved cooperation. . . .
>
> More striking still, the British handed over to the Americans a mass of scientific secrets for war, including that for a controlled nuclear explosion. The Americans had the industrial resources to develop this. . . . The British received no acknowledgement or reward, other than a personal promise from Roosevelt to Churchill that Great Britain should share fully in all nuclear advances. This promise lapsed on Roosevelt's death, and the British had to start out again on their own. The British in fact assumed a more or less permanent merger of the two countries. The Americans accepted only a short-term combination and tried to put it on a business footing.

However, at Arcadia the United States and Britain merged more fully for war than had any two countries and far more than Germany and Japan, which had no coordinated strategy. The United States stuck resolutely to the ABC-1 doctrine that Germany, as the principal enemy, must be defeated first. This decision determined the course of the war. It was taken with little discussion, but it followed naturally from previous habits of thought when Germany had been the enemy and Japan had not. Moreover, both the United States and Britain were disturbed at the prospect of a German victory in Europe, or a Russian victory there, or a compromise—any of which might have happened had they stood aside.

There certainly was no grand Axis design. Despite Anglo-American fears, neither Germany nor Japan contemplated joining forces across the wide expanses of the Middle East. Moreover, the war in the Pacific was a matter for the American navy, while the American army wanted to get into action in North Africa and Europe. It could only do this by supporting Britain, which was already committed to those theaters. This

Engines of War. Despite Britain's richly deserved wartime reputation as the greatest natural aircraft carrier in the world, it was North Africa that provided the first base for the American and British assault of Axis-occupied Europe. Photographs such as this of men and materiel being assembled for the invasion of Sicily from North Africa assumed a status of icons, especially when by angle and silhouette the photographer turned the subjects into monumental hulking shapes as menacing as anything the enemy could devise. (Library of Congress).

produced a series of ironies: Britain had to leave the fate of its Pacific lands to the United States, and Britain was not fighting Germany except in the air. The United States, having decided not to go first for Japan, which was perceived as the less important enemy, was, like Britain, soon drawn into a war against Italy, which was even less important.

Also at Arcadia, Churchill and FDR defined their war aims by issuing the Declaration of the United Nations on January 1, 1942, thus reaffirming their commitment to the purposes and principles set out in the Atlantic Charter. The term *United Nations* was first coined by FDR.

Initially, twenty-six nations fighting the Axis powers signed the declaration and another twenty nations joined during the war. In the declaration, these nations pledged that they would accept the principles of the Atlantic Charter and not sign any separate armistice or peace treaty with the common enemies.

Despite the agreement that Germany had to be defeated first, Churchill and his generals were united in their reluctance to fight Germany head-on in northwestern Europe. It was, says John Keegan (1944), a viewpoint derived from Britain's "status as a sea power, informed by memories of the Battle of Trafalgar [1805] and the Peninsular [War], and re-inforced by a determination never again to suffer a Passchendaele." This view was also determined by two strategic decisions made in the summer of 1940. The first was that Germany could be reduced to a state of confusion and then collapse by aerial bombardment. Belief in the efficacy of strategic bombing was popularized by Major Alexander de Seversky and fully endorsed by Air Chief Marshal Sir Arthur ("Bomber") Harris. As the war progressed, Harris became convinced that a cross-channel assault on Europe was unnecessary. He argued that Germany's will to fight would be broken by an aerial bombardment of civilian targets.

Harris knew his hastily assembled crews could not bomb with any precision and that they must strike at barnyard doors and anything else close by if they were to hit anything at all. However, the more crews were used on indiscriminate bombing, the more likely it was that precision bombing would be postponed indefinitely. Moreover, Harris's offensive was largely a public-relations exercise to impress the British and American governments and peoples. Furthermore, unless Harris used his aircraft, they would be put at the disposal of the navy; and production might shift from bombing planes to fighters, tanks, and landing craft. Thus, targets were selected for their publicity value. Neither Lübeck (March 28, 1942) nor Rostock (April 24 to April 27) was important to the German economy; however, they were medieval towns with many timber buildings that burned well. On May 30, Harris caused a sensation when he sent one thousand bombers over to Cologne. In time, Harris's American counterpart, the commander of the United States Strategic Air Force Europe, General Spaatz, came to share Harris's faith in aerial bombardment. He too thought that an invasion of northwestern Europe was unnecessary. Nevertheless, Spaatz contended that the key to victory lay in the destruction of German industry, most notably its production of oil.

The second influential strategic decision was to make the Middle East the focus of Britain's military effort. The thinking and planning of most British strategy in the war was the result of these two decisions. One major conclusion was to avoid a frontal assault on western Europe, if at all possible. Instead, the enemy's strength and resolve were to be weakened by naval blockade and, even more pertinently, by aerial bombardment. Moreover, Germany's military capacity was to be weakened by launching diversionary attacks and fighting periperhal campaigns. The Mediterranean was the main theater for such campaigns. In keeping with this strategy, it was suggested at Arcadia that British and American forces should combine in joint military action in North Africa.

While American military leaders gave their approval to this proposal, they also stated their firm commitment to a cross-channel invasion of France. In so doing, they were subscribing to a traditional American strategy of bringing maximum force to bear upon the enemy. By engaging the German army head-on, they sought to deliver one stupendous blow that would end the war in Europe and release men and supplies for engagement in the Far Eastern theater.

When Dwight D. Eisenhower was appointed American commander in chief in Europe on June 25, 1942, he immediately submitted a plan that would bring about the proposed invasion of Europe. The program was divided into three phases: first, "Bolero," the transference of forty-eight American divisions to England by 1943; second, "Roundup," the supplying and training of these troops; and third, "Sledgehammer," the emergency landing of British troops in Europe in the event of either the collapse of Germany or, as was thought more likely, the imminent surrender of the Soviet Union.

Not surprisingly, the British opposed "Sledgehammer." They saw it as nothing short of national suicide. Eisenhower's proposal for a joint Anglo-American invasion in 1943 also met with opposition from the American naval command that, having borne the brunt of fighting in the Pacific, was demanding a more immediate effort from the army. They were supported in this by the American people who, after months of sacrifice at home and bad news from the Pacific theater, were impatient for some military success. The American navy also wanted the war in Europe to be brought to a swift conclusion so that men and resources could be diverted to the Pacific theater. Admiral King, while always subscribing to a strategy of defeating Germany first, was inclined to give priority to the war against Japan. Ever mindful of the public mood, FDR inclined toward Churchill's view that something positive had to be done in 1942. He may also have been influenced in this decision by the arrival in Washington, D.C., in June 1942 of the Soviet foreign minister, Vyacheslav Molotov. Molotov pleaded on Stalin's behalf for some early military initiative in the west.

However, the only feasible option open to the Allies was the already muted attack on North Africa. Although the British had most to gain from a commitment of American forces to the North African theater and American military leaders remained opposed in principle to such a diversionary campaign, the United States had, nevertheless, important strategic interests in the area. The strategic importance of the bulge of Africa had been recognized even before Pearl Harbor by Secretary of the Navy Frank Knox. In a memorandum of April 24, 1941, he stated, "Too few of us realize, and still fewer acknowledge, the size of the disaster to American hemisphere safety if Germany . . . should establish herself in Dakar. . . . From there, with surface ships, submarines and long range bombers, a victorious Germany could substantilly cut us off from all commerce with South America and make the Monroe Doctrine a scrap of paper."

The North African Campaign

The Anglo-American amphibious invasion of North Africa, codenamed "Torch," was set for early November 1942. By destroying German forces there, the Allies hoped to free the Mediterranean for their shipping and provide themselves with a key base from which to attack Italy and occupied France. The invasion of North Africa and putative invasions of Italy and France would also assure Stalin that the United States and Britain were taking the offensive on a second front. Furthermore, Germany would have to divert military and air resources from the Russian front and northern France in order to rescue Italy from disaster. Thus, a North African campaign would be a substitute for a second front and, also, a preparation for it.

British troops in North Africa already had been forced to retreat by

"British infantry chase Axis troops out of Egypt" was the original caption when this photograph was first published to proclaim the success of the British war effort; and, indeed, the excitement of pursuit amid the raging heat and dust of Africa are caught in the image. (Library of Congress).

the German Afrika Korps, brilliantly led by Field Marshall Erwin Rommel, the "desert fox." (Although, in time, Rommel outran his supplies.) Mussolini went to Libya, expecting to lead a triumphal entry into Cairo on a white horse. On July 25, 1942, Rommel tried—and failed—to break through British lines at El Alamein. The British Eighth Army was responding to the new leadership of Lieutenant General Bernard Law ("Monty") Montgomery. His troops were dug in along defensive lines at El Alamein, about sixty-five miles from Alexandria and the Suez Canal, an essential water route to Asia.

Montgomery (1887–1976), knight and later first Viscount Montgomery of El Alamein, was the most widely publicized British commander of World War II. His initial reputation was as a tough and efficient leader who had had a distinguished record in World War I. He first led a division in France in 1940 and then commanded the troops in southeast England at the time German invasion seemed imminent. The keys to his success in North Africa, where he was commander of the British Eighth Army, were the building up of overwhelming supplies of materiel and the restoration of morale among the troops. His critics, however, charged him with overpreparation, lack of innovation, and with exasperating his colleagues' patience. Some believed his reputation was based upon British propaganda, the authors of which were determined to promote a war champion equal to Rommel.

Erwin Rommel (1891–1944) had earned rapid promotions in the Prussian-German army on account of his courage, his insight into men, and his natural gift for leadership and teaching, exemplified by his book *Infantry Attacks*, published in 1937. Dispatched to command German troops sent to aid the faltering Italian army in Libya, it was his audacious surprise attacks in North Africa that led to his being called the "desert fox." Ironically, while he was fighting with Italians, it was his British enemies who were much more to his liking. Indeed, Rommel was most popular among the Arab nations, which regarded him as their liberator from British rule. Yet, despite Rommel's great skill as a commander and the superior quality of his troops, victory in North Africa would fall to Montgomery and Eisenhower and the superior supplies and materiel of their forces provided by the American war machine.

Ironically, however, operation Torch began not with an attack on Germany, America's declared enemy, but on France, its oldest ally. During this period, huge convoys of men from America and Britain arrived off the North African coast. From November 8, 1942, about 200,000 American troops, led by Lieutenant General Dwight D. ("Ike") Eisenhower, disembarked at Casablanca on the Atlantic coast of French Morocco and at Algiers and Oran on the Mediterranean coast of Algeria. They quickly seized Oran and Algiers from the French, but French forces at Casablanca resisted them for several days. However, Eisenhower eventually convinced the ranking Vichy officer, Admiral Jean François Darlan, to cooperate with the Allies. Darlan took advantage of Hitler's occupation of Vichy France after the North African invasion and on December 1 ordered all French forces to end their resistance. Darlan's new position as French chief of all North Africa was bitterly resented by those who knew him as a fascist and a virulent anglophobe. Nevertheless, Eisenhower knew that Darlan's cooperation had saved him many casualties. Churchill agreed, and FDR tried to convince the American public by issuing a none-too-convincing statement on the necessity of "temporary expedients" in wartime.

Charles de Gaulle. The redoubtable French general became a symbol of French resistance to Hitler in the mid-1940s. He was also the strong-willed champion of French independence from America and Britain as much as was possible in World War II and mightily so thereafter, notably when he became first president of the Fifth French Republic in 1959. This portrait of 1942 was published by the United Nations and the Office of War Information during the war as an icon of Gallic self-assertion. (Library of Congress).

Having realized their initial objectives, American forces were to march eastward and meet with Montgomery's Eighth Army. Monty had been prepared to wait for several months until he had accumulated enough men and materiel, including four hundred American Sherman tanks, before striking back. Then in ten days, beginning on October 23, 1942, the British Eighth Army routed Rommel's forces and sent them stumbling back in disorder in the momentous battle of El Alamein, a decisive turning point in the war. At El Alamein, Monty had planned a set-piece battle. He had put all his weight in a match at the enemy's strongest point. But in so doing, he lost more tanks than did the Germans and Italians; and the proportion of casualties among men on the front line was as heavy as casualties had been on the Somme. Because of the steady flow of supplies through the Suez Canal, Monty could afford such losses. However, Rommel could not because of the destruction of Axis convoys coming from Malta. El Alamein was finally won on November 4, 1942, three days before the landing of Anglo-American forces in French North Africa.

Hitler and Mussolini provided Rommel with massive reinforcements from Italy and Sicily, and he struck at the American forces. While they were not always successful in advancing from the west, Montgomery with his British and Commonwealth troops were also moving in on Rommel from the east. Thus by May 1943, the German and Italian forces were trapped. Rommel himself escaped; but over 250,000 enemy soldiers were captured, and the Axis forces were eliminated from North Africa.

At this point in the war, Franco-American relations, especially those involving Darlan, Charles de Gaulle, and FDR, had a considerable impact on the outcome of the war in North Africa and France. De Gaulle had first become known beyond the French army through a BBC broadcast of June 18, 1940, in which he called on Frenchmen to resist the Nazis and the Vichy government of collaboration. In 1934 he had written a book in which he criticized the inadequacy of the French system of defense, which was based on fortifications and foot soldiers. Instead, he proposed mobile armored units. While the French commanders did not take him seriously, the Germans did. In fact, they had adapted de Gaulle's tactics to roll their troops across France's supposedly impregnable frontier in 1940. After de Gaulle fled to London in 1940, the Vichy government declared him a traitor and signed his death warrant. While Churchill was willing to recognize, and work with, de Gaulle, FDR was not. Roosevelt's political doubts about de Gaulle were reinforced by a deep personal dislike of the willful, egotistical general. Perhaps later FDR came to realize, albeit grudgingly, that de Gaulle's stubbornness was based on a determination to prove to French people everywhere that he was truly independent of the United States and Britain.

As mentioned previously, Darlan had presented himself to the American military command in Algiers and, claiming full legitimacy as Vichy commander in chief in the area, had signed the Clark-Darlan agreement, ordering his troops not to oppose the landing. The question now turned upon who the Americans should recognize as head of state in the "liberated" Vichy territories. Of course, de Gaulle suggested that the North African territories be placed under the jurisdiction of his provisional government. However, American policy makers had little faith in him because they thought he held only minuscule support among the French people. They were also aware that the men in North Africa with whom they were now dealing were united by an uncompromising hostility toward de Gaulle. Indeed, Darlan had stipulated that the Allied operation in North Africa would be forcibly opposed if Gaullist troops were involved.

When Darlan was assassinated on December 24, 1942, the Americans began a search for another figurehead with whom the pro-Ally French could identify. The State Department considered the credentials of Generals Weygand (commander in chief of Vichy forces in North Africa from June 1940 to November 1941); Giraud; and the veteran statesman of the Third French Republic, Herriot. With the strong backing of the British, de Gaulle put forward his own case, and, finally, it was agreed that he and Giraud be established as co-leaders in North Africa. De Gaulle quickly outmaneuvered his politically naive colleague, and Giraud withdrew from the North African stage.

On the eastern front, "General Winter" finally came to the aid of the Russians. The great thrust of German forces in Russia in the summer and autumn of 1941 was finally halted by a mix of ferocious Russian resistance and just about the worst winter weather and snow in fifty years.

The siege of Leningrad lasted nine hundred days—from September

1941 to January 1944. There may have been a million civilian deaths during that terrible period caused by disease, cold, and starvation. Over 100,000 bombs were dropped on the city and over 150,000 shells fired upon it. Yet the devastation of the elegant northern city conceived as the new capital of the tsars by Peter the Great was communicated to the West in a most original form that dramatized the terrors of war and the heroism of the gallant Russian people. This took the form of the Seventh Symphony, the *Leningrad* (1941), by Dmitri Shostakovich (1906–75).

Shostakovich's successful early career as Russia's preeminent resident composer had gone into a bitter eclipse when Stalin had had his opera *Lady Macbeth of Mtsensk* (1934) denounced by *Pravda* as "chaos instead of music" and withdrawn from performance in 1936. Yet Shostakovich won back critical and public acclaim with his *Leningrad* Symphony. Largely composed before the German invasion of Russia, it seemed to criticize the way Stalinism was laying waste to culture, symbolised by Shostakovich's own city of Leningrad. Yet its message was transformed by the terrible circumstances of the war into a condemnation of fascism and militarism for which Shostakovich had found appropriate musical forms—notably the repetitive, plodding march tune that extends along a crescendo of 280 bars. The work's first performance by a scratch orchestra in early 1942 during the darkest days of the siege was dramatic evidence of the triumph of the human spirit over tyranny and adversity as was the symphony's exultant finale.

The score was put on microfilm, taken by plane to Tehran, and thence smuggled to the United States. It received a rapturous reception when it was first performed live on radio in America by the NBC Symphony Orchestra under Arturo Toscanini and heard by millions of listeners. Its use as propaganda is evident from the record of over sixty concert performances across the United States alone in 1942–43.

Thwarted at Leningrad in the north and at Moscow in the center, Hitler decided to drive German troops to the south. His immediate objective was to capture the oil fields of the Caucasus and the key area of the lower Volga River. Thus, he sent a large force of 300,000 under General von Paulus to take Stalingrad, a vital strategic point on the west bank of the Volga. The siege of Stalingrad began on August 19, 1942,

Mass execution of Russian Jews by *Einsatzgruppen* of the advancing German army; the first slaughters were by shooting. (Library of Congress).

with an artillery bombardment that destroyed much of the city. Russian soldiers and civilians fought the Germans in the streets, houses, and ruins in a battle generally accounted the worst for face-to-face slaughter in the entire war. On November 23, 1942, the Russians succeeded in halting the Germans, whom Hitler forbade to retreat even for essential regrouping.

Despite heavy snowstorms, the Russians counterattacked the German Sixth Army in two deep pincer operations and gradually succeeded in cutting the Germans off. Almost without supplies and losing men to the relentless weather with its terrible subzero temperatures, as well as to persistent Russian pressure, on January 31, 1943, von Paulus was forced to surrender the tattered remnants of the once-mighty Sixth Army that had earlier subdued the Low Countries of Holland and Belgium. Von Paulus's surrender of the Sixth Army was the symbol of the first major defeat of German forces in the war. While Russia had the prestige of this truly significant victory, it had been achieved at considerable cost. Russia lost more men in this one titanic struggle than the United States was to lose in combat in all theaters of the war.

The defeats for Germany at El Alamein and Stalingrad were, in all probability, the turning point in the war. Hitler's character became more brooding and perplexed. Hitherto, the sort of success that he had imagined in his mind had been largely realized; but to preserve the world of fantasy from defeat and failure, he increasingly isolated himself from the reality around him. He never visited bombed cities nor read reports of setbacks. He became dependent on a variety of medical injections administered by his physician, Theodor Morell. He could still react vigorously to special problems, as in the decisive action he took to rescue Mussolini from the jaws of defeat in July 1943. However, his failure to respond realistically to the situation in Russia and to withdraw led to far greater losses. It was inevitable that his relations with his commanders would deteriorate, especially as he gave greater importance to the SS. Furthermore, the failure of the U-boats in the Atlantic and increased bombing of Germany had reduced a chance of any victory at all.

Defense to the last ditch. Valiant women of Leningrad use picks and shovels to cut ditches to ensnare German tanks as part of their defense precautions against the invader. (British official photo; Library of Congress).

The Casablanca Conference

With Montgomery's victory at El Alamein and American troops safely and securely settled in North Africa, FDR and Churchill met at Casablanca to discuss where next to apply the pressure against Germany. However, no hard and fast agreements were reached at this meeting, the "Symbol" conference of January 14 to January 25, 1943. Secretary of State Hull did not attend the Casablanca conference, a fact that we can interpret as the earliest unequivocal evidence of Roosevelt's determination to act as his own foreign secretary during the war.

Roosevelt had tried to persuade Stalin to attend the Casablanca conference, but he refused to meet FDR and Churchill until the Americans and British provided positive evidence that they would tackle Germany's armies by land, instead of letting Russian troops bear the full brunt of the fighting. There existed a widespread suspicion among Russian leaders that the United States and Britain wanted Germany and

Russia to fight it out and devastate one another so that Anglo-American capitalism could dominate Europe.

At Casablanca the Americans restated their commitment to a cross-channel expedition, while the British argued for an extension of Mediterranean operations. In the end, they compromised. They could continue to build up forces in Britain for the invasion, with autumn 1943 or, more likely, spring 1944 as the target date. They would also continue operations in North Africa, with Sicily chosen as the next target for an invasion of the mainland. Moreover, they set no precise dates for either operation, partly because the Axis forces had yet to be expelled from Tunisia and partly because any invasion of Europe depended first on Allied victory in the battle of the Atlantic.

Despite American fears to the contrary, it was not operations in the Mediterranean that were responsible for the delaying of Operation Overlord. Rather, it was the U-boat offensive in the Atlantic and other unforeseen difficulties in transportation and supply that caused the postponement of the cross-channel invasion until June 1944.

Two other important decisions were made at Casablanca. First, the Combined Chiefs of Staff gave top priority to winning the battle of the Atlantic. Second, FDR announced that the Allies would fight on until they received the unconditional surrender of the Axis powers. It is sometimes reputed that this was a spur-of-the-moment decision. In reality, FDR had discussed the issue at length with his advisers. It was inspired primarily by FDR's wish to dispel Stalin's fears that, in the aftermath of the Clark-Darlan agreement, the Allies would make a deal with Hitler. FDR also had told Churchill in advance, and Churchill had informed his own war cabinet. Perhaps FDR's announcement about unconditional surrender also reassured the American public that there would be no new Darlan deal. In fact, the Axis leaders probably supposed that they would still make peace on compromise terms. In the end, both Italy and Japan surrendered under somewhat elaborate conditions.

Critics charged that such a policy only served to unite the enemy more solidly and make its resistance more determined. Some Germans claimed that the policy delayed the overthrow of Hitler. Roosevelt undoubtedly was influenced by German misconceptions about their defeat in World War I and wanted to leave no doubt in anyone's mind that the defeat of Germany must be military and complete. Moreover,

The triumph of music over chaos. Dmitri Shostakovich, the composer whose opera *Lady Macbeth* had once been condemned by Stalin as "chaos instead of music," was responsible for the war's most heroic cultural achievement, his Seventh Symphony, the *Leningrad* Symphony. This work not only found musical forms for the cacophony of war but also was given its premiere during terrible conditions in the midst of the siege of Leningrad, an event that in itself symbolized a people's ability to confront invasion and attack with art of great intensity. (Office for Emergency Management; Library of Congress).

An exhilarating cavalry charge by horsemen of the Red Army in the midst of the German infantry sometime in 1942—a terrifying experience for German foot soldiers and one that contributed to the devastating decline in German morale on the Russian front. (British official photo; Library of Congress).

Germany would not be allowed a government based on any form of nazism. If FDR's policy of unconditional surrender served to prolong enemy resistance, it also encouraged Allied solidarity. Moreover, the policy of unconditional surrender proved to be the last in the history of modern large-scale wars.

Victory at Sea and War in the Air

In the summer of 1943, the Allies finally turned the tide against the U-boats in the war in the Atlantic. March 1943 was the worst month of either world war with 477,000 tons of shipping sunk and only twelve German submarines destroyed in the North Atlantic. In July there was a dramatic change, with only 123,000 tons of shipping sunk but thirty-seven U-boats destroyed. In the last three months of 1943, 146,000 tons of shipping were sunk and fifty-three U-boats.

There were many reasons for this sudden shift in Allied fortunes. The United States had produced a flood of destroyers for convoy—260 in 1943. Britain diverted bombers to escort duties and to attack U-boats in the bay of Biscay. Then the United States began to use aircraft carriers for escort. Moreover, Portugal allowed Britain and the United States to use the Azores as an air base and thus closed the gap in the mid-Atlantic. Germany's only battleship, the *Tirpitz*, was badly damaged on September 23, 1943, by two British midget submarines at Alten Fjord. Germany's only remaining battlecruiser, the *Scharnhorst*, was sunk by the *Duke of York* on December 26. As a result of these various factors, British imports greatly increased; and this was absolutely essential since Britain could no longer maintain itself on its own resources. In 1941 the United States supplied only 10 percent of the munitions for the British Empire; in 1943, 27 percent; in 1944, 28.7 percent. In early 1942, American munitions production was less than British; by the end of 1943, it was four times as great; in 1944, it was six times as great.

British bombers carried on a campaign of indiscriminate bombing in 1943, attacking the industrial towns of the Ruhr (March to June); Hamburg (July to November); and Berlin (November 1943 to March 1944). Of the attack on Berlin, Harris remarked, "We can wreck Berlin from end to end if the USAAF, will come in on it. It will cost us 400 to 500 aircraft. It will cost Germany the war." In fact, indiscriminate bombing was aimed at the centers of towns, where it destroyed houses, rather than at the suburbs, where most factories were located. The few German factories destroyed were usually old ones producing civilian goods because the war factories had been hidden and dispersed. Germany was not producing to maximum capacity, and random bombing compelled German industrialists to make production more concentrated and cost-effective. The bombings also revived German morale. German munitions production doubled between early 1942 and late 1943 and went on rising until the summer of 1944. Indeed, Germany was better stocked with munitions in June 1944 than at any other time in the war.

Because the Americans and British could not agree, there were two separate air offensives in 1943 and early 1944. The Americans believed their heavily armed bombers could operate in daylight against precise targets. However, they failed, partly because their "Flying Fortresses" could not match the German fighters. Thus, Harris wanted the United States to join in the British night attacks. The Americans thought differently and wanted a major air battle against the Luftwaffe. Harris deliberately and skillfully misinterpreted a May 1943 Washington directive and dismissed the strategy of selective bombing and continued to concentrate on indiscriminate bombing.

Experts conclude that the damage to German war production by Allied bombing was, at most, 9 percent, while the demands of bombing on Allied war production were far greater—about 15 percent in the United States and 25 percent in Britain. Harris stuck to his positon, although by March 1944 he had to admit that the rising scale of casualties inflicted by German night fighters made further attacks on the then-present model impossible. However, Harris's days were over. The United States had perfected a long-range fighter airplane that could take on the *Luftwaffe* in direct combat. Moreover, the time for invading northern France was drawing nearer; and on April 13, 1944, Harris was told, much to his chagrin, that bomber command was now under Eisenhower, the supreme commander of Operation Overlord. Independent British bombing was at an end.

Invasion of Italy

By May 1943 the battle of the Atlantic was all but won, and the war in North Africa was over. A precise timetable for future operations could now be devised.

At the "Trident" talks, held in Washington, D.C., from May 12 to May 25, 1943, the British again proposed to extend action in the Mediterranean. As Churchill argued, a successful invasion of Sicily would precipitate the collapse of the Italian government. He won his point, but General Marshall demanded, and gained, certain concessions of his own. First, operations in the Mediterranean were in no way to hamper or delay the invasion of Europe—now codenamed Operation Overlord. Second, the Allies set May 1, 1944, as the date for the invasion. Third, the Allies agreed to assemble twenty-nine divisions in England in preparation for Operation Overlord, and seven of these divisions were to come from the Mediterranean theater. The sudden,

American forces take leave of North Africa en route for the invasion of Sicily; U.S. Coast Guardsmen load ambulances, or "mercy trucks," aboard their transport ship. (Library of Congress).

badly prepared entry of numerous GIs into Britain was another contributory factor in the dislocation of the island kingdom during the war. The common British complaint about the Yanks was that they were "overpaid, oversexed, and over here." While British strategists acceded to American demands at the "Trident" talks, they were again successful in winning the American military over to their view on extending operations in the Mediterranean. Once again, Eisenhower was to be commander in chief in this theater. He was given two objectives: to hasten Italy's elimination from the war; and, at the same time, to draw off from France and to tie down the maximum number of German divisions.

With this working brief, Eisenhower recommended that should Sicily fall quickly after an Allied assault, then the initiative should be driven home with an invasion of the Italian mainland via the straits of Messina. Of course, Churchill approved, while Marshall, who was increasingly wary of being embroiled in a diversionary war, suggested only an invasion of Corsica and Sardinia.

Sicily was, indeed, invaded on July 10, 1943. This strike was intended to hit the Axis forces at their most vulnerable point. The invasion of Sicily, codenamed "Husky," was the largest amphibious operation of the early years of the war and included the United States Seventh Army under General George S. Patton, Jr., the British Eighth Army under General Bernard L. Montgomery, several Canadian units, large air forces, and both American and British paratroops. Most of the ships were British.

General George Smith Patton, Jr., was the most controversial American commander of World War II. Born in San Gabriel, California, in 1885, he graduated from the United States Military Academy in 1909 and served as a second lieutenant in the cavalry, taking part in General Pershing's ill-fated expedition against Pancho Villa in Mexico in 1916. He served as a member of Pershing's task force in France in 1917 and organized the American Tank Center at Langues. Tank warfare became Patton's speciality, and he commanded the 304th Tank Brigade at Camp Meade, Maryland, after the war. He served in the office of the chief of cavalry in Washington, D.C., from 1928 to 1931, graduated from the Army War College in 1932, and served with the Third Cavalry at Fort Meyer, Virginia, from 1932 to 1935. The Second Armored Division, which he commanded in World War II, became known as the toughest outfit of the army. He organized the desert training center at Indio, California. Under Eisenhower, he was in charge of task force troops in the North African campaign in 1942 and commanded the Seventh Army in its successful invasion of Sicily in 1943. It was during the Sicilian campaign that a widely publicized incident cost him a reprimand from Eisenhower. He had slapped a hospitalized soldier suffering from battle fatigue whom he suspected was not ill but simply malingering. This cost him his command and delayed until August 1944 his promotion to the permanent rank of major general.

To Carlo D'Este, author of *Bitter Victory: The Battle for Sicily, 1943* (1988), the invasion of Sicily was precisely that. The first major step in reclaiming Europe from Hitler and Mussolini, it was also most bitter, characterized by divisions between American and British points of view.

An American soldier wounded by shrapnel during maneuvers following the invasion of Sicily is given blood plasma by Private First Class Harvey White on the street in the presence of islanders. (Library of Congress).

These divisions arose partly from the circumstances in which operation "Husky" was conceived. At that time such senior officers as Eisenhower and Sir Harold Alexander were still preoccupied with "cleansing" North Africa; thus, planning of the invasion of Sicily was left to inexperienced junior officers.

When he saw the original plans, Montgomery was appalled. They called for an American landing in northwest Sicily and a British landing in the southeast. Montgomery called the scrambled plan a "dog's breakfast." He revised it to have American forces under Patton brought ashore next to the British under himself. Sir Harold Alexander, deputy supreme allied commander under Eisenhower, showed little interest. Thus Montgomery overrode his colleagues' objections and had Captain Walter Bedell, Eisenhower's chief of staff, persuade Eisenhower that

109

his plan was more practicable. (The meeting between Montgomery and Smith took place in a headquarters latrine outside Algiers.)

The coastal landing of July 10, 1943, was successful. The huge invasion fleet landed along a broad front of 105 miles of coast and the ground troops were welcomed everywhere. Patton's Seventh Army and Montgomery's Eighth had achieved all their principal objectives by the end of the first day. Italian forces surrendered gladly. However, the story in the air was different. High winds and imperfect navigation took a bitter toll. Only 12 out of 147 British gliders carrying troops landed where they were intended to land. American paratroopers found themselves scattered over a thousand square miles.

Nevertheless, the success of the ground landing swelled Montgomery's arrogance. He persuaded Alexander to broaden the role of his Eighth Army. Instead of driving to Messina along the eastern coast, he would send one corps on a northwest route around Mount Etna. The trouble was that this route had already been assigned to Patton. On July 13, Alexander agreed that Montgomery should supersede Patton along the Vizzini-Caltagirone highway. It is possible that, from his vantage point, Montgomery believed this was the best strategy to take the whole island and the crucial port of Messina, the staging post for the invasion of mainland Italy. However, Alexander should have realized that Patton was far better placed to make effective use of the road. By giving Montgomery priority, Alexander was relegating Patton to a subsidiary position guarding Montgomery's rear. However, Patton obtained a crucial concession from Alexander and this shifted the tactical balance between the two commanders: he would drive west and take the ancient town of Agrigento. On July 16 he took Agrigento. Then he moved his forces to Palermo, which he took on July 22, and moved across the northern coast to Messina, which he entered before Montgomery. For his part, Montgomery had found German forces in eastern Sicily harder to defeat. Consequently, his advance was delayed. While both generals wanted to prevent the Germans' escaping to the mainland from Messina, sixty thousand German troops did escape with all their guns and equipment before either Patton or Montgomery's forces reached the port. This was despite the fact that the combined Allied forces greatly outnumbered them, with 450,000 men. Nevertheless, any resistance to the Allies in Sicily was ended on August 17, 1943.

Carlo D'Este lays the blame for the bitterness of the victory squarely at Alexander's door, finding him strong in appearance and charm but weak in strategy and leadership. He calls him "one of the most intellectually lazy men ever to hold high command."

The political repercussions of the invasion of Sicily were even more striking than the military aspects. Mussolini's government was both inefficient and corrupt and was generally regarded with contempt. His colleagues on the Fascist Grand Council, alarmed by the successful invasion, voted to remove him from office. Mussolini looked to the king, Victor Emmanuel III, for support; but on July 25, 1943, the king told Mussolini that the people no longer supported him and that his government was finished. Mussolini was thus deposed, placed under arrest, and interned, first, on various islands in the Mediterranean and, later, in a hotel in the mountains of central Italy.

Unfortunately, for both the invaders and the Italian people, the fall of Mussolini was not exploited politically quite fast enough. The king appointed Marshal Pietro Badoglio, a somewhat devious old soldier, as head of the new government. Badoglio played a double game, trying to convince the Allies that Italy deserved something better than unconditional surrender, while trying to maintain an impression before German agents and forces that Italy was still committed to its old Axis partner. The Germans had had time to move extra forces into Italy. The Allies could only land, crablike, in the extreme south. They were lucky to take Naples; they could not take Rome. As a result of Badoglio's duplicity, negotiations between Italy and the Allies dragged on for several weeks until Eisenhower, exasperated beyond measure, began to bring pressure on Badoglio by heavily bombarding Rome and other cities. Thus on September 3, 1943, Badoglio agreed to unconditional surrender, although the formal announcement was delayed until September 29, after the full Allied invasion of mainland Italy. On October 13, Italy declared war on Germany. Meanwhile, on September 3 and 4, the British and Canadian Eighth Army had already fought its way ashore in Calabria, opposite Messina in Sicily. Six days later the United States Fifth Army, composed equally of American and British units, went ashore at Salerno as part of an amphibious assault on the port of Naples. Meanwhile, British paratroopers seized the Italian naval base of Taranto on the Adriatic. Although the Allies began to move inexorably northward and had occupied Naples by October 1, the Germans found they could defend the Italian terrain with its mountain spine and meandering

American forces pass through the Sicilian town of Scoglitti and begin their advance inland. The image has many resonances, including that of a swarm of insects in honeycombs. (Library of Congress).

rivers farther north. The Germans gave clear notice that they would fight to the last by a daring commando raid led by Colonel Otto Skorzeny on September 9 on the mountain town where Mussolini was being held prisoner. The Germans freed Mussolini on September 12 and carried him to northern Italy, where from September 15 he then led a new fascist regime that was, in effect, a puppet government under German supervision. Mussolini's only function was to legitimize continued resistance to the Allies in the south.

The First Quebec Conference

While Sicily was being secured, the Allies met in Quebec to decide future strategy at the "Quadrant" conference of August 14 to August 24, 1943. This was probably the most crucial Anglo-American strategic meeting of the entire war. It was here that the conflict of opinions concerning Operation Overlord and the Mediterranean theater came to a head. It was here, also, that the differences were resolved.

The fall of Mussolini on July 25, 1943, and the news that the new regime of Marshall Pietro Badoglio was offering assistance to the Allies (transmitted via Madrid, August 16, 1943) strengthened Churchill's resolve to extend operations in the Mediterranean. He now recommended extension of operations into the Aegean. According to his rationale, Italian garrisons in Greece, Yugoslavia, and the Aegean Islands could be persuaded to join the fight to drive the Germans from the Balkans. However, it would be necessary to use Allied troops. The key to the operation would be the Dodecanese Islands and, specifically, Rhodes. If Rhodes were taken, then the Allies could use it as a base from which to bomb German communications and Rumanian oil fields, to supply Yugoslav and Greek partisans, and to supply the Soviet Union via the Dardanelles. Also, the taking of Rhodes would, according to Churchill, persuade Turkey to enter the war on the Allied side. This— the winning of Turkish support—seems to have been something of an idée fixe with Churchill. Perhaps it proceeded from the respect he had for Turkish military prowess, a respect derived from Churchill's own painful experiences as the author of the disastrous Dardanelles campaign of 1915 in World War I. It was certainly central to his plans for extending the Mediterranean operations into the Balkans.

Churchill's aims were to create a diversion that would draw German divisions away from western Europe; to keep those divisions tied down; and, eventually, to drive them from the Balkans and, in so doing, open up the whole southern flank of the Third Reich. To achieve the initial advantage in the Aegean, Churchill was willing, if necessary, to postpone Operation Overlord for weeks and even months. The British intended to confront German forces in western Europe only when Germany itself had been weakened to the point of collapse.

As had been the case in previous Anglo-American meetings, the

British delegation arrived at Quebec well briefed on their objectives and well prepared to expound on their arguments and parry American objections. By their effective organization in committee, the British had been able to win over recalcitrant American military leaders to their schemes for extending the war in the Mediterranean. However, on this occasion Marshall and his team were prepared to resist any further British demands in this area.

Thus, when Churchill proposed the attack upon the Dodecanese, Marshall and his team rejected the scheme out of hand. American suspicions that the British were ready to sacrifice operation Overlord in order to further their own interests in the Balkans blinded the Americans to the strategic and political merits of the proposed Dodecanese enterprise. They were quite adamant that nothing should now divert Allied energies away from the cross-channel invasion. While the Americans were willing to push ahead with the proposed invasion of mainland Italy, which they saw as the logical extension of the whole Mediterranean operation, they were totally opposed to action in the Aegean.

At Quebec the Allies avoided an open breach by agreeing to leave a Dodecanese landing on the list of possible future operations. Nevertheless, it was being put well down the list of priorities and was effectively struck off the list by the Combined Chiefs of Staff (CCS) even before the Quebec conference adjourned. The CCS did this on August 23, 1943, when it commandeered landing craft originally set aside for the assault

Artist Justin Murray extended his bird satires upon leading statesmen to Josef Stalin, whom he depicted as an outsize bird of prey with ambiguous tendencies. The legend reads:

JOSEF STALIN
(Protectus Defendus)

Range: Unpredictable.

Habitat: Enjoys subzero temperatures. Remarkably mobile, he is frequently found far behind his enemies' nests.

Identification: A large, tough bird—much tougher than anyone imagined.

Voice: Seldom heard.

Food: Feeding habits are almost entirely beneficial to man, since its diet is largely composed of destructive rodents and führer-bearing animals.

(Library of Congress).

on Rhodes and dispatched them to the Far East and then assigned the British forces already under training for the landing to duty in the Italian theater instead.

Thus, the Quebec conference marked the turning point in Anglo-American military relations. The tail would, thereafter, cease to wag the dog. As Edwin Packer has observed, "the Americans had at last succeeded in dominating the conference table, and were putting a stop to British demands for diversionary forces."

The Cairo and Tehran Conferences

On September 8, 1943, Stalin at last agreed to meet FDR and Churchill, suggesting Tehran in Persia (Iran) as the venue. FDR requested that Jiang Jieshi (Chiang Kai-shek) also attend, but Stalin opposed this. In response, FDR suggested that Jiang meet with FDR and Churchill at Cairo prior to the first Big Three conference in Tehran.

At the Cairo or "Sextant" conference of November 22 to November 26, 1943, the Americans again argued for an absolute British commitment to Operation Overlord. The British, however, were still seeking support for an extension of the Mediterranean operation into the Aegean. Since the last Allied meeting, Churchill had pressed ahead with the Dodecanese operation. On September 14, 1943, British troops had landed on the Dodecanese island of Kos. While this operation had met with little initial resistance from the Germans, it had been staunchly opposed by the American military staff. Eisenhower, who was responsible for the disposition of forces in the Mediterranean, made it clear at the time that under no circumstances was the Dodecanese gambit to be allowed to influence the conduct of other campaigns in the region. Therefore, the British could rely only upon very limited air and naval support. Thus, with the advantage of aerial supremacy in the Aegean, the Germans launched their own attack on Kos on October 3, 1943. With the Kos garrison on the point of collapse, Churchill asked FDR for reinforcements for the proposed landing on Rhodes, set for October 23, 1943. Eisenhower relayed the message to Washington that such reinforcements were not available. Then, at a meeting of the Combined Chiefs of Staff on October 9 and 10, 1943, the Americans made it clear that the British could not hope to receive any support for their operations in the Dodecanese. The only course of action was, as they recommended, to evacuate the islands.

However, the Dodecanese debacle failed to dampen Churchill's enthusiasm for future operations in this theater. At Cairo he requested troops and landing craft for an amphibious assault behind the German Gustav line in Italy. This landing was designed to outmaneuver the Germans and enable the Allies to take Rome in January 1944. Having secured Rome, the troops and landing craft could then be used in an assault upon Rhodes in February 1944. Again Churchill argued that, with Rhodes under occupation, the Allies could better supply Greek and Yugoslav partisans, persuade Turkey to enter the war, and, thus, perhaps bring about the defection of the Axis satellites—Bulgaria, Hungary, and Rumania. To achieve these ends, Churchill was ready to delay Operation Overlord until the late summer of 1944.

This debate continued without resolution throughout the Cairo meeting and was resumed at the Tehran conference of November 28 to December 1, 1943.

Iran was a safe venue. The country provided a last secure land route for supplies, notably of munitions and oil, between Russia and Britain. After Hitler had invaded Russia and the shah of Iran refused to expel Nazi agents from the country, Britain and Russia invaded Iran on August 25, 1941, in order to safeguard the oil and their supply routes. They deposed the shah on September 16 and exiled him, first to Mauritius and then to South Africa where he died. In his place, the British promoted the crown prince, Reza Shah Pahlavi, then an inexperienced youth of twenty-one, whom they intended to reign as their puppet. Russia entered Tehran on September 17, 1941; and both Britain and Russia maintained troops in the south and north of the country, respectively, to guard their interests.

The Tehran conference was the first of the two momentous war conferences between the Big Three leaders that was to decide the shape of the postwar world. The first joint meeting of Roosevelt and Churchill with Stalin brought home to the western allies in the most forceful way possible that they would have to examine their own strategy in the most fundamental way in the light of the basic objectives of Soviet military strategy and foreign policy. This involved coming to terms with the needs of the complex ruler of the Soviet Union.

In the period 1928–53, Joseph Stalin probably exercised greater political power than anyone before or since in any country. It was Stalin who ensured that the industrialization of the Soviet Union was completed; who supervised the collectivization of its agriculture; who led it to victory against Hitler in World War II and extended its territorial control of a belt of satellite countries in eastern Europe; who created a military-industrial complex and moved Russia forward into a nuclear age. Yet, despite these monumental if controversial achievements, his name has become synonymous with two other most doubtful achievements — the suppression of individual freedom and delayed individual prosperity for millions of Russian people. During his lifetime, he was honored in the Communist world with a cult of veneration bordering on fanaticism. As early as 1925, he had the city of Tsaritsyn renamed Stalingrad. (The city was renamed Volgograd as part of the policies of demystification put into effect after his death.)

Of all the political giants of the first half of the twentieth century, Stalin's reputation remains the most controversial. To Robert C. Tucker, an American specialist on Russian affairs, Stalin was no better than a twentieth-century Ivan the Terrible. To British historian E. H. Carr, Stalin was ruthless and rigorous but completely lacking in originality — a mediocrity pressed into awesome achievement by the sweep of the Russian Revolution itself.

It was Stalin's position as secretary general of the party's central committee from 1922 until his death in 1953 that provided him with the sinews of control from which he could flex the muscles of dictatorship. Whether on Politburo or interlocking committees, he outmaneuvered his more intellectual rivals for the leadership, such as Leon Trotsky and Grigori Zinoviev, both before and after the death of Vladimir Lenin in January 1924. In addition to the personal rivalries between Stalin and Trotsky, and among Stalin and his triumvirs Zinoviev and Kamenev,

Stalin's megalomania was an incidental satire in Russian pioneer director Sergei Eisenstein's epic film *Ivan the Terrible*, Parts 1 and 2 (1943–46), in which the brutal power of the sixteenth-century Russian despot was captured with operatic emphasis so intense that its parallels were not lost upon contemporary audiences. This undoubtedly led to the Soviet authorities delaying the release of Part 2 until Stalin himself was dead. (Museum of Modern Art Film Stills Archive).

there were profound ideological differences. Whereas the others looked to support from revolutions worldwide, Stalin advocated "socialism in one country," meaning that the Soviet Union (so named from 1924) must, instead, concentrate on creating its own viable political and economic model. Stalin's preferred strategy was well received by the pedestrian party managers whom Stalin was promoting within the middle ranks of the hierarchy. He isolated, dismissed, and disgraced political rivals such as Zinoviev and Kamenev. Most notoriously, Trotsky was exiled from the Soviet Union in 1927 and assassinated in Mexico in 1940.

In 1928 Stalin instituted the first of a series of five-year plans for industry and agriculture—an economic revolution more profound than the political revolution of 1917. Eventually, an estimated 25 million households were compelled to amalgamate in collective farms. Those who remained obdurate and uncooperative were arrested, exiled, executed, or imprisoned in concentration camps where they were worked to death. Collectivization was anything but efficient, causing a great famine in the Ukraine. It is thought that perhaps 10 million peasants died from the devastating effects of the strategy and punishment. When plans for industrialization also fell short of expectations, industrial managers were arraigned in show trials. Despite the terrible cost in human terms, the country was industrialized at an astonishing rate. By 1937 Stalin had increased the total industrial production of the Soviet Union to a level that was second only to that of the United States. Yet, the momentous industrial achievement was not used for the material benefit of the Soviet peoples by way of consumer goods or even for the production of the basic amenities of an industrial society. An overwhelming proportion of national wealth was deployed by the state to maintain military might, the terrifying apparatus of a police state, and renewed industrialization. Many commentators believe that the Soviet Union could and would have industrialized itself by more humane means in any regime other than Stalin's. The collectivization of agriculture was successful as a means of asserting state control over the recalcitrant peasants but was unsuccessful in purely economic terms—often disastrously so.

Perhaps the most durable of Stalin's achievements was the elaborate system of interlocking bureaucracies based upon ties between the Communist party, ministries, legislatures, labor unions, police, and armed forces. It was this cumbersome form of administration that provided the levers of government from the 1930s to the 1960s.

In 1934 Stalin unleashed the first of a series of terrible purges upon the party members who had helped him seize power. The pretext was the assassination of Stalin's principal colleague and potential rival Sergey Kirov, whom Stalin himself had had murdered. The purge continued through show trials of leading officials Zinoviev and Kamenev in August 1936. In fact, their confessions of counterrevolutionary activities had been fabricated. Both were sentenced to be executed by firing squad. Two further major trials followed in January 1937 and March 1938. In June 1937, Marshal Mikhail Tukhachersky, the most prominent and highly regarded military official, was court-martialed with other generals on various charges of treason and was also executed.

Thus by persecution did Stalin curb both the Communist party and the Soviet elite, eliminating veteran Bolsheviks, industrial managers, soldiers, and party leaders who continued to show independence. Even the police organization, the NKVD, yielded a high number of victims. The terror continued to his death, albeit in less dramatic form, and, in all, claimed tens of thousands of victims.

Stalin's wartime agenda was clear: to eliminate Hitlerism and to work Roosevelt and Churchill round to committing men and materiel to a second front in the west in order to take the pressure off Russia in the east. Thereafter, Stalin was committed to the creation of satellite blocs to the west to shield the Soviet Union from further invasion and to spread socialism ever wider across Europe.

The Tehran conference was preceded by a preliminary meeting of the foreign ministers (Cordell Hull, Anthony Eden, and Vyacheslav Molotov) in Moscow. Secretary of State Hull, in his only major task during the war, emphasized the need for a postwar international organization to keep the peace. This time, unlike the ill-fated League of Nations, the United States and the Soviet Union would have to play important roles. However, Russia was reluctant to accept the Roosevelt-Hull thesis that China should be one of the four major police powers to maintain the peace. Stalin told Hull that Russia would join the war against Japan once Germany had been defeated.

With the British and Americans at loggerheads over the extension of Mediterranean operations, FDR, who chaired the Tehran discussions, passed the question on to Stalin. Stalin was well aware of the advantage of bringing Turkey into the war. It would enable the Soviet Union to take delivery of urgent supplies through the Dardanelles. However, his fundamental objective lay in winning an absolute commitment from the British and Americans to a second front in western Europe. Thus, much to his satisfaction, the Allies promised a cross-channel invasion in May 1944; and he, in turn, agreed to launch a Soviet offensive to coincide with Operation Overlord. As English historian A. J. P. Taylor (1965) concludes, "final decision for a Second Front was the great outcome of the Tehran conference: a decision imposed by Stalin and the American generals on Churchill, on the British generals and, to some extent, on Roosevelt."

Churchill and Stalin argued over the future of Poland. Churchill wanted a strong and independent Poland with the government in exile in London as the basis of the postwar government. Stalin denounced the London Poles and claimed that their agents in Poland were killing partisans trying to fight the Germans.

Another bone of contention was France. Roosevelt and Stalin were both skeptical about its military competence, and both showed an aversion to powerful fascist elements in the French army. In short, they viewed the French inability to resist Germany in 1940 as symptomatic of fundamental flaws in the French national character. FDR's dislike of European colonialism in general and of de Gaulle in particular led to his proposal for what had been French Indochina. He suggested that Laos, Cambodia, and Vietnam should be placed under a four-power trusteeship of Britain, China, the United States, and the Soviet Union. Stalin readily agreed, adding that Indochinese independence should follow in due course. However, it was clear, given the composition of the trusteeship, that the French landowners would remain while the Viet Minh, a local force of guerrillas led by Ho Chi Minh, and the Communists would be excluded from power. Churchill disliked the precedent of thus removing a French colony.

As to Germany, the Big Three discussed various plans of dismemberment. Churchill proposed a new federation of central European states, based on Prussia and southern Germany. Roosevelt suggested the permanent weakening of Germany by dividing it into four or five self-governing units, with such important industrial areas as the Ruhr and the Saar placed under an international trusteeship. Stalin had no specific Russian proposal, but he thought Churchill's plan was far too lenient.

"Thanksgiving in Berlin 1943." Clifford Berryman was as shrewd a satirist of the evil empire of the Third Reich as he was of America's political titans. In his cartoon of 25 November 1943, Göring, Hitler, and Goebbels contemplate a dead bird on the table while the city of Berlin is aflame with the mayhem wrought by bombing raids. (Library of Congress).

Moreover, Roosevelt and his advisers had come to regard the British Empire as an anachronism. Roosevelt was fully convinced of the need for national self-government for colonial peoples throughout the world. In addition, he believed that if the Big Three or the United Nations did not help subject peoples attain independence, then there would be continuous strife across the world. He communicated such ideas to Churchill periodically, much to Churchill's irritation.

The clearest indication of Britain's reluctance to grant independence to its colonies was its hesitation about freeing India. Indeed, such

123

Indian patriots as Gandhi, Nehru, and other leaders in the Indian Congress were imprisoned from September 1942 until the end of the war. FDR believed, like most Amerians, that if the United Nations were fighting for freedom, then India should be free. Toward India Britain was both obstinate and vain. Since all costs in the war in India were borne by Britain, at a cost of £1 million per day, Britain incurred a great debt and many casualties for a country it had promised to free at the end of the war. Of course, Britain needed India as a base for the reconquest of Burma and Malaya, and this reconquest had to be pursued to show that Britain was still a great power. However, the fundamental reason for staying in India was habit. Britain wanted to continue to behave as an imperial power. Nothing else could have been expected of Churchill. Churchill had announced, "I did not become His Majesty's First Minister in order to preside over the dissolution of the British Empire." However, FDR could have trumped this declaration with one of his own — that he was not fighting the war in order to preserve it.

Roosevelt and his team were both suspicious about, and optimistic toward, Stalin and the Soviet Union. They were wary of the Soviet Union's ambitions in eastern Europe. They were unsure of what the revolutionary movements in certain countries could accomplish and what influence the Soviet Union would exert upon them. It was clear there were strong underground revolutionary movements that adhered to socialist and Marxist ideology in both Italy and France. Their political commitment was in part a reaction against the fascist or quasi-fascist nature of their governments before the war.

Churchill did not return to London totally empty-handed. He did win approval for an amphibious landing behind the German defensive screen in Italy. However, the Americans exacted a price for their agreement by insisting that, after the Italian campaign, the troops and landing craft would be used in an amphibious assault upon southern France.

Churchill's project went ahead on January 22, 1944; but the Fifth Army failed to break out at the landing point, Anzio, and was bottled up on its beaches — a tantalizing thirty-seven miles short of Rome. Similarly, the Allied advance up the Italian peninsula foundered on the German Gustav line. The Italian mountains were the source of Italy's rivers; thus, the American and British infantry had to cross what seemed like an endless series of valleys, rivers, and ridges, each held by hardy German troops, and fight a series of bitter battles in order to advance

Greek troops rest in the mountains of Albania from their guerrilla warfare against the Germans. The composition of the photograph in which the sharply angled line of men is silhouetted against the snow recalls medieval snow scenes by the Flemish painter Bruegel. (Office of War Information; Library of Congress).

up the Italian spine. When Eisenhower was recalled to England to plan the cross-channel invasion, he took his best generals with him — Patton, Montgomery, and Omar Bradley. This damaged the foot soldiers' morale even further. After Eisenhower's departure, the Middle East and Italian commands were united under Sir Henry Maitland Wilson, with Sir Harold Alexander in command in Italy. Thus, the Mediterranean command became a British affair. It was a war of attrition fought in the worst winter in Italian memory, in mud by day and in ice frozen solid at night. The bodies of the dead were wrapped in bed sacks and bound together in stacks with Signal Corps wire. Feral dogs scavenged among the dead. Trench foot and frostbite were epidemic.

For three months the keystone of the German defense system, Monte

Cassino, withstood incessant ground and air attack. The most controversial act of the Allies was the devastation of the Benedictine abbey at Monte Cassino, a medieval treasure house that was thought to be a prime sanctuary of German arms. Not realizing that the Germans were not using the great stone monastery itself, the Australian commander, General Bernard Freyberg, insisted on its destruction. Despite pleas from various quarters, Allied bombers reduced the great abbey to rubble. This proved a tactical as well as an artistic mistake, since German troops hid themselves in among the broken stones and were even more difficult to dislodge than before. Finally, on May 15, 1944, Hitler ordered a retreat from the Gustav line. Three days later, Polish troops entered the monastery at Monte Cassino. On May 23, 1944, the Allies at last broke out at Anzio. Rome, which Churchill had envisaged taking in January, finally fell to the Allies at midnight on June 4, 1944.

The entry into Rome should have caused a sensation across the world, but it was eclipsed by the landing of Allied armies in northern France. A. J. P. Taylor comments, "With this, the taking of Rome, and indeed British strategy in the Mediterranean, lost all significance." By then, the Italian campaign was, as the Americans had always intended it to be, a sideshow. Operation Overlord was about to be launched. Planning for the invasion had begun in March 1943 under the direction of a British officer, Lieutenant General F. E. Morgan, who had been appointed COSSAC, or chief of staff to the supreme Allied commander. A command structure had been agreed upon, and Eisenhower had now been appointed supreme Allied commander at the Cairo conference. Originally, the Americans wanted a single supreme commander for all operations against Germany in northern and southern Europe, and they probably would have chosen Marshall. However, the British objected on the grounds that this appointment would virtually eliminate the Combined Chiefs of Staff. Thus the Americans acquiesced, and FDR chose Eisenhower instead. FDR had already singled out Eisenhower to lead the European theater after learning of his successful organization of army maneuvers in Louisiana in 1941. Here he thought was the sort of commander who could lead the most difficult of all wars—war by coalition.

Dwight David ("Ike") Eisenhower, the future thirty-fourth president (1953–61), was born in Texas in 1890 and grew up in Abilene Kansas. Having graduated from the United States Military Academy in 1915, he

In January 1944, General Dwight D. Eisenhower arrived in England to assume his post as supreme commander of Allied Expeditionary Forces. Here "Ike" encourages the men of the 502d Parachute Infantry Regiment, 101st Airborne Division, shortly before the D Day invasion of Normandy in 1944. This publicity photograph captures him in conversation with Lieutenant Wallace C. Strobel. Because of the tent, some authors have mistakenly placed this photograph in the earlier North African campaign. (Library of Congress).

served with the Nineteenth Infantry at Fort Sam Houston, Texas (1915–17); and during World War I organized Camp Colt for training tank troops, attaining the rank of captain. In 1933 he became special assistant to General Douglas MacArthur, the chief of staff, and served MacArthur as assistant adviser (1935–39) to the Philippine Commonwealth. His success led to promotions and his being appointed chief of the War Plans Division in the office of chief of staff in February 1942. Eisenhower's distinctive and special talents lay in his ability to work with varied temperaments among commanding officers and to weld their different aims into a cohesive strategy. His campaigns were well planned with tactics wisely modulated within a particular strategy. His relaxations were golf, for which he had a passion, collecting objets d'art from the great European houses he stayed at on his successful drive to Germany, and his dalliance with his British chauffeuse, Kay Sumersby Morgan, whom he found more spirited than his wife, the dour Mamie Doud. Eisenhower, inwardly a somewhat cold man, was outwardly the average American's idea of what an American soldier should be — fair-minded and canny, modest and alert. On January 16, 1944, he took up his duties; and on February 8, 1944, the plan for Operation Overlord was confirmed at Allied headquarters.

While the plan for the cross-channel invasion was accepted unanimously, one bone of contention did arise. It was an issue that was to reveal just how strained had become the once special relationship between the British and the Americans. Predictably, it centered upon Mediterranean operations. The decision to invade southern France had been made at Tehran. There, Stalin won approval for his suggestion that this assault — "Anvil" — occur two months before Operation Overlord. The British had accepted earlier the proposal as the price they had to pay for winning American approval for a continuation of the Italian campaign. However, as the target date for Operation Anvil drew nearer, Churchill and Chief of Imperial General Staff General Brooke fought tooth and nail against the scheme. In Brooke's opinion, it would bring to nothing all that had already been achieved at such considerable cost in the Italian campaign. Moreover, Brooke thought it would reduce by half the war effort in that theater. In addition, the ten divisions transferred from Italy would be slaughtered if Operation Anvil were launched prior to the main invasion of northwest France. Brooke was also preoccupied with the possible political repercussions. In his view, the only beneficiary of the operation would be Stalin. By calling a halt to operations in Italy, Britain and America would lose the opportunity of both chasing the Germans out of northern Italy, the Adriatic region, and the Balkans and, therefore, influencing the political complexion of those zones in the postwar period. Brooke, it appears, harbored no illusions either about Stalin's trustworthiness as an ally or his postwar intentions. Churchill supported Brooke's position and pleaded with FDR to cancel the assault. A compromise was reached when it was agreed to go ahead

One of the classic photographs of the Normandy landings shows American servicemen about to be discharged from the vessel that has carried them to the shore. Seen purely as image, the photograph has a disturbing trompe l'oeil effect. Is the shore about to be swallowed by the jaws of the landing craft as they open like a giant shovel? Is it the sea itself that is about to disgorge its special cargo ashore in a giant belch? (Library of Congress).

with Operation Anvil only when the Allies reached the Pisa-Rimini line in Italy. When the Allied advance in this theater foundered on the Gustav line, the debate ended as to whether Operation Anvil should or should not be launched prior to Operation Overlord. However, the arguments concerning the advisability of such an operation were soon to be resumed.

The Invasion of France

Despite demands for starting a second front earlier, the invasion of France on D Day, June 6, 1944, could not have been launched until the U-boats had been overcome in 1943 and thus came at the most appropriate time. Furthermore, though Germany was hard pressed, it was by no means finished. The Germans were preparing new weapons —U-boats with snorkels, pilotless planes, and rockets—that the Allies could not answer immediately. Moreover, without a second front to compensate for this, the morale of the American and British people would have been greatly strained. Fortunately, Germany's new weapons came too late. The fast U-boats and jet aircraft were never used on a large scale, and use of the pilotless planes was delayed by the bombing of their stations and launching pads.

There were two key factors that brought success to Operation Overlord: first, by spring 1944 the Allied air forces enjoyed a superiority of planes over the Luftwaffe of thirty to one. For six months prior to D Day, German defenses and lines of communication had been hammered from the air. During the Normandy landings, Allied aircraft provided essential cover while beachheads were established. Indeed, on D Day over 11,000 missions were flown. Allied command of the skies was so complete that not one plane was lost to the Luftwaffe. Second, by carrying out a complex campaign of disinformation, the Allies were able to fool Hitler into believing that a major army group under Patton's command would launch the Invasion at the Pas de Calais. The main body of German forces were concentrated there to receive the supposed assault, while a meager fourteen divisions were left to defend the Normandy beaches. In fact, the invasion and the battles that followed were by no means fought as planned.

D Day was set for June 5, 1944. However, foul weather caused yet another delay. On June 6, 600 warships and 4,000 supporting craft did set sail to escort 176,000 Allied troops on the Normandy beaches. The British Second Army was to land on the eastern section of the Normandy coast at beaches named Gold, Juno, and Sword. The United States First Army was to land at the base of the Cotentin Peninsula farther west at beaches named Omaha and Utah.

The First Army under Lieutenant General Omar Bradley was assigned to the western flank. At Utah beach, the United States Seventh Corps under Major General J. Lawton Collins met with little resistance and lost only twelve men during D Day. However, at Omaha Beach, Major General L. T. Gerow's Fifth Corps were slaughtered at the water's edge and by midnight hanging on grimly to a thousand-yard strip of shoreline.

Rommel, now entrusted with the defense of the French channel coast, developed a special inventiveness in creating coastal fortification. He understood that if German forces were to have a chance of warding off the combined Allied attack that the enemy must be prevented from establishing beachheads, that strong reserve forces should be assembled behind coastal defenses ready for counterattacks, and that, unless the Allies could be driven back into the sea, the eventual outcome of the invasion would be decided on the first day. However, his insights fell upon deaf ears.

The defenses constructed by the German armies were considerable. They had mined all the beaches, laid tank traps under the shallow waters of the beach approaches, and built concrete emplacements to permit a dead cross fire. However, despite numerous casualties, the Allies were successful. The sheer weight of Allied forces quickly delivered within a narrow front, the overwhelming preliminary pounding from air and sea, and the strategic sealing off of the area by airborne troops dropped behind beach defenses played a vital part in the assault's success. Allied air forces met with very little opposition and worked closely with troops on the ground. Moreover, German organization suffered from divided and competitive chains of command and the stubborn orders of the intuitive, irrational, and megalomaniac führer. The German commanding officer, General Gunther von Kluge, wanted to retreat to avoid encirclement, but Hitler stubbornly refused to allow any retreat. Von Kluge was quickly relieved by Field Marshal Model and took poison rather than face court-martial and execution.

In the first week of the campaign, the Allies landed 326,000 men, 50,000 vehicles, and over 100,000 tons of supplies. They established a beachhead fifty miles in length and from five to fifteen miles in width. By July 23 the battle for Normandy had been won, and the battle for France began. At the end of July, Patton's Third Army had broken out into Brittany. On August 20, 1944, the Third Army established a bridgehead across the Seine. Meanwhile, Operation Anvil, the amphibious assault on southern France, had been launched on August 15, 1944.

Even after D Day, the federal government was reluctant to embrace de Gaulle. Henry Stimson, secretary of war, recorded in his diary that FDR "believes that de Gaulle will crumble and that the British supporters of de Gaulle will be confounded by the progress of events. . . . The

President thinks that other parties will spring up as liberation goes on and that de Gaulle will become a very little figure."

As Paris awaited liberation in the summer of 1944, rumors abounded concerning American attempts to install a puppet government. The United States had refused to equip the French Forces of the Interior (FFI), located in Paris and under the command of pro-Gaullist General Delestraint, with sufficient arms to overthrow and expel the Nazis by themselves. FDR had already informed Churchill that he would not provide "a white horse on which he [de Gaulle] could ride into France and make himself master of a government there."

De Gaulle pleaded with Eisenhower to allow French forces to advance on Paris. Eventually, Eisenhower complied. But even this concession could not have allayed de Gaulle's fears of American duplicity, for the French division assigned to the liberation of Paris comprised 12,000 so-called Free French, loyal to de Gaulle, and 15,000 "others," including a large number of officers who had fought the British in Syria and who had been fervent supporters of Pétain. De Gaulle hastened to Paris to arrive in the immediate wake of this spearhead, with the intention of establishing himself as head of a coalition of resistance groups and presenting the United States with a fait accompli. On August 25, 1944, Paris was liberated by the Allies with General Jacques Le Clerc leading the procession through the streets.

Paris surprised its liberators. It did not look like a capital freed from slavery. In fact, it was more prosperous than London. Not only had the French textile industry flourished during German occupation but the French also had been developing the first practical television transmitters and sets. The most famous dress designers were in business, and their clientele were buying full skirts and mutton-legged sleeves, fashions impossible to produce in those countries like Britain and the United States where clothes were subject to rationing. One couturier told an American reporter, "What shall I do with all this nonsense going on? All my best customers are in concentration camps because of course they were working for Vichy." Indeed, the Gaullists and the French Resistance had compiled lists of 700,000 collaborators, including girls who had had sex with German soldiers. The girls had to submit to having their heads shaved. Many other collaborators escaped reprisals or bought their way out.

In October 1944 the United States begrudgingly granted recognition

Invasion troops land on the coast of Iwo Jima in 1945. (Library of Congress).

to de Gaulle's provisional government. Nevertheless, Washington did all that it could to diminish de Gaulle's status and the role played by France in the continuing conflict. All American aid to FFI forces still fighting the Nazis was brought to an end. American military leaders also encouraged the recruitment of FFI troops into the regular French army. French army units were then assigned to largely noncombatant roles in isolated theaters.

Why were relations between de Gaulle and the United States, especially Roosevelt and his advisers, so fraught? Initially, FDR and his advisers were convinced that de Gaulle commanded only very limited support among the French people. In the period from June 1940 to December 1942, de Gaulle's adventurism had seriously jeopardized American attempts to remain on good terms with the Vichy regime. The most serious incident occurred in December 1941 when de Gaulle ordered Free French forces to occupy the Atlantic islands of Saint Pierre

133

and Miquelon, off of Newfoundland. This order ran counter to an agreement the United States had made with Admiral Robert, Vichy commander in Martinique, that neither party would entertain a change in the status quo of any part of the Western Hemisphere.

Moreover, FDR had no intention of supporting de Gaulle's ambition to restore France to the status of a great power in the postwar period. At his various meetings with Churchill, FDR poured contempt upon the French, asserting that their initial performance in the war had permanently disqualified them from claims to such status. Moreover, he was resolutely opposed to allowing the French to reassert their precious authority over their overseas possessions, something to which de Gaulle was totally committed. Roosevelt also was opposed to de Gaulle's proposal to establish France as the leader of a European third force in postwar relations. When de Gaulle announced that "the unity of Europe should be built round these poles: London, Paris and Moscow," FDR interpreted this as an endorsement of the "balance-of-power" principle. Such a principle was totally discredited in the eyes of FDR and played no part in his plan for peaceful coexistence among the great powers in the postwar world.

Among those Americans who praised de Gaulle and his resistance movement was columnist Walter Lippmann. In his column "Today and Tomorrow" of 17 September 1940, he denounced those Frenchmen who had made "the terrible mistake of thinking that they could ingratiate themselves with the victors by rendering themselves completely helpless." Disturbed by deteriorating relations between the Free French in Washington, D.C., and de Gaulle in London, Lippmann wrote a series of sharply worded columns, trying to persuade the federal government that de Gaulle's organization was a "necessary and critical move in the

1066 and 1944. The inspiration for the cover of the *New Yorker* designed by illustrator Rea Irwin to commemorate the Allied invasion of western Europe in June 1944 was the Bayeux Tapestry of the eleventh century, which depicted, in serial form, William the Conqueror's successful invasion of England in 1066. Illustrator Irwin reversed the order of passage, with invasion forces from England conquering Normandy. He has FDR, Churchill, and King George VI in conference *(upper left)* and Montgomery and Eisenhower *(upper right)* planning the slings and arrowshots of the new Normans in the war against tyranny. (Library of Congress).

development of a western front in Europe" (16 July 1942). He told a French-American Club dinner in New York on October 28, 1942, that de Gaulle was "as much the acknowledged leader of the French war of independence as General George Washington was the acknowledged leader of the American." While Lippmann outwardly compared de Gaulle with Washington, inwardly he compared him to Theodore Roosevelt.

De Gaulle never forgot how shabbily he was treated by Roosevelt. Lippmann was inspired to make an outspoken defense of the "greatest living soldier of France" in his column of 10 July 1943. The administration's prejudice was "rapidly making this man, already the symbol of French national resistance, the symbol of French, and not only of French but of European independence." His warning took on even sharper meaning twenty years later: "Let us not imagine that Europe can be resettled and restored without the full participation of France and without the influence which France alone can exert. If, therefore, we pursue a policy which estranges her and divides her, there will be no great friendly power in the whole of Europe from the Atlantic Ocean to the frontier of Soviet Russia. But there will be a focus of disorder and of antagonism which bodes only ill for our dearest hopes." American confusion toward France suggests something of the problems that would follow the Allies' failure to clarify, understand, and appraise realistically their postwar aims.

The Liberation of Europe

As the problems of the war multiplied and as Hitler's megalomania and mental derangement became increasingly apparent, the few soldiers and civilians in Germany ready to remove Hitler in order to negotiate terms for Germany grew desperate. Several attempts on his life were planned in 1943 and 1944; the most nearly successful was on July 20, 1944. Colonel Claus von Stauffenberg exploded a bomb in a valise at Hitler's headquarters in East Prussia. However, because the suitcase had been moved accidentally from its site, when the bomb exploded the intended victim escaped with only minor injuries. All those implicated in the plot were barbarously executed by being hanged slowly with piano wire—a gruesome spectacle photographed for the depraved entertainment of the führer and as a warning to others. The failure of the plot led Hitler to eliminate the last vestiges of the army's independence from his control. Henceforth, Nazi politicians were appointed to all military headquarters.

Despite his fatigue, Hitler never relaxed his control of the party and the army and continued to exercise hypnotic control of his immediate subordinates, although any hope of victory or even negotiated surrender was now but a lunatic vision.

Erwin Rommel was a professional soldier of considerable integrity. He was not, and did not consider himself, a politician. Yet he knew Hitler was losing the war and that he was not prepared to accept or deal with the fact. In 1944 several acquaintances advised Rommel that he should become head of state once Hitler had been overthrown. Those who planned to eliminate Hitler did not tell Rommel they were determined to assassinate the führer. Rommel did not reject the suggestion that he should take over. Once Europe had been invaded, Rommel tried at different times to persuade Hitler to come to terms with surrender while negotiation was still possible. On July 17, 1944, at the height of the fighting during the invasion, Rommel's car was attacked by British fighter bombers and was forced off the road. The car keeled over, and Rommel was injured with serious head wounds. The assassination attempt on Hitler came on July 20, 1944, while Rommel was still recuperating in the hospital. Investigations after the assassination attempt disclosed Rommel's contacts with the conspirators. Hitler could not have his greatest war hero, the invincible *Volksmarschall* (people's marshal), arraigned, condemned, and officially executed as he had had the others. Instead, Hitler sent two generals to Rommel who was now recovering at home. They revealed what was known and assured him that if he took his own life by poisoning the facts would remain hidden, and he and his family would remain innocent in the eyes of the world. If he refused, he would be sent to trial. On October 14, Rommel took poison and died. As far as the public was concerned, he had died of his injuries. He was buried with full military honors.

By the fall of 1944, there were over 2 million Allied soldiers in France—three-fifths of them Americans. On September 1, 1944, American forces crossed the Meuse; on September 3, 1944, the British Second Army liberated Brussels; and, on the following day, the Second Army marched into Antwerp. On September 11, 1944, the United States

The ebullient FDR dominated the Quebec conference of 1944. Here the president is flanked by Prime Ministers Winston Churchill of Britain and McKenzie King of Canada. (Library of Congress).

First Army crossed the German frontier near Aachen. Thus it was that within six weeks of the breakout from Normandy, France had been cleared of German forces. D Day and its sequels raised American and British morale. Now people expected unconditional surrender; yet, the end of World War II was far less abrupt than was the end of World War I.

While June, July, and August were months of triumph for the Allied armed forces, military and diplomatic relations between Britain and America reached a nadir. Again, it was the proposed invasion of southern France that drove a wedge between them. As we know, it had been agreed in the spring of 1944 that Operation Anvil should commence when the Allies in Italy had reached the Pisa-Rimini line. Then operations on that front were to be curtailed while ten divisions were made ready for the attack on southern France. Generals Alexander (Great Britain), Clarke (United States), and Juin (France) were deeply disappointed that, having at last taken Rome, they were not to be allowed to pursue the enemy and drive home their advantage. Churchill shared this view. With the Allied forces firmly established at the Normandy beachhead, Churchill now argued that Operation Anvil was superfluous. He suggested that the German divisions assigned to the defense of southern France could be tied down there by a series of feints, while the offensive in Italy could be resumed. These proposals were rejected at a meeting of the Combined Chiefs of Staff on June 13, much to Churchill's chagrin. The Americans insisted that the Italian advance should halt at the Apennines and that Allied forces in that theater be diverted to one of three operations: Anvil; an amphibious landing at the bay of Biscay; or an amphibious landing at the head of the Adriatic. This last option was the brainchild of the British delegation. Churchill was now thinking in terms of an attack upon Istria and Trieste, the clearance of northern Italy, and then a march on Vienna via the Ljubljana Gap in Yugoslavia. His thoughts now focused not only on the defeat of Hitler but also on future bargaining with Stalin on the postwar settlement of eastern Europe.

However, there was little hope that the American military would consent to such an operation. On June 28, 1944, Churchill tried to win FDR over to his side. In a wire sent to Washington, he explained that the more he contemplated Operation Anvil the "more bleak and sterile it appears." He regarded the operation as completely destructive of all Allied efforts in the Mediterranean. It was his hope that FDR would not allow the operation to be forced upon the British. FDR remained unmoved by this personal appeal. He sent word that he would support Eisenhower in his refusal to depart from the grand strategy laid down at Tehran. This, despite the fact that Stalin had failed to fulfill his promise of a Soviet offensive to coincide with Operation Overlord. FDR was also influenced by domestic considerations. This was an election year, and Roosevelt knew he could not afford to alienate public opinion by committing American troops to a British-sponsored adventure in the Adriatic. As he informed Churchill, "I should never survive even a slight setback in Overlord if it were known that fairly large forces had been diverted to the Balkans."

Thus at the beginning of July 1944, Churchill decided to bite the bullet and gave orders to the British commander in Italy to prepare forces for an attack upon southern France on August 15, 1944. However, the successful breakout of Allied forces from the Normandy enclave served to rekindle Churchill's hopes of avoiding Operation Anvil. When FDR again proved unsympathetic, Churchill turned his attention to Eisenhower. For ten days he pleaded with and cajoled the supreme commander. According to Eisenhower, he was "stirred, upset and even despondent." On one occasion he even talked of resigning the premiership. For his part, Churchill accused America of playing the "big, strong and dominating partner" in the alliance. The meetings ended, according to Eisenhower's naval aide-de-camp Captain Harry Butcher, with the general "saying No in every form of the English language at his command."

On August 10, Churchill finally gave the order to proceed with Operation Anvil. The invasion of southern France, first called "Anvil" and later "Dragoon," began with landings on the Mediterranean coast near Toulon and Cannes on August 15, 1944. More than fifteen hundred ships delivered the American Seventh Army, under Lieutenant General Alexander M. Patch, and parts of the French First Army, under General Jean de Lattre de Tassigny. The invaders soon seized the vital ports of Marseilles, Toulon, and Nice. Supported by FFI resistance fighters, the Allies moved inexorably northward to Lyons and Dijon.

The Allies did not have things all their own way. At this stage, in an attempt to turn the tide for the Nazis, Hitler unleashed a series of hitherto secret weapons. The first was the V-1 robot bomb, a small pilotless plane carrying about one ton of explosives and moving on a preset course at 350 miles per hour. The bombs were used first against London just after the first Normandy landings on June 13, 1944. The British devised balloon barrages and increased their antiaircraft defenses to intercept the V-1s. Although only about 27 percent of 8,000 V-1 rockets reached London, they caused 6,184 casualties, while wounding thousands more and destroying many buildings.

Then from September 8, 1944, Hitler began using the second of these weapons, the V-2. Unlike its predecessor, the V-2 carried its explosives at supersonic speeds and at such heights that it could be neither seen nor heard. Thus, the V-2s claimed far more lives and caused more damage than the V-1s in London, until their flights were ended by the Allied capture of the main launching pads. Thereafter, V-2 rockets

Allied commanders discuss their final strategies against Germany. *Left to right:* Sir Alan Brooke, Eisenhower, Montgomery, Major General B. Anderson, and Lieutenant General Omar N. Bradley. The wisdom of Eisenhower's crucial decision to move slowly but surely on a broad front to Germany was confirmed by hindsight, despite the British preference at the time for a quick drive to Berlin. (U.S. Army photograph; Library of Congress).

were sent from other launching ramps against Belgian cities in Allied hands. Altogether, 5,000 V-2s were fired in the war, of which 1,115 came down over England and 2,050 over Brussels, Antwerp, and Liège, claiming 2,500 lives. Had they been deployed earlier, the V-1 and V-2 rockets would have hampered the Allied war effort. The V-2s were sometimes known as "Bob Hopes" because civilians had to "Bob down and hope for the best."

With the Allies triumphant in France, the generals had to choose how best to exploit the situation. By the end of August 1944, the

German army in the west was in a state of complete disarray. Of the fifty-eight infantry divisions involved in action between June 6 and August 25, 1944, perhaps only twelve were now fit to stand and fight. With Hitler's reserve committed to the war of attrition on the eastern front, the road to Berlin seemed to be open.

The Allies were not prepared for such a situation. When planning Operation Overlord, they had assumed that their aerial supremacy would deter Hitler from committing his western armies to one titanic effort to throw the expeditionary force back across the English Channel. They had, indeed, expected his generals to withdraw gradually, fighting a yielding defensive action. As such, the Allies had laid down plans to advance slowly on a broad front. The British were to take the coastal route through Belgium, skirting the northern extremity of the Ardennes Forest, while the Americans were to swing eastward, south of the Ardennes. Eventually, both wings would breach the Siegfried line at separate points and then converge to encircle the Ruhr. Therefore, it was expected that the Allies would cross into Germany in early 1945.

Hitler's unexpected decision to launch all his forces against the Allies in July and August rendered this plan redundant. By mid-August it was apparent to the British commander, General Sir Bernard Montgomery, that if the original plan were adhered to, then the opportunity of striking into Germany and ending the war in 1944 would be lost.

On August 17, 1944, Montgomery met with General Omar Bradley to explain a new strategy. He suggested ordering General Patton's Third Army to halt its eastward advance so that supplies could be concentrated upon Montgomery's own British force. This force, augmented by some American divisions, could then thrust eastward, north of the Ardennes and along the shortest land route into the heart of the Reich. Initially, Bradley appears to have been impressed by the scheme. However, the idea was anathema to Patton; thus, Bradley, who had once served under the charismatic general, quickly withdrew his support for Montgomery's proposal. Undaunted, Montgomery took his case to Eisenhower on August 22, 1944. Eisenhower accepted the view that the original plan now had to be revised, but he rejected Montgomery's quick thrust into Germany. The most obvious reason for his resistance centered on the difficulty of supplying the advance force. With the French railway system destroyed by preinvasion aerial bombing, the Allies were dependent upon long-haul trucks for their supplies. There

"Bombs away at Meuçon" on September 23, 1944. An instance of the strategy of saturation bombing by the Allies in the last years of the war, a strategy intended to bring Germany to its knees. (Library of Congress).

were simply not enough of these vehicles available for a rapid advance along a narrow front. Supply difficulties were also exacerbated by the fact that the channel ports were either shattered or still in German hands.

It must also be pointed out that Eisenhower's decision may well have been influenced by the fact that the American people would have been outraged had the American military been forced to enter Germany on the coattails of the victorious British forces. (Could FDR's devious hand be detected in this? 1944 was an election year, and FDR already had voiced his fears about alienating the electorate by mishandling Operation Overlord.)

As it was, Eisenhower's refusal to go along with Montgomery's proposal poisoned relations between the two men for the next six months. Eisenhower was determined to carry on the policy of a broad advance —to clear the Scheldt Estuary in order to enable the Allies to use Antwerp as an entrepôt; to capture Dunkirk and Calais; and to overrun V-1 and V-2 coastal emplacements. However, he did agree to Montgomery's Operation Marketgarden, an airborne assault upon the Rhine bridges at Eindhoven and Arnhem. The operation was a catastrophic blunder that put an end to Montgomery's further requests for a rapid assault on Germany in 1944.

By mid-December 1944 the channel ports had been cleared; Patton had breached the Siegfried line's heaviest fortifications; and the Allied armies stood poised on the German border. Hitler gambled that, by discreetly withdrawing crack units from other portions of the front and concentrating them against the tightly held Allied front in the Ardennes area of Belgium, he could penetrate Allied defensives, capture bridges across the Meuse, and then retake Antwerp. This was what German forces tried to do, beginning on the morning of December 16, 1944. Against all expectations, General Runstedt launched an attack through the Ardennes, aimed at splitting the Allied forces and recapturing Antwerp. The attack advanced fifty miles before the Allies could mount significant resistance. The Battle of the Bulge ended on January 15, 1945, with the Germans thrown back from whence they came. Rundstedt had lost 120,000 men, 1,600 planes, and most of his armor. Asked what turned the tide, Montgomery, now not at all sympathetic to the United States, admitted, "the good fighting qualities of the American soldier."

As a result of the Battle of the Bulge, the Allies enjoyed a new tactical advantage. The battle had shattered Hitler's crack troops and had made it almost impossible for the Germans to withstand the subsequent Allied advance. Moreover, the battle had used up the reserves essential to combat the Russians in the east. Nevertheless, it took the Allies almost one month to fight their way back to their earlier positions; and, in the process, they suffered 100,000 casualties and irreplaceable losses in tanks, planes, and supplies. By the end of January, Eisenhower had regrouped his armies and was ready to push onward to the Rhine and beyond.

The Battle of the Bulge was followed by the disintegration of German forces and the reduction of Berlin, Hamburg, Dresden, Essen, Düsseldorf, Nuremberg, and Frankfurt to rubble by Allied bombing and shell-

Britain ravaged by bombing. The Guards Chapel, London, was damaged beyond repair in 1944. The protective shield of the roof covering the sanctuary has been torn away, and a shambles is all that is left. (Library of Congress).

ing. The Anglo-American firebombing raids on Dresden of February 13 and 14, 1945, were militarily unnecessary and incinerated 135,000 people. In fact, Berlin was the original target, and the switch to Dresden was a last-minute decision. It was not possible to pass the bombing of Dresden off to the public as an essential strategic operation in which a few civilians were killed only by a regrettable accident. To exculpate themselves, Churchill and his cabinet saddled Harris with sole responsibility for the entire strategy of indiscriminate destruction. In all, 593,000 German civilians were killed by bombing during the war.

On the eastern front, in 1944 the Soviet armies began to expel the Germans from Russian soil and the Soviet First Army entered Poland on July 17. By May they had expelled all German soldiers from the Soviet Union and had invaded Hungary and Rumania. Russian forces now totaled 5 million men in 300 divisions. Several weeks after the Normandy invasion of June 1944, Stalin launched a new and larger offensive; and by early 1945, the Russians stood on a line from Memal on the Baltic in the north to Vienna in the south. By the time the Allies were poised before the Rhine, the Russians were at Frankfort on the Oder.

FDR and Churchill had met only once throughout the climactic year of 1944. At the second Quebec, or "Octagon," conference of September 11 to September 16, 1944, the focus of military discussion shifted away from Europe and onto the Far East. However, the British once more proposed an extension of operations into the Adriatic. Predictably, the Americans vetoed this idea.

When the Allies next met, at Malta from January 31 to February 3, 1945, the Adriatic issue was raised again. Once more, it was opposed by the Americans. Attention then turned to the war in northwest Europe. The British revived Montgomery's plan for a single thrust into the heart of the Reich. For their part, the Americans held fast to Eisenhower's plan for a broad advance to the Rhine to be followed by a pincer movement aimed at encircling the Ruhr. Again, the British were forced to give way. Eisenhower was authorized to put his plan into action. He did this in three stages: the advance to the Rhine from the end of January to March 21, 1945; the encirclement of the Ruhr leading to the entrapment and surrender of 325,000 German troops between March 21 and April 14, 1945; and the annihilation of further pockets of enemy resistance, from April 14 to May 7, 1945.

London children evacuated from new terrors of war from the air in the spring of 1944. (Library of Congress).

Yet even this successful campaign was not achieved without a high degree of acrimony. It was an argument over strategy that, once settled, pointed up Britain's subordinate status in its morganatic relationship with the United States and, ultimately, helped define the postwar balance of power in Europe.

The campaign began with yet another blow to British prestige. On March 28, 1944, Eisenhower announced that, once the Ruhr was encircled, the United States Ninth Army, which had been fighting under Montgomery's command, would return to American control. Thereafter, Montgomery's truncated force was to play but a supporting role, guarding Omar Bradley's northern flank in the general advance to the Elbe. There, on the banks of that great river, the Allied advance in the west was to halt.

Churchill was incensed because Eisenhower had, by his treatment of Montgomery, affronted the British military and wasted the opportunity of driving on to Berlin. On April 1, 1945, he cabled FDR, urging him to order Eisenhower on to Berlin. According to Churchill's argument, a rapid British and American assault on, and capture of, Berlin would shatter the German will to fight on. It would also rob the Russians of this, the greatest prize of the war. As he stated, the Russians were already in Vienna. If they also took Berlin, then they could later argue that this was positive proof that they had shouldered a disproportionate share of the burden of fighting. Churchill also was aware that it would be difficult to get the Soviets out once they were ensconced in the German capital. This, as he told FDR, might hold "grave and formidable difficulties" for the future.

Yet, again, FDR proved unresponsive to Churchill's request for strategic change. On April 12, 1945, the United States Fifth Armored Division, in the vanguard of the Allied advance, reached the Elbe. Standing only fifty-three miles short of Berlin, the men of the Fifth assumed that they were to drive on to the capital. When Eisenhower learned of their position, he asked Bradley for a general estimate of casualties in an assault on Berlin. Bradley suggested something in the region of 100,000 men. To Eisenhower, the prize was not worth the cost. He reiterated his order to halt at the Elbe.

With Patton's Third Army driving all before them on the southern flank, the British General Staff now turned their attention to Prague. In conversation with their American counterparts, they pointed to the possible political advantage of having Patton installed in the Czech capital. Marshall passed this idea on to Eisenhower, adding that he, himself, was unwilling to sacrifice American lives for purely political purposes. Eisenhower shared this opinion. It was a typical response, for, throughout the war, the American military had taken the defeat of German armed forces as their primary objective. They had not been concerned about political perspectives. Their opposition to British proposals had been inspired by a prevailing suspicion of British motives. Even when these proposals had positive strategic merits, American military leaders held out against them for fear that they were being used as pawns in some greater game. By mid-April, the American forces were on the point of achieving their objective. In the opinion of the American military leaders, who took Berlin and Prague was irrelevant. The limited strategic advantage offered by each capital was not especially important in comparison with the effort. If the Russians were

The small town of Würzburg, a repository of all that was best in German culture, is no better than a shell after Allied bombing raids. The only brilliance left is the sunshine that penetrates the craters of its badly deformed visage. (Library of Congress).

willing to pay this price, then Eisenhower was willing to let them have the prize.

There was one dissenting voice among American military leaders. In the final weeks of the war, Patton pleaded with Eisenhower for permission to drive on to Prague. Finally, Eisenhower's resistance crumbled; and, on May 4, 1945, he informed Red Army Chief of Staff General Antonov that he was about to unleash Patton's Third Army. Antonov responded by telling Eisenhower that, in order to avoid a "possible confusion of forces," he should refrain from giving the order. Eisenhower complied and thus allowed the Red Army to liberate Prague and, indeed, much of Czechoslovakia.

The Russians had assembled 2.5 million soldiers (the largest military force ever to gather in a concentrated front) at the line of the Oder River and moved steadily to Berlin, which they entered on April 22 and finally captured on May 2, 1945. They had to sustain casualties of more than 100,000 in bitter street fighting.

Now the end in Europe came suddenly and bitterly. On April 28, Mussolini and his mistress were shot by Communist partisans, and their bodies were hung upside down in Milan. On April 29, German forces in Italy surrendered unconditionally to Alexander. On April 30, Hitler and his former mistress, Eva Braun—now his wife—committed suicide. Their bodies were burned in the yard outside their bunker.

Hitler's closest aides also came to sorry ends. Goebbels also committed suicide with Hitler—after he had killed his wife and six children.

Although Himmler had put down the July 1944 conspiracy against Hitler with the utmost ruthlessness, a few months later he was secretly attempting to negotiate terms of surrender with the Allies, thus expecting to be able to save himself. Hitler expelled him from the Nazi party. In 1945 Himmler tried to escape but was captured by British troops and committed suicide by taking poison.

Before Hitler committed suicide, he named Grand Admiral Karl Dönitz as his successor as chancellor of a pocket Reich. However, it was Field Marshal Alfred Jodl who was escorted to Eisenhower's headquarters in Reims on May 7, where he signed the document of Germany's unconditional surrender. Dönitz would have preferred to end the war in the west while continuing to fight Russia. However, the Allies rejected this, and the Germans signed unconditional surrender on all fronts at Eisenhower's headquarters. To accommodate Russia, the surrender was ratified at Zhukov's headquarters in Berlin at 11:30 P.M. on May 8. In a final (but typical) muddle, the Western Allies celebrated V-E Day (Victory in Europe) on May 8, while the Russians celebrated victory on May 9.

Much of the myth about which power would first get to Berlin is based on a misconception that the nation first past the post of the Brandenburg Gate then would have refused to yield to the other Allies their zones of occupation. However, after they had taken Berlin, the Russians, as previously agreed, gave up the various sections of the city to the American, British, and French forces. At about the same time, the Allies yielded to the Russians those other areas of Germany that they were holding but which had previously been allocated to the Russians.

Churchill did suggest that American forces should seize areas previously allocated to the Russians as a means of trading Russian agreement on Poland, but State Department officials advised him that this would set a dangerous precedent that the Russians could exploit in areas closer to American and British interests.

[4]

THE WAR IN ASIA

The War Against Japan

THE ATTACK on Pearl Harbor was the terrible climax of deteriorating American-Japanese relations. Final military and aerial plans by the Japanese began on November 26, 1941, when six Japanese carriers and their escort met in the Kurile Islands. At the same time, American military intelligence received reports that large forces of Japanese troop transportation vessels were seen steaming southward from Formosa. Japanese aircraft finally took off for the attack on Pearl Harbor on December 7, 1941, at 6:00 A.M. They reached their target at 7:55 A.M. and dropped the first bombs.

By the end of the day, 2,403 Americans had been killed; 149 American planes had been destroyed. The USS *Arizona* was sunk; five American battleships, including the USS *Oklahoma* were badly damaged. However, Pearl Harbor was not the disaster that it might have been. For the U.S. Pacific Fleet's aircraft carriers—the *Lexington*, the *Enterprise*, and the *Saratoga*—were all at sea when the Japanese attack took place.

The Japanese attack on Pearl Harbor by carrier-based planes was a dramatic demonstration of the potential uses of aircraft carriers, which

Emperor Hirohito of Japan (1901–89) whose part in the tragic events of the dark valley has remained obscure. Was he, as this photograph of the 1930s suggests (with the divine emperor in the headdress of a priest), no more responsible for the terrible dramas of high-power politics than a statue in a shrine? (Library of Congress).

became the dominant combat ships of the war. The aircraft carrier was a naval vessel from which airplanes could take off and onto which they could land. It was originally conceived of by the British who built the *Argus* in World War I, although the war ended before the *Argus* could be put into operation. However, the idea was quickly adopted by the Americans in March 1922 with a converted carrier, the USS *Langley*, and also by the Japanese.

Essentially, aircraft carriers were airfields at sea with many special features necessitated by limitations in size and conditions at sea. To facilitate short takeoffs and landings, airspeeds over the deck were increased by turning the ship into the wind. Catapults flush (or level) with the flight deck assisted in launching airplanes. For landing, air-

American attempts to understand events from the Japanese point of view were not helped by a propaganda film, *The Japanese Soldier*, in which common stereotypes of totalitarian society were expressed, such as the inculcation among schoolchildren of unswerving obedience to militarism. (Library of Congress).

planes were fitted with retractable hooks that engaged transverse wires in the deck, thereby braking the planes to a quick stop. The vital control centers of the aircraft carriers were situated in special islands on one side of the flight decks. Landings were guided by hand signals on deck.

General Douglas MacArthur called the enemy "the Jap." To most Americans they were "Nips," short for *Dai Nippon*, the Japanese word for the home islands. Even after the lightning devastation of Pearl Harbor, Americans consoled themselves with an ill-founded racial stereotype of Japanese soldiers as bespectacled, bandy-legged men in baggy clothes. In fact, they were absolutely fearless, deadly accurate sharpshooters. Their ships were faster; their guns were bigger; and their airpower was superior to anything the United States could provide in 1941 and 1942. Secretary of War Henry L. Stimson maintained how "we'll defeat the Japanese in the end, but we shouldn't look at the war with them through rose-colored glasses. There are reports that the Japanese . . . are badly trained troops, ill equipped. The cold truth is that the Japanese are veterans and they are well equipped. The Japanese soldier is short, wiry and tough. He is well disciplined."

Perhaps the most potent cause of anti-Japanese feeling lay in the fact that in late 1941 and early 1942, Japan appeared to be winning the war. On December 10, 1941, the pride of the British Far East Fleet, the *Prince of Wales* and the *Repulse*, were sunk by Japanese aircraft off Manila. On December 22, 1941, Japanese forces landed at Lingayen Gulf on the island of Luzon in the Philippines. On December 23, American forces surrendered at Wake Island. On December 25, Hong Kong fell. On January 2, 1942, Japan took Manila. On January 11, Japan invaded the Dutch East Indies. On January 24, the Japanese occupied Borneo and Celebes. On February 15, Singapore fell. On February 27 and 28, the Allied fleet lost eleven of fourteen vessels in action with Japanese warships off the Java Sea. On March 9, Japan occupied Java. On May 6, American resistance at Bataan and Corregidor ceased.

The surrender by General Perceval and 60,000 British troops in Singapore on February 15, 1942, was the greatest capitulation in British history and a blow from which British prestige never recovered in the Far East. The loss of Singapore was the result of Britain's foolhardiness in bidding way beyond its strength. Churchill survived this great setback, although he was himself much to blame, and won a vote of confidence in the House of Commons because clearly there was no one better to take his place.

At the start of the war in the Pacific the American navy had to make do with obsolete charts. Some sea battles were abandoned because no one knew where the bottom was. The Marine Corps had to survey the Solomon Islands as they fought for them. They began on the wrong river, thinking it was the Tenaru, when it was, in fact, the Hu. Until that time such islands as Wake, Midway, and Iwo had little value. It was the wide use of aircraft that now made them strategically valuable.

At the Arcadia conference in Washington, D.C., in December 1941, FDR, Churchill, and their military advisers had agreed that the first aim of the united war effort must be the defeat of Hitler. Even if Italy or Japan were defeated, the main threat to world peace—Germany—could survive. With Germany defeated, the Axis powers would be destroyed. It was also accepted that, because of shortages in men, munitions, and supplies, a strategy of active defense be adopted against Japan. Thus, the Allies were to fight a holding operation in defense of the Malay barrier, Burma, and Australia until reinforcements became available and the American program of naval constriction became more productive. However, the original defense perimeter collapsed in the face of the concerted Japanese advance in the first months of the war.

The Philippines, stretching almost 1,110 miles to Borneo, were the key to Japanese hegemony over Southeast Asia and the South Pacific, being directly astride the principal trade routes to the Dutch East Indies. MacArthur originally tried to prevent Japanese landings on Luzon, but he lacked enough airplanes and ships. Many Filipino units disintegrated after the Japanese invasion, and strong Japanese forces moved toward Manila from the north and east. MacArthur decided to remove all troops from the capital, Manila, and declared it an open city. From December 27, 1941, he concentrated all available American forces on the Bataan Peninsula on the west side of Manila Bay and made the island of Corregidor in Manila Bay his headquarters. American troops and Filipino Army Scout units fought to delay the Japanese conquest of the archipelago, but their supply ships were sunk by the enemy. By January 1942, they were running out of food and drugs. On April 8, 1942, 12,500 Americans and 60,000 Filipinos surrendered unconditionally at Bataan. On May 6, 1942, Corregidor fell with the surrender of 11,000 American troops and 50,000 Filipinos. FDR ordered MacArthur to quit Corregidor on March 11, 1942. MacArthur escaped—but only just—via a torpedo boat and vowed to return to the Philippines in triumph.

Pushed back in successive stages, American forces in the Pacific theater now made the defense of Samoa and Hawaii their top priority and tried to hold the line protecting sea and air communications with Australia and New Zealand.

In the north, the Japanese air force bombed Dutch Harbor and Alaska, and Japanese infantry seized the islands of Attu and Kiska in the western Aleutians. In Southwest Asia, Japanese troops moved easily and quickly through Thailand and into Burma. Once they had captured

The sprawling deck of a mighty aircraft carrier, its top guns ready for the attack on a mission to Attu Island. (Library of Congress).

Mandalay, they had severed the Burma Road supply route to China. In the extreme south, Japanese troops invaded British North Borneo and seized its oil fields. They also landed in New Guinea and Rabaul in New Britain. Japanese ships carried troops to Java in the Dutch East Indies and completely destroyed a combined fleet of American, British, Australian, and Dutch cruisers and destroyers in the battle of Java Sea (February 27, 1942). Thus, the Allies failed to save the Dutch East Indies. Having captured the Dutch East Indies, Japan consolidated its gains in New Britain, the Gilbert and Admiralty islands, and parts of New Guinea and even bombed the naval base of Port Darwin, Australia.

The only successful Allied venture in the Pacific theater in early 1942 was the Doolittle raid on Tokyo of April 18. This was only a

After the victorious epic battle of Midway, American servicemen honor their dead in a mammoth memorial service. (Library of Congress).

tactical move to throw the enemy off balance. Lieutenant Colonel James M. Doolittle led sixteen army medium bombers from the deck of the aircraft carrier *Hornet*, eight hundred miles off Tokyo, to the Japanese capital where they bombed military installations. Most of the planes then landed in China and were rescued. Some of the pilots and crews that were not rescued were executed.

Battles of Coral Sea and Midway

Continuing his seemingly inexorable advance upon Australia, Admiral Yamamoto, a strategist of genius, was determined to engage and destroy the U.S. Pacific Fleet. He was aware that this coup de grace had to be delivered before American production of fighting ships reached its peak and gave his enemy overwhelming numerical supremacy in the Pacific. It was Yamamoto's contention that a decisive Japanese victory at this juncture would persuade the supposedly soft American people to withdraw their support for the war.

Yamamoto failed to achieve his aim. At the battle of the Coral Sea (May 7 to May 8, 1942), a numerically inferior American fleet, under the command of Rear Admiral Jack Fletcher, fought the Japanese to a standstill and halted the advance upon Australia. The Japanese had to abandon plans to land troops at Port Moresby in Dutch New Guinea and had to curtail their conquest of the extreme South Pacific. Moreover, the battle of the Coral Sea was the first naval battle in which opposing forces attacked each other entirely by air strikes.

Yamamoto then assembled all the naval resources at his disposal and threw them forward in an attack upon Midway Island, the proposed staging point for future attacks upon Pearl Harbor and the Hawaiian chain. American bombers first attacked the enemy fleet and transport ships without suffering much damage. Realizing that the Japanese carriers must refuel and rearm their planes, Admiral Raymond A. Spruance used torpedo and dive bombers from the carriers *Hornet* and *Enterprise* to hit the Japanese again before they could get their planes in the air. Although most of the slower torpedo bombers were shot down, the dive-bombers inflicted heavy damage and many casualties. Three Japanese carriers were destroyed or sunk with their planes still on deck, and a fourth carrier was badly damaged. Over the next four days successive American action from army bombers stationed in Midway and from submarines continued to inflict losses on the Japanese, while the United States lost only the *Yorktown* and one destroyer. Once again, naval forces engaged one another only through the air. Unlike the battle of the Coral Sea, the battle of Midway of June 4 to June 7, 1942, was an overwhelming victory for the United States. Yamamoto was repulsed, and he withdrew. A supreme Japanese force had been outmaneuvered at sea and air, humiliated by heavy damage and numerous casualties. The battle of Midway was the first naval defeat for Japan since the late nineteenth century.

Guadalcanal

While the immediate threat to the Hawaiian Islands had passed, the Japanese were continuing their advance upon Australia. By July 23, 1942, Japanese forces were established at Buna and Gona on the north coast of New Guinea. They were also rapidly constructing airfields at Guadalcanal in the Solomon Islands. This was to be their springboard for an assault upon the forward Allied base at Espiritu Santo. On August 7, 1942, the First U.S. Marine Division landed in the Tulagi-Guadalcanal area with the objective of overrunning the airstrips and clearing the zone of Japanese forces. In all, seven major naval engagements were fought as both sides strove to reinforce their land forces. On Guadalcanal, the U.S. Marines managed to hold their ground and then gradually forced the Japanese to retreat. Like the battles of Stalingrad and El Alamein, both of which were reaching their climaxes at the same time as Guadalcanal, the battle of Guadalcanal was acquiring a psychological significance quite out of proportion to its strategic importance. In each of these battles, both sides fielded huge forces because both had decided to commit all, confident that they could win all. However, here was one of several occasions when, despite MacArthur, FDR would not commit absolutely everything because he still had to consider his wars in the Atlantic and Mediterranean. Nevertheless, the Japanese were eventually to evacuate their forces from Guadalcanal on February 9, 1943. They had been taken by surprise—something that would never happen again.

By now the American military had turned their attention to planning for offensive operations.

This official Marine Corps photograph of forces en route to the island of Tarawa, which was held by the Japanese, draws together several images of a type that have become deeply etched on our historical consciousness of American operations in the South Pacific theater. As the landing craft plows the water, one anxious marine looks back while another fondles a GI pinup. (Library of Congress).

Strategy in the Pacific Theater

While FDR's military advisers agreed upon the necessity of defeating Hitler before committing the bulk of Allied forces to the war against Japan, Admiral Ernest J. King, commander in chief of naval operations, was always inclined to give priority to the Pacific theater. Although he accepted the principle of Germany first, he continually pressed for a greater share of resources for the Pacific theater and insisted that the navy receive the lion's share of these resources.

After long and detailed discussion, King and Marshall reached a compromise on the division of responsibility in, and the offensive strategy for, the Pacific theater. MacArthur was made commander in chief of the southwest Pacific area, while Admiral Chester A. Nimitz was made commander in chief of the central Pacific zone. The division of the Pacific theater into two zones was put to FDR who, at the Casablanca conference of January 1943, set the proposal before Churchill and his advisers. The British accepted the proposal and, furthermore, agreed to leave all future strategic decisions in this theater to the American Joint Chiefs of Staff.

The most influential of all commanders in the Far East was MacArthur. MacArthur was, in fact, the most widely publicized American commander of the century. General Douglas MacArthur (1881–1964) has been rightly called the "American Caesar" by one of his biographers, William Manchester (1978). Born in Little Rock, Arkansas, he graduated from the United States Military Academy in 1903 and served in the Philippines (1903–04) and Japan (1906–07) and then as aide de camp (1906–07) to President Theodore Roosevelt, whose magnetic personality left a profound impression upon him. He was determined to fulfill the role of charismatic military leader, and luck and opportunity ensured his success. During World War I he became, in rapid succession, chief of staff of the Forty-second ("Rainbow") Division, commanding general of the Eighty-fourth Infantry Brigade, and commanding general of the Forty-second Division. Twice wounded in action in major American offensives, he served with the army of occupation in Germany from November 1918 to April 1919 before taking up an appointment as superintendent of the United States Military Academy (1919–22), com-

Marines on Tarawa shelter behind sand dunes and sandbags in front of a pillbox occupied by Japanese soldiers, as one marine prepares to throw a hand grenade at the target. (U.S. Marine Corps photo; Library of Congress).

mander of the Manila District in the Philippines (1922–25), and commander of the Philippine Department (1928–30).

In 1930, at the rank of general, MacArthur was appointed chief of staff, a post he filled until 1935 when he became director of the Philippine Department, becoming a field marshal in the Philippine army in the following year. When he retired in 1937, it seemed he had fulfilled a complete and honorable career as a professional soldier and that the only blot on his escutcheon was his unfortunate part in the breaking up and razing of the bonus army camps in Washington, D.C., in 1932 and the dispersal of the army veterans.

The growing threat of war prompted MacArthur's recall in July 1941 as commander of American forces in the Far East. This appointment led

163

to his greatest days and widest fame, first as author of the highly skilled "island-hopping" strategy by which the Japanese were ousted from the Pacific; second as the "American Caesar" who arbitrated Japanese affairs (1945–50) after the defeat of Japan and supervised the restructuring of Japan's political, social, and military order; and third, as commander of the United Nations forces fighting Asian communism, in the Korean War of 1950–53. MacArthur possessed daring fluency in military maneuvers, sure-footed command of logistics, and overwhelming inspirational confidence.

Chester William Nimitz (1885–1966) graduated from the United States Naval Academy in 1905 and later served as chief of staff to the commander of the United States Atlantic Submarine Fleet during World War I. In 1939, he became chief of the Bureau of Navigation at the rank of rear admiral. It was after the attack on Pearl Harbor that he took over command of the Pacific Fleet and the Pacific Ocean areas, with the rank of admiral. His initial strategy was to defend the approaches to Hawaii and maintain lines of communication across the mainland. Following what was MacArthur's lead, he was given considerable credit for the success of the strategy of "island hopping"—a strategy that began with his amphibious-landing offensive at Guadalcanal in August 1942 and the decisive victory in the naval battle of Guadalcanal (November 12 to November 15, 1942). At the time of Japan's surrender, Nimitz was in command of 6,256 ships and 4,847 combat aircraft, the largest flight fighting team in history. He accepted the Japanese surrender in Tokyo Bay. In essence, Admirals Ernest J. King and Chester W. Nimitz were disciples of the nineteenth-century American naval historian Alfred T. Mahan. They wanted victory at sea by a single concentrated strategy—to pursue, encounter, and destroy the Japanese fleet in the Pacific. However, Japanese naval strategy was not predicated on command of the sea by naval power alone but, rather, on dominating a stretch of ocean and its numerous, varies islands by a mix of land, sea, and air power. Thus, had they persisted in their original aim of victory at sea alone, the strategy of King and Nimitz would have resulted in a stalemate through mismatch. It was to his everlasting credit that MacArthur hit upon the far more sophisticated strategy of "island hopping," thereby "leaving the enemy to wither on the vine" and setting in motion a campaign that devastated the Japanese oceanic empire.

Agreement on strategy was finally reached at the Pacific Military

Conference, held in Washington, D.C., in March 1943. It was decided that Nimitz and a predominantly naval force should secure the Marshall and Gilbert islands and then take the Marianas. Simultaneously, MacArthur and the bulk of the American army forces in the Pacific would begin clearing the enemy out of New Guinea, then New Britain, and, finally, the Solomon Islands. The two forces were then to converge for an attack upon either the Philippines or Formosa.

After Guadalcanal, there was a five-month lull in fighting before the proposed American offensive began. Then, on July 30, 1943, Mac-Arthur launched Operation Cartwheel, a series of amphibious operations against the Japanese in the southwest and South Pacific toward the Solomon Islands. By the end of July 1943, the American navy had won command of the seas around the central Solomon Islands, and the American land forces began a successful advance, aimed at clearing New Guinea and New Britain and securing the main passage from the Coral Sea, through the Bismarck barrier, to the western Pacific.

To achieve his aims, MacArthur conducted a series of "leapfrogging" or "island-hopping" operations—landing forces beyond heavy concentrations of enemy troops; building airfields that would give him the capacity to cut the enemy garrison's lines of communication and supply; and bombing and bombarding them until they were either willing to surrender or too weak to resist an amphibious assault. In the words of Rear Admiral Theodore S. Wilkinson, American forces were "hitting 'em where they ain't." By March 25, 1944, the Bismarck barrier had been broken, and MacArthur had embarked upon a "leapfrogging" campaign along the north coast of New Guinea that by mid-September would leave American forces within bomber range of the Philippines.

Meanwhile, Admiral Nimitz was meeting with similar success in the central Pacific. Having secured the Gilbert Islands in November 1943, on January 31, 1944, he invaded Kwajalein Atoll and other islands in the Marshall group. By February 5, 1944, American troops were dispensing with the last vestiges of Japanese resistance on Kwajalein Atoll.

The Pacific was known for the great natural beauty of its islands—dense rain forests with white orchids and cockatoos and smoking volcanoes that set the sky alight—and for the myth of South Seas sexuality, as erroneously described by anthropologist Margaret Mead and lived by such fictional characters as Sadie Thompson. For American marines, the grim reality was ferocious fighting in jungles infested with mosqui-

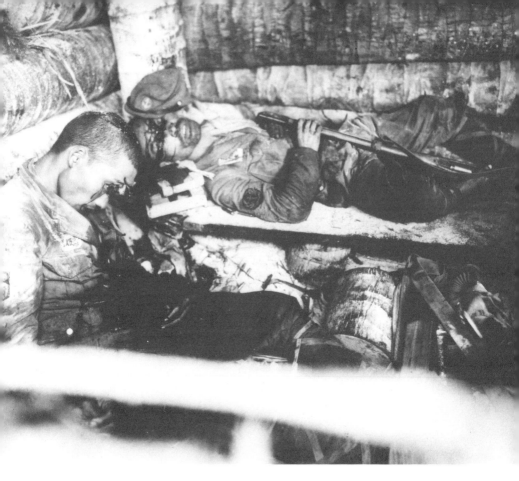

Death rather than dishonor for these Japanese soldiers cornered on the island of Tarawa who killed themselves by pressing the triggers of their rifles with their toes. (U.S. Marine Corps photo; Library of Congress).

toes carrying malaria. The battles were fought under terrible conditions in which the ground itself heaved. Guadalcanal was rocked by an earthquake; parts of Iwo Jima were suffused by volcanic steam. In Bougainville, bulldozers disappeared in bottomless swamps; on Peleliu at the height of the fighting, the temperature was 115 degrees in the shade; sixteen inches of rain fell in a single day at Cape Gloucester; and the battle of Leyte Gulf was interrupted by a double monsoon.

In early June 1944, an attack force under Vice Admiral Richmond Turner assembled at Hawaii to transport 71,000 troops to assault Saipan in the Marianas. Such an attack, if successful, would breach Japan's inner defensive ring; cut the air route between the home islands and New Guinea; and provide the USAAF with a base from which to bomb

Japan. To neutralize this threat, the Japanese High Command was willing to commit all its naval forces in one climactic sea battle. On June 11, 1944, United States *Task Force Fifty-eight* began the process of softening up defenses on Saipan. On June 15, 1944, American marines were landed and pressed forward against heavy opposition. On June 19, the Japanese located the American invasion fleet and the aircraft carrier *Task Force Fifty-eight*. The battle of the Philippines Sea had begun. By the end of June 20, 1944, Japanese forces were in full retreat, having lost some four hundred aircraft; and fourteen warships were either sunk or damaged, including three aircraft carriers. American losses were slight: seventeen aircraft and two slightly damaged battleships. The Japanese were now unable either to reinforce the Marianas or to provide air cover to their beleaguered garrisons. By August 9, 1944, the main islands in the Marianas chain—Saipan, Tinian, and Guam—were securely in American hands. The loss of Saipan was enough to bring down the cabinet of Tojo Hideki in July 1944.

The jungle was savage to defeated Japanese soldiers. Cut off from supplies, all they had to eat were ferns and one another. They had to share the dense jungle with deadly snakes and crocodiles. Thus even if they had an escape route, they still had little chance of survival. Only one man in five was fit to serve after Admiral Mori's retreat across the Huon Peninsula in New Guinea; and during General Horii's disastrous retreat across the Owen Stanley Mountains, the general himself was drowned.

Battle of Leyte Gulf

Among the American commanders, the debate now centered upon where next to apply the pressure. Admiral King argued for an invasion of Formosa that would put American forces on the very threshold of the Japanese home islands. Conversely, MacArthur insisted that the line of advance should be through the Philippines to Luzon, thus cutting Japanese lines of communication southward and establishing bases from which could be launched air attacks upon Japan and the ultimate invasion of the home islands. Nevertheless, both commanders were united in their opposition to a Joint Chiefs of Staff (JCS) proposal of

Rubber craft speed the landing of American and Canadian forces on the island of Kiska on August 15, 1943. (Library of Congress).

June 1944 for an attack on Japan that would bypass both Formosa and Luzon.

On September 1, 1944, the JCS decided to postpone any decision until its logistical committee had made a thorough study of each plan. However, before this report was submitted, Admiral ("Bull") Halsey, who was conducting carrier strikes in Philippine waters, reported that enemy resistance in this region was remarkably weak. To exploit this weakness, he recommended that MacArthur's proposed attack on Leyte Gulf in the Philippines, provisionally arranged for December 20, 1944, be brought forward immediately. Accordingly, the JCS, then in conference with their British counterparts at Quebec, decided to launch the Leyte Gulf operation on October 20. MacArthur announced his return to the Philippines in typically dramatic fashion by splashing ashore from a landing craft.

To the Japanese, the possible loss of the Philippines would be a disaster second only to attack upon the home islands. If the Americans succeeded in taking the Philippines, then Japan's access to its precious source of oil in the Dutch East Indies could be cut and the Imperial Japanese Navy immobilized. Japan must, therefore, answer this threat; and it responded in an all-out measure, the battle of Leyte Gulf, the greatest sea battle in history.

With American land and sea forces thus committed to the battle for Leyte and the subsequent push through the Philippines, King and Nimitz abandoned their plan for an invasion of Formosa. In its place, they proposed a revised strategy for the central Pacific: a push northward from the Marianas to the tiny volcanic island of Iwo Jima in the Bonins in January 1945 and then on to Okinawa and nearby islands in the Ryukyus early in March 1945. On October 3, 1944, the JCS accepted this plan and issued directives for MacArthur's invasion of Luzon on December 20, 1944.

The whole strategy in the Pacific now hinged upon the success of the Leyte landing. On October 20, 1944, Leyte Gulf was invaded by a combined central Pacific force (led by Nimitz and Halsey) and southwest Pacific force (led by MacArthur and Admiral Kinkaid). This, the most formidable armada yet to sail in Pacific waters, was soon to be engaged by every remaining battleship and aircraft carrier in the Imperial Japanese Navy. The three-day battle of Leyte Gulf began on October 23, 1944. This was certainly one of the most decisive naval engagements in history. The Japanese lost three battleships, fourteen cruisers, and nine destroyers. The American navy lost three carriers and three destroyers but gained total command of Philippine waters.

The land battle for Leyte was another matter and lasted for over two months, during which the Japanese defenders fought with suicidal fervor. Of more than 65,000 Japanese troops committed to the battle, only 15,000 survived it. American marines met with the same fanatical opposition when Nimitz launched his delayed attack on Iwo Jima on February 19, 1945. In a last desperate effort, the Japanese mustered a task force, including their last battleship, the *Yamamoto*, with screening cruisers and destroyers, to protect the island. However, they were intercepted near home waters by the aircraft carrier *Task Force Fifty-eight*, whose planes sank the *Yamamoto* and five of her screening vessels and damaged others. Thus, the Japanese fleet no longer existed.

However, Iwo Jima proved a more formidable target; and the struggle for it lasted from February 19 to March 15, 1945, during which 20,000 marines were killed and wounded in a painful step-by-step progress. One notable incident was preserved for posterity. This was the triumphant raising of the American flag by four marines at the summit of Mount Suribachi, on February 19, 1945, a moment photographed by Joe Rosenthal of the Associated Press. It became the most widely used photograph of World War II and won Rosenthal a Pulitzer Prize.

Okinawa

What the Americans wanted was a series of secure island bases from which to launch the final attack upon Japan. As part of this strategy, Nimitz's task force then descended upon Okinawa. This island in the Ryukyus, three hundred miles from Japan, was itself an integral part of the southern Japanese archipelago. American forces would at last be fighting upon Japanese soil. Their opponents were willing to die before allowing it to be occupied by the enemy. Japanese defensive strategy was enshrined in the battle slogan of the Thirty-second Army, stationed on Okinawa: "One plane for one warship. One boat for one ship. One man for ten enemy. One man for one tank." On Okinawa the Japanese had converted even burial vaults to pillboxes for snipers, while caves housed (and hid) heavy artillery that moved in and out on railroad tracks.

The invasion began on Easter Sunday, April 1, 1945, and the fighting continued until June 22, 1945. The eighty-two-day battle resulted in the end of the Japanese navy as an effective fighting force. It also resulted in the death of 110,000 Japanese troops. For its part, the United States Tenth Army suffered 7,613 killed or missing in action, 31,807 wounded, and over 26,000 nonbattle casualties. American naval casualties were also alarmingly high: 9,731, of which 4,907 were killed. The naval casualties were almost all victims of kamikaze attacks.

Joe Rosenthal's prize-winning photograph of U.S. Marines hoisting the American flag on Iwo Jima, a legendary incident at the start of the campaign against the Japanese in the South Pacific and now commemorated in sculpture in Washington, D.C. (Office of War Information; Library of Congress).

Japanese pilots had begun flying the *tokkai tai* (special attack) missions during the Philippine campaign. However, it was at Okinawa that the kamikaze became a fundamental feature of Japanese defensive operations.

Kamikaze rocket planes carried a 2,645-pound bomb housed in a wooden winged casing twenty feet in length and were equipped with three rocket motors capable of delivering 1,700 pounds of thrust. The mother plane carried the rocket within fifty miles of the target and then released it with the pilot to glide onward at less than 250 miles per hour toward the target. The pilot then ignited the rockets that burned for ten seconds and increased the speed to 600 miles per hour until it crashed and exploded, killing the pilot and devastating the target. Of the 1,900 kamikaze attacks launched at Okinawa, 14.7 percent were successful. In all, 25 Allied ships were sunk (but none was larger than a destroyer); 157 were damaged by hits; and 97 were damaged by near misses.

The Japanese code was absolute—to commit suicide rather than surrender—and this led to bizarre scenes of immolation. Faced with certain defeat, officers would round up their men for final, senseless, banzai suicide charges. Men who could not walk were given hand grenades with which to blow themselves up. On Saipan, five-year-old Japanese children were placed in circles and then tossed grenades to one another until they were all killed. The Japanese also thought it was shameful for their enemies to surrender; thus, they inflicted gruesome penalties on their captives. After the American defeat at Corregidor, the survivors were led on a death march in which the weak and wounded were deliberately marched to death. The Japanese beheaded marines captured on Makin Island. At Mine Bay, they impaled Australian prisoners on their bayonets, cut off their penises, and sewed the foreskins to the prisoners' lips. They left them underneath a slogan, "It took them a long time to die." Such treatment brutalized American soldiers who treated Japanese soldiers (but not women and children) with disregard for the traditional show of chivalry to a defeated enemy. In the Admiralty Islands, American soldiers used defeated Japanese troops hiding in the bush for target practice.

A dramatic photograph of a crewman dominating an airplane, *My Girl*, which he is directing as it is about to take off from Iwo Jima. (Library of Congress).

Toward an End in the Pacific

If the taking of Okinawa made clear to Japanese military leaders that defeat was inevitable, then it also impressed upon the Americans how costly would be a frontal assault upon other islands in the Japanese homeland.

173

In the meantime, British forces had entered Rangoon, Burma, on May 3, 1945, and were ready to go farther. The British wanted to push themselves into the war in the Far East not only for strategic reasons but also to show that they could still be of use to the Americans. It was also important from Churchill's point of view that "Stage 2," the defeat of Japan, should be prolonged in order to ensure the continuation of supplies of lend-lease material for Britain that could help the domestic transition from war to peace. Many politicians expected the war against Japan to last eighteen months beyond the defeat of Germany.

The taking of Okinawa and the rapid construction there of a vast air and naval base effectively closed the ring on the Japanese homeland. USAAF B-29s could now bomb Tokyo and other towns and cities at will from their bases in the Ryukyus, the Philippines (liberated July 5, 1945), and China. Bombing raids culminated in the deaths of about 100,000 people in a raid on Tokyo of March 9, 1945. Once great cities were overrun by refugees, who were living in shantytowns and were racked by tuberculosis and malaria.

With total command of air and sea, the Allies now had to decide how to end the war in the Far East, the JCS already had devised military strategy. On April 3, 1945, MacArthur (now appointed commander in chief of United States Armed Forces—Pacific) was ordered to formulate a plan for the invasion of the Japanese homeland. It was fully approved by the JCS on May 25, 1945. "Downfall," as it was codenamed, comprised two operations: the invasion of the southernmost island, Kyushu, on November 1, 1945; and a much larger invasion of the main island, Honshu, on March 1, 1946. It was expected that the first thirty days of the Kyushu operation would claim between 30,000 and 50,000 American casualties. Moreover, in an off-the-cuff remark, Secretary of War Henry L. Stimson estimated that the entire "Downfall" operation would cause one million casualties.

American military leaders hoped that this price would not have to be paid. There were various options to frontal attack: one was conditional surrender. In mid-June 1945, the Japanese Supreme War Cabinet authorized the foreign minister, Togo, to approach the Soviet Union with a view to arranging terms, leading to the cessation of hostilities in September 1945. On July 12, the Japanese informed the Kremlin of their desire for peace and on July 21 asked the Soviet Union to mediate on their behalf. Stalin refused, and the embryonic peace process broke

+56310A

Bombs over Burma. Tons of bombs speckle the sky above Rangoon, Burma, as they descend from 20th Bomber Command "Superfortress" planes. Their target was a large Japanese supply depot near Mirgaladon Air Field near Rangoon. (U.S. Army Air Force, Washington, D.C.; Library of Congress).

down. However, Washington was fully aware of the Japanese peace moves. Having broken the Japanese cipher early in the war, Harry S. Truman, Roosevelt's successor as president (1945–53), and his advisers knew that Tokyo was willing to surrender on condition that imperial institutions be preserved. Truman refused to pursue this option. Emperor Hirohito had, like Hitler and Mussolini, been presented to the American people as a symbol of all that was antithetical to democratic values. Truman was well aware that public opinion would have been outraged had he, in the last days of a titanic struggle, reached an accommodation with the enemy. Therefore, the fight was to continue

175

until unconditional surrender had been achieved. Furthermore, Truman's secretary of state-designate, James F. Byrnes (1945–47), influenced the new president's decision by arguing that any concessions by the United States would be seen as a symptom of American weakness. An apparent lack of resolve to continue the war to the bitter end on Truman's part would thus strengthen the position of the hawks in Tokyo.

A second option was a reliance upon blockade and bombing. Generals Spaatz, Curtis Le May, and Herbert H. Arnold, Admiral Leahy, and others among Truman's military advisers were convinced that the Japanese would be forced to surrender by a war of attrition accomplished by naval blockade and strategic bombing. A third option was the entry of the Soviet Union into the war against Japan, thereby adding to the forces arrayed against the empire. In early June 1945, the War Department's Operations Division agreed that a Soviet declaration of war would hasten unconditional surrender by the Japanese, either in itself or in combination with a landing or the imminent threat of a landing. This was the opinion General Marshall offered to Truman in mid-June. By mid-July, the Joint Chiefs of Staff Intelligence Committee stated explicitly that an entry of the Soviet Union into the war would finally convince the Japanese of the inevitability of complete defeat. Nevertheless, it is most unlikely that the Japanese government was unaware of Russia's imminent entry into the war. On April 5, 1945, the Soviet Union renounced the Russo-Japanese Neutrality Pact. By July the Red Army had 1.5 million troops stationed on the Russo-Manchurian border. They were certainly not there to augment the Soviet customs service. The other, perhaps most terrible, option to end the war was the use of the atomic bomb against Japan.

The United States and China

The war against Japan was fought by the Allies as two separate conflicts. The United States took responsibility for operations in the Pacific theater, while Britain was responsible for operations in Southeast Asia. However, there was an American military presence in Southeast Asia.

At the outbreak of the Sino-Japanese War in July 1937, the Chinese government invited a recently retired American Army Air Corps captain, Claire L. Chennault, to become its adviser on aeronautical affairs.

Japanese devastation of a defenseless Chinese town, its religious and cultural artifacts smashed like so many broken toys. (Library of Congress).

Chennault was an expert in the theory of aerial combat, but there was little he could do with Jiang Jieshi's ramshackle air force. In early 1941 he persuaded Jiang to form a special air corps, comprising veteran American fighter pilots. To this end Chennault visited the United States and, by the early summer of 1941, had signed up some ninety former servicemen plus ground crew. Simultaneously, China took delivery of 100 highly efficient P-40 American fighter planes as part of their lend-lease supply of war materiel.

By December 1941 the American Volunteer Group (or "Flying Tigers" as they were popularly known) had absorbed Chennault's tactical combat system and were trained to perfection. When the United States declared war on Japan, the American Volunteer Group pilots remained as mercenaries in the employ of the Chinese government. They were paid far higher wages than ordinary American servicemen, received a

177

$500 bonus for every Japanese plane brought down, and were contracted to fight for Jiang until July 1942.

By December 1941 the Japanese had cut off the bulk of Jiang's forces from the eastern Chinese seaboard. Jiang's only contact with the outer world now lay via the Burma Road that crossed the Himalayan peaks from Kunming in Yunnan to Lashio in Burma. Throughout the early months of 1942, the American Volunteer Group engaged and repulsed Japanese bomber aircraft that had been sent to close the vital line of communication.

FDR wanted to see Britain leave its Raj in India. Moreover, he had no intention of allowing the French to reclaim their colonial possessions in Indochina (the three states of Vietnam, Cambodia, and Laos). He wanted to see Asia decolonized by means of a trusteeship system that would eventually bring independence to the various indigenous populations. He hoped that, during the transitional period, countries would be supervised by international control. It was also FDR's hope that China would emerge from the war as the supreme power in Asia. Thus, throughout the war he strove to support Jiang Jieshi's supposedly democratic regime and to win for the generalissimo a place alongside the Big Three. FDR was equally determined to keep China actively engaged in the struggle against Japan. He also thought that Chinese involvement would help the Allies win the war as quickly as possible. He wanted Jiang's army to tie down the maximum number of Japanese troops, partly to relieve pressure on beleaguered American forces in the Pacific theater and, partly, to give American forces time to prepare and launch their own offensive in that theater. FDR also hoped that Jiang's troops would play an important part in the overall defeat of Japan.

Roosevelt's overly optimistic casting of Jiang as one of the four world policemen of the postwar period disconcerted American diplomats and military staff in China. They recognized how inefficient and corrupt were Jiang's regime and his armies and how his party, the Kuomintang, was rapidly losing popular support. They were also disturbed by the steadily growing strength of the Chinese Communists under Mao Zedong in the north and Jiang's response that it was his primary duty to contain his internal political opponents while the United States saw to the defeat of Japan.

However, FDR had no spare American troops available to bolster the Chinese war effort. All FDR could offer was continued delivery of lend-

Generalissimo Jiang Jieshi (Chiang Kai-shek, *right*), together with his wife, Song Meiling, and a group of American flyers awarded the military order of China for their contribution to the war against the Japanese in Chungking in 1942. At the front left is Brigadier General Clayton Bissel, who later died in a domestic air crash in the United States. (U.S. Army Signal Corps and Office of War Information; Library of Congress).

lease supplies and a military mission under the direction of Lieutenant General Joseph W. Stilwell. On his arrival in China in March 1942, Stilwell was appointed chief of staff to Jiang Jieshi. By then, Jiang had accepted the Allied invitation to become commander in chief of the China theater. While Stilwell served as Jiang's chief of staff, he was also commander of the American task force in China. As such, he was responsible for supervising lend-lease deliveries, increasing the effectiveness of American military assistance to China, and improving the combat efficiency of the Chinese armed forces by advising on training and tactics and rationalizing the command structure.

The situation in the China theater deteriorated drastically in April 1942 when the Japanese overran Burma and thus cut Jiang's last line of land communication with the Allies. Jiang now could be supplied only by airlift, which entailed a hazardous five hundred–mile journey (known as "the Hump") across the Himalayas from Assam in North India. As the shortage of supplies reached a crisis point, Stilwell decided that all available resources be channeled into his efforts to build the Chinese army into an efficient fighting force. The decision troubled Chennault (now promoted to brigadier general of the Chinese air force), who argued that his American Volunteer Group was being starved of vital fuel resources and ammunition.

The dispute over allocation of resources poisoned relations between the two leaders and caused discontentment among the pilots flying with the American Volunteer Group. When these pilots' contracts with the Chinese government expired in July 1942, the majority returned home. However, Chennault took a commission as brigadier general with the United States Army Air Force. Regular military pilots filled the vacuum caused by the departure of these mercenaries. The role once played by the American Volunteer Group was assumed by the newly formed China Air Task Force under Chennault's command.

The controversy between Chennault and Stilwell became even more heated when Chennault proposed that his pilots alone should be allowed to drive the Japanese out of China. He argued that if the China Air Task Force were given all available supplies, then, with command of the air, it could bomb and strafe Japanese ground troops until they were forced to withdraw to the home islands. Stilwell rejected this plan. He believed that if the Chinese army remained weak, then the Japanese would easily overrun Chennault's air bases. He also took as his main objective the reopening of the Burma Road. This could only be achieved by an offensive conducted by China's land forces. Stilwell was willing to divide supply deliveries between the air force and the army forces, but he refused to grant Chennault's request.

This decision displeased Jiang who liked Chennault almost as much as he disliked the irascible "Vinegar Joe" Stilwell. Jiang was anxious to keep Chinese casualties to a minimum and thus opposed the idea of an offensive in Burma. However, Stilwell had the support of both the chief of staff of the United States Army, General George C. Marshall, and the commanding general of the United States Army Air Force, General Henry H. Arnold. To resolve the impasse on allocation of resources, Jiang went above Marshall's head to appeal directly to FDR on Chennault's behalf. In March 1943, FDR ordered the lion's share of resources to be given to the China Air Task Force. Chennault's pilots quickly gained complete control of the skies above central China and began bombing Japanese positions in the previously unassailable eastern provinces. Such was the success of his strategy that at Cairo (December 1943), FDR and Jiang agreed that America's new weapon, the B-29 "Superfortress," be shipped out to Chennault who could then start bombing the Japanese homeland. The first such sortie was launched on June 15, 1944.

However, by then the Japanese had fulfilled Stilwell's prophecy and had begun a land assault to capture Chennault's air bases. The offensive began in May 1944, and, by June, Jiang's underfed, poorly equipped, and inadequately trained troops were in full retreat. By mid-August their resistance in eastern China had completely collapsed. Desperately in need of reinforcements, Stilwell now went to Jiang to demand the incorporation of Chinese Communist troops into the regular army. Jiang refused for he could not comply with the Communists' conditions that they be allowed to keep command of their eighteen divisions and that they keep governmental control of the territory in which they were now firmly settled. Jiang also frustrated Stilwell's efforts to draw off the troops then engaged in a blockade of these Communist-controlled areas.

FDR realized then the folly of his decision to back Jiang and Chennault in opposition to Stilwell, Marshall, and Arnold. On July 4, 1944, he cabled Jiang, requesting that he put Stilwell in full command of all Chinese armed forces. While Stilwell was already chief of staff to Jiang, in reality he had no staff to whom he could dictate his orders. Because of the chaotic state of the Chinese military command, he had little access to Jiang's various war-area commanders. He also had difficulty gaining an audience with the generalissimo. When he did gain Jiang's ear, his words were ignored. In despair, Stilwell appealed to Marshall to intervene on his behalf. Marshall duly drafted a message, which FDR signed, requesting that Stilwell be made once more commander of all forces in China. The message was delivered in person by Stilwell in early October. Jiang interpreted this as an act of gross insubordination. In his reply to FDR, he demanded Stilwell's immediate recall. As a result, "Vinegar Joe" was relieved of his command on October 18, 1944.

In his place as chief of staff to Jiang came Major General Albert C. Wedemeyer. Relations between Jiang and Wedemeyer were, in fact,

Chinese doctors minister to a victim of Japanese violence, felled in the street. A scene from the war in northern China. (Library of Congress).

quite cordial. Indeed, the generalissimo expressed an interest in cooperating with his American chief of staff. Whereas he had constantly opposed Stilwell's efforts to reorganize the Chinese armed forces, Jiang now gave enthusiastic support to the establishment of a combined Sino-American staff for the China theater. In December 1944, the generalissimo also agreed to Wedemeyer's proposal that all senior Chinese commanders in the field work in concert with a team of American advisers. Those commanders who habitually ignored their American advisers were threatened either with replacement or with the cutting off of vital American assistance. By working through these advisers and the newly formed Sino-American military council, Wedemeyer managed to achieve operational control in the China theater.

However, by early 1945, FDR had lost faith in Jiang Jieshi and the prospect of future Chinese preeminence in Asia. Jiang's treatment of

Stilwell had cast a dark shadow over Sino-American relations. Americans stationed in China only served to deepen the gloom with their reports of corruption, venality, and inefficiency at the heart of the generalissimo's regime. Such reports also indicated that, far from emerging as a great power, China would, in the postwar years, have to endure civil war. American disillusionment also proceeded from the fact that Jiang had failed to deliver the goods on the field of battle. For much of the war, Jiang appeared to maintain an unofficial truce with the Japanese, while preferring to fight his Communist compatriots instead. As the war in the Far East moved toward its conclusion, FDR turned not to Jiang but to Stalin for support in driving the Japanese out of China and delivering the final blow against their home islands. On the eve of the Yalta conference of February 1945, the president expressed his disillusionment with Jiang when he told Churchill "that three generations of education and training would be required before China could become a serious factor." Having thus decided to leave the sleeping giant to its slumbers, FDR went off to Yalta to barter China's commercial, territorial, and military interests in return for Stalin's promise to declare war on the Japanese.

[5]

GOD BLESS AMERICA
Mobilization and the Home Front

WORLD WAR II was as much a contest between the industrial capacity of the participants as a struggle between their armed forces. In 1943 Stalin admitted at Tehran that, without American production, the Allies could not win the war. Not only was American production on a scale sufficient to wage war across two oceans and furnish its allies with war materiel but also to raise the standard of living at home. Furthermore, Americans did not suffer the extreme privations that the Asians and Europeans did. As commentator Edward R. Murrow observed, "we live in the light, in relative comfort and complete security. We are the only nation in this war which has raised its standard of living since the war began. We are not tired, as all Europe is tired." There was, perhaps, something disturbing about the fact that between 1939 and 1945 the United States could field an army of 12 million against two evil dictatorships, construct a navy larger than the combined navies of its allies and its enemies, and still afford a 20 percent increase in civilian spending.

At first the war united Americans from all classes and regions. It seemed to most American citizens that Japan and Germany had, without

In his expressionist watercolor, *Soldiers Dancing at 99 Park Avenue*, artist Reginald Marsh captures the poignancy of young people in their few tender moments of lyrical social pleasures.

Reginald Marsh was the son of mural painter Frederick David Marsh. Born in Paris but raised in Nutley, New Jersey, and a Yale graduate, he was a pupil of John Sloan and George Luks at The Art Students' League in New York City. As a staff illustrator for the *New York Daily News*, Marsh continued the newspaper's particular tradition of realistic art but one that, in this instance, was tinged with considerable melancholy. (Library of Congress).

any provocation, attacked the United States as part of a plan to enslave the world. For its part, the United States had no selfish ambitions of its own but only wanted to ensure freedom and security for people everywhere. Ronald Steel (1980) recounts how "with the nation at war the old arguments over intervention became irrelevant. Isolationists were now apostles of total victory. War orders flowed into long-silent factories, the jobless went back to work, and the pessimistic drift of the thirties gave way to national enthusiasm and sense of purpose."

Mobilization

One of the first priorities was raising a fighting force of soldiers, sailors, airmen and marines. The government had begun preparing for war fifteen months before Pearl Harbor. Despite opposition from isolationists, the Burke-Wadsworth Selective Service Act was passed on September 16, 1940, which introduced the first peacetime conscription in American history. The act required the registration of all men between twenty and thirty-six years of age. Selective service was set up under the administration direction of General Lewis B. Hershey by means of six thousand local draft boards that could give deferments on grounds of physical disability, occupation, or number of dependents. Those men who were not deferred were called up by means of a lottery, as in 1917. The first year of military service expired before Pearl Harbor, and FDR's proposal for its renewal for an extra six months met with more resistance. Congress approved renewal by only 45 votes to 30 in the Senate and 203 votes to 202 in the House, an astonishingly narrow margin.

After Pearl Harbor, Congress passed a new draft law widening requirements to all men between the ages of eighteen and sixty-five, of which only those between twenty and forty-four were liable for military service; those above forty-four were eligible for labor service—a provision that never was used. All men currently in the armed forces had to serve for the duration of the war and six months beyond. In 1942 the age of those liable for military service was lowered from twenty to eighteen in order to expand the forces beyond 5.5 million. Moreover, it proved impossible for some local boards to draft men according to priorities—of, respectively, single men, married men, and fathers—and thus the law operated unevenly across the nation. In all, some 31 million men entered selective service, of whom about 10 million were actually drafted. Altogether, 15 million men and women served. There was no question of college students obtaining special exemptions. Everyone who was fit went to war.

In 1945 the army and air force accounted for 8.2 million men, of whom two-thirds served overseas. The navy and the marines accounted for 3.9 million and the Coast Guard for about 250,000. The extensive use of women in the armed services was an innovation. The Women's Army Corps (WAC) was established in May 1942, and the Marine Corps established the Women's Reserve in 1943.

Compared with the citizens of the countries they served in, GIs were well paid, though not out of line with costs in the United States. American privates received $50 a month in basic pay and an extra $10

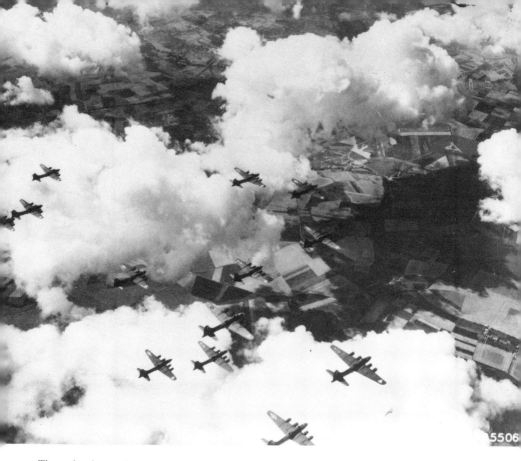

The splendor and might of American P-51 planes of the 375th Fighter Squadron, 361st Fighter Group, as they soar in formation practice in the skies above England. (U.S. Army Air Force photo; Library of Congress).

if they were serving overseas. Paratroopers received an extra $50 for hazardous duty; enlisted men who flew regularly in the air forces received an extra $25 a month. Halfway through the war Congress decided that infantrymen should receive an extra $10 a month and extended the paratroopers' extra pay to glider troops. Of the officers, a second lieutenant received $216 a month (more if he was married), with an extra 10 percent for service overseas, 50 percent extra if a flyer, and $100 if a paratrooper.

The air forces were considered the most glamorous of the services. Men in ground units envied airmen their higher pay, easier promotion, and more comfortable living conditions. Furthermore, by a flexible rotation policy, after flying thirty missions, an airman could return to the United States. Comedian Bob Hope quipped of the army's rotation policy, "Every two years they put your name in the hat and you go home at the end of the war."

Correspondent Ernie Pyle in *Here Is Your War* (1943) and *Brave Men* (1944) described GIs who embodied the sort of quintessential traits that Americans most liked to believe they possessed. Pyle's soldiers were democratic, individualistic, optimistic, and, forsaking ethnic, racial, and class divisions, united in a glorious common purpose: "The battle-field does produce a brotherhood. The common bond of death draws human beings toward each other over the artificial barriers of rank." No matter what was its original composition, hardly any unit retained a strong regional flavor as successive intakes of men from all sections of the country began to blur the distinctions between regular army divisions, the National Guard, and selective-service divisions.

Nevertheless, black citizens served in totally segregated units. These were mainly service units but also included tank and artillery battalions, a fighter-bomber group, and two infantry divisions. When the need for extra troops became most pressing in 1944–45, Eisenhower succeeded in having 4,500 black volunteers, some of whom were reduced from ranks as high as master sergeants to privates, brought into the white sections. They fought in the Sixth Army Group as provisional companies and in the Twelfth Army Group. The army also kept three other ethnic groups separate: Norwegian Americans who could not speak English served in a special infantry battalion; Japanese Americans, the *Nisei*, fought in a special regimental combat team; and Filipinos were assigned to special units known as "Philippine Scouts."

In World War II an American foot soldier on combat duty carried 84.3 pounds of equipment, including his uniform, helmet, M-1 rifle, bayonet, knife, canteen, a combination pick and shovel, a first-aid kit, a web belt with cartridge magazines, and hand grenades. He also had his pack, comprising a poncho, Primacord fuses, a mess kit, and, probably, cigarettes and Zippo lighter, and writing paper. Moreover, he had to carry part of his outfit's communal weapons, such as a Browning automatic rifle, a light or heavy machine gun and their tripods. He should have had, but did not, a shelter for night, a blanket, and extra socks. As GIs accumulated wet mud in European theaters, they ran the risk of trench foot. The pain was excruciating. When doctors cut off their shoes, their feet sometimes swelled to the size of footballs and amputation was sometimes necessary.

Emergency rations came in three varieties: The K-ration consisted of a small cardboard package containing a can of cheese, a mix of ham and eggs or beef hash, a fruit or candy bar, and four cigarettes, hard crackers, toilet tissue, and fruit juice or coffee concentrate. The 10-in-1 ration was made up of dehydrated or canned food in a large package, enough for ten men for one day. A soldier in combat had one free packet of cigarettes a day.

The gap between officers and enlisted men disturbed many soldiers, although it was wider in rear units than at the front where officers shared the same dangers and living conditions as their men. The armed forces drew officers from the service academies at West Point and Annapolis, the ROTC in over one hundred universities and colleges, and the National Guard and special ninety-day officer candidate schools.

Airplanes and Armory

World War II was notable for the invention or further development of a whole range of planes, weapons, and ships that helped determine the outcome of the war and had momentous consequences for the atomic age that followed it. Robert J. McNamara, assistant professor of business administration at Harvard, was among the first to discern peacetime potential in such things as radar, prefabricated housing, frozen foods, diesel power, and catalytic cracking of crude oil.

As airpower came to dominate the war, aircraft of all sorts became the major instrument of offense and defense in the air and was essential for protection of ground forces. Events repeatedly proved that the side with superiority in the air would enjoy a decisive advantage over the enemy. During the war the pace of aeronautical development was astonishing: the maximum speed of fighters rose from 360 miles per hour to 540 miles per hour and that of bombers from 290 miles per hour to 460 miles per hour. Their performance in range and altitude also increased.

All nations learned that formations of unescorted bombers could not survive in daylight in the face of a well-equipped and determined fighter opposition. These were lessons drawn by the German Luftwaffe during the battle of Britain and by the United States Army Air Force in 1943. However, attack under cover of darkness had its own problems. The darkness that hid the bombers also hid their targets. At first, Royal Air

Force Bomber Command pilots tried to locate targets by what was called dead reckoning—flying straight ahead on a calculated reading but taking account of wind. In wartime the margin of error was about 10 miles in every 100. Thus in a flight of 300 miles, say from Lincolnshire to the Ruhr, the plane would be lucky to arrive within 30 miles of its objective. Close to target, bombers flew hither and thither in a deadly game of blindman's bluff with the predictable result that most bombs fell nowhere near their intended target. An analysis of 350 photographs taken during British night raids in June and July 1941 disclosed that only one in three crews had dropped their bombs within 5 miles of the target, and, in the case of the most difficult target, the Ruhr, the figure was one in ten. Not for nothing did novelist Gore Vidal subsequently remark of the airplane's ease at bombing indiscriminately and without mercy that "the natural aviator is a fascist."

First the British and then the Americans profited from a series of German radio and radar techniques that assisted bombers in finding their targets. The American and British GEE system used three ground transmitters, each about 100 miles from the others. These transmitters acted in unison and radiated a complex train of pulses in a set order, providing navigators in aircraft with a special radar receiver that allowed the navigators to measure the time difference between the reception of the various signal pulses. By referring these differences to a special GEE map, the navigator was able to determine his position within 6 miles as far as 400 miles from the most distant transmitter. In effect, GEE transmitters laid an invisible radio grid across Europe. By listening to the character of the transmissions, the GEE navigator could determine on which lines of the grid his aircraft lay. The device was first used on a large scale for an attack on Essen of March 1942. The proportion of successful sorties—those in which the crews released their bombs within 3 miles of the aiming point—rose from 23 percent to 33 percent.

Subsequently, in the H2S radar device, radar equipment on a plane could take a picture of the ground based on centimetric wavelengths of echoes from the ground. This system was first used during an air attack on Hamburg of January 30, 1943; but the set produced problems of its own, which led bombers to confuse lakes close to the city. As a result, of 344 crews who thought they had attacked Hamburg, only 17 had in fact done so. A new device, "Oboe," based on beacons in Dover and

"See an Elephant Fly? Jumbo Dumbo." Walt Disney's classic animated film of the young elephant with outsize ears ridiculed by all and sundry until he is given the confidence to fly included this parody version of early World War II flights by cumbersome planes from aircraft carriers. His little friend the mouse presses reluctant blackbirds into service to propel the timid rogue elephant into space by pushing him off a cliff. (Walt Disney Productions; Museum of Modern Art Film Stills Archive).

Cromer, made use of the fact that a radar set could measure the range of an object to within very fine limits and that the accuracy did not diminish with distance—giving bombing accuracy within 200 yards. After successive improvements, the proportion of bombers releasing bombs within 3 miles had reached three-quarters by June 1944. By December 1944, when most of the aircraft in Bomber Command had been fitted with H2S radar, the proportion of planes releasing bombs within one mile of the target was nine-tenths.

Bombing operations began as diffuse, inaccurate, and ineffectual raids by a few score of aircraft. They developed swiftly and dramatically into a series of sledgehammer blows of many hundreds of heavy bombers, weaving complicated patterns over Europe, stricking accurately and devastatingly whether bombing blindly or not. The flyers were confident in the knowledge that the enemy's defenses were being blinded and deafened by an invisible thunder of radar and radio jamming.

The first jet-propelled airplanes also made their appearance in the war. Although Frank Whittle had made the first turbojet in England on April 12, 1937, it was the German Heinkel, He 178, that was the first jet-propelled airplane to fly, on August 27, 1939. Both Britain and Germany worked to perfect jet fighters as quickly as possible. By 1944 the Royal Air Force Gloster Meteor and the German Messerschmidt, Me 262, were both in operation. They and other jet aircraft played only a small part in the fighting; but their high speed and high ceiling in operations indicated that, with improvements, they would supersede the traditional piston-engined combat airplane. In 1945 a Meteor increased the world airspeed record from 469 to 606 miles per hour.

Another air development was the helicopter, an aircraft lifted into the air and propelled by one or more overhead lifting rotors, turning horizontally about a vertical, or nearly vertical, axis. Because of its design, a helicopter could take off and land vertically, hover, or move horizontally in any direction without a corresponding change in heading. The first truly successful helicopter prototype was designed by Igor Sikorsky, a Russian American who had immigrated in 1919. It was flown for about one hour and a half on May 6, 1941, although Sikorsky and others in America, Germany, and Russia had been experimenting with different designs since 1909. The helicopter was a crucial development, but one that was not fully exploited in World War II and had to wait until the late 1940s and the Korean War of 1950–53 for fuller development. Sikorsky regarded the helicopter as a useful tool for air commerce and for rescuing people caught in natural disasters. He did not appreciate its future use as an offensive military weapon.

The range of terrible weapons included a series of lethal gases. Germany had first used chlorine gas on the Russian front in Poland in 1915 and then mustard gas in 1917. By the end of World War I, half of the German shells were filled with poisonous gases. The choking gases chlorine, diphosgene, and carbonyl chloride affected the respiratory system by attacking the soft, unprotected lining of the lungs, first producing coughing as the lungs tried to expel the irritant and fluid.

Anti-Aircraft Battery from the Coast Guardsman's Marshall Islands Notebook by Ken Riley. Aboard a Coast Guard–manned transport ship in the South Pacific a 40-millimeter antiaircraft battery goes into action against Japanese bombers winging overhead. Ken Riley, a young combat artist in his mid-twenties, was assigned to one of the U.S. Coast Guard–manned transport ships that took part in the invasion of Tarawa and the Marshall Islands. (U.S. Coast Guard; Library of Congress).

Tear gases affected the eyes. Blister gases (or vesicants), including distilled mustard, N-metylebisamine (2-chlorethyl) (or nitrogen mustard), and lewisite, attacked the skin, causing burns, destroying skin tissue, and forming painful raw ulcers. All these gases could cause extensive damage, leading to death; but the most severe and lethal were carbon monoxide, cyanide, and cyanogen chloride. All interfered with the uptake of oxygen by the hemoglobin in the blood, causing profound physiological suffocation.

Wartime chemistry also devised chemical (rather than gas) grenades, notably the phosphorous bomb, which contained an explosive charge and a quantity of white elemental phosphorus. These bombs were used

Destruction by remote control. At the request of ground forces, a fighter control center in Europe determines bombing missions far behind enemy lines. (U.S. Army Air Force photo; Library of Congress).

as incendiaries by both sides in air attacks on large cities. As the charge exploded, the bombs scattered fragments of white phosphorus over a large area; and the particles ignited spontaneously on contact with the air. The particles of phosphorous stuck to bare skin and caused painful flesh wounds that took a long time to heal. In the meantime, the patient's care would be excessively demanding of limited and over-stretched medical services. Thus, these phosphorous bombs not only burned and destroyed property but also burned and maimed those people they did not kill outright.

The most damaging incendiary was an extension of the so-called Molotov cocktail, a grenade made out of a bottle containing petrol, which was not an especially effective incendiary, as it dispersed and evaporated too quickly. Assiduous research found a way of forming the petrol into a gel, a jellolike substance, napalm, through a mix of palmitic and napthalemic acids. It had the effect of turning the petrol into a viscous jelly, the basis of a highly efficient incendiary material that burned fiercely for longer than ordinary petrol. Once napalm came into contact with any organic material (such as skin), it continued to burn with a violent, intense flame. If it went off close to human beings, it turned them into torches of flame. It was widely used by the Allies against soldiers on battlefields and against civilian populations in large towns and cities.

Medicine

As well as leading to the development of more terrible weapons, the war accelerated huge advances in medical knowledge and surgical techniques. Because the war produced so many appalling casualties and created adverse conditions in which diseases could flourish, it provided the medical profession with a great challenge to which doctors across the world responded. The war hastened the revolution in research into sulfonamides that had led already, in November 1939, to the uncovering of the compound sulfapyridine, the first truly effective drug against bacteria, produced as M and B 693, and then sulfathiazole, M and B 760.

The United States led the field in developing means of protecting its military forces and civilians against medical, biological, or chemical attacks. For example, American doctors produced an ointment, M5, to neutralize the poison of mustard gas. A British discovery, DTH, was effective for preventing burns and poisoning by lewisite, and the Du Pont laboratories produced it in great quantities in both liquid and ointment forms.

The most famous wartime development was the production of the antibiotic penicillin, in which Dr. H. Raistrick of Britain greatly expanded the early accidental findings of Sir Alexander Fleming and, as a result of assiduous research and a vigorous campaign, ensured its widespread cultivation. In 1942 American researchers began to investigate the possibility of large-scale production of penicillin in vats, instead of in bottles (including milk bottles), as used in Britain. In 1944, American researchers began production of penicillin by a new deep-fermentation process. However, not until the invasion of northwest Europe was there enough penicillin to use for prevention of infections as well as their treatment. The penicillin was used primarily to treat severe wounds.

Another pivotal development was in plastic surgery, the art of repairing severe skin disfigurement. Here cruel necessity was the mother of invention, and important advances were made in all major countries. Many badly wounded men and civilians, notably burn victims, were treated who might have been passed over in peacetime as beyond hope.

The Russian surgeon Filatov invented the crucial "walking-stalk" operation, a masterpiece of surgical thinking. This technique involved the development of a new technique for skin grafting, which had often failed in the past when a transplanted area of skin had refused to take on its new site. Filatov discovered that it was possible to detach a section of skin on three sides of a rectangle, leaving it attached at one end. The detached section was then rolled into a tube and sutured (that is, joined at the edges by stitches) in that position. In the meantime, the section was pulled over to the damaged area requiring a skin graft and secured until it had joined firmly. The other end was then detached and looped across to the original region. Thus, by a series of maneuvers over several weeks, successive sections of skin were looped from one part of the body in such a way that the sections never lost contact with the original tissues that nurtured them. Finally, when the graft had settled, the cylinder was opened flat and the skin sutured into its new site. The British plastic surgeon whose feats equaled those of Filatov was Archie McIndoe.

Other surgeons carried out major operations in which limbs were repaired after severe damage; new tongues were made and stitched into position; nerve trunks were encouraged to grow and reproduce. Russian doctors also led research into biogenic agents to encourage healing and regrowth with such chemicals as dicarboxylic acid. To aid surgery and medicine, blood banks were instituted. In 1940 the rhesus factor—Rh —was discovered, completing the basis of understanding on which the discipline of transfusion could develop. During the 1940s the cross-matching and storing of blood became widespread.

The war also spurred on production of tablets to prevent malaria, first made possible by the German use of atebrin in 1933. This drug was later called mepacrine when it was used by Sir Neil Hamilton Fairley in

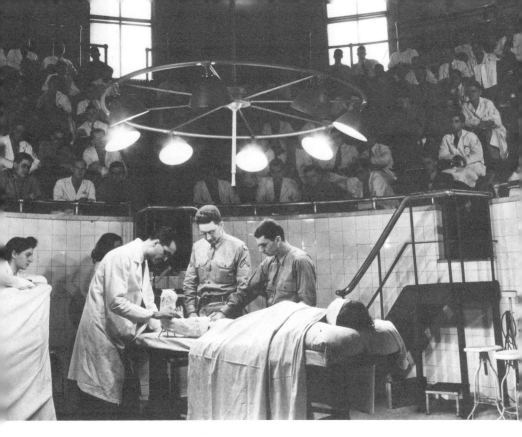

World War II spurred on advances in medicine and medical education alike. This was especially true in the U.S. Army where fully qualified surgeons were required in all theaters of the war. Here a surgeon in white coat *(left)*, with experience of war injuries stretching back to World War I, supervises two army medical students as they diagnose a leg injury. Fellow students watch their progress from the amphitheater. The photograph was taken at Bellevue Hospital in New York City, where army medical students, registered at New York University, were given practical experience of all manner of injuries. (Library of Congress).

the southwest Pacific in 1942. Other antimalarials included chlorgunide in the United States and paludrine in Britain. Tetanus, a dangerous disease for people in earlier wars, was also brought under control by prophylactic treatment by injection.

Whether the theater was the Middle East, the central Mediterranean, or northwest Europe, it took, on average, fourteen hours for a soldier to be brought in for surgery after being wounded. Casualties were first treated (and recorded) by a medical aid man and then at a battalion aid station where a doctor performed limited emergency surgery. The casu-

Marines ferry two of their colleagues wounded at Tarawa to safety. One marine lies at the bottom of the boat, the second on the hatch, covered with a towel to keep flies out of his wounds. (U.S. Marine Corps photo; Library of Congress).

alty was then moved by ambulance to a division-collecting company and then to a field (or evacuation) hospital. Whereas in World War I, 8.1 percent of American soldiers who had to receive medical treatment died, in World War II, the mortality rate of American soldiers was 4.5 percent.

For identification in case of death, every GI wore two metal tags ("dog tags") around his neck bearing name, service serial number, next of kin, and religion. Upon death, one tag remained with the body; the other went with the GI's personal effects. Bodies were encased in a cotton mattress cover and were laid in a temporary cemetery to be transferred after the war.

The Battle of Production

The battle to organize the American economy to meet the demands of total war was begun eighteen months before the attack on Pearl Harbor. In response to the German offensive in the west, FDR, on May 10, 1940, asked Congress for $1 billion to mechanize the army and greatly expand aircraft production. Congress replied with a grant of $1.5 billion. At the end of May 1940, as British troops were being evacuated from Dunkirk, FDR warned Congress that events "necessitate another enlargement of our military program." Congress duly voted to spend a further $1 billion for the army and $700 million to provide the United States with a two-ocean navy. In all, in the two years prior to America's military entry into the war, some $64 billion was appropriated for ships, planes, and guns; $7 billion was assigned to the lend-lease program; and $3 billion was injected into the coffers of the Reconstruction Finance Corporation in order to facilitate the expansion of defense industries.

The amount and range of American production were truly astounding. Between 1940 and 1945 the United States produced 296,429 warplanes; 102,351 tanks; 872,431 pieces of artillery; 2,455,964 trucks; 87,620 warships; 5,425 cargo ships; 5,822,000 tons of aircraft bombs; 20,086,061 small arms; and 44 billion rounds of small ammunition. In *The American Character* (1944), Denis Brogan declared that part of the explanation of this immense production, and its effective deployment, lay in the American national character that took a different view of the war than did the Europeans. "To the Americans war is a business, not an art; they are not interested in moral victories, but in victory. . . . The United States is a great, a very great corporation whose stockholders expect (with all their history to justify the expectation) that it will be in the black."

This was an overseas war, and the United States was dependent on ocean shipping to transport men and supplies. American industrialists adapted their mass-production techniques to ship construction and expanded shipyards to a point where in 1942 they produced 18 million dead-weight tons of merchant shipping. Between 1941 and 1945 they produced 55 million tons of shipping, about half of them in Liberty ships constructed by assembly-line methods. From mid-1943 industrialists began producing a more specialized kind of shipping, notably landing craft—LSTs, LCTs, LCI(L)s, and others—first for use in a cross-channel invasion and then in the Pacific and Mediterranean. During the first 212 days of 1945, American shipbuilders built 247 cargo ships.

Industrialists Henry Kaiser and Howard Hughes became partners in aviation construction. They became celebrities who were widely known for encouraging their executives, designers, and workers to achieve the impossible. Furthermore, in September 1942 Kaiser set a world record by launching the *John Fitch*, a Liberty ship of 10,000 tons, just twenty-four days after laying the keel. In all, America's merchant fleet rose from 34.84 million tons of dry cargo shipping on January 1, 1943, to 67.36 million tons on August 1, 1945. Thus, the United States could deploy 5 million of its army of 8 million overseas in all theaters of war by may 1945, 3 million of them in the war against Germany.

What the British then called administration, the Americans called logistics, meaning almost all military activity apart from strategy and tactics. Logistics was the science of getting the right forces and equipment to the right place at the right time. Logistics, military planning of the moving of supplies, was the task of the Army Service Forces (ASF), headed by General Brehom B. Somervell, an engineer-officer with considerable drive who did not mind offending others in order to get things done quickly. The ASF motto was "We do the impossible immediately. The miraculous takes a little longer." The entire system of production, transportation, delivery, and stocking was based on an essential continuous pipeline of supply with new articles put in at one end of the pipeline as similar articles were removed from the other. This applied to factories, storage depots, and theaters of war. Once an authorized level had been established, a regular supply was maintained, with individual needs computed according to official tables of organization and equipment (TOEs).

If the United States really was to serve as "the arsenal of democracy," as Roosevelt had promised in his fireside chat of December 1940, then what was required was a bureaucratic infrastructure that would direct the development of the burgeoning defense program. As was the case with funding, FDR began the groundwork at the time of the capitulation of France. On May 28, 1940, FDR created the National Defense Advisory Commission. In the months that followed, he established the Office of Production Management (OPM) in January 1941, the Office of Price Administration and Civilian Supply (OPACS) in April 1941, and the Supply Priorities and Allocations Board (SPAB) in August 1941.

Between January and December 1941, munitions production increased by 22 percent. However, such growth did not dispel doubts about the efficiency of the defense program. Its critics found their views represented in the report submitted by the Senate Special Committee to Investigate the National Defense Program in January 1942. According to the committee's chairman, Senator Harry S. Truman of Missouri, industry was not converting from the manufacture of consumer goods to munitions production fast enough and government was failing to apply the force needed to expedite this change. Truman's first point was valid. Business was booming in 1941, and America's entrepreneurs were unwilling to sacrifice a newly buoyant market in consumer goods for the uncertain gains promised buy military production. They were providing most recalcitrant about converting existing plants and using their supplies of scarce comodities, such as steel, in order to turn out rifles instead of vacuum cleaners. As such, despite the vast amounts of money earmarked for defense, actual spending on munitions amounted to only $18 billion in 1941.

On January 16, 1942, FDR responded to this crisis by issuing Executive Order 9024 that brought into being the War Productions Board (WPB). Its chairman, Donald Marr Nelson, came to the board from his post as vice president of Sears, Roebuck and Company with its salary of $70,000. Nelson had previously been "borrowed" from Sears in the years 1933–35 to work as adviser to the NRA. He had also been coopted by government in 1940 to coordinate purchasing for the National Defense Advisory Committee (NDAC) and had stayed on in the same role when the committee became the Office of Production Management. His brief with the War Production Board was to develop policies governing all aspects of production and to "exercise general responsibility over the nation's economy." His authority was confirmed by the passing of the Second War Powers Act of March 1942. This act gave the president power to allocate resources and declare priorities throughout the economy as the needs of national defense determined them. Thereafter, he was responsible for deciding who could, or could not, have access to steel, copper, rubber, gasoline, and other scarce commodities. He also was empowered to prohibit the manufacturing of ultimately over three hundred items deemed inessential in the war effort, including cars, refrigerators, and household hardware. He had authority to force manufacturers to convert plants to war production or expand existing facilities, to force them to accept war orders, and, in extreme cases, to commandeer their plant.

Such severe measures were never applied. Instead of coercion, Nelson tried to get the cooperation of business by offering irresistible inducements to join the battle for production. These came in the form of subsidies or low interest loans for enlarging plants and constructing new facilities. Government encouraged industry with tax benefits to take account of the depreciation of defense plants, at a rate of 20 percent per annum, and the "cost plus" contract, by which the government and contractor agreed on a profit over and above the "cost" of production to be included in the overall price of a contract. Unfortunately, this led to widespread abuse by which all sorts of expenses were included in the basic cost until exposure by Truman and his committee led to some curtailment of the worst abuses. The government also promised contractors that new facilities built at government expense for war production would be available at knockdown prices at the end of the war.

In addition to these incentives, in March 1942 FDR approved the suspension of all antitrust actions and investigations involving those companies cooperating with the war effort. The stratagem proved successful. As much new industrial plant was built in the three years following Pearl Harbor as had been constructed in the previous fifteen years. In the first six months of 1942, federal orders amounted to some $100 billion worth of war equipment. By June 1942, 50 percent of America's manufacturing output was in war materiel.

If such growth was good for the generals, it was just as good for the captains of industry. In the war years, big business boomed in harmony with the guns. On the eve of America's entry into the war, 75 percent of all contracts in the defense program were lodged with only fifty-six large companies. Economic centralization continued apace in the ensuing years. From the onset, Nelson had sought to prevent this. He wanted an equitable distribution of procurement contracts to ensure that small entrepreneurs benefited from war production. However, he found himself powerless to impose his will. The largest demand for munitions came, quite obviously, from the War and Navy departments. These

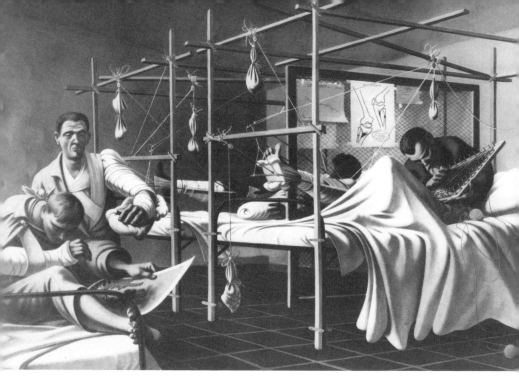

Fracture Ward. Artist Peter Blume, known for his corrosive satire of Italy as prey to an evil jack-in-the-box Mussolini, here demonstrated his unerring ability to portray the wrenching effects of political violence on these victims of war—their limbs set anew but their inner understanding of the horrific nature of war fueled by a fire that cannot be quelled by medication. (Library of Congress).

agencies jealously defended their right to choose with whom they would deal. Invariably, they chose to deal with big business.

Why was this so? First, in order to avoid the confusion over standardization that had dogged the production effort in World War I, they placed their contracts not with a multiplicity of manufacturers but with the corporate giants. Second, big business was the most attractive option because it had the resources, equipment, expertise, capital, and organizational experience to meet the demands for production on a mammoth scale. Third, giant corporations had expert lobbyists pleading their case within the administrative branch of the armed services and the War Productions Board. Perhaps the most influential advocate of big business was Secretary of War Henry L. Stimson. An avowed enemy of New Deal liberalism and a staunch Republican, Stimson came to the War Department in 1940 from a New York City law firm that dealt almost exclusively with clients from big business. As head of the War Department, he continued to defend their interests. To justify such favoritism, he explained that, when waging war, "you have got to let business make money out of the process or business won't work."

Others of lesser rank were equally as willing to favor what they saw as their own constituency. Foremost among these were the so-called dollar-a-year men. These individuals were recruited from big business to staff the executive branch of the War Production Board. To assuage their fears concerning their status once hostilities ceased, it was agreed that they should be allowed to remain upon the payrolls of the corporations from whence they came. With one eye open to the opportunity for postwar advancement, they were naturally inclined to deal leniently with their corporate employers. They included not only Donald Nelson and various executives in the War Production Board but also William S. Knudsen who left General Motors to become director of the War Department and banker James V. Forrestal who became secretary of defense, Robert A. Lovett who became assistant secretary of war for air, and Edward Stettinius, Jr., who left General Motors and U.S. Steel eventually to become secretary of state. The Truman committee gave substance to doubts about their impartiality when it condemned the War Production Board's "dollar-a-year men" for not enforcing conversion to war production. The most obvious case came in the automobile industry. In 1941, Detroit was enjoying its first prosperous year since the onset of the depression. In August of that year, 88 percent more automobiles were being produced than in the same month of 1940. However, a halt was called when the War Production Board decreed that no more cars or light trucks be constructed after January 31, 1942. Despite this decree, and, in the face of the obvious need for military transport, the board granted an exemption that permitted the production of a further 250,000 automobiles. The extension was attributed to the influence wielded by the "dollar-a-year men." It was only in spring 1942 that the government ended such policies toward automobile producers in Detroit.

By tying business, military, and government closely together, FDR was preparing the ground for the construction of what became known variously as the power-elite, the military-industrial complex, and the warfare state. The center of such activities and the symbol of American military power was the Pentagon, a huge five-sided building in Arlington County, Virginia, just outside Washington, D.C. Designed by George

Edwin Bergstrom and built in the period 1941–43, it later became the headquarters of the Department of Defense, including all three services that had been housed previously in widely scattered buildings. When completed, it was the largest office building in the world, covering thirty-four acres and providing 3.7 million square feet of usable floor space. The design was based on five concentric pentagons, or rings, with ten spokelike corridors connecting the whole. In order to conserve steel for the war effort, which would have gone normally into the construction of the inner frame and the elevators of a high building, the Pentagon was deliberately designed as a low (but extensive) building with numerous ramps for easy movement.

Controversy about contracts, personnel, and, most notably, supplies of previous materials generated an undercurrent of popular dissatisfaction with the planning and implementation of the war-production effort. Further doubts about the efficiency of the board were raised when contractors complained that they were failing to achieve maximum output because they were not being provided with adequate supplies of scarce raw materials. In June 1942, the board attempted to solve this problem by instituting the Production Requirement Plan. In accordance with this scheme, each factory under government contract submitted its own individual demand for resources. This bargaining-free-for-all proved to be a failure; in November 1942, the board replaced it with the Controlled Materials Plan. Under the new plan, each of the claimant agencies—the War and Navy departments, the Lend-Lease Administration, the Maritime Commission, and the Office of Civilian Supply—submitted its own requirement order to the War Production Board. The board then allocated the designated scarce materials—copper, aluminum, and steel—to the agencies, which, in turn, distributed them at their discretion to the contractors. By introducing the Controlled Materials Plan, the board broke the log jam in copper, aluminum, and steel allocations. It could do nothing in 1942 to redress the shortage of that other vital material, rubber. The way this problem was eventually solved was a testimony to governmental initiative. It also illustrated the way in which the morganatic relationship between state and big business operated during the war years.

Japan's conquests in Southeast Asia effectively interrupted America's principal supply of raw rubber. The administration adopted two measures to make up the shortfall: petrol rationing to curb automobile wear and tear of rubber tires and a scrap-rubber drive that garnered 450,000 tons of used rubber in only four weeks. However, the only real solution lay in developing America's synthetic rubber production. Here, there was much to be done. In 1941 American industry had the capacity to produce only 40,000 tons of synthetic rubber. By 1944 actual output exceeded 800,000 tons and accounted for 87 percent of all rubber produced in the United States. To achieve this transformation, the federal government spent $700 million constructing fifty-one centers for synthetic rubber production. To enlist the cooperation of industry, the government leased these plants to rubber manufacturers at a nominal price and operated them on the customary cost-plus-fixed-fee basis.

The battle for production was won by the end of 1943. In November of that year $6 billion of war materiel rolled off American production lines. In the following month, the War and Navy departments began to return funds appropriated for munitions. From then until June 1944, one million workers were laid off from war and war-related industries. In the aftermath of the successful Normandy landings of June 1944, Nelson began urging war contractors to reconvert to peacetime production. He was opposed in this both by the armed services that sought to maintain high levels of military production and by the businesses that had grown fat upon lucrative munitions contracts. These businesses were most unwilling to comply, and they were strengthened in their resistance by support given by the War Production Board's vice chairman, Charles Wilson. As the controversy grew in acrimony, FDR decided to jettison Nelson. Instead of firing him, he sent him to act as Chinese leader Jiang Jieshi's economic adviser. Nelson left for China in July 1944 and resigned officially from the board in September. He was replaced by a former board official, Julius A. Krug, who avoided a collision course with Nelson's adversaries by allowing industry to reconvert to peacetime production at its leisure.

The balance sheet of war production suggests the scale of the achievement and also who gained most from it. Between June 1940 and September 1944, government expenditure on war-related industries totaled $175 billion. Of this, some 66 percent went to only 100 companies. Similarly, two-thirds of the $1 billion invested by Washington in research and development was channeled toward just sixty-eight large corporations; and 40 percent of this sum found its way into the coffers of the nation's ten leading business concerns.

The grapes of wrath became the grapes of plenty for the Okies—migrants from the Dust Bowl who came to find work in California—in the state's burgeoning aircraft industry. This photo by Hollem of a western aircraft plant of the Consolidated Aircraft Corporation has a line of partly completed Consolidated B-24 bombers and C-87 transport planes extending to the horizon under seemingly endless rows of fluorescent lights. (Office of War Information photo of October 1942; Library of Congress).

The cost was borne by the lesser. During the war 500 small banks went out of business; over half a million modest businesses in the retail, service, and construction sector went to the wall. Commenting on the further consolidation in industry, Geoffrey Perrett (1973) declares: "The net result was that before 1950 big business was stronger, more firmly entrenched and more monopolistic than ever before in American history." Thus in 1940, 175,000 companies produced 70 percent of American manufactured goods; in March 1943, 100 companies produced 70 percent of American manufactured goods.

The trend was to ever bigger companies. For example, in 1939 firms with less than 500 workers employed 52 percent of those engaged in manufacturing; firms with over 10,000 workers employed 13 percent of those engaged in manufacturing. In 1944, firms with less than 500 workers employed 38 percent of those engaged in manufacturing; firms with over 10,000 workers employed 31 percent of those engaged in manufacturing. Furthermore, in 1940 corporate profit was $6.4 billion; in 1944 corporate profit was $10.8 billion.

A direct consequence of the federal government's control of the war effort and the battle for production was a dramatic and rapid increase in personnel. During the New Deal era, the federal government's manpower increased by 60 percent. During the war, the number employed in federal agencies increased by 300 percent.

Moreover, it was World War II that finally and irreversibly transformed farming into a large business enterprise. Farmers used larger amounts of fertilizer, better hybrid seeds, and improved pesticides and understood much more about soil conservation. The most singular development was the wider use of ever larger and better machines. New row-crop loaders for harvesting carrots, onions, potatoes, and beets almost entirely displaced the old stoop labor in the fields. The Bureau of the Census took a sample count in 1945 and discovered a pronounced trend toward fewer but much larger farms. In short, farming became agribusiness. Geoffrey Perrett comments, "No one had prospered more in wartime than the farmers had." On the face of it, this is somewhat ironic for, between 1940 and 1945, farm population fell by 17 percent. However, the productivity of each individual involved in agriculture rose by 25 percent. The increase was largely due to mechanization, fertilization, and the consolidation of small holdings into larger units of production. Thus, the number of sharecroppers and tenants fell by 33 percent. As a result, in 1945 the income of America's farmers was 250 percent higher than in 1939.

Employment and Economic Problems

The battle for production provided a solution to the central problem that had confounded FDR's first two administrations—the problem of unemployment. By December 1942, less than one million able-bodied men were idle. In all, some 17 million new jobs were created during World War II. Thus, despite the undoubted gains made by business and the farm bloc, it can be argued that the chief beneficiary of the war boom was the previously disadvantaged working man.

By 1945–46, over 40 percent of the population was in the middle-class income bracket of $2,000 to $4,000 per annum. The following breakdown of income increases is based upon the division of American society into five sectors determined by annual income prior to Pearl Harbor. The income of the poorest fifth of the population rose during the war annually by 68 percent; the next poorest fifth experienced as increase in annual income of 59 percent; the middle sector had an increase of 36 percent; while the two more affluent fifths of the population enjoyed an annual income increase of 30 percent and 20 percent, respectively. Moreover, during wartime nearly 30 percent of all earnings were saved in the form of bonds, private bank accounts, and so on.

However, while the defense program provided a solution to one problem, it raised the specter of another—inflation. Policy planners were confronted with the task of stabilizing a newly buoyant economy in a way that averted the sort of fiscal crisis that had occurred during World War I. During that conflict, Americans became accustomed to paying $4 for a steak and $20 for a pair of shoes. Between 1917 and 1920, the cost of living had risen by 51.7 percent. In the months prior to Pearl Harbor, there were ominous signs that increased defense spending had once more set the inflationary spiral in motion. From 1939 to the spring of 1942, the cost of living increased by 15 percent. Treasury advisers concerned about the sudden climb identified the problem as the inflationary gap—the gap between disposable income and available consumer goods. In short, too much money was chasing too few commodities. This resulted in a rise in prices, a subsequent demand for wage increases, an increase in the cost of production, another rise in prices, and so on, ad infinitum.

The man assigned to the task of keeping down the cost of living was an economist and former director of research and planning with the National Recovery Administration, Leon Henderson. An ardent supporter of the New Deal, Henderson had been director of the prewar Office of Price Administration and Civilian Supply (OPA). In January 1942, he was made head of the newly formed Office of Price Administration. His powers were enhanced by the passing of the Emergency

These glistening Hamilton Standard propellers were photographed in front of the big United mainliner plane at United's central maintenance base at Cheyenne, Wyoming, where engines, propellers, and planes were serviced and reconditioned after every 725 hours of flight. (Library of Congress).

Price Control Act (EPCA) of January 1942, which authorized the OPA to impose price ceilings upon consumer goods. One crucial exemption was granted, one that vitiated the OPA's efforts to arrest inflation. As a result of pressure exerted by the farm bloc, Congress agreed that the ceilings should not be applied to agricultural produce. Thus, the price of foodstuffs remained unrestricted.

The passing of the EPCA had little immediate impact upon the rising cost of living, partly because the price of foodstuffs continued to rise and partly because the OPA was equal to the task of assessing and imposing a fair price limit upon each of the thousands of consumer goods on the American home market. This particular problem was solved in April 1942 by the OPA's introduction of the General Maximum Price Regulation. This required merchants to accept the highest prices charged for goods in March 1942 as a price ceiling. Again, farm produce was exempt from these restrictions. "General Max" was roundly condemned by businessmen who complained that they were being asked to freeze prices at too low a level. The OPA's critics in Congress carpeted Henderson. To them, "General Max" was not only a dictatorial measure, it was also a failure. With the cost of living rising by 7 percent in the first six months of 1942, Henderson's critics wanted to know if he had any solution other than that of persecuting businessmen. In his defense, Henderson explained that price control was pointless unless he could lift exemptions on foodstuffs and impose a wage freeze. His conservative critics in Congress reluctantly accepted the logic of his argument. The Stabilization Act of October 2, 1942, broadened the OPA's power to enforce price controls and placed responsibility for price fixing on all foodstuffs, including fresh fish and vegetables, under its jurisdiction. The act also granted the agency a free hand to introduce rationing. Congress thus grudgingly accepted the OPA as the instrument to combat inflation, but its members demanded a price for their cooperation—Henderson's subsequent resignation.

In early 1943, the OPA's old system of price ceilings across the board was abandoned on many commodities in favor of regular monthly readjustments that varied from region to region, taking into account local conditions of supply and demand. The agency insisted that all revised prices be posted in full view of the public, and it was empowered to take all violators to court.

The OPA proved to be the most unpopular of all wartime agencies. Democrats and Republicans alike saw it as a source of spoils and corruption. Businessmen damned it as a restraint of trade. To the man in the street, the chief irritants were its efforts to ration consumer goods. In 1942 ten such programs were instituted, involving, among other products, gasoline, coffee, shoes, sugar, butter, and a variety of processed foods. The aim was to achieve an equitable distribution of these scarce commodities. It was achieved by allocating each citizen aged sixteen and over a fixed monthly quota of ration stamps. These were to be used, along with cash, to purchase the individual's quota of the restricted commodities. To offset the possibility of hoarding, the stamps carried an expiration date. If they were not used within this set period, they became invalid. In order to be able to restock their shelves, retailers had to present the stamps taken over the counter to prove that their stocks really were exhausted. Rationing was deeply resented and unpopular. For one thing, it was regarded as an extension of bureaucratic control at the expense of individual freedom. Moreover, it was condemned for creating artificial shortages. People frequently misplaced their ration cards and then had to plead their case to local ration boards in order to receive their quota of essential consumer goods. Officials on the local rationing boards were sometimes accused of favortism—when the Jones family thought the Smiths were getting a more generous allocation than they really were, they invariably accused administrators of nepotism and petty graft. Finally, the Americans were now, after years of depression, a newly prosperous people, impatient to enjoy the pleasures of affluence. They opposed rationing because it enforced a state of austerity that few citizens thought necessary.

The Office of Economic Stabilization (OES) was established in October 1942 to oversee all aspects of the economy. Its principal function was to arbitrate in disputes between the various governmental agencies and, of most immediate importance, to shield the OPA's unpopular anti-inflation campaign from further congressional criticism. It was headed by James F. Byrnes, a liberal southern Democrat and former senator who had represented South Carolina for over twenty years, only recently appointed to the bench of the Supreme Court. Byrnes still commanded the respect of his former colleagues in Congress, and FDR hoped that he would be able to win a hostile Congress over to the administration's battle against inflation. According to Richard Polenberg (1972), "Byrnes speedily assumed jurisdiction over any and all matters relating to the economy."

The Office of War Mobilization (OWM) was created in May 1943 with Byrnes as its director. The OWM served as "a court of last appeal, a body that adjudicated disputes between the military and civilians or between competing civilian interests." In practice, Byrnes never trusted Donald Nelson (chairman of the War Production Board) and tended to give support to big business and the military. FDR invested Byrnes with great trust and responsibility, allowing him to serve as his representative to the military establishment. Indeed, he has been described as "a kind of assistant president."

With the almost complete elimination of unemployment and the rise in working-class wages, the government had to find ways of absorbing excess capital, otherwise available for discretionary spending, if it were ever to narrow the inflationary gap. The government adopted two strategies, both of which had the added virtue of helping it finance the war effort. The first was the sale of war bonds. From the onset of war, many of FDR's closest advisers urged him to establish a compulsory savings scheme. Secretary of the Treasury Henry Morgenthau opposed this plan. Instead, he envisaged the selling of war bonds as a means of involving the public in the war effort. By organizing the scheme on a voluntary basis, he reasoned, the American people would be able to feel that they were making their own positive contribution to the war effort. Through advertising and other promotional campaigns, the citizen would be alerted to the patriotic virtue of saving. Morgenthau's argument carried the day.

In all, there were seven bond drives, each of one month's duration. The first, which began in December 1942, yielded $12.9 billion. By the end of the war, a total of $135 billion had been raised. Although these bond drives helped pay for the war, they were only partially successful in soaking up citizens' excess capital. Most sales were made to large financial institutions, such as banks, insurance companies, and industrial corporations. The smaller bond issues, those priced between $25 and $50, remained disappointingly undersubscribed. When the initial wave of patriotic fervor subsided, the newly affluent workingman chose not to save but to spend what he had earned and enjoy material comforts. When it came to a choice between guns for the nation or butter for himself, he was inclined to spend his wages on butter.

The second government strategy to absorb excess capital was by taxation. In 1939, only 4 million Americans paid taxes. By the spring of 1942, the tax system had been revised and extended to cover nearly 30 million citizens. As that year progressed, it became apparent that, with the continued growth in government spending and the parallel rise in wages, inflation could only be controlled by a further extension of the tax system.

Veteran New Dealer Henry Morgenthau considered fiscal policy an instrument of social reform. The proposed revision of the tax structure was, to him, a useful device, not only for stabilizing the economy and paying for the war but also for narrowing the gap between rich and poor. In March 1942, he recommended to FDR an increased surtax on personal income and a rise in corporate income tax. He called for a tightening of the terms applicable to payment of excess-profits tax, an increase in estate and gift taxes, and a higher excise tax on scarce commodities and luxury goods. He also called for an immediate hike in social security taxation. FDR passed the proposition onto Congress, which damned it as a reform measure aimed at soaking the rich.

The Revenue Act of October 1942 devised by Morgenthau did strike at the rich, but the blow carried by the increase in corporate and personal income tax was light. The bill's most innovative feature, the so-called victory tax, sloughed the burden of financing the war firmly upon the shoulders of the poorer members of society. This measure, which imposed a 5 percent gross income tax upon all annual incomes in excess of $624, extended liability to 20 million workers in the lower income bracket. The act lowered the personal allowance—the money on which tax was not paid—to $500 for single men and women and $1,200 for married couples. Thus was income tax made a truly mass tax. In 1939, only 4 million people paid income tax; by 1943, the new act had increased the number of people paying income tax to 43 million; and by 1945, the number was 50 million. However, not only were the middle- and lower-income tax groups brought into the new tax structure, but the upper classes were also required to pay more. The normal tax in the upper brackets rose from 4 percent to 5 percent, and the surtax was increased from 77 percent to 82 percent.

Thus, in 1939 a married man with no children who earned $2,000 paid no tax; in 1945, he paid $202. In the period 1939–45, the tax on an income of $5,000 rose from $80 to $844; on an income of $10,000, it rose from $415 to $2,370; and on an income of $25,000, it rose from $2,489 to $9,955. Corporate taxes rose from 31 percent to 40 percent, and excess-profits tax went up to 90 percent. The act of 1942 also increased taxes on inheritances and gifts and introduced sizable excise taxes on communications, luxuries, and transportation that were to remain after the war. Accordingly, government revenues rose from $7.5 billion in 1941 to $46.5 billion in 1945.

Until the act of 1942, income-tax payments were always made twelve months in arrears. Thus, taxes to be paid in 1943 were based upon incomes earned in 1942. However, if taxation were ever to operate as an effective weapon against inflation by syphoning off expendable income, then this traditional system of payment had to be revised. Wage levels for 1943 and tax rates for that year would be higher than they had

The final stages of the assembly line for army trucks as water is poured into the radiator and gasoline into the fuel tank so that each truck can run off the production line under its own power. (Office of Emergency Management photo by Palmer; Library of Congress).

been in 1942. Thus, after having met their tax obligations for 1942, Americans, in 1943, would still have money in their pockets. To put the bite on personal incomes, it was proposed that the citizen pay income taxes for 1943 currently, while simultaneously filing returns for 1942. For obvious reasons, this proposition met with little enthusiasm. One other solution was proffered by Beardsley Ruml, chairman of the Federal Reserve Bank of New York. This solution simply involved the cancellation of all tax obligations for 1942. Despite the Treasury's protest against losing a whole year's revenue, Congress approved the plan.

The Current Tax Payment Act of 1943 subsequently wrote off all obligations for 1942 that amounted to $50 or less, forgave 75 percent of the rest, and made taxpayers current in the payments as of July 1, 1943. Popularly called "Pay as you go," the act required employers to deduct federal taxes from their employees at source and to turn over these deductions to the collector of internal revenue every three months. Those who were self-employed had to compute and pay their own tax estimates on the same basis.

As this controversy waned, a new one waxed on the Treasury's horizon. With the cost of the war still spiraling and the necessity of combating inflation still urgent, the Treasury devised a new tax bill for 1943 that set as its target a sum of $12 billion. Wary of sending such a request to Congress, FDR told Secretary of the Treasury Henry Morgenthau to reduce the target figure. Morgenthau's revised plan aimed at raising $10.5 billion, of which $6.5 billion would come from personal income tax; $1 billion from corporate taxes; $2.5 billion from excises; and the rest from estate and gift taxes. FDR passed the proposal on to Congress, where the House Ways and Means Committee dismissed it out of hand. Left to its own devices, the committee devised a plan to raise only $2 billion. To FDR the measure was not only inadequate, but it was also inequitous for it granted lucrative tax favors to business in general and the mining and lumber industries in particular. Nonetheless, the measure was passed by the House in November 1943, and the Senate gave its approval the following January.

On February 22, 1944, FDR vetoed the bill, describing it as "not a tax bill but a tax relief bill providing relief not for the needy but for the greedy." Undaunted, the House decided by 299 votes to 95 to override the veto. In the Senate, the vote was equally emphatic — 72 votes to 14. For the first time in American history, Congress had passed a revenue law over a presidential veto.

While this controversy constituted a humiliating defeat for FDR, he had by then won the overall battle against inflation. Victory had in fact been assured by mid-1943, when the requisite economic controls had been established and made operative. Although price and wage ceilings provoked politicians and public alike, and people remained reluctant to invest in war bonds, and although the extension of taxation aroused much petty discontent, these measures did bear fruit. From 1942 to 1945, the rise in the cost of living was held down to only 9 percent.

Social Changes

In wartime Americans were a people in motion. Sixteen million men left home to join the armed services; 15.3 million others uprooted themselves to be near their loved ones or, in the vast majority of cases, to find work.

The hand that wrote the military procurement contracts gave direction to the great internal migration. In 1942 the population of New Orleans rose by some 20 percent, an increase generated by the demand for labor in the city's naval shipyards. The defense program gave a similar stimulus to the growth of other cities across the nation. Between 1940 and 1943 the population of Charleston, South Carolina, rose by 37 percent; that of Norfolk, Virginia, by 57 percent; and that of Mobile, Alabama, by 61 percent. As John M. Blum suggests when he quotes a federal report in *V was for Victory* (1976), "scarcely a section of the country or a community of any size escaped the impact of this great migration." The greatest impact was registered in California. The promise of work in the burgeoning munitions industry attracted 1.4 million people to the Golden State. By the end of the war, Californians comprised 10 percent of the population of the United States and, in turn, accounted for the production of 20 percent of the nation's manufactured goods. As Geoffrey Perrett explains in his *Days of Sadness, Years of Triumph* (1973), the "industrial growth of twenty-five to fifty years had been achieved in less than three."

Small towns as well as big cities were affected by the arrival of war installations and defense plants. A typical example was the Mississippi coastal community of Pascagoula. Prior to Pearl Harbor, its six thousand inhabitants enjoyed a lifestyle into which the most modern and progressive aspects of the twentieth century rarely intruded. Its fine harbor played host to a handful of small fishing craft. The war came to Pascagoula in the form of a new shipyard and an influx of outside labor. By war's end, the town's population had risen fourfold.

In the boom towns, the inevitable tensions between old stock and newcomers were accentuated by the breakdown or sheer absence of civic amenities and essential services. In many cases, the existing medical, sanitary, educational, and transport services simply could not meet the demands of a greatly expanded population. The most immediate problem facing the migrant work force lay in the shortage of accommodation. The short-term solution came in the form of the trailer, described by the Federal Security Administration as "a slum on wheels." Huge trailer parks sprung up almost overnight near military plants and bases. Life there was both dangerous and dirty. Few had fire safety regulations, adequate sanitation, or a pure water supply. While conditions were bad in the boom towns, accommodation problems were also confronted by those who sought work in the city. Indeed, in January 1945, 98 percent of all American cities reported a shortage in single-family dwellings.

The most vulnerable members of the transient families were the children. They suffered overcrowding in the home and in the classroom. The problems caused by the influx of pupils to both big-city and small-town schools were exacerbated by a growing shortage of teachers. Teachers' pay did not, in the war years, keep pace with wages in industry. Predictably, many teachers quit in order to seek more lucrative employment. In turn, the profession was unable to attract suitably qualified new recruits to fill their places. In response, understaffed school boards began demanding only part-time attendance from their pupils. Many youngsters dispensed with even a part-time education. An estimated one million youths dropped out of school in 1943.

The crisis in the classroom was identified as a primary cause of one of the wartime's most serious social problems — juvenile delinquency. At a time when the adult crime rate fell, there was an alarming increase not only in juvenile lawlessness but also in the teen-age tendency toward serious violent crime. According to reports from one New York City classroom, the issue of juvenile delinquency was linked, quite literally, with the teacher shortage. In this single instance, pupils had tortured their teacher to death.

Almost as alarming as the rise in teen-age violence was the upsurge in youthful promiscuity. Young girls could be seen making their own individual contribution to the war effort, loitering around military installations and bus depots, offering the ultimate in hospitality. The most celebrated of these "Victory girls" was seventeen-year-old Josephine Tencza. She was arraigned before a New York City court and charged with operating a vice ring employing some thirty girls, aged between twelve and fifteen.

The blame for such delinquency was placed not only upon the failure of the education system but also upon the collapse of family life and the disintegration of traditional communities.

A people in flux escaped the constrictions upon behavior once imposed by traditional culture and its socializing institutions. In the case of American youth, wartime social change further undermined what had been the most crucial source of behavioral guidance—parental authority. If millions of children lost their fathers to the services, then many also lost their mothers to industry. Before the war, the number of American women at work stood at 12 million. By 1943, this figure had risen to 17 million. In the past, women had been confined generally to the domestic service and clerical sectors of the job market; but now, because of the manpower shortage, they were absorbed into industry. Between 1940 and 1944 the number of women employed in manufacturing rose by over 140 percent. In that former all-male preserve, the steel industry, females came to constitute 10 percent of the work force.

Although by 1944 married women comprised 50 percent of the female work force, child-care facilities remained rudimentary. Federal funding for day-care centers met the needs of only 100,000 children (or 10 percent of those requiring supervision) while their mothers were at work. The rest remained unsupervised and undisciplined and entered the national consciousness as the "eight-hour orphans" and the "latch key children."

"Adolescents" disappeared and "teen-agers" took their place. Lester Markel, editor of the *New York Times Magazine*, began using the word *teen-ager* in various articles, but the term did not catch on with the public until after the war. Here was a new socioeconomic group, defined by age and by its newfound ability to consume. The group was ripe for exploitation by the worlds of fashion and entertainment. For example, in 1944 young people were delighted by the marketing of an invention of Biro, a Hungarian refugee in Argentina, a pen first called a Stratopen that used a ball bearing instead of a point and soon was known as a ball-point pen.

Because young girls wore short socks, they were called bobby-soxers. Disdaining the saddle shoes and cardigan sweaters of the swing generation, they wore loafers with flat soles, Sloppy Joe sweaters, and men's white shirts outside blue jeans. Their capacity for fads was not different from the middle-class adolescents of the 1930s; the only difference was in older people's inclination to indulge them. There was another change in teen-age fashion with the appearance of the zoot suit, which combined high-waisted trousers billowing to narrow cuffs with a swallowtail jacket, worn with a wide-brimmed felt hat, bow tie, and long watch chain. Such suits were taken both as a badge of independence and as a uniform to identify a gang. Zoot suits were also associated with ethnic minorities, who became targets for racial attacks. In the "Zoot Suit Riot" of 1943 in Los Angeles, mobs of servicemen and civilians attacked Mexican-American youths who were scapegoats for the large number of Mexicans moving into wartime jobs in California.

Dress designers began to get their ideas for women's clothes from military uniforms, a clear indication of where women's minds were. Eisenhower jackets were models for evening wraps or blouses with drawstring waists. Berets, based on those worn by British commandos, made stylish hats for daytime wear. Girls also wore copies of WAC hats decorated with sequins. One evening gown carried a huge, swooping Air Corps wing of gold lamé from the hip to the opposite shoulder across the breast. Taking its cue from cloth shortages, the Dido was an outside romper suit for play by day and for wearing as pajamas at night.

The war led to the erosion of ethnic solidarity in a number of ways. Not only were the numbers of migrants large but also many of them moved several times and over longer distances. The rate of migration was highest for young people between the ages of twenty and twenty-four. No one compiled statistics to show how this group was composed in terms of ethnic origins. Nevertheless, it is likely that many of these young people were attached to some ethnic group or other. They were the people most likely to set down roots in new communities. Thus, as Richard Polenberg explains in *One Nation Divisible* (1980), "the sense of ethnic attachment, which drew support from the fixed social structure of the immigrant community, waned as wartime mobility disrupted old neighborhoods."

Those institutions that encouraged immigrant culture, especially foreign-language newspapers and radio programs, began to decline. Moreover, to prevent the broadcast of subversive material, the Federal Communications Commission (FCC) required stations broadcasting foreign-language programs to approve scripts in advance, to monitor programs, and to investigate the backgrounds of radio personnel. These restrictions were troublesome to the radio stations. Not surprisingly, the

Workers assigned to special wartime duties in industry stroll amid the trees and buildings of their temporary homes around a production plant in Arlington, Virginia, in sight of the Washington Monument in the nation's capital. (Office of War Information; Library of Congress).

number of stations broadcasting programs in foreign languages declined from 205 in 1942 to 126 in 1948.

The foreign-language press also began to suffer as revenue declined from advertisements by steamship lines, foreign-exchange banks, and foreign governments. In addition, the foreign-language press relied on using copy verbatim from European papers. As the war interrupted the flow of foreign copy, foreign-language papers in America started to place more emphasis on domestic stories; and in this they had to compete with the more substantial English-language press. Thus, because of a whole series of factors, they began to lose much of their distinct character and appeal. Between 1940 and 1945, about 165 foreign-language publications, or 15 percent of the total, closed down.

Between 1939 and 1941, the war encouraged greater ethnic solidarity among immigrant groups; but from 1942 onwards, it did the reverse. Few immigrants could enter the country during the war; and with the rush of alien residents becoming naturalized citizens, the proportion of aliens fell sharply. Statistics on naturalization provide a good index of assimilation. Between 1934 and 1939, an average of 148,291 resident aliens were naturalized each year; between 1940 and 1945, the average was twice as high at 295,872. Thus 1.75 million aliens became American citizens in those six years, with almost 442,000 in 1944 alone. The federal government also devised a simplified naturalization procedure for aliens in the armed forces, waiving such requirements as residency for legal immigrants who were recommended by their superior officers.

Despite the way the federal government began to turn away from the New Deal and, in some instances, dismantle it, and the related Republican resurgence in Congress, throughout the war the state did frequently intervene to defend the citizen's welfare. However, these measures were applied with different intent from those implemented by the despised "long hairs" who had descended upon Washington in the 1930s. They were devised not with a view to transforming society on an a priori basis. Instead, they took the form of a series of improved responses to new social problems.

Congress first gave notice of its willingness to redress the shortcomings of boom-town life by passing the Community Facilities Act in 1940. This piece of legislation, popularly known as the Lanham Act, made federal funds available for the development of civic amenities and the provision of essential services in the boom towns. The Office of Defense, Health, and Welfare was established in November 1940 to develop programs financed by these allocations. In early 1943, this agency was transformed into the Office of Community Services (OCS). Of its two main branches, one was to provide social protection and was responsible for ensuring that each community had an adequate number of doctors, dentists, and teachers. The organization was also responsible for cleaning up the trailer parks and shanty towns and providing them with such amenities as child-care centers and kindergartens. The other branch was responsible for recreation. Its assignment was to provide the communities with adult-education centers, play parks, theaters, teen-age recreational centers, and the organization of outdoor activities.

To help alleviate the housing shortage, the National Housing Agency was set up in February 1942. Its initial objective was to analyze how and where resources should be allocated. In the first months of its existence, much of the agency's energy was expended in providing temporary shelter to migrant families. However, by the end of the war, federal spending on this problem reached $2.3 billion; and, with the help of the private sector, housing was provided for 9 million migrants.

To assist those who were unwilling, or unable, to purchase a home, the Office of Price Administration froze all rents in twenty defense areas in March 1942. To the chagrin of landlords who sought to exploit the housing shortage, the rent freeze was extended to three hundred areas in the following month. In all, an estimated 86 million tenants benefited from this freeze.

In the realm of health care, the most immediate beneficiaries of state spending were the millions of servicemen who were equipped with glasses and dentures, fed, often for the first time, on a nutritious, well-balanced diet, and nursed in sickness at federal expense. The families of those servicemen in the lower-paid grades also qualified for medical support. In all, one million service wives received state-assisted medical, hospital, and nursing care. In the boom towns, a Social Protection Division of the federal government was responsible for providing communities with doctors and dentists. The responsibility for building community health centers fell to the Public Health Service.

An embarrassing but wholly necessary feature on the boom-town landscape was the veneral-disease clinic. Thousands of these centers were set up across the country. The public was alerted to the dangers, symptoms, and treatment of the dread disease by pamphlets, films, and radio broadcasts, issued by the Social Protection Division and the Veneral Disease Control Division of the Public Health Service. Congress lent its support to the campaign. The May Act of July 1941 empowered authorities to close down brothels located near military installations. By 1944, the same fate had befallen red-light districts in some seven hundred American cities. In that same year, thirty states were requiring couples to undergo blood tests before marrying. Such was the determination of the various governments to curtail the spread of veneral disease. Unfortunately, the campaign met with only partial success. The rate of infection was higher among servicemen stationed at home than it was among those sent abroad.

Prohibitionists attempted to explain this embarrassing statistic by blaming booze. In search of a dry stick to beat the wets, they also ascribed the successful surprise attack on Pearl Harbor to servicemen's hangover. The attack came on Sunday morning when soldiers were supposedly sleeping off Saturday night's excesses. However, the public was not ready for another bout of abstinence. Nevertheless, three states (Kansas, Oklahoma, and Mississippi) did pass wartime laws prohibiting the sale of liquor.

By 1945 the federal government was spending $1.1 billion per annum on the nation's health. Despite this commitment, liberal reformers were unsuccessful throughout the war period in forcing an expansion of the rudimentary system of national health insurance. Any such proposals were quickly damned as a restraint of trade by the powerful American Medical Association. Its opposition was finally overcome not by Congress but by ship-building magnate Henry J. Kaiser. All of Kaiser's 125,000 shipyard workers were enrolled in a company health plan. By 1943 Kaiser was operating the largest prepaid medical insurance scheme in the United States. The American Medical Association held that Kaiser was acting in restraint of trade and took him to court. It also ostracized those of its members who treated Kaiser's employees. The battle in the courts ended with a Kaiser victory. In breaking the American Medical Association's monopoly, he opened the door to what, in postwar years, evolved into a sophisticated system of corporate welfare. He also encouraged the development of the then-embryonic Blue Cross and Blue Shield medical insurance plans.

Besides enjoying certain benefits of state subsidized health care, many new recruits were also offered opportunities in higher education

The port of New York was a prime point of departure for servicemen and materiel sent to Europe. So extensive was the supply of men and machines that the army had a veritable "navy" of its own by way of small craft to supplement the needs of its troop ships. (Library of Congress).

that were closed to those in civilian life. For instance, the army agreed to send several hundred thousand high-school graduates to college for two years before enrolling them at officers' candidate schools. In another scheme, the Army Specialized Training Program (ASTP), gifted recruits were sent to college for nine months to take courses in such subjects as engineering, foreign languages, and dentistry. The navy's U-12 program operated in a similar way, but its courses lasted for two years. By the end of 1943, the ASTP alone had 140,000 student soldiers on its rolls. This figure constituted a fraction of the total of individuals that eventually benefited from this veiled form of federal aid to education. As Geoffrey Perrett (1973) has estimated, "more than 1,000,000 young men in wartime received college degrees or credits towards degrees at the taxpayer's expense." Here was another example of social welfare in disguise.

As in the relationship between government and industry, the chief beneficiaries of state aid to education were the large institutions. The greatest rewards were reaped by those colleges awarded contracts by the Office of Scientific Research and Development (OSRD). Invariably, these were the institutions that already had established a reputation in the field of scientific research. Harvard, Columbia, the Massachusetts Institute of Technology, and the California Institute of Technology had the facilities and the expertise to cater to the requirements of the OSRD. In turn, the OSRD underwrote the cost of expanding these facilities and constructing new ones. Thus, while smaller colleges teetered on the brink of bankruptcy, these renowned seats of learning consolidated their position at the apex of the American educational system. Thus, also, began the collaboration between these colleges and (what would become known as) the military-industrial complex, an alliance for which college authorities would be pilloried by student radicals in the 1960s.

By far the most important and far-reaching wartime enactment of social legislation came in the form of the GI Bill of Rights. This measure was promoted by the American Legion, was passed unanimously by Congress in March 1944, and was signed into law by FDR in June 1944. The bill gave veterans priority in many sectors of the job market, provided them with occupational guidance, and gave them a monthly allowance until they found satisfactory work. In addition to federal aid, some twenty-one states gave, as a token of gratitude, their own bonuses to returning GIs. In all, these state bonuses amounted to some $2.4

billion. Of more lasting impact was the provision that authorized the Veterans Administration to guarantee 50 percent of all loans required by former servicemen for the purchasing of homes or the buying or setting up of farms or businesses. By 1955 the value of home loans granted to veterans amounted to $33 billion. If the householder died, then his family was supported by a government-subsidized life insurance plan. When he was buried, the state paid for the funeral and laid him to rest in a veterans' cemetery.

The doors to other institutions were also opened to him by the GI Bill. If a serviceman wished to complete his education, then the government would pay the full cost of tuition and provide supplementary allowances during the period of his enrollment. In all, nearly 8 million GIs learned a trade, took a degree, or simply completed high school at the taxpayers' expense. By 1955 the GI Bill had infused some $14.5 billion into the American educational system. As a result of the GI Bill of Rights, 16 million veterans plus their dependents had their lives irrevocably altered by governmental largess. Indeed, by 1950 it had touched the lives of approximately 33 percent of the population. They were the lawyers, teachers, doctors, dentists, artisans, and entrepreneurs of postwar America. As Geoffrey Perrett (1973) has stated, "they and their children are the bedrock of America's modern middle class."

The Citizens' War

The American declaration of war upon Japan received almost unanimous support from the people of the United States. Only one vote was cast against the declaration in Congress on December 8, 1941—that of the veteran pacifist Jeannette Rankin of Montana. Some days later, the motion declaring war upon Germany and Italy was passed without opposition. In the country as a whole a sense of outrage about Japanese treachery, a concomitant hatred of the enemy, an awareness of great danger, and a spirit of sacrifice united the citizenry in patriotic fervor. As thousands of young men hurried to recruiting stations, millions of citizens offered their services on the home front.

By February 1942, 5 million volunteers were enrolled in local organizations. This urge to contribute to the war effort gathered momentum throughout the spring. By April 1942, 6 million Americans were tending their "victory gardens." Because farmers needed to concentrate on feeding the armed services, Secretary of Agriculture Claude R. Wickard had recommended that civilians plant "victory gardens" of vegetables in every available plot, including backyards, derelict parking lots, and empty playgrounds. The most unusual sites were the zoo in Portland, Oregon, Ellis Island, and Alcatraz. By 1943 one-third of the country's fresh vegetables were being grown in 20 million "victory gardens." In the countryside, the Farm Security Administration launched its own campaign on the principle of providing "an acre for a soldier." The nation's yachtsmen joined the so-called hooligans' navy and went on submarine patrols. Forty thousand pilots enrolled in the Civil Air Patrol; 600,000 civilians joined the Air Warning Service. Thousands of others gave their time as auxiliary firemen and nurses. By midsummer 1942, 11,000 local defense councils had been established; and, in all, some 40 percent of the population was engaged in voluntary war service on the home front.

The War Production Board exploited this spirit of sacrifice by setting the public to work, salvaging scrap paper, scrap metal, and scrap rubber. The people were asked to "Give Till it Hurts," and, in the first year of the war, did so with an alacrity that surprised those who had asked them to "back the attack." War service volunteers not only salvaged rubber and metal but also the farm crops of 1942. In the first year of the war, recruitment to the armed services and the steady drift of the agricultural work force to munitions industries created a severe manpower shortage in the fields. Harvesting the crop of altruism and public spiritedness, the federal government appealed for volunteers. In response, a small army of workers from the YMCA, the High School Victory Corps, and the American Womens' Voluntary Service made up the shortfall in agricultural labor.

At times the citizenry proved overzealous in its urge to help the war effort. On the West Coast the blackout was enforced by the half brick and the fist. Mobs smashed the windows of illuminated premises, and beat up motorists who drove with headlights glaring.

As the first shock of war subsided and as the threat of aerial bombardment and invasion passed, war fever waned. Indeed, as 1942 progressed the public's mood turned sour. Bad news from the war front, rumors of inefficiency in the defense program, the effect of inflation and the unpopular measures devised to combat it provoked a general feeling of frustration and disappointment. This mood found its outlet in criticism of wartime agencies and open condemnation of what Geoffrey Perrett describes as "probably the most despised political body in twentieth-century American history," the Seventy-seventh Congress.

The change in public mood and growing dissatisfaction with the way the war was being run is perhaps best gauged by Gallup polls taken throughout 1942. In May 1942, polls indicated that in the November congressional elections the Democrats could expect gains of thirty-eight seats. By August, projected Democratic gains had fallen to eight seats. In September, Gallup polls were predicting Republican gains of twenty-one seats. In actuality, the Republicans took forty-four seats in a landslide victory.

By the time the new members took their seats, the home front was totally secure against enemy attack; and the economy was booming in synchronization with the faraway guns. It was clear, therefore, that American citizens would remain untouched by real deprivation. Unlike the citizens of all other belligerent nations, they would experience none of the war's catastrophic effects. Of course, the American people did suffer anxiety, loneliness, and grief. In the first year of the war, communities posted lists of combat casualties. However, this practice was quietly dropped after 1942. One constant reminder of the conflict's terrible aspect did remain. Families with members in active service displayed pennants bearing blue stars in their windows. The blue star was replaced by a golden one when the telegram brought news that a loved one would not be returning from overseas. While the possibility of bereavement was constant, the real threat of war remained in the abstract. Without nocturnal visitations from the Luftwaffe and without the pathetic spectacle of long armies of refugees, the American people were, as one commentator said, "fighting this war on imagination alone."

The relative security and real prosperity enjoyed by the American people served, inevitably, to dull that imagination. In order to sustain public commitment to the war effort, the government repeatedly called for renewed sacrifice, self-denial, and cooperation. It also strove to make each citizen feel capable of making a significant contribution to victory over the Axis powers. To this end, FDR spoke on the radio and told Americans, "Not all of us can have the privilege of fighting our enemies in distant parts of the world. But there is one front and one battle where everyone in the United States, every man woman and child is in action. That front is right here at home."

The scrap metal, paper, and rubber drives were organized upon this premise. So too were the "victory gardens." The Office of Civilian Defense led the campaign for gasoline and food conservation. Its campaign to encourage car sharing carried the slogan "An empty seat is a gift to Hitler." Its appeal to shoppers to buy only that which was necessary was reinforced by the message "Hoarders are on the same level as spies." Perhaps the most ambitious of the government's attempts to engage citizens in the war effort came with the bond drives. When the first bond issue was being organized, FDR's closest advisers urged him to institute a compulsory savings scheme. Secretary of the Treasury Henry Morgenthau disagreed. In his opinion, the bond sales afforded the government the perfect opportunity for actively involving the public on a voluntary basis. He won the day and, with the aid of the media, promoted bond sales by emphasizing the patriotic virtue of saving.

His strategy was only partly successful. While the seven bond drives raised a total of $135 billion, a disproportionate share of the sales went to big business, insurance companies, and the banks. Quotas allocated for private citizens were undersubscribed. Individual purchases accounted for but 25 percent of all sales, and the sale of bonds in the $25 to $50 range remained particularly disappointing. Eventually, the government resorted to the practice of manipulating public emotions in order to stimulate demand. On the eve of the fourth bond drive, news of the Battan death march, which actually had occurred two years previously, was at last released to the press.

By then, the American people perceived the war neither as a mortal threat to the homeland nor as a righteous crusade for democracy. It was, a *Fortune* magazine staged, seen simply as "a painful necessity." The American public's lack of a clear appreciation of the nation's war aims was revealed by one opinion poll conducted in 1942. Here nine out of ten interviewees failed to name one provision of the Atlantic Charter. The passage of time brought little in the way of enlightenment. A similar

Airplane parts hoisted high by cranes aboard ships that will take them from the port of New York to supply the European theater of war. (Library of Congress).

survey taken in 1944 indicated that four in ten Americans had no real understanding of what the war was about.

One fundamental cause of the public's incomprehension lay in Franklin Roosevelt's refusal to traffic in the idealistic phraseology favored by Woodrow Wilson in World War I. During World War II, there was little talk of making the world safe for democracy; there were few overt references to building some postwar international utopia. FDR's fundamental aim was to win the war as quickly as possible. He knew the limits of American altruism, and he was well aware of the dangers inherent in aggravating the spirit of isolationism that had shattered Woodrow Wilson's hopes. For the duration, he was "Dr. Win-the-War." "Dr. Win-the-Peace" would be a persona to be assumed at a later date.

If FDR failed to provide a clear-cut rationale for American involvement in the war, then so, too, did the governmental agencies from which such guidance might have come. Initially, FDR was wary of creating a ministry of propaganda. His reluctance was inspired by memories of the hate campaigns conducted by the Committee on Public Information during World War I. However, FDR was aware of the need for a centralized coordination and distribution of information. As the international crisis deepened throughout 1941, the people demanded details of day-to-day events, while Washington was overrun by newspapermen ever willing to accommodate this demand. By the time Japanese bombs fell on Pearl Harbor, newsmen were making daily rounds to the Division of Information in the Office of Emergency Management, the Office of Government Reports, and the Office of the Coordinator of Information. The most influenced of all these information services was the Office of Facts and Figures (OFF), set up in October 1941 under the direction of Archibald MacLeish, then librarian of Congress. This body was established as the prime source of information pertaining to the defense program. After Pearl Harbor, its responsibility was expanded to include the provision of basic factual details on the war effort at home and abroad. MacLeish was in agreement with FDR as to the function of the OFF. It was not to serve as a conduit for propaganda; it was not to implant ideas upon the collective consciousness. Instead, it was charged with the task of providing the American people with the factual material from which they could construct their own conception of how and why the war was being fought.

The OFF almost immediately fell foul of the nation's newspapers.

Editors and reporters resented having to rely upon OFF functionaries for their information. That information was often meager. Newsmen had to scan the special pamphlets that OFF writers devised if they wanted the facts on a given situation. Given the anti-Roosevelt sympathies of many of the leading newspapers, the facts carried in these pamphlets were often selected judiciously and used to criticize the administration for mismanaging the war effort. MacLeish also drew fire from members of his own staff, who doubted the efficacy of simply telling the truth. They and other experts in the fields of communications, psychology, and public relations argued that the national emergency necessitated the implementation of a program of democratic persuasion. MacLeish recognized democratic persuasion as a euphemism for propaganda.

His task was made even more difficult by his lack of control over other outlets of information. The State, War, and Navy departments, the coordinator of the inter-American affairs, the aforementioned Division of Information, and other agencies ignored MacLeish's appeals for a coordinated response to news dissemination. This discordant orchestra of voices drew much criticism from a special White House task force. In March 1942, this investigative team told FDR that bulletins and press releases were being published not with the aim of enlightening the public but with the goal of glorifying the agencies from whence they came. It concluded that intermural rivalry prevented cooperation between the various departments and gave issue to a welter of confusing and contradictory statements.

In the collective judgment of this team, what was required was a new agency with explicit authority to administer the dissemination of news and information. In response, FDR issued an executive order on June 11, 1942, creating the Office of War Information (OWI). Its director was veteran journalist and radio broadcaster Elmer Davis. He and his staff were called upon by FDR to "coordinate the dissemination of war information by all federal agencies" and via the various forms of mass media "to facilitate the development of an informed and intelligent understanding, at home and abroad, of the status and the progress of the war effort and of the war policies, activities, and aims of the government."

Some of the old problems posed by interagency rivalry were solved simply by integrating the OFF, the Office of Economic Stabilization's Information Division, and the Office of Government Reports with the

Domestic News Branch (DNB) of the new agency. Simultaneously, the Foreign Information Service attached to the Office of the Coordinator of Information became the Overseas Branch of the OWI. The primary function of the OWI lay in keeping the public abreast of the progress of the war effort. The responsibility here lay with the OWI's Domestic News Branch. Its officials worked round the clock, collecting the data and pronouncements on policy that emanated from the multitude of civilian government departments. From these myriad sources, the DNB pieced together the press releases that fed the public's appetite for news. For news from the combat zones, the people had to rely upon the military departments. Not surprisingly, the War and Navy departments were rarely forthcoming in providing this information. In the face of their obstinate resistance to Davis's appeals for a more candid approach, relations between the OWI and the service chiefs remained strained.

If the OWI were responsible for keeping the public updated on developments on the domestic front, it was also charged with the task of sustaining the public's interest in, and commitment to, the war effort. A multitude of programs were devised to boost morale and encourage greater efforts in the field of vigilance, self-sacrifice, and cooperation. The OWI's messages were delivered by movies, radio, newspapers, posters, billboards, and pamphlets. On the issue of propaganda, Davis shared FDR and MacLeish's preference for presenting an unlaundered version of the truth. It was argued that through the presentation of factual information, people would draw their own conclusions on the righteousness of the fight and the necessity of contributing to swift victory. To this end, Davis assembled a group of predominantly liberal writers who endeavored to set forth the basic details of the origins of the war, the issues involved in the struggle, and the United States's objectives after victory.

However, the advertising executives employed by OWI did not share the intellectuals' faith in the reasoning powers of the American public. They were, of course, committed to telling the truth but, as they recommended, only "in terms that will be understood by all levels of intelligence." To the OWI's writers, the war was being fought to prepare mankind for the world envisaged by those who framed the Atlantic Charter. To the advertising men, the battle was joined to preserve the world encapsulated in the drawings of Norman Rockwell. In time, the homespun image won out against the high-minded ideal. In April 1943, the writers resigned from the OWI en masse, voicing their disgust at the agency's efforts "to soft-soap the American public."

If by April 1943 the OWI was drawing scorn from disaffected liberals, then it was also the target for vehement criticism from conservatives in Congress. From the onset, its opponents had objected to the OWI's mandate "to facilitate the development of an informed and intelligent understanding . . . of the war policies, activities, and aims of government." To conservative politicians, this was construed as a license to propagandize in behalf of the Democratic party. The agency was accused of lionizing FDR, providing apologies for his domestic policies, and preparing the electorate for his 1944 campaign for a fourth term of office. The campaign against OWI reached its climax on June 18, 1943, when Republicans and southern Democrats in Congress voted to stop all funds to the Domestic Branch. The Senate Appropriations Committee sealed its fate by granting it a mere $3 million, none of which, according to the terms of the grant, was to be spent on publications, movies or radio scripts. When Congress reduced this sum further by $250,000, the Domestic Branch was effectively rendered redundant. In wielding its ax, Congress had, in the words of historian John Morton Blum (1976), "returned to the media and to those who bought advertising space the whole field of domestic propaganda."

Advertising During the War

At the time of Pearl Harbor, it was widely expected that war would bring a decline in living standards and a severe shortage in basic domestic goods and services. In such circumstances, what would be the role of advertising? What was an industry committed to persuading people to spend more than they could afford upon more than they needed to do at a time when conservation and self-denial were at a premium? One Office of War Information executive offered this answer: "The job of advertising is not to influence [the citizen] to the point of spending his money for a 'product' but to invigorate, instruct and inspire him as a functioning unit in his country's greatest effort." The adman had thus to serve his country's need by making the war itself the "product" that he sold to the people. Simultaneously, he had to satisfy his corporate clients' future economic need to keep their products in the public eye throughout the war.

He achieved these aims by associating his clients' brand names with the war effort. It was hoped that the advertisers' displays of patriotism would reinforce bonds of consumer loyalty that would, in turn, reap dividends in the postwar period. Thus, bond drives were promoted by, advertisements in newspapers placed by banks, department stores, and other public-spirited businesses. The Ford Motor Company exhorted people to greater sacrifices with the slogan "Truly there's a great day coming." Undoubtedly, the authors of this prose hoped that in the coming great day, Americans would recall the patriotic efforts of the Ford Motor Company.

When it came to direct advertising, manufacturers strove to establish a firm link between their products and the war effort. For example, the American Tobacco Company, makers of Lucky Strike cigarettes, began packaging their product in a plain white carton. Their marketing slogan, "Lucky Strike Green has gone to war!" was based upon the fiction that the supply of chrome green used on the cigarette packet had been diverted for use in the war effort. In truth, the new plain white package was a marketing ploy devised to attract women smokers.

As we have already observed, in the summer of 1943 Congress passed the responsibility for disseminating domestic propaganda onto the advertising industry. To meet the challenge, big business set up its own War Advertising Council. Despite the shortages of many consumer goods—such as radios, refrigerators, and automobiles—and despite the constant appeals for self-denial, conservation, and revenue saving, Madison Avenue's business was booming. Instead, even as Allied troops were assembling for the invasion of France, the advertising industry was recording its largest budget in history.

By the time the troops landed in Normandy, Madison Avenue had switched its attack to preparing the public for a postwar boom. A typical tactic was employed in the advertising campaign for Johnston and Murphy footwear: "When our boys come home . . . among the finer things of life they will find ready to enjoy will be Johnston and Murphy shoes. Quality unchanged." According to Madison Avenue, it was for the right to enjoy such material comforts that the GI was fighting. The American way of life depicted by the advertising agencies was one

The Andrews Sisters (Maxine, Patty, and Laverne), perhaps America's prime chanteuses of swing music and boogie-woogie during the 1940s, were regularly pressed into service to boost morale at home and abroad with upbeat musical interludes in such privates-on-parade movies as this Abbott and Costello vehicle, *Buck Privates* (1942). (Universal Pictures; Museum of Modern Art Film Stills Archive).

based upon consumption, comfort, and materialism. When an advertisement carried the rhetorical question "Is This Worth Fighting For?" it presented a picture of an old-fashioned living room with a blazing fire and a beautiful pinewood decor. There was no mention of the four freedoms and no attempt to contrast Nazi tyranny with democratic modes of government. In the words of John Morton Blum, what advertising prepared people for was "a brave new world of worldly goods."

Thus, if Americans lacked a clear conception of war aims, it was partly because government and propaganda failed to provide them with the necessary guidance. However, the fault also lay with the American people. The impression gained from the most recent secondary literature on the home front is that the American citizen made a determined effort to ignore the war and to carry on in a state of willful obliviousness to its broader issues. As Richard Polenberg (1972) avers, "as the initial wave of patriotic emotion passed, as sacrifices became more demanding, as the danger of invasion disappeared and victory grew more certain, people became more likely to look out for themselves. The longer the war lasted, the more the balance shifted from public and collective to private and personal concerns." Geoffrey Perrett (1973) concurs, "Community involvement in the war followed the same curve as war production, paralleling its spectacular rise and subsequent decline."

It would be erroneous to say that Americans settled down to live normal lives as their enthusiasm for the war effort waned. In the twelve years prior to Pearl Harbor, normality had been characterized by austerity and poverty. In wartime, Americans wanted to enjoy the material benefits of full employment and high wages. Thus, they came to regard such war emergency measures as extended taxation and rationing as violations of the citizens' inalienable right to spend their money as they chose.

Despite rationing, millions of Americans found ways of exercising that right. It was estimated that between 25 and 50 percent of all business was conducted on the black market. Perhaps it was a legacy of national prohibition or perhaps it was simply a manifestation of the American tendency toward anarchistic individualism, but there was no social stigma attached to dealing on the black market. Whatever the cause of this petty infraction of the law, it was symbolic of the triumph of self-interest over the appeals to sacrifice in the name of the national interest.

If the shortage of gasoline curtailed the citizens' mobility, it forced them to rediscover the delights of inner-city night life. Downtown bars, nightclubs, dance halls, theaters, and cafes enjoyed a popularity they had not known since the 1920s. So too did bootleg liquor. At a time when there was no production of alcoholic liquor, consumption increased by 30 percent. According to Geoffrey Perrett (1973), "by the fall of 1942 . . . the country looked as if it were out on a permanent celebration." The Americans were spending their way out of the psychological depression that war threatened to impose upon society. Inevitably, the federal government intervened to take its cut by levying a 30 percent tax upon live entertainment. A collective cry of outrage greeted this measure, and forced the government to reduce its take to 20 percent.

The merrymaking continued through 1943 and reached a climax in the summer of 1944. By then the Allies were ashore in Normandy, and there was talk of the war being over by October. The blackout was lifted; and, with gasoline more plentiful, the coastal resort towns came back to life. The motor car also brought business back to the racetrack. The mutual machines at the nation's racetracks took $1 billion in bets in 1944, which was two and a half times the sum taken in 1940. In California, legal betting at the one functioning track amounted to an average of $420,000 per day. Illegal gambling operating via bartenders, barbers, and the like was estimated at $10 million per day.

The simple act of spending seems to have become a leisure pastime in itself. As one Philadelphia jeweler explained, "people are crazy with money. They don't care what they buy. They purchase things . . . just for the fun of spending." To cater to this need, there appeared what was to become a permanent feature of the American urban and suburban landscape—the supermarket. In 1939 there were only 4,900 of these monuments to consumerism in the United States. Despite the wartime scarcity of building materials, by 1944 some 16,000 had been constructed.

In the summer and fall of 1944, it was quite possible for Americans to forget that there was a war being fought in Europe and Asia. Rationing restrictions were still being enforced, yet the total of all goods and services available to citizens was greater than in 1940. However, the harsh reality of war reasserted itself with a vengeance just as the people were preparing to celebrate what would be the last Christmas of the war. The Battle of the Bulge (launched by von Rundstedt on December 16, 1944) put overconfident predictions about an imminent German collapse into the correct perspective and dispelled some of the complacency that had characterized the mood on the home front. Manufacturers, who had started to produce for the domestic market, were ordered to reapply their efforts to defense programs. The government attempted to call a halt to the revelry of the previous months by closing the racetracks and imposing a midnight curfew on bars, nightclubs, and theaters. The majority of Americans objected to this infringement upon their right to pursue happiness. Rather than reduce their intake of alcohol, they simply speeded up their rate of consumption. At midnight they spilled out onto the streets to do in public parks and doorways what they would otherwise have attempted in the dark corners of dance halls and nightclubs. Others found sanctuary in that great American institution, the speakeasy. Like national prohibition, the curfew order failed to reinforce public morality. Instead, it brought into sharp focus the tendency of some Americans toward hedonistic excess.

The curfew lasted for three months. By the time it was lifted, Americans were concerned not with winning the war, which was a foregone conclusion, but with preserving affluence in the face of an expected postwar depression. To defend their wartime gains and ensure job security, workingmen ripped up the no-strike pledge. By the spring of 1945, industry was hamstrung by the impact of between thirty to forty strikes a day. GIs were still laying down their lives as workingmen laid down their tools. Yet those in dispute saw nothing treacherous in their actions. They were simply fighting on the home front to achieve the war aim that had inspired the country throughout hostilities—namely, to enjoy the benefits of the advertising man's brave new world of worldly goods.

[6]

LOVE'S LABORS WON
Labor, Reform, and Dissent

Labor in World War II

THE MASS UNEMPLOYMENT and abject poverty of the Great Depression were reduced significantly by the economic revival accompanying World War II. The demand for labor suddenly soared following the election of 1940. In 1940, according to official statistics, 8.12 million people were unemployed, or 14.6 percent of the civilian labor force. Unemployment fell sharply in the war from 5.56 million (9.9 percent) in 1941 to 670,000 in 1944 (1.2 percent), and then rose slightly in 1945 to 1.04 million (1.9 percent).

Those who had work were more prosperous than ever before. Between 1941 and 1945 the percentages of family income increases across the five main socioeconomic groups from poorest to richest were, respectively, 68, 59, 36, 30, and 20 percents. The share of national income owned by the richest 5 percent fell from 23.7 percent to 16.8 percent. The number of families with incomes over $5,000 went up more than four times.

Nevertheless, a significant proportion of people remained poor. In 1944 about 10 million workers, about one-quarter of those in industry,

241

earned less than 60 cents an hour or $24 for a forty-hour week. The
federal administration opposed allowing employers to provide increases
up to 65 cents (instead of 50 cents as then allowed). Certain sections of
the population suffered, notably those living on social security pensions,
clerical workers who did not have any opportunity to work overtime,
and craftsmen whose special skills were of no account when factories
converted to unskilled war production. These were the people who were
"not able to live the way Americans ought to live," as Senator Claude
Pepper remarked to Bernard Baruch.

Workers whose wages had remained static since 1937 swiftly began
to press for improved pay and conditions. A National Defense Mediation
Board was created by FDR to try and lessen industrial unrest, but the
government was becoming increasingly disaffected with labor demands
and more hostile to working-class militancy. When 12,000 members of
the United Auto Workers struck at the North American Aviation factory
in Los Angeles, federal troops were dispatched to take over the site.
Elsewhere, conservative politicians and newspapers decried the wave of
strikes as "treacherous" and "Red."

Moreover, unprecedented wartime production led to a level of involvement by the federal government in relations between management
and labor that the New Deal had never achieved. By bringing the unions
into the war effort and by presenting itself as a benevolent intermediary,
the federal government embarked on a program that would profoundly
affect the organs of the American labor movement.

As was usual for the Roosevelt administration, the crucial tactic was
the creation of a new agency. The National War Labor Board (NWLB),
established in January 1942, comprised four representatives from labor,
four from business, and four civilians. The first steps toward gaining the
cooperation of the unions were taken in the two weeks after Pearl
Harbor, when representatives from business and labor met to pledge
that there would be no lockouts and no strikes for the duration of the
war. The main threat to this tenuous peace lay in management's assault

Gordon Parks's classic photograph of two women welders at the Landers, Frary,
and Clark plant in New Britain, Connecticut, taken in June 1943 remains a
tribute to the unity of purpose of workers on the home front in World War II.
Generosity and determination are reflected on the first woman's face, optimism
and repose on the second. (Office of War Information; Library of Congress).

upon, and labor's defense of, the union shop. In the summer of 1942, the NWLB defused tension by formulating a policy that guaranteed "maintenance of union membership." In accordance with this agreement, each worker was allowed fifteen days to resign from his union; thereafter, he would remain enrolled until the termination of the contract between union and business. Management was not to discriminate against union members, and unions were to recruit only as a means of maintaining membership levels.

"Maintenance of membership" provided that neither labor nor management could take advantage of the wartime emergency to advance its own cause. Although the union continued to act as the bargaining agent, new employees could choose to join, or not to join, the union, as they preferred. Those workers who were union members could not give up their membership without losing their jobs. Thus, management could not break the union by taking on many new and, perhaps, temporary workers to displace the old. But labor could not exploit the living of new workers as a means of forcing newcomers to join. Just how much middle ground was occupied by the maintenance-of-membership compromise is shown by the fact that of about 6.5 million additions to the labor force, 3.5 million decided to join unions and 3 million decided not to.

At the same time as it was negotiating maintenance of membership, the NWLB was also prevailed upon to address itself to the highly sensitive issue of wage fixing. In July 1942, the issue was forced by a strike involving those who worked in the nation's smaller steel mills. They were demanding a wage increase of $1 per day. When called upon to arbitrate, the NWLB took as its gauge the 15 percent rise in the cost of living for the period January 1, 1941, to May 1942. It then ruled that wage claims were legitimate where salaries had not kept pace with the rate of inflation. The workers in dispute had had a pay rise since January 1, 1942, but it had been less than the level of inflation. Therefore, to redress the imbalance, they were entitled to a rise of 5.5 percent, or 44 cents, per day. With the dispute thus settled, representatives of national labor organizations agreed that, thereafter, the so-called Little Steel principle would apply to all disputes. However, the 15 percent ceiling would not affect wage increases that were decided as a result of free collective bargaining between management and labor.

The Little Steel agreement was a forward step in the war against inflation. Because of his anxiety about alienating labor, Roosevelt was unwilling to sanction any further moves. However, in the face of the ever-rising cost of living—it rose another 2.6 points between May and October 1942—the president closed all loopholes in the Little Steel formula by extending it to all wage increases. Then, in April 1942, he tightened control by relieving the NWLB of its authority to revise the Little Steel agreement.

If labor was willing to accept such financial stringency, it was because the wage ceiling applied only to hourly rates of pay. While hourly rates were being held down thus, incentive bonuses, overtime pay, and fringe benefits remained unrestricted. As a result, average take-home pay actually rose by 70 percent during the war.

Safe from open-shop drives and economic recession, organized labor increased its membership. During World War II, trade-union membership rose from 8.69 million in 1941 to 12.56 million in 1945. This included 5.17 million in the AFL in 1941, rising to 6.89 million in 1945, and 2.65 million in the CIO in 1941, rising to 3.92 million in 1945. Although the unions had obtained a previously inconceivable level of protection and security, they had abandoned labor's most effective bargaining tool—the strike. As a result, the bureaucratic and autocratic trends that appeared in unions in the late 1930s were accelerated by the new alliance of government administrator, employer, and union boss. In *Labor's War at Home* (1982), Nelson Lichtenstein argues that the protection offered to the quiescent union leadership by FDR's administration "reinforced the ideological commitment that most CIO leaders already had to the mobilization policies of the president, but also trapped them in a Rooseveltian political consensus that soon put them at odds with the immediate interests of their rank and file."

However, workers on the shop floor, and especially in the nation's coal mines, were far from enthusiastic about the suggestion that they give up their most powerful weapon. A succession of sudden, unofficial, wildcat strikes plagued industry throughout World War II, despite the efforts of union leaders to enforce the no-strike pledge. "Workers who engaged in unofficial strikes," writes James R. Green in *The World of the Worker* (1980), "were not necessarily unpatriotic or unwilling to make sacrifices for the war effort; they simply refused to allow management to abuse them by taking advantage of the war situation."

There was, of course, one notable exception to the cozy relationship between the government and the upper echelons of organized labor. In October 1942, John L. Lewis withdrew the United Mine Workers from the CIO—the very body his union had helped to create. The miners' leader rejected the uncritical stance of Phil Murray, Sidney Hillman, and the other union leaders toward the government, not because it smacked of class collaboration, but rather because it conflicted with what Lewis considered to be the conventional—or bread-and-butter—concerns of trade unionism. Ironically, by holding tight to traditional voluntarist principles, Lewis became an important source of militant opposition to the president's mobilization of industry.

However, it was among the rank and file that the greatest wartime militancy originated. Nearly 2 million workers were involved in 3,752 wildcat strikes during 1943. When miners walked out in Pennsylvania, Lewis involved himself in the revolt and led a long and bitter confrontation with the Roosevelt administration. "The mine worker is at a great disadvantage working under the present wage structure," Lewis argued at a wage conference in New York City. "His compensation is insufficient to enable him to maintain his living standards, and it contains no protection against the vicissitudes of tomorrow." One study found that food prices in mining towns had risen by an average of 124.6 percent since August 1939. Lewis wanted an increase of $2 per day. Roosevelt himself was unimpressed by the miners' claims of hardship. Reacting angrily to the stoppages, Roosevelt condemned them as "not mere strikes against employers of this industry to enforce collective bargaining demands. They are strikes against the United States government itself." On May 1, 1943, he ordered troops to take possession of the nation's bituminous mines. Lewis, knowing that the prospect of federal management appalled the mine owners almost as much as did the strikes, preempted FDR's orders by calling on his men to return to work while negotiations progressed. In the end, the miners were awarded $1.50 per day and certain fringe benefits.

Meanwhile, in Congress, conservatives were drafting the Smith Connally War Labor Disputes Bill that Congress passed over FDR's veto in June 1943. The bill allowed strikes only after a secret ballot held after a thirty-day "cooling-off" period; it provided for criminal prosecution of individuals proposing strikes; and it forbade union contributions to political campaigns. The public opposed strikes; yet, despite the government's skill in devising more flexible wage formulas while controlling prices, there was almost persistent industrial unrest in the last years of the war. Nevertheless, the NWLB handled 18,000 labor disputes, and only about one-seventh of one percent of working time was lost during the war because of strikes.

During World War II, 1.15 million blacks entered the armed services; and many fought overseas. However, since the armed forces were totally segregated, the black press continued to emphasize similarities between fascist persecution of the Jews in Europe and racial segregation in the United States. Throughout the war, the Red Cross kept "white blood" and "black blood" in separate containers.

Although chiefs of staff would have preferred to think the armed services were immune from racial conflict, they came under increasing pressure to abandon their ironclad segregation code of 1941. By the terms of this code, blacks could not enlist in the Marine or Air Corps. In the navy, blacks could serve only in menial tasks. The Army did admit blacks but maintained segregated training facilities and units and retained black troops primarily in a supportive capacity rather than in combat. Black officers were assigned to so-called Negro units and had to serve under white superiors. No black officer could ever be superior to a white in the same unit. The army rationalized this policy partly on the sophistry that blacks were poor fighters, partly on the grounds that the army was not a laboratory for social experiments, and partly in the belief that integration would destroy the morale of white soldiers. The War Department insisted that it could not ignore the social relationships between negroes and whites which have been established by the American people through custom and habit." However, as the numbers of black soldiers increased sevenfold, from 100,000 in 1941 to 700,000 in 1944, so did their dissatisfaction with military segregation.

Black recruits came primarily from the North because southern blacks were usually neither sufficiently healthy nor well educated enough to pass induction tests. Northern blacks were less likely to accept Jim Crow. Black leader Edgar Brown advised FDR in a letter of May 20, 1942, how "many of these young people have lived all of their lives in New York, Detroit, Philadelphia, Chicago and other metropolitan areas where their civil rights have never before been abridged." Thus gradually (and reluctantly) chiefs of staff came to accept that military segregation was wasteful of manpower, that it was exposing the armed services to liberal criticisms, and that it was depressing morale of an ever larger section of the army. Somewhat shamefaced, the army began to use blacks in combat; and the navy introduced a program of cautious integration. Nevertheless, the army remained totally segregated. The agitation for integration led Army Chief of Staff George C. Marshall to declare, "My God! My God! . . . I don't know what to do about this race question in the army. I tell you frankly, it is the worst thing that we have to deal with. . . . we are getting a situation on our hands that may explode right in our faces."

The Great Migration of blacks from south to north, which had started in 1915, partly stilled by the depression, resumed as southern blacks sought new opportunities in the North. During the 1940s, 1.24 million blacks left the South.

In the North blacks could vote and there was not the same blatant segregation of blacks and whites as existed in the South. In fact, in Chicago a larger proportion of blacks than whites went to the polls. Nevertheless, the war and renewed migration upset the delicate balance of institutional racism in South and North. As a result, race relations became most tense in the crucial areas of housing, transportation, employment, and military service.

In Chicago, blacks were excluded from some eleven square miles of residential districts either through restrictive covenants (under which householders agreed neither to sell nor to lease property to blacks) or by informal agreements by landlords and real estate operators. As to employment, blacks were restricted to the dirtiest and least desirable jobs, partly because of color prejudice, partly because of inadequate training, and partly because of opposition from trade unions. Thus, in Chicago blacks accounted for 8 percent of the labor force and 22 percent of the city's unemployed.

The number of blacks working in industry, public utilities, and transportation increased from 700,000 in 1940 to 1.45 million in 1944. In the same period, the number of blacks working for the federal government rose from 60,000 to over 200,000. Despite continuing resistance to giving blacks highly skilled jobs or supervisory roles, those who worked as skilled workers or foremen doubled during the war. At the same time almost 550,000 black workers joined labor unions, usually those affiliated with the CIO.

Whereas white migration was at its peak in 1943, black migration peaked in 1945. Moreover, once blacks began to move, they did so in greater proportions than whites and tended to settle permanently in their new homes. The prime centers of black migration were usually centers of war production, such as Chicago and Detroit in the North; Norfolk, Charleston, and Mobile in the South; and Los Angeles, San Francisco, and San Diego on the West Coast. In the period 1940–44, the total population of the ten largest centers of wartime production increased by 19 percent; but the black population in these areas rose by 49 percent.

Discrimination against blacks in defense industries was somewhat curbed by the persistent need for extra manpower. Unions that excluded blacks found it difficult to sustain such open racism when the federal government announced that it would refuse to certify them as the accredited agent for collective bargaining unless they accepted minorities. Also, in 1943 the War Labor Board outlawed wage differences based exclusively on race.

White workers looked on askance as blacks joined them on the factory floor and dreaded that they might lose their cherished illusion of superiority. The white workers protested the upgrading of blacks by walking out, beating up black workers (as shipyard workers did in Mobile, Alabama), or going on strike (as trolley-car workers did in Philadelphia). White workers in a munitions plant in Baltimore stopped work rather than share washroom and cafeteria facilities with blacks. Railroad unions tried to protect their white members by insisting on a union contract that restricted both the jobs open to blacks and their chances of promotion.

What did the federal government do? In Philadelphia the government dispatched federal troops to run the trolley cars, thereby persuading the strikers to give up the dispute and go back to work. However, in the other cases, the government responded timidly, settling differences by compromise rather than with justice. In Mobile, the Fair Employment Practices Committee (FEPC) agreed to a segregation of the shipyards in which blacks could work in certain categories, such as welders, riggers, and riveters, but not in others, such as electricians, machine operators, or pipe fitters. In Baltimore, the FEPC allowed a munitions company to construct a larger cafeteria and washroom and to assign whites and blacks separate spaces at opposite ends of the rooms. As Louis Ruchames shows in *Race, Jobs, and Politics* (1948), where the government thought intervention to promote equal opportunity might threaten war production, it took no action. Thus, the railroad unions deliberately ignored an FEPC order against discrimination and retained their restrictive contract until the Supreme Court declared it unconstitutional in December 1944. The movement of so many people to only a few centers led to especially heightened tension over housing. In certain northern cities, black ghettos were filled well beyond capacity and began to burst beyond their boundaries, thus upsetting traditional lines of demarcation. White householders, disturbed at the prospect of being engulfed by a black tide, took matters into their own hands. However, when they tried to stop blacks moving into federal housing projects, they received the appropriate adverse publicity. In Buffalo, New York, threats of violence induced the government to cancel plans for a housing project. In February 1942, a mob of whites armed with rocks and clubs menaced fourteen black families and deterred them from moving into the Sojourners Truth Homes in Detroit until April, when they were protected by a police escort.

The worst riots since 1919 occurred in 1943 as whites, enraged by the black penetration of formerly white neighborhoods, took the law into their own hands. Troops were called in to restore order in Mobile after a riot broke out when black workers were promoted in a shipyard. Two people died after a disturbance in Beaumont, Texas; and a small-scale riot in Harlem was sparked off by rumors that a black soldier had been shot by a black policeman. By far the worst incident took place in Detroit, where thirty-four people died in a riot after a fist fight between a black man and a white man quickly spread. Moreover, police brutality toward blacks in the Detroit riot stunned the nation. Seventeen blacks had died at the hands of the police, and there was a preponderance of blacks arrested over whites.

Persistent industrial unrest mirrored the enormous changes that the work force underwent during World War II. Masses of new workers were introduced into basic industry to meet wartime production demands. Eight million women became wage earners, thereby increasing their proportion in the work force from 25 percent to 36 percent. The war shattered many ideas about the woman's place being in the home, as "Rosie the Riveter" went to work in shipyards, munitions plants, and lumber mills. Through the NWLB, several unions obtained equal-pay clauses in contracts to protect the new female workers (of whom 75

"And in my spare time . . ." proclaims the mother of little children who is also a dab hand at ship repairs in this cartoon by Bob Barnes satirizing society's expectations of women pressed into service on the American home front as they still managed their family responsibilities. (Library of Congress).

percent were married). However, the male leadership of the AFL and CIO were less determined when it came to actually fighting wage discrimination in the factories. At the end of the war, women's earnings in manufacturing were still less than two-thirds of those of men.

The foothold obtained by women and blacks in the core production sectors of the economy was of vital importance to the future of the women's and civil rights movements, but it also created difficulties for labor. Most of the new workers had no trade-union experience. While this undoubtedly contributed to the spontaneous character of many wildcat strikes that employers and union officials found difficult to contain, the volatility of the work force tended to undermine the primary work groups of long-term employees, who had previously provided much of the base so crucial to the CIO's advances in the 1930s. More than 15 million workers changed jobs, as companies, always anxious to increase already soaring profit margins, competed vigorously for labor. In this unstable environment, militants found it virtually impossible to build organized alternatives to the burgeoning bureaucratic machinery of the mainstream trade unions.

Employers looked to the union bosses to police their members and maintain the high production levels. In one case, the president of the United Rubber Workers, Sherman Dalrymple, expelled seventy-four workers for having taken part in strikes at Goodyear and the General Tire and Rubber Company. Without union cards, the workers were then fired by the companies under the maintenance-of-membership agreement that obliged firms not to employ workers out of favor with the union. In addition, as *Business Week* reported, "General and Goodyear are expected to notify the appropriate local draft boards of the dismissals, and the change in occupational status may subject them to reclassification."

The CIO's commitment to Roosevelt's administration was increased a stage further in 1943 with the creation of the Political Action Committee (PAC). Headed by Sidney Hillman of the Amalgamated Clothing Workers, PAC endeavored to mobilize working-class support for the president in the forthcoming election campaign of 1944. Spending $1.32 million and obtaining endorsements from every constituent union, the CIO was credited with a key role in securing FDR's victory. However, the political importance of trade unions to the Democratic party had been declining since the early 1940s. As the end of the war drew near, a number of factors cast grave doubts on the hopes that union leaders held for an equitable postwar alliance among business, labor, and government.

Despite the remarkable militancy of certain sections of workers, as a group workers exhibited far more patriotism and support for the government than had their counterparts in World War I. Many radicals seemingly relegated the class struggle at home to second place behind the fight against fascism abroad. In contrast to the determined stand of Eugene Debs's Socialist party in 1918, the Communist party took a militant prowar posture once Hitler had invaded Russia in 1941. Even as the conservative forces in the nation were mobilizing against them, Communist leaders approved of the federal suppression of their Trotskyite rivals and opposed workers who rejected the no-strike pledge. Denied any radical political alternative, the working class soon proved as responsive to claims of Communist "totalitarianism" as they had to nazism and fascism. The experience of welfare capitalism in the twenties and the New Deal in the thirties had apparently been as effective as overt repression in keeping Americans innoculated against radicalism. Even when workers episodically halted the wheels of industry to demand their rights (an enormous wave of wildcat and other strikes erupted again when wartime restrictions were relaxed in 1945–46), "the government" remained peculiarly separated from "the management" in most workers' minds.

The development of organized labor in the 1930s had helped to dampen class consciousness. According to labor historian Nelson Lichtenstein (1982), the experience of trade unions during World War II "formed a crucial stage in the transition from their institutionally fluid, socially aggressive character in the 1930s to the relative accommodation and bureaucratic stability of the postwar years." The support given by most union leaders to the government in this era allowed for a significant increase in numerical strength. By 1945, approximately 36 percent of the nonagricultural labor force was organized. However, the power of the labor movement as a whole was diluted as a result of various changes in policy and structure. Internal debate and grass-roots influence were stifled by the birth of a cohesive autocracy of labor in the postwar years. Union leaders pointed to the improved standards of living enjoyed by their members and the influence that they exerted on government. It is true that union membership brought with it some considerable economic advantages over other workers (a trend that grew rapidly in the following decades); but with the majority of labor still unorganized, this tended to increase working-class divisions instead of solidarity. Similarly, with union cooperation less important once the war ended, business leaders and government officials were ready to withdraw many of the basic concessions granted during the New Deal. Roosevelt and his successor, Harry Truman, found that it was more important to retain the political support of conservative southern Democrats than it was to oblige union leaders who, by now, were committed to supporting the Democratic party.

Radio in World War II

World War II was the first war Americans followed through broadcasting. It was a radio war, just as the war in Vietnam would be a television war. Since radio drew a mass audience, it contributed to the shaping of the public's response to events during the war. Radio news was quite extensive, even in its coverage of the war before Pearl Harbor. The way that radio brought the news and actual sounds of the conflict in Europe into so many American households must have been a factor in countering any inclination toward isolationism—to shut the door and forget the noise. Yet, nearly two decades of expansion and consolidation had proved that Americans preferred an open door on the sounds of as many events as possible.

Since America was technically neutral when World War II began, the news organization of CBS and NBC were ideally placed to offer American listeners a commentary on the war as seen from all sides. Eyewitness accounts of the air raids on London came from Ed Murrow of CBS, who presented a nightly "This is London" report, while William L. Shiver reported from Berlin. NBC tried to offer similar coverage of the early stages of the war. Then radio recorded the actual entry of America into the fight. Sunday afternoon programs on December 7, 1941, were suddenly interrupted at 2:31 P.M. with a news report about the Japanese attack. Subsequently, American broadcasting was rapidly made subject to wartime restrictions; for example, weather forecasts ceased. In June 1942, the Office of War Information (OWI) was established, and its Radio Bureau was concerned with the flow of war propaganda and general information on, for example, rationing through commercial radio. The bureau produced series like "You Can't Do Business with Hitler."

The OWI and commercial radio enjoyed a smooth relationship. In fact, radio did not need prodding to broadcast patriotic programs. Variety shows, such as the Mutual Network's "This Is Fort Dix" and NBC's "Army Hour," were based in military camps. Frank Sinatra was the rising singing star of the war years, and his broadcasts and concerts in America and to the troops overseas entertained legions of young teenage girls, or "bobby soxers." Drama shows referred to the war in a variety of ways. In popular soap operas, as actors were drafted the characters they portrayed would similarly go off to the army camp or the front leaving proud and anxious loved jones. Japanese and Nazi villains entered the thriller series. Drama-documentaries about the war, such as "Pacific Story" and "First Line of Defense," were produced jointly by the networks and the government. The tension-breaking quality of silly quiz shows, involving members of the public, proved increasingly popular during the war. Examples of this type of show were "Blind Date" (an ancestor of the present-day "Dating Game"), which catered to lonely soldiers, and the gambling gameshow "Double or Nothing." The growing success of quiz shows during the war laid the initial foundation for their phenomenal success on television in the postwar period.

More than ever before radio became indispensable, for it alone could bring up-to-the-minute news about how the war was going on its many different fronts and, more importantly, whether victory was in sight. Despite the critical shortages of radio sets, spare parts, and even of technicians to repair old sets, 4 million additional households tuned into radio during the war.

American intervention stimulated the number of radio news programs, which increased from about 66 newscasts per year in 1941 to 108 in 1942. Actual yearly hours of news on all of the networks grew to 5,552 by 1944; whereas in 1940, the figure was 2,376 hours. Yet the number of news broadcasts declined in early 1945 when victory seemed imminent. The war made the evening news a considerable feature of American broadcasting. At first, censors restricted live newscasts of events but eventually allowed greater freedom. Thereafter, American radio journalists followed American and Allied forces through every stage and in every theater of the war, scoring their own journalistic

Irving Berlin (b. 1888), the most prolific of all American songwriters, composed over one thousand songs, the words and music of which celebrated homespun values and national pride. During the war, "God Bless America," as sung by Kate Smith, was received as a second national anthem. (Library of Congress).

victories. Webley Edwards reported from the "island-hopping" campaign in the Pacific and live from an air bombing of Japan. George Hicks of CBS followed the troops during the D Day landings.

The hero of the hours throughout the war was Eghbert Roscow ("Ed") Murrow, originally of Washington State. Murrow had spent five years working for the Institute of International Education traveling across Europe and watching Hitler's rise to Continental mastery. He devised a program that rescued ninety-one German scholars from Nazi persecution. Although Murrow was employed by CBS to establish a European broadcast operation, he did not himself become a radio broadcaster until pressed into service the day Hitler entered Vienna. This was to be the first of over five thousand broadcasts. During World War II, he took to the skies, flying twenty-five missions over Germany. Murrow's radio reports signaled the emergence of the most important English-speaking broadcaster of the period, a man whom biographer A. M. Sperber shows in her *Murrow* (1986) to have been a man who served his public, his profession, and his country with rare dignity and courage in the period from 1938, the year he broadcast about the Austrian and Munich crises, to 1965, when he died of cancer. On nights of heavy bombing, Murrow provided the BBC with its links with the street, becoming what one BBC man called "a messenger from hell." "You burned the city of London in our houses and we felt the flames that burned it," observed poet Archibald MacLeish of Ed Murrow's wartime broadcasts. "You laid the dead of London at our doors and we knew that the dead were our dead . . . were mankind's dead . . . without rhetoric, without dramatics, without more emotion than needed be. . . . You have destroyed . . . the superstition that what is done beyond 3,000 miles of water is not really done at all." Film maker and critic George Steven, Jr., declares, "Murrow had acquired an unusual grasp of the dynamics of history. He also understood the raw power of broadcasting. Although he believed radio should not be used as a privileged pulpit, his broadcasts had a point of view."

In April 1945, two significant broadcasts were made within days of each other. On April 12, 1945, a character in a children's evening adventure serial suddenly said, "Just a minute, kids—President Roosevelt just died." Afterward, for four days, radio went into mourning, deleting all commercials, broadcasting solemn music and tributes for the dead president, and, finally, covering the funeral. On April 15,

1945, Ed Murrow gave Americans his impressions of a visit to the concentration and extermination camp at Buchenwald near Weimar in defeated Germany: "I pray you believe what I have said about Buchenwald. I have reported what I saw and heard, but only part of it. For most of it I have no words. Dead men are plentiful in war, but the living dead, more than twenty thousand of them in one camp. . . . If I've offended you by this rather mild account of Buchenwald, I'm not in the least sorry. I was there on Thursday, and many men in many tongues blessed the name of Roosevelt. . . . These men who had kept close company with death for many years did not know that Mr. Roosevelt would, within hours, join their comrades who had laid their lives on the scales of freedom." Finally, by playing the first three short notes and then the first one long note of Beethoven's Fifth Symphony, radio signaled the final victory.

Radio news was not the only aspect of radio to flourish as a result of the war. Radio advertising boomed; the impetus was a 90 percent excess-profits tax on American industry to prevent profiteering on war contracts. However, excess profits used in advertising were taxable at normal, or extremely low, rates. In effect, a dollar's worth of advertising time cost only ten cents. Moreover, paper rationing meant smaller newspapers and less space for advertising, so many firms shifted the bulk of their advertising to radio. Radio passed newspapers as the national advertising medium in 1943. Radio's share of advertising dollars went up from 12 percent in 1941 to 18 percent in 1945. Consequently, from 1940 to 1945, the revenues belonging to the networks rose from $56.4 million to $100.9 million. Therefore, the close and profitable relationship between the broadcasting and advertising businesses was further cemented during the war. Broadcasting had become a stable industry, for while one-third of all stations reported losses in 1939, only 6 percent were still in trouble in 1945.

Even so, in 1943 American broadcasting underwent a major change. In early 1942, Mutual (the affiliation of six local stations into a national network) and the Justice Department had filed antitrust suits against CBS and NBC and had forced an appeal to the Supreme Court, where both networks lost their case. NBC was forced to sell off its Blue Network. It was sold to Edward J. Noble, a man who made his fortune from making Life Savers candies. In 1945, when the deal was finalized and the war was over, the new American Broadcasting Company (ABC) was formed. Thus, another prominent feature of postwar broadcasting was established.

The war suspended immediate developments in broadcasting, but there were many opportunities for long-term, postwar planning. People rapidly came to believe that radio and television broadcasting were going to enjoy a massive postwar boom. Therefore, in every year of the war the number of applications for new radio and television-station licenses mounted, awaiting the end of wartime restrictions. The FCC was faced with a renewed need to settle the future allocation of frequencies for AM, FM, and television stations. The situation was complicated further by a number of other factors. FM radio and television demanded the same right to use the VHF band. Yet government officials realized that the new international postwar status of the United States would require extra-spectrum space for civil, diplomatic, and military communications. Furthermore, the advocates for television were divided, some calling for the immediate arrival of television while others urged that the industry should await further technological developments. Overall, relatively starved by wartime restrictions and tantalized by advertising promises, consumers expected a wave of new goods and services once the war was finished.

The FCC settled the dispute between the supporters of FM radio and television by siding with television. Claiming that at the lower frequencies FM sound quality would be ruined by interference caused by sunspot activity, FM was moved up the VHF band to 88 to 106 megahertz. Armstrong and other FM broadcasters had gained more channels, but all their equipment and the receivers previously sold were now obsolete. Having experienced radio for over twenty years, the public was far more enthusiastic and expectant about the prospect of television than the sound improvement FM offered. The FCC's decision was politically advantageous. As a result, the introduction of FM radio was delayed yet again.

As to postwar television standards, RCA, with its proven and publicly available technology, was ranged against CBS, which proposed its not fully developed high-picture definition and color-television system. CBS asserted that it would be foolish to allow the technology of 1941 to determine future television standards, but CBS lost its case. RCA had the support of the entire manufacturing industry and had already won the issue in 1941. Again, the principal obstacle that defeated CBS was the tremendous public demand for television as soon as possible. It has to be remembered that throughout the decade of 1935–45, the public had been told by the inventors, various publicists, the federal government, and the broadcasting industry in general that the advent of television was just around the corner.

In January 1945, the present-day structure of American television broadcasting was created. Television was assigned only twelve VHF channels; the rest had been awarded to the government and to FM. The allocation was divided between six channels in the 44 to 80 megahertz band and, then, six more in the 180 to 216 megahertz band. In addition, the CBS proposal was rejected. The FCC had made a poor and expedient decision, for the twelve channels it had given to television were inadequate for the full-fledged exploitation of television that it had also authorized.

Another feature of postwar broadcasting in evidence before the war was unionization. Under its new national president, James Caesar Petrillo, the American Federation of Musicians (AFM) became militant and flexed its industrial muscle. After negotiations collapsed over the level of musicians' fees, Petrillo imposed a complete ban on recording for the radio and record companies. Although the union was accused of endangering national morale and was approached by President Roosevelt to end the dispute, the union held fast. Eventually, in late 1943 and 1944, the union succeeded in forcing the recording and broadcasting industries to accept its demands. Later, in 1944 and 1945, Petrillo prepared to take on the enlarged postwar broadcasting business. He started to campaign for AFM members to be employed as platter turners, the technicians who placed the records on the turntable. Furthermore, he instructed his members to stop playing for FM radio until the networks and stations agreed to employ duplicate orchestras for FM stations rather than use the same orchestras for both FM and AM.

Hollywood in World War II

In the fall of 1941, the film industry was condemned by the Senate Commerce Committee for producing movies with a distinctly anti-Nazi bias. Champ Clark, the isolationist senator from Missouri, held that Hollywood was "turning 17,000 movie theaters into 17,000 nightly mass

Hollywood's support of the British war effort drew together artists and themes associated with quintessential values of the British urban and pastoral scene, notably the stiff upper lip of heroism whether the setting was war or peace. In his first American film, a version of Daphne du Maurier's Gothic romance *Rebecca* (1940), director Alfred Hitchcock *(left)* elicited sterling but stereotyped performances from British regulars Joan Fontaine and Laurence Olivier as the married couple threatened by the malign posthumous influence of the husband's first wife. In order to heighten Joan Fontaine's sense of terror and sharpen her performance, cast and crew treated her meanly during filming. When she told Olivier that she had recently married Brian Aherne, he asked "Couldn't you do any better?" (United Artists; Museum of Modern Art Film Stills Archive).

meetings for war." If Hollywood did stop making such movies in the wake of these hearings, it was due not to political pressure but, rather, to market forces. They were, it seems, unpopular with audiences.

However, the film industry did continue to contribute to the defense program. In early 1940, 10,000 exhibitors were organized to form the

Committee Cooperating for National Defense. Their aim was to collect funds for the war effort and ensure that more screen time was dedicated to newsreels. After Pearl Harbor, this body became the War Activities Committee–Motion Pictures Industry and was placed under the supervision of Colonel Darryl F. Zanuck. The committee took as its responsibilities the organization of war bond and service fund drives and the production of training films. The film community was committed to educating the public about what they could expect from the war. To deter possible air raids, expected in America as they had been in Europe, special-effects artists designed a miniature suburban community on the roof of the Lockheed aircraft factories. It was hoped that this camouflage would confound enemy bombing crews. To boost morale, each weekend celebrities played host in their homes to servicemen stationed on the West Coast. Film stars also boosted morale by making all manner of public appearances and christening ships and bomber aircraft. In addition, leading stars John Garfield and Bette Davis founded the Hollywood Canteen. Stars such as Deanna Durban, Linda Darnell, Marlene Dietrich, Lana Turner, and Ann Miller served drinks to, and danced with, the numerous servicemen who passed through the canteen's doors. Moreover, these and other stars paraded their talents on the GI vaudeville circuit, visiting encampments and playing to as many as 100,000 troops at a time. Most of Hollywood's famous names appeared in the hundreds of propaganda shorts, exhorting the people to further efforts of sacrifice and endeavor.

The most popular cause in Hollywood appears to have been the bond drive. Stars were mobilized to make public appearances, promoting each of the seven campaigns. Such stars as James Cagney, Humphrey Bogart, and Lionel Barrymore appeared in short films, reminding cinema audiences that it was their duty to buy bonds. In one such propaganda short, Cary Grant stared accusingly into the camera and with thinly disguised scorn asked, "Can you say that you can't afford to buy victory bonds?" Hollywood also gave its support to the scrap drives. Short films asked people to "back the scrap" and "slap the Japs with your rubbish scraps." Even Jack Benny, eponymous star of *The Meanest Man in the World* (1943), demonstrated his support by donating his old Maxwell automobile.

Some film stars actually were involved in the fighting. Over fifty leading men wore the uniforms of the fighting services; and some

The Sullivans. Powerful death scene of the first of five brothers who became heroic victims in World War II. The first son to die expires in the presence of his four brothers, whose stoicism conceals their inner realization that this too might be their fate—as indeed happens. (Twentieth Century Fox; Museum of Modern Art Film Stills Archive).

distinguished themselves, such as Captain Clark Gable, Navy Commander Douglas Fairbanks, Jr., Lieutenant Commander Robert Montgomery, Marine Captain Louis Hayward, and Colonel James Stewart. For devising the series of seven *Why We Fight* movies, commissioned by General George C. Marshall to indoctrinate "the pleasure-loving soft citizens' army, fifty to every one professional soldier," director Frank Capra was the recipient of the Distinguished Service Medal, the highest award the army could bestow upon a civilian. Walt Disney gave much of his time and applied his talents in the art of animation to the creation of special training films for the armed forces. In all, he produced over one million feet of training film—more than all the other studios combined. The military took over Hal Roach's studios to produce its own training films, in which the highest ranking performer at Fort Roach was Ronald Reagan. In all, Hollywood produced 982 movies during the war and sent 34,232 prints overseas.

Hollywood was anxious to present itself as an integral part of the war effort, partly because the studio bosses lived in fear of the possibility that the government would begin producing its own movies. Moreover, an industry so dependent upon sustained public goodwill had to present itself in the most favorable way. By helping to win the war, Hollywood sought to win the confidence of the people. Furthermore, the film community, comprised as it was of so many hyphenated Americans, was ever sensitive to charges of disloyalty and cosmopolitan un-Americanism.

During the war, cinema attendance rose by 50 percent over the totals for 1940. During the depression, working-class people could not always afford to visit the cinema. Wartime affluence enabled them to go to the movies not just once but four or five times a week. Gasoline rationing curtailed pleasure driving and obliged Americans to seek their diversions in their neighborhood movie theaters.

Along with radio, cinema provided citizens with the most readily accessible avenue of escape from fears of bereavement, grievances about wartime restrictions, and the pressures of working eight hours a day, six days a week. Moreover, it was escapism that the public wanted. If movies make their money in peacetime by pandering to the median taste, then in wartime that taste was for saccharine. Hollywood gave the nation the most popular song of the war, "White Christmas" by Irving Berlin, in the 1942 feature film *Holiday Inn*. "White Christmas" remains the best-selling song in the history of popular music. *Holiday Inn* was but one of the hundreds of musical comedies that came to the wartime cinema. Prior to Pearl Harbor, this genre accounted for 20 percent of Hollywood's output. However, during the war, 40 percent of all film releases were of this type.

It seems people craved titillation as well as escapism. Their movie heroes duly accommodated them with both performances on screen and in the courts. Throughout the winter of 1942–43, Errol Flynn's statutory rape case dominated the front pages of the nation's newspapers. Two years later, it was a Charlie Chaplin paternity case that pushed the war to the inner pages. The war also struggled to assert itself on the cinema screens. By 1944, less than one-third of all motion-picture releases dwelt on themes related to the conflict. Those that did adhered to the

Supporting actor Ronald Reagan *(left)* was frequently cast in the role of best friend in Hollywood films. Here he assists that redoubtable roué Erroll Flynn *(second from right)* in a "spot of espionage" as a pastime to while away their *Desperate Journey*, a piece of war hokum in which Van Heflin *(center)* and Alan Hale *(right)* also appeared. Why are they dressed like Nazis? It seemed like a good idea at the time. (Warner Brothers—First National; Museum of Modern Art Film Stills Archive).

guidelines found in the Office of War Information's *Government Information Manual for the Motion Pictures* (1942). One of the OWI's main priorities was for the movies to emphasize the polyglot aspect of the armed forces. Studios were advised to enlist black servicemen and soldiers with foreign names into their fictional platoons. The intention here was to help defuse racial tensions at home and project the message of American egalitarianism to the world.

By and large, war films served to reaffirm their audiences' assumptions about the conflict. Germans were sadistic, Italians cowardly, and Japanese subhuman. A mere handful of American GIs was all that was necessary to dispatch whole regiments of enemy soldiers. When death

265

came to an American soldier, it was clean and painless. Before expiring, the hero often managed to utter some cracker-barrel philosophy on the righteousness of the fight and some message to be relayed to loved ones back home. As cinema historian Eric Rhode (1970) has written, "most of the actual war films produced by Hollywood during the war were intended to reassure wives and girlfriends, like letters home from the front." Those films that might have caused distress by depicting the cruel face of war were suppressed. John Huston's documentary treatment of *The Battle of San Pietro* (1944) not only showed GIs falling under enemy fire but also had footage of their corpses being bagged, ready for burial. Here soldiers trudged slowly toward death through drizzle and devastatingly accurate enemy mortar fire. At the end of the day, they had advanced a mere six hundred yards. This harrowing vignette of the Italian campaign was, on its arrival in America, designated as unsuitable for general release. So too was Huston's *Let There Be Light* (1945), which focused upon those who had been psychologically crippled by the conflict.

Even when Hollywood pulled out the sentimental stops, suffering was deemed to be subversive of the war effort. *The Sullivans* (1944) was based upon the real tragedy that befell five brothers — Albert, Francis, George, Joseph, and Madison Sullivan. Their story on screen gives special emphasis to the common decency, brotherhood, and close ties of love that bind all members of a family together. The film reaches its climax with the arrival at their home in Iowa of an old family friend (Ward Bond) who has called to give the news that all five sons have been killed by one Japanese torpedo. In the final reel, their father (Thomas Mitchell) passes the water tower that, in childhood, the boys had scaled to wave him off to work. Tearfully, he salutes their memory. Tearfully, the audience watched as the five departed Sullivans materialized in the heavens to return his salute. This emotional tour de force was just too heartrending, and cinema owners across the country withdrew it from exhibition.

Like the majority of Americans, the film community gave loyal and productive service to the war effort. Yet, like its audience, Hollywood chose to ignore the brutal aspects of the conflict. In the movies, as in everyday life, war clouds hovered ominously on the horizon; yet, they never threatened to obliterate the American citizen's natural optimism nor his passion for self-indulgence. Hollywood continued to give the

American people what it thought they wanted. However, in the opinion of some high-minded critics, it failed to provide them with what they needed. As poet Archibald MacLeish averred, motion pictures were "escapist and delusive." By feeding its audience a daily diet of musical comedy, melodrama, westerns, period-piece epics, and comic-book heroism, Hollywood, as historian John Morton Blum (1976) concludes, contributed "to the failure of Americans to understand either the origins or the objectives of the war."

The Enemy Within—Aliens and Dissenters

In the immediate aftermath of the declaration of war, the American people were seized by a spirit of patriotism. However, there was little evidence of overt xenophobia. Italians, Japanese, and Germans, resident in the United States, may have been subjected to some verbal abuse; but it seemed that they had little to fear from mob violence. Nevertheless, their freedom was curtailed. On December 8, 1941, FDR issued an executive order designating them as enemy aliens. The order suspended all naturalization proceedings, prohibited aliens from traveling without prior permission, and barred them from areas close to strategic installations. Simultaneously, the FBI began rounding up 3,000 Japanese, Italians, and Germans on suspicion that they were a threat to national security.

At the outbreak of war, there were some 599,000 Italians resident in the United States. For the vast majority, the executive order of December 8 was a source of irritation and inconvenience, rather than a form of oppression. As the war progressed, they easily dispelled doubts as to their loyalty and won the trust of the other American people by espousing and displaying total commitment to the war effort.

The loyalty of the vast majority of the 204,000 German aliens should never have been in doubt. Most of them were Jewish refugees from Nazi tyranny. If these people did experience hostility, it was because of their Jewishness and not their German origins. A belief that Jews were not contributing fully to the war effort persisted throughout the war. Indeed, they were often accused of profiteering. Also, despite Selective Service head General Louis B. Hershey's testimony to the contrary, it was believed that Jews avoided the draft.

Such slander proceeded from the vein of anti-Semitism that ran through American society. Its depth was revealed by reports from the Fair Employment Practices Committee that indicated widespread discrimination against Jews on the labor market. Such bigotry had its more obnoxious aspect in Chicago's Gentile Cooperation Society, formed to "halt growing Jewish power." Even worse were the teen-age gangs that roamed the Boston suburbs of Roxbury, Dorchester, and Mattapan, desecrating synagogues and terrorizing Jewish businessmen. Their hatred was fueled by such anti-Semitic tracts as *The Broom* and *X-Ray*. The most influential hate sheet was Father Charles E. Coughlin's inappropriately named *Social Justice*, in which Communists and Jews were blamed for tricking America into the war. One of his editorials was freely adapted from a speech by Nazi propaganda minister Joseph Goebbels. *Social Justice* and other right-wing publications were damned by the liberal press as a fifth column of fascist sympathy. Amidst growing demands for their curtailment, Attorney General Francis Biddle resisted calls to invoke the Sedition Act of 1918 to suppress *Social Justice*. Instead, he prevailed upon Archbishop Mooney of Detroit to order Coughlin to cease his inflammatory outbursts.

The German American Bund had 25,000 members, with Nazi uniforms and swastikas, and expressed even more gross forms of anti-Semitism. According to Sander A. Diamond, in *The Nazi Movement in the United States, 1928–1941* (1974), Bund leader Fritz Kuhn declared: "We do not consider the Jew as a man." And one of Kuhn's thugs spoke of the eventual need "to wipe out the Jew pigs." In their very different ways, both Coughlin and Kuhn tried to link Jews with international communism and tried to malign attempts to draw the United States into war on the side of Britain and France.

After the *Kristallnacht* of November 1938, more European Jews than ever tried to enter the United States and far more than the permitted quota of 27,000 immigrants from Germany and Austria. Thus in February 1939, sympathetic liberals in Congress proposed a measure to allow only 20,000 additional children under the age of fourteen to enter the United States over a period of two years. The bill ran into a storm of criticism. Its opponents charged that the initial figure would become the opening boulder in an earthquake of renewed immigration. Public opinion polls suggested that two-thirds of Americans were opposed to the measure. Some Jewish spokesmen within the United States were afraid that a sudden influx of Jewish immigrants, even children, would further inflame anti-Semitism. Richard Polenberg (1972) declares how "the bill was so emasculated in committee that its sponsors decided against bringing it to a vote." The wife of a commissioner of immigration caught the essence of public disquiet when she remarked "that 20,000 children would all too soon grow up into 20,000 ugly adults."

Throughout the summer of 1940, FBI director J. Edgar Hoover led those concerned about possible Nazi "fifth-column" activities in the United States. They included conservatives and liberals. In its issue of 22 June 1940, the *Nation* warned of "our enemies within" and asserted that "treasonable elements are feverishly at work." The editors called for a group libel law to allow the government to eradicate fascist sympathizers. In *Faith for Living* (1940), Lewis Mumford favored "keeping every fascist group or pro-fascist speaker off the air, denying the use of the United States mails to every fascist publication . . . and finally putting into jail—or sending into exile—the active ringleaders of fascism, under a law which would make the espousal of fascism itself an act of treason against democracy."

The intention of the Bloom-Van Nuys bills of 1941 was to provide for a thorough review of all applications for entry into the United States and for rejection of any candidates who "because of their mental philosophy" might serve as enemy agents. However, it was the Smith Alien Registration Act of June 1940 that required the 4.9 million alien residents to register, have their fingerprints taken, and declare their membership in any organizations. The act followed the deportation of those who belonged to a communist or fascist group "at any time, of no matter how short duration or how far in the past." Attorney General Frank Murphy, hitherto a known advocate of civil liberties, now described the confused, angry nature of public opinion. "Unless we are pudding headed," he said, "we will drive from the land the hirelings here to undo the labors of our Fathers." Finally, the Smith Act made it illegal for anyone to conspire to advocate or to propose the violent overthrow of the government.

This was the period of the so-called little red scare. In October 1940, Congress required the registration of any organization that was "subject to foreign control" or favored violent revolution. Several states, including California, barred parties with communist connections from the ballot. The Department of Justice used all powers possible to put those

Silence is golden. The American war effort at home and at the front depended upon solidarity of purpose from all the American people, and this included discretion about their individual work in the war. The *Victory Bulletin* was a government publication to educate people that loose talk costs lives. Millions of copies were produced of various posters such as this one that frames the endangered sailor within a ship's porthole like a halo. (Library of Congress).

it considered dangerous behind bars. Fritz Kuhn of the German American Bund was accused of misappropriating $500 of organization funds and was sentenced to imprisonment in Sing Sing. Earl Browder, head of the Communist party, was charged with a technical infraction concerning his passport. Browder was convicted and sent to prison for between two and four years.

However, unlike the Wilson administration during the Great Red Scare of 1917–21, the Roosevelt administration tried to reassure the public and to check the hysteria. In fact, FDR, while accepting tight controls on freedom of speech and association, defused attacks he thought might have further eroded free speech, curbed dissidents, and deprived aliens of civil liberties. Moreover, in World War II Americans were more concerned with the threat of fascism than communism. Anti-Communist hysteria was at its peak during the Russo-Finnish War of 1939–40 and soon abated after the German invasion of Russia in June 1941.

Not only did fear of fifth-column activities derive from the course of the war but also from enduring ethnic loyalties and rivalries that were simply being reinforced by the war. Ironically, such ethnic divisions, although most noticeable in the early years of the war, proved the most easy to reconcile, whereas those social tensions arising from the class structure and racial segregation would prove far more difficult to resolve.

In October 1942, Attorney General Francis Biddle decreed that Italian aliens would no longer be classified as aliens of "enemy nationality" and thus exempt from the restrictive regulations. Such a gesture was never extended to German aliens. The Democrats reckoned that it was worth trying to entice the Italian American vote at home and, perhaps, encourage Italians in Italy to reject Mussolini. However, they did not use such arguments for Germans and German Americans. According to Biddle, FDR remarked, "I don't care so much about the Italians. They are a lot of opera singers, but the Germans are different; they may be dangerous." In public, FDR praised German Americans in 1944, noting "how many good men and women of German ancestry have proved loyal, freedom-loving, and peace-loving citizens." Moreover, he was also implying—and rightly—that ethnic loyalties were losing much of their force in the social turbulence and upheaval of the war.

FDR, who had considered taking legal action against the *Chicago*

Tribune and the *New York Daily News* for editorials attacking America's allies, put pressure upon Attorney General Biddle to make an example of the ultraright-wing press. The action finally came to the courts as *U.S. v. McWilliams, et al,* on April 17, 1944. In all, some thirty fascist sympathizers were indicted under the Espionage Act of 1917 and the Smith Alien Registration Act of 1940. The trial quickly degenerated into farce. The counsel for the defense wasted the court's time challenging jurors and raising countless frivolous motions. At one point, it was requested that the trial be adjourned until FDR and Adolf Hitler were available to testify. In displays of irreverence and showmanship (anticipating the behavior of the so-called Chicago Seven of 1968), the defendants harangued the bench and appeared in Halloween masks, bearing placards announcing "I AM A SPY." The farce ended in tragedy when, on November 30, 1944, the sorely tried Justice Eicher died of a heart attack. The case was then dropped in order to spare the American legal system further embarrassment.

If these fascists escaped being sent to prison, other less blameworthy American citizens were not so fortunate. A provision inserted into the Selective Service Act of 1940 exempted from combat duty anyone who "by reason of religious training and belief is conscientiously opposed to participation in war in any form." These conscientious objectors were to be assigned to noncombatant duties. Those who opposed any form of military service were to be set to work in civilian public-service camps.

The majority of America's total of 42,973 conscientious objectors accepted noncombatant service. However, some 11,950 opted to work in the civilian camps. Life for these individuals was arduous. They were set to work for fifty hours each week under strict military discipline. During World War I, inmates in similar encampments had been paid for their labor. In World War II, the financial burden was passed from the state to the individual or the church of which he or she was a member. It was stipulated that conscientious objectors (COs) had to reimburse the authorities for expenditures on their food and clothing. Conditions were so harsh that, by 1943, many COs were choosing prison rather than work in the camps. Some COs were not even given the choice. Moreover, a prison sentence awaited those whose claims to religious commitment were rejected by the authorities. In all, some 5,500 were sent to jail. At the start of the war, five years was the normal sentence. In 1945, a conscientious objector might still expect to go to jail for four years. In prison, the COs received poor food and experienced frequent physical abuse. Hundreds of those sent to Fort Leavenworth in Kansas were kept in solitary confinement for periods of up to sixteen months.

Members of the Jehovah's Witnesses constituted 75 percent of all COs sent to prison. Draft boards rejected their claims to pacifism because of their avowed intention to fight in the coming battle of Armageddon. This was a cosmetic device that disguised a deep-seated popular distrust of the sect. Antipathy boiled over into mob violence against Jehovah's Witnesses at Little Rock, Arkansas, and Springfield, Illinois. Jehovah's Witnesses were persecuted by the people and were harassed by the authorities. In 1942, the Supreme Court ruled in the case of *Jones* v. *Opelika* that municipal authorities could levy a peddlers' tax upon literature distributed by the sect. The Court then upheld the civic authority's right to ban all such literature from the mails. However, in the case of *Murdock* v. *Pennsylvania* on May 3, 1942, the Court overruled the *Jones* decision by five votes to four. The Court now decided that a city ordinance requiring all persons taking orders, or delivering goods from, door to door to obtain a license from the city and the tax of $1.50 on peddlers were unconstitutional. "A state may not impose a charge for the enjoyment of a right granted by the federal Constitution."

Oppressive though they were, such violations of citizens' rights paled in comparison to the treatment meted out to America's Japanese minority. At the time of Pearl Harbor, there were some 127,000 people of Japanese descent resident in the United States. Of these, 112,000 lived on the West Coast, with 93,717 in California. Approximately 33 percent of these were designated as enemy aliens. These first-generation immigrants, the *Issei* (47,000), had been born in Japan and, as a result of the Immigration Act of 1924, had been barred from taking out papers of citizenship. However, their children, the *Nisei* (80,000), were American citizens. The middle-aged *Issei* produced over half of California's fruit and vegetables; the *Nisei* in their teens and twenties were native-born, were educated in public schools, and talked, behaved, and dressed like white Americans of the same age.

With the onset of war, the *Issei* were subjected to the same restrictions as those imposed upon German and Italian aliens. Initially, they suffered little persecution and escaped being held responsible for the act of treachery that had brought America into the war. The popular mood soon turned sour as a movement demanding the total evacuation of all Japanese from the West Coast gathered momentum. In the vanguard of this movement was the head of the Western Defense Command, General John De Witt. To him there was no difference between a Japanese resident in Tokyo and one resident in Seattle. Congressmen from California, Oregon, and Washington State added their voices to his call for the removal of both the *Nisei* and the *Issei*. They were supported in this by many West Coast city mayors, the American Legion, and spokesmen for farm, labor, and business, and California's attorney general, Earl Warren.

What explains this upsurge of anti-Japanese hysteria in the weeks immediately after Pearl Harbor? First, people on the West Coast were, to a much higher degree than their counterparts in the East, susceptible to the fear of enemy attack. Numerous false air-raid reports and the actual shelling of the coast by a Japanese submarine on February 23, 1942, heightened these anxieties. Second, every Japanese was seen as a potential saboteur. The many important war installations and the construction of new munitions factories on the West Coast made the inhabitants particularly sensitive to fear of sabotage. Their suspicions were strengthened by the findings of the official investigation into the attack on Pearl Harbor. This, the Roberts Report of January 24, 1942, detailed the existence of a highly organized fifth column among Hawaii's Japanese community. The attack itself seemed to lend credence to the image of the Japanese as treacherous and untrustworthy. Third, as in the case of the Jews (and, also the Jehovah's Witnesses), the crisis of war brought into sharp focus any residual intolerance toward minorities. The anti-Japanese sentiment that erupted in late 1941 and early 1942 had its source in the Nativist movement and the American Protective Association of the 1870s and 1880s. Finally, some of those who demanded Japanese removal saw in it an opportunity for personal gain. With Japanese residents being forced to leave their homes at short notice, these individuals would be able to acquire their businesses and property at bargain prices.

However, perhaps the most potent cause of anti-Japanese feeling lay in the fact that in early 1942 Japan seemed to be winning the war, taking Wake Island (December 23, 1941), Hong Kong (December 25,

Evacuation of the *Nisei*. American citizens of Japanese descent, among a contingent of 664 and the first to be taken from their homes in San Francisco in April 1942, await buses to transport them to the so-called Santa Anita reception center of Arcadia and thence to war relocation centers for the duration of the war. (U.S. War Relocation Authority; Library of Congress).

1941), and Manila (January 2, 1942). The Japanese invaded the Dutch East Indies (January 11) and occupied Borneo and Celebes (January 24), Singapore (February 15), Java (March 9), and Bataan and Corregidor (May 6). In the meantime, the Allied fleet had lost eleven of fourteen vessels in action against Japanese warships off the Java Sea (February 27 to February 28, 1942). It is true that news from the European theater was just as depressing. The crucial difference lay in the fact that American forces were not on the receiving end of the *Wehrmacht's* bludgeon. In the Far East, however, GIs were losing and dying. The American public was nonplussed, angry, and frustrated. They wanted a scapegoat, and they found it in the *Nisei* and the *Issei*.

Throughout January 1942, Attorney General Francis Biddle ignored the mounting clamor for Japanese removal. Finally, when FDR denied him his support, Biddle succumbed. Ironically, the repression was advocated by men usually praised for their freedom from bigotry, such as Earl Warren, Walter Lippmann, Henry L. Stimson, Abe Fortas, Milton Eisenhower, Hugo Black, and John J. McCloy. Without a scintilla of evidence or a fragment of logic, Earl Warren used convoluted reasoning to justify repressive measures. For example, Warren contended that the fact that there had *not* been any acts of sabotage by Japanese Americans just showed how devious was their plotting. Furthermore, "opinion among law enforcement officers in this state is that there is more potential danger among the group of Japanese who were born in this country than from the alien Japanese." Among those who did plead for compassion were such known conservatives as FBI director J. Edgar Hoover and Senator Robert A. Taft of Ohio (son of the president).

On January 29, the attorney general announced that all enemy aliens were to be removed from the West Coast. Four days later all aliens were ordered to register with the Western Hemisphere Command. Even so, the anti-Japanese lobby was unappeased. They wanted the order to be extended to apply not only to alien Japanese but also to their offspring. To them, there was no distinction between *Nisei* and *Issei*. On February 14, De Witt informed Washington that "the Japanese race is an enemy race and while many of them have become 'Americanized' the racial strains are undiluted." He was supported in this by a characteristically vitriolic campaign in the Hearst press. Its squalid cause was dignified by a series of syndicated articles by veteran progressive journalist Walter Lippmann that appeared in February 1942. The extension of the order was also supported by state and federal officials who demanded that the army be authorized to evacuate anyone deemed to be a threat to national security.

On February 19, FDR acceded to their demand. By signing Executive Order 9066, he authorized the War Department to designate military areas and to exclude any or all persons from these zones. On March 2, 1942, De Witt issued a proclamation requiring all aliens, all *Nisei*, and all individuals suspected of subversive activity to move from the West Coast. In four weeks, 9,000 migrants left California, Oregon, and Washington State to settle in the interior. This was their intention, but they met with little success. The recipient states (Arizona, Arkansas, Kansas, Montana, and Colorado) refused them entry. In the face of this breakdown in the removal program, De Witt called a halt to voluntary evacuation on March 27, 1942. Thereafter, the army began enforcing and transporting evacuees to assembly points, pending transfer to permanent facilities. By June 1942, the program was almost completed. One hundred thousand *Nisei* and *Issei* had been forced to leave the West Coast. Ironically, Hawaii had a much higher proportion of Orientals, but Japanese-American leaders there cooperated closely with the FBI and no charges were preferred.

The *Issei* and *Nisei* of California forfeited their bank accounts and investments. The *Issei* lost $70 million in farm acreage and equipment, $35 million in fruits and vegetables, almost $500 million in annual income, and countless savings, bonds, and stocks. They had no right of appeal. They were also forbidden to take with them their pets, personal items, and household goods. Government officials agreed to store personal possessions but refused to guarantee their safety. As such, many evacuees chose to sell off their goods for a pittance.

The task of accommodating the evacuees fell to the War Relocations Board, established under the direction of Milton Eisenhower in March 1942. Initially, Milton Eisenhower conceived of the camps as a kind of wartime Civilian Conservation Corps. Each small enclave of evacuees would, he hoped, become self-sufficient in foodstuffs and, perhaps, develop small-scale manufacturing enterprises. Such plans did not come to fruition. The land assigned to the camps was invariably too arid for arable farming. As far as the proposed manufacturing enterprises were concerned, evacuees were actively discouraged and often prohibited from competing with local businessmen. Indeed, the receiving states— California, Texas, Arkansas, Utah, and Wyoming—curtailed the rights of Japanese-American citizens to trade, own land, and vote. Moreover, Milton Eisenhower's plans met with the opposition of the army. The

War Department simply did not have the manpower resources to police a multitude of small encampments. For the sake of convenience, evacuees were concentrated in ten huge camps in seven states. Each encampment housed 10,000 to 12,000 inmates.

The conditions there were penal. The camps comprised row upon row of wooden barracks. Each family was assigned to one room in these blocks. For warmth, they were each given an army blanket. Light was provided by a bare light bulb. Toilet, bathing, and dining facilities were all communal. Guard dogs patrolled the barbwire fence that marked the perimeter of each encampment.

The whole process of relocation added immeasurably to existing strains within the Japanese-American community. The older generation of *Issei* were trying to preserve traditional Japanese culture, in which filial piety, respect for tradition, and the importance of hierarchy remained essential group values. The younger *Nisei* were adopting the sort of individual values and self-assertion they thought were truly American values. Menial work in the relocation centers undermined the authority of order of people whose skills and education now went for little. Moreover, to give a specious appearance of democratic organization, the camps were allowed a limited degree of self-government. However, at first only Japanese-American citizens could assume elective office; and, therefore, it was young men, usually in their early twenties, who became the official leaders of the community. The older generation, deprived of their traditional roles in their households and in the community at large, were overwhelmed by a sense of futility.

Also, the *Issei* and *Nisei* were divided over the policy of internment. Some accepted the policy, believing that compliance would result in their eventual return and assimilation with the rest of American society. Others deeply resented internship, and clashes between the two groups sometimes led to outbreaks of violence. The most serious disturbance occurred at Camp Manzanar, California, in December 1942. Such disorder was interpreted by the authorities as the work of subversives. In July 1943, the War Relocations Board began segregating "loyal" from "disloyal" inmates. Some 18,000 "disloyal" inmates were assembled at the special camp at Tule Lake. Harsh discipline and poor food served only to increase the alienation of its inmates, and further rioting ensued. In 1944 Congress passed the Denationalization Act that made it possible for 5,766 *Nisei* who did not want to enlist in the American army to renounce American citizenship.

The detention of Japanese Americans was contested in the courts, most notably in two cases that went to the Supreme Court. In the first, *Hirabayashi* v. *United States*, the Supreme Court decided unanimously on June 21, 1943, that a curfew of Japanese Americans was not a violation of their civil rights. While admitting "it is jarring to me that U.S. citizens were subjected to this treatment," Chief Justice Harlan Fiske Stone declared, "In time of war residents having ethnic affiliations with an invading enemy may be a greater source of danger than those of a different ancestry."

In the second case, *Korematsu* v. *United States*, decided by a vote of six to three on December 18, 1944, the Court upheld the removal of Japanese Americans to relocation centers. For the majority, Justice Hugo Black stated that the removal program was within the combined war powers of the president and the Congress. Moreover, the Court held that military necessity warranted the racial classification.

Those inmates who were regarded as loyal to the United States were in time allowed to leave the camps. However, they had to prove to the War Relocations Board that they had a job to go to and that they could be assimilated into the proposed receiving community. By the end of 1944, some 35,000 of the best and brightest evacuees had left the camps.

In 1944 there remained little justification for continuing the policy of detention. The always exaggerated military threat to the West Coast had long since passed. Yet FDR refused to disband the camps. He judged that popular opinion ran counter to such action, and he feared that returning Japanese would provoke civil disorder. He also was aware that, if he authorized their return, he might alienate the electorate in the 1944 election.

It was only when FDR was returned safely to the White House after the election of 1944 that he rescinded the exclusion order in December 1944. Ironically, although they were now free to leave, many of the detainees were reluctant to do so. Dispirited, demoralized, resentful, and fearful of attack, most of those who stayed on were the elderly *Issei*. In June 1945 they were still clinging to camp life, for they had little reason to leave. It is estimated that the Japanese evacuees suffered

Early victims of the abandonment of some civil rights in war, these *Nisei* citizens are in line to register for evacuation from San Francisco in April 1942 and then to be transported to camps for the rest of the war. Their expressions mix apprehension and stoicism, as they prepare themselves for years of uncertainty. (U.S. War Relocation Authority; Library of Congress).

property losses of $350 million. Many had no homes to return to, and, eventually, half of them began new lives in areas other than the West Coast.

Astonishingly, the natural affection and patriotism of the Japanese Americans to the United States remained unaffected by their maltreatment in what the American Civil Liberties Union was to call "the worst single wholesale violation of civil rights of American citizens in our history." With much stoicism and fortitude, they assembled each morning to raise and salute the American flag, take courses in English and in American history, and plant trees.

On January 28, 1943, Stimson announced that the army would accept

Nisei volunteers, and by 1945 17,600 of them had joined up. *This Fabulous Century* (vol. 5, *1940–1950*), edited by Maitland A. Eden, quotes Bill Maudlin as saying, "To my knowledge and the knowledge of numerous others who had the opportunity of watching a lot of different outfits overseas, no combat unit in the Army could exceed them in loyalty, hard work, courage, and sacrifice. Hardly a man of them hadn't been decorated at least twice, and their casualty rates were appalling." During the Italian campaign, the 442d Infantry, which included *Nisei* soldiers, lost three times its original numbers and won 3,000 Purple Hearts, 500 Oak Leaf Clusters, 810 Bronze Stars, 342 Silver Stars, 47 Distinguished Service Crosses, and 17 Legion of Merit awards.

What drove these soldiers to the most audacious heroism was the hope that once the story of their bravery was carried across America, attitudes to their families would improve and their possessions would be returned to them. The hope was forlorn; the trust misplaced. The Hearst press, a notable pioneer of virulent xenophobia, ensured that white Californians retained their loot; and, when *Nisei* soldiers returned, they risked discrimination by restaurants and barbershops and even beatings.

Ironically, the abuse of the *Issei* contributed to the slightly better treatment afforded the Chinese in the United States. Because the government was emphasizing so-called racial traits to justify its policy to Japanese Americans, it had to distinguish most carefully between people of Japanese and Chinese descent. After all, China was a wartime ally in urgent need of support. Through careful propaganda, the government encouraged sympathy for China. This sympathy reached its peak in 1943 when Madame Jiang Jieshi visited the United States. She was invited to address Congress, where, according to *Time* magazine, "tough guys melted." The Citizens' Committee to Repeal Chinese Exclusion was hastily formed and lobbied Congress to repeal the Chinese Exclusion Act of 1882. FDR advised Congress that repeal would "silence the distorted Japanese propaganda," and Congress complied in the fall of 1943. Nevertheless, while the new act allowed Chinese immigrants to become American citizens, it established a diminutive annual quota of 105 for all "persons of the Chinese race" no matter where they were born. Thus, Chinese from Hong Kong were not to be included in the British quota, and Chinese wives of American citizens and their children could enter the United States only as part of the quota.

Politics During Wartime

FDR's fundamental concern lay with defeating the Axis powers as quickly as possible. All other considerations were wholly secondary to the achievement of this aim. As he said, "the war effort must come first and everything else must wait." Democratic party boss Ed Flynn concurred. "In the face of war, politics are adjourned," he said.

Nevertheless, for all his efforts to create a bipartisan front, FDR was, in 1942, not wholly averse to political maneuvering in defense of his party's interests. In the early months of 1942, with one eye on the November congressional elections, he staunchly opposed Leon Henderson's call for a freeze on wages. Such an action might, in FDR's opinion, alienate the labor vote. Also, considering public opinion, he refused to impose strict gasoline rationing. He knew that such a measure would be highly unpopular with the electorate. He was also aware that the states dependent upon revenue accruing from gasoline taxation would be outraged by the strict enforcement of a federal tax on gasoline. Thus he waited until after the November elections before enforcing this restriction. However, FDR was unable to prevent the Democratic party from being trounced at the polls. The Republican victory was overwhelming. They gained forty-four seats in the House, seven in the Senate, and won the gubernatorial contests in practically all the important states.

The defeat of the Democratic party was ascribed to apathy among its traditional supporters. Only 28 million out of an electorate of 80 million actually went to the polls. To some observers, this apathy portended the breakup of the New Deal coalition. They pointed to such things as the disaffection of southern Democrats who were alienated by the Fair Employment Practices Commission; liberal disconcertion with FDR's accommodation of big business; the anger of the farm bloc over the eventual application of price restrictions on farm produce; and the defection of the ordinary workingman. The newly affluent worker was now less inclined to see the Democratic party as the protector of his or her interests. Another factor that influenced the electorate was a general undercurrent of dissatisfaction with the way the war was being run. Shortages in butter, coffee, meat, and so on were attributed not to genuine scarcity but to bungling by the Office of Price Administration (OPA). The OPA was pilloried by the press, politicians, and the general public. The administration's inability to control inflation and the unpopular measures adopted to combat the problem, such as price fixing, wage freezing, and taxation, contributed to the general public truculence. Moreover, a series of serious military setbacks and industry's complaints that it was not being allocated sufficient supplies of raw materials created the impression that the defense program was failing.

The Seventy-eighth Congress was fairly evenly balanced between Democrat and Republican members. However, the balance was tilted in favor of the Republicans by the southern Democrats' habitual defection from the party line. To this powerful conservative bloc, the November election result was seen as a mandate to roll back and wind up the New Deal. By then, the New Deal was an almost indefensible target. It had obviously failed to fulfill its principal functions—that is, lead the country out of the depression and end mass unemployment. In 1939, 16.5 million Americans were drawing welfare. It was clear that they would have remained on the welfare rolls had it not been for the stimulus given to the economy by the defense program. Supporters of the New Deal had little else with which to justify their position.

If the New Deal was thus ailing prior to Pearl Harbor, then it died the death after America entered the war. Why did it finally expire? First, many of the New Deal's job-creation programs became redundant with the advent of near full employment. Second, funds that had once been allocated to help support New Deal agencies were required to meet the more pressing need of paying for the war effort. Third, with the balance of power in Congress being held by the Republican–southern Democratic alliance, the responsibility for allocating such funds passed into the hands of those who were avowed opponents of New Deal liberalism. By the end of 1943, such agencies as the Federal Writers Project, the Civilian Conservation Corps, the Works Progress Administration, the Farm Security Administration, the Rural Electrification Administration, and the National Youth Administration had been either abolished or made inoperative through shortages of funds.

Perhaps the most prized scalp on the conservative belt was that of the National Resources Planning Board (NRPB). The NRPB's task was to formulate plans for using financial resources and establish public works projects. In 1943, the board signed its own death warrant by proposing extensive postwar expansion in federal aid to medical care, education, housing, and social insurance. The plan outlined in the document *After the War: Toward Security* constituted a firm commitment to improving the lives of the disadvantaged classes in America once hostilities ceased. In a preemptive strike, Congress took the cudgels to the NRPB in August 1943 by slashing its appropriations and effectively closing it down.

Even those agencies created to meet the demands imposed by the emergency of war proved vulnerable in the face of conservative critics in Congress. Republicans and southern Democrats had long suspected that the Office of War Information (OWI) had been established to serve as a propaganda wing of the New Deal. In retaliation, all funds allocated for the OWI's domestic program were stopped on June 18, 1943. Of all wartime agencies, the Office of Price Administration (OPA) bore the brunt of congressional anger. Its critics in the Seventy-seventh Congress harassed, harangued, and finally forced the resignation of the OPA's first director, Leon Henderson. Its opponents in the Seventy-eighth Congress ruled that no OPA official could officiate upon price-fixing levels unless he had had at least five years experience in business.

FDR presided over the dismantling of the New Deal because he had neither the energy nor the time to defend it against its critics. Such a defense would have entailed mobilizing public opinion as a counterweight to the conservative bloc in Congress. However, FDR could not afford to become embroiled in partisan issues on the home front because from Pearl Harbor onward his priority lay in winning the war. His tuned political antennae told him that the mood of the country was not conducive to a campaign in defense of social reform. To the chagrin of his liberal allies, in December 1943 FDR announced that "Dr. New Deal" had outlived his usefulness and that he now had to make way for "Dr. Win-the-War." At approximately the same time, *Life* magazine reported that "the U.S. is now a Republican country. . . . The Republicans are now the majority party."

Such news made for depressing reading to Democrats entering a presidential election year. It was apparent to them that, whether as "Dr. New Deal" or as "Dr. Win-the-War," FDR was the only real guarantee they had against a Republican victory in November 1944. By remaining above domestic party politics, FDR had succeeded in ensuring that he would not be identified with the defeat of New Deal liberalism. While the political and economic institutions with which his past administrations were so closely associated suffered wholesale condemnation, FDR remained a popular figure. If the war went well in 1944, then it was FDR as commander in chief, rather than as Democratic leader, who would be assured of a fourth term.

William Manchester describes FDR's charismatic persona during the war in *The Glory and the Dream* (1973):

> He certainly didn't look like a military genius. In his flannel shirt, old hat, and carelessly knotted bow tie—his invariable costume when visiting troops— he looked more like a hearty grandfather casually dressed for a weekend of trout fishing. . . . General Eisenhower might be dazzled by the President's gift for terrain, for grasping and remembering all the features of a countryside; to GIs and bluejackets, however, his greatest gift was his warmth, his concern, his appearance on the world scene as a shirt-sleeved President in a shirt-sleeved America. . . . Nothing is more illustrative of the Roosevelt touch, of his sensitivity to the needs of people, than his visit to a military hospital in Hawaii. . . . Before he left, he asked to be wheeled through the ward for combat victims whose arms and legs had been amputated. He smiled and waved; he said nothing; his presence said everything. Here was a man who had lost the use of both legs. He knew their bitterness; he had shared it. Yet he had overcome it to become President, and there was no reason for them to despair of their prewar dreams.

The Election of 1944

There was never any real doubt as to whether FDR would seek a fourth term of office in 1944. The only real question revolved around who would be joining him on the ticket. Throughout the war, the vice president, Henry Wallace, had moved progressively leftward, while the nation in general had become more conservative. Long identified as the defender of the interests of agriculture and labor, Wallace was unacceptable to what were now the twin shibboleths of the national party— the conservative Democrats of the South and the party machines of the northern cities. Roosevelt refused to endorse Wallace and, instead, left the decision on the vice presidency to the Democratic National Convention, held in Chicago in July 1944. There, in the face of strong grassroots support for Wallace, the party power brokers gave the nomination to a reluctant Senator Harry S. Truman.

A compromise candidate, Truman was all things to all men. The southern Democrats saw the man from Missouri as, if not one of their

Cartoon of FDR as a bird *(Unitus Andguidus)* by Justin Murray with the ornithological inscription:

Range: In or near water, sometimes as far as mid-Atlantic, sometimes farther.

Habitat: On the radio by your fireside.

Identification: If you can see him through that mob in his office, you're a better bird than I.

Voice: A familiar "My friends."

Food: Nazis, Fascists, Republicans, etc. Relishes particularly third and fourth term-ites. This bird was one of the finest of our feathered friends.

(Library of Congress).

own kind, then an acceptable son of the middle border. A protégé of Kansas City's Boss Tom Pendergast, he was acceptable to the politicians who operated the big-city machines. Having established his reputation on the Senate Special Committee to Investigate the National Defense Program as a critic of big business, he was seen by liberals as their own champion. However, events would prove that Truman had none of FDR's vision as an international leader.

Paradoxically, the true champion of liberal reform stood among the Republican ranks. Wendell Willkie, who had fought and lost as the Republican presidential candidate in 1940, had every intention of running again in 1944. He had begun his campaign in 1940 by offering guarded support for American involvement in the war against Hitler. Nevertheless, by the end of the race he was castigating FDR's foreign policy with a venom characteristic of the most ardent isolationists. By 1943, his perception of America's global role and responsibility had changed completely. He now urged America to work in concord with other nations to preserve peace in the postwar period, to dismantle formal empires and informal spheres of influence alike, and to aid the social, economic, and political development of the emerging nations. His views, set out in the book *One World* (1943), excited great popular interest. Indeed, *One World* was supposed to have sold faster than any book in the history of American publishing. With a year of its release, 2 million hardback copies had been purchased.

Willkie's forays into foreign policy formulation offended the Republican old guard. So too did his pronouncements on domestic affairs. His support for civil rights, his attacks not only upon big government but also upon big business, and his pledge to protect the rights of minorities and provide absolute guarantees against unemployment and want caused by old age, injury, and incapacity effectively alienated Republican leaders. By September 1943, these leaders had decided to dump Willkie. Undeterred, the nominal head of the Republican party decided to go over their heads to galvanize public support for his candidacy. He carried on in the hope that he might still steal the nomination. His challenge ended abruptly on April 4, 1944, when in the Wisconsin primary his delegates won no more than 16 percent of the popular vote. Thus repudiated, Willkie withdrew from the race. He died of a coronary thrombosis on October 8, 1944.

The easy victor in the Wisconsin primary, Governor Thomas Dewey of New York, went to the Republican National Convention in June 1944 as the firm favorite to win the presidential nomination. Chicago played host to a dispirited, lackluster affair in which a deep sense of defeatism pervaded the proceedings. As expected, Dewey won on the first ballot. Forty-two-year-old Dewey had come to national prominence in the late 1930s as a racket-busting special prosecutor in New York City. Swept along by the wave of resurgent Republicanism, he had won the governorship of New York in November 1942. As governor, he had a useful record as a social reformer. To balance the ticket, Robert A. Taft's protégé, John W. Bricker, the conservative governor of Ohio, was chosen as Dewey's running mate.

Reporters who took to the campaign trail in search of sensation found Dewey's manner to be stiff, that he lacked any original ideas, and that his speeches were somewhat stupifying. He seemed quite unwilling to engage in political controversy. He was reluctant to attack either social reform or FDR's war record. With the Republican's committed to American involvement in a postwar international organization, Dewey's future plans for foreign policy differed little from his opponent's. The only issue that Dewey would openly discuss was age. He depicted himself as a vigorous, youthful alternative to a tired and aged FDR. Doubts about Roosevelt's health were truly justified. On March 27, 1944, he had undergone a thorough general physical examination at Bethesda Naval Hospital. The findings by Lieutenant Commander Howard G. Bruenn were grim. As well as acute bronchitis, the president was suffering from high blood pressure, hypertension, hypertensive heart disease, and heart failure in the left ventrical.

While FDR was undeniably in need of rest and recuperation, by unintentionally emphasizing Roosevelt's experience and thus personalizing the campaign, Dewey simply played into the president's hands. FDR was quite content to fight the campaign on his image as commander in chief. The successful D Day landings in June 1944 enhanced his reputation as a great war leader. His much publicized meetings with the other free-world leaders at Bretton Woods (July 1944) and Dumbarton Oaks (August 1944) added luster to his reputation as a great statesman. In that summer, a wave of optimistic excitement swept the nation. After the liberation of Paris on August 25, 1944, it was thought that "Dr. Win-the-War" might complete his assignment by October. When these hopes were dashed, public spirits and FDR's political collateral were raised by the timely American landings at Leyte in the Philippines in late October.

By then Dewey and Bricker had abandoned all respect for political niceties and were embarked upon what FDR described to Harry Hopkins as the dirtiest campaign in his experience. Dewey popularized the view that FDR had egged the Japanese on to bomb Pearl Harbor. Bricker made similar accusations, embellishing them with the charge that war was the only way that failed New Dealers could extricate the nation from depression. There were all the old canards, notably that FDR wanted to be dictator for life, plus some new ones, according to which FDR was the dupe of international communism; that before he made any decision, he made sure that his advisers went to "clear everything with Sidney" (Hillman of the CIO). FDR was also supposed to be dying of cancer or syphilis. Truman got off lightly; he was simply (and in fact) a former member of the Ku Klux Klan. The nadir came with the song of Franklin to Eleanor—"You Kiss the Niggers / I'll kiss the Jews / And we'll stay in the White House / As long as we choose."

Even the *New York Times* supported FDR, albeit with "deep reluctance and strong misgivings." Walter Lippmann wanted a change of president but thought the country could not afford Dewey. "I cannot feel that Governor Dewey can be trusted with responsibility in foreign affairs," he wrote in "Today and Tomorrow" of 21 October 1944. "He has so much to learn, and there would be no time to learn it, that the risk and cost of a change during this momentous year seems to me too great." However, the Hearst press inevitably joined in scandal mongering. So too did certain radio stations. It was noted that, among others, stations in Detroit, Los Angeles, and Cleveland had a tendency either to follow or preface a news item relating to FDR and his family with a sensational story of scandal, corruption, or Communist subversion.

Stung into reaction, FDR went on radio on September 23, 1944, to denounce "the Republican fiction writers in Congress and out." However, despite the intensity of this virulent campaign, FDR was confident of victory and was determined to leave his own campaigning until but two weeks before polling day. He had two aims: to silence rumors as to his health and to get the sleeping Democratic vote to the polls. He achieved the first on October 21, 1944, when he was scheduled to participate in a four-hour open-car motorcade through New York City. When the heavens opened, FDR saw it as a blessing. Against the good counsel of his advisers, he went ahead with the tour. Newspaper photographers, newsreel cameramen, and millions of New Yorkers saw him drenched to the skin but smiling and jaunty—the FDR of old. One of his speech writers, Robert Sherwood, saw him afterward. He was neither sick nor ailing but in a state of "high exhilaration" at having gained a major publicity coup over his rivals.

As to the problem of getting his supporters to the polls, he did—to a degree—clear it with Sidney. Hillman's Political Action Committee (PAC) was organized in 1943 as an instrument for keeping Henry Wallace on the Democratic ticket and as a counterweight to the burgeoning antilabor bloc in Congress. In the run up to the 1944 election, PAC took on the responsibility of mobilizing the labor vote for FDR. Throughout the campaign, Republicans castigated it as a Communist front organization. In the aftermath of the election, it was accredited with getting 6 million blue-collar workers to the polls.

The Democrats devised another strategy aimed at getting the supporters out. On the eve of the election, all four radio networks broadcast the party's victory train special. It opened with statements from representatives of practically every sector of society. The old and the young, veterans of both world wars, a housewife, a beneficiary of the New Deal in the form of a Tennessee Valley Authority farmer, and one of its supposed enemies in the guise of an industrialist—all explained why they were going to vote for FDR. Then the chorus and the orchestra struck up a locomotive rhythm, and the "Roosevelt Special" set off on its imaginary whistle-stop tour of the country. The passenger list bore such names from the world of entertainment as Irving Berlin, Lucille Ball, Tallulah Bankhead, and Joan Bennett, who came to the microphone to pledge their support for the president. There was scant reference to issues or policies, yet the conventional wisdom among Democratic party leaders believed that this extravaganza was worth one million votes to FDR. With the opinion polls on the eve of election showing Dewey closing fast upon his opponent, it was clear that every vote was vital.

The new prosperity of the war years was having unfortunate electoral repercussions for FDR in the election. He had always appealed frankly to the class interests of blue-collar workers, disadvantaged groups, and the poor. But in a period of dwindling unemployment and greater prosperity, his plangent appeals lost something of their old urgency. Public opinion specialist Hadley Cantril, who was employed by the White House, began to notice rising dissatisfaction with the Democrats among blue-collar voters who "now feel more secure economically [and] are disturbed by the taxes they are paying for the first time."

In the event, far fewer votes were cast in 1944 than in 1940. FDR took 25,606,585 votes (53.5 percent), and Dewey took 22,014,745 votes (46 percent). In the electoral college, FDR's victory was more pronounced. He won 432 delegates to Dewey's 99. Roosevelt's victory of 3.6 million popular votes over Dewey was the lowest of any victor since 1916. His share of the popular vote had fallen from 54.7 percent in 1940 to 53.4 percent in 1944. While the Republican vote had fallen by 300,000 since 1940, the Democratic loss was greater at 1.64 million.

Nevertheless, the overriding factor in 1944 was the war and people's desire for continuity. However, the movement of blacks to the North in New York, Michigan, and Illinois and their commitment to the Democrats probably made a decisive difference to FDR's plurality in these pivotal industrial states. The CIO was also effective in getting apathetic labor people to the polls. Diehard isolationists, such as Congressman Hamilton Fish of New York and Senator Gerald P. Nye of North Dakota, were roundly defeated. A new generation of internationalists entered the Senate, including Wayne Morse of Oregon and J. William Fulbright of Arkansas.

[7]

AN END AND A BEGINNING

THE GREAT POWERS had become involved in World War II for reasons that made their immediate strategic objectives perfectly clear. While Britain had gone to war with Germany nominally to free Poland, its underlying motive was to prevent German domination of Europe. In Southeast Asia, Britain's various colonies, dominions, and dependencies were under attack or threat from Japan, and it had to protect them as best it could to prevent its raw materials and supply routes being seized by the Japanese. Russia had finally been forced into the war when Germany invaded its territory. The United States had finally gone to war against Japan because of the attack on Pearl Harbor. It had already been heavily involved on Britain's side in the war against Germany. Moreover, its various economic and diplomatic responses to the increasing militarization of Japan had played a part in the deteriorating world situation. The Grand Alliance was, therefore, committed wholeheartedly to the elimination of Germany and Japan as aspirants to the status of first-class powers.

While none of this changed in the course of the war, the Allies found common justification in what was, initially, a war of self-defense in the doctrine that nazism, fascism, and all forms of right-wing military totalitarianism must be eliminated from the Axis powers and the world.

The pivotal event in the shared experience of the Grand Alliance at war was the Holocaust, the destruction of the European Jews. The full extent of the tragedy became apparent when Russian forces moving from the east and Anglo-American forces moving from the west liberated a series of death camps in eastern Europe, such as Auschwitz, Dachau, and Buchenwald in the fall of 1944 and spring of 1945.

The Holocaust

Raul Hilberg first described the Holocaust in *The Destruction of the European Jews* in 1961 and, after further investigations and revisions, in a definitive form published in three volumes in 1985. Hilberg notes that chronic and widespread anti-Semitism among European Christians had taken such forms as Christian policies of converting all Jews and state policies of expulsion, notably the Russian pogroms at the turn of the century. However, such policies had never included total annihilation. As David Wyman, author of *The Abandonment of the Jews: America and the Holocaust 1941–1945* (1984), puts it, "it took Hitler, the Nazis and the Third Reich to plunge into the abyss of savagery." Whereas Christian missionaries had said, in effect, "You have no right to live among us as Jews," secular rulers had said, "You have no right to live among us." As Raul Hilberg writes, "The German Nazis at last decreed: You have no right to live. . . . The German Nazis, then, did not discard the past; they built upon it. They did not begin a development; they completed it."

The process of destruction began with wide-ranging sophistical distinction of who the Jews were, expropriation of their property, and the concentration of the victims in camps. It concluded with their annihilation. In this terrible affair, as in the Grand Alliance, the crux of the matter occurred in Poland. The devastation of Polish Jewry was a catastrophe that led to the deaths of 2.6 million of Poland's 3.5 million Jews and the extinction of a traditional center of Jewish culture.

What is sometimes called the "final solution," euphemistically by the Nazi racists and ironically by their critics and later historians, began with the German invasion of Russia in June 1941. As the Wehrmacht moved across Russian territory, special mobile killing units *(Einsatzgruppen)* followed close behind the front lines. Their task was to round up Jews by the thousands and to slaughter them by shooting. For eighteen months, the *Einsatzgruppen* did their work in Russia and eastern Poland, thereby eliminating 1.3 million Jews. The Germans were now committed to the total annihilation of the Jews. Despite chronic labor shortages throughout the territory held by the Axis powers, they proceeded to eradicate what would have been a prime source of labor.

Herman Friedrich Graebe, manager of a branch of a German building firm in Sdolbuman in the Ukraine, recorded his impression of one series of incidents of mass shootings; and it has been preserved on 78 rpm phonograph records. He recalled how, on October 5, 1942, his foreman mentioned that some Jews from Dubno had been shot in three large pits, about thirty meters long and three meters deep. He understood that all five thousand Jews living in Dubno were to be liquidated. Herr Graebe went to see for himself and came to pits surrounded by Ukrainian militia and several trucks. Forced to dismount from the trucks, the victims, all wearing the regulation yellow patches on their clothes, were then told to undress by an SS man who had a dog whip. They had to sort out their clothes according to shoes, top clothing, and underclothing—about eight hundred pairs of shoes and great piles of clothing. Without any demonstration or weeping, the victims stood in family groups and kissed one another. Herr Graebe walked over to the tremendous grave. He could see that "people were closely wedged together and lying on top of each other so that only their heads were visible. Nearly all had blood running over their shoulders from their heads. Some of the people were still moving. Some were lifting their arms and turning their heads to

German troops have arrived in the French town of Metz in 1940. This photograph juxtaposes military and commonplace elements to bizarre effect, as the shadows lengthen inexorably for this hapless small town. (Library of Congress).

Himmler was on hand to oversee the evacuation of French citizens from the French town of Metz in the summer of 1940. The Library of Congress has no precise data on the photograph apart from its date and location. The cowed people may be French Jews, awaiting an even worse fate than evacuation.
Although it was said Himmler could not stand the sight of blood, it was he who established and supervised the systematic genocide of European Jews. (Library of Congress).

show that they were still alive. The pit was already two-thirds full. I estimated that it already contained about a thousand people." The executioner was an SS man who sat at the edge of the pit with a tommy gun, smoking a cigarette.

The new group of victims, "completely naked, went down some steps which were cut in the clay wall of the pit and clambered over the heads of the people lying there, to the place to which the SS man directed them. They lay down in front of the dead or injured people; some caressed those who were still alive and spoke to them in a low voice. Then I heard a series of shots." Herr Graebe continued, "I looked into the pit and saw that the bodies were twitching or the heads lying motionless on top of the bodies which lay before them. Blood was running away from their necks." Those who remained alive had to pack the corpses more tightly into the pit and then lie down themselves to be shot in the neck.

And so the apparently endless cycle of butchery continued with ever new groups of victims following the other dead.

It was similar elsewhere. On September 17, 1941, 3,400 Jews in the small Lithuanian town of Eisiskes were herded by the *Einsatzgruppen* into the Jewish cemetery, forced to undress, and then shot at the edges of a series of trenches. One sixteen-year-old youth, Zvi Michalowski, fell into a trench unscathed, a split second before bullets killed his father and the other adults beside him. After nightfall, he climbed out of the grave and ran naked and spattered with blood to a house nearby. The owner denied him shelter, crying "Jew, go back to the grave where you belong." Having been refused by several others, the youth returned to the house of an old widow who had already turned him down once. This time he cried out to her, "I am your Lord, Jesus Christ. I came down from the cross. Look at me — the blood, the pain, the suffering of the innocent." Crossing herself, the crone fell at his feet, took him in, and sheltered him for three days. Eventually, the young man joined a band of partisans in the forest and survived the war to give pitiful testimony of what happened.

To eliminate the Jews who were not in Russia and eastern Poland, the Nazis established six killing centers in Poland. Here they built the gas chambers to which Jews from across Europe were deported in the period 1942–44. The six terrible death camps were Auschwitz; its larger neighbor Birkenau; Treblinka; Belźec; Chelmno; and Sobibóv. The

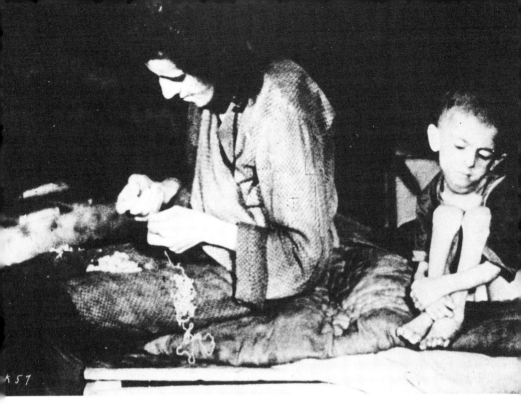

Heart-rending scene of a desolate mother and child in the Warsaw Ghetto. A film still from *Mein Kampf*, a documentary film subsequently released by Columbia Pictures in the United States. (Columbia Pictures, 1961; Museum of Modern Art Film Stills Archive).

camps were usually near munitions plants but in sites that could be easily camouflaged. The victims were given railway tickets but were forced to travel on closed and bolted freight cars. They were deprived of food and were refused sanitation. When they arrived, they were paraded before SS doctors who decided which among them was fit to work. The average proportion of able-bodied was only between 25 and 30 percent. After arrival at the death camps, prisoners were tatooed; their heads were shaved if they were Jewish; and they were assigned triangular badges to denote status—red for a political prisoner and green for a criminal.

The camps, which were surrounded by electrified wires and were surveyed by watch towers, were a series of gigantic barracks built of either bricks or wood by the prisoners themselves. One prisoner described a barrack interior thus:

297

The block was filled to capacity by four rows of low berths, looking like a three-tier chicken house. It was always damp and cold inside, even in hot weather, and the aisles between the berths were covered with slimy mire. The straw in the berths came from thatched roofs of the adjacent farmhouses which had been pulled down. The straw was rotten and stinking in the lower berths where it was mixed with mud and looked like dung. The best thing was to find an upper berth, but these were already taken. Some of the middle lower berths were vacant, here and there, but they had no straw. . . . The floors of the upper berths were not made of flat boards but of round joists; no wonder that fragments of rotten straw would continually fall upon us from the upper berths. Indescribable dust everywhere. To protect our heads from litter of rotten straw, from above, we covered them with our clothes. We used our shoes and caps as pillows. The stink, thirst and hunger made sleep impossible.

According to Raul Hilberg, the German bureaucracy killed 5.1 million Jews; and it took large numbers of German officers, soldiers, and workers to perpetrate the outrage. Hilberg also believes that various Jewish councils, faced with horrible dilemmas, tried to cooperate with the Germans and, unintentionally, facilitated the slaughter.

Over Europe the pattern of annihilation was uneven. The deportations included three-quarters of Dutch Jews, but four-fifths of Italian Jews survived. The destruction of the entire Jewish population in Serbia was early and complete. In Rumania the bureaucracy moved unbelievably from the most hideous massacres to an unreliable, lethargic lack of interest. In July 1944, the Hungarian government ended the deportation of Jews, thereby saving 120,000 Jews. By August the government would have allowed Hungarian Jews to leave Europe, but the Nazis refused to let them go. The grossness and enormity of the massacres was not, at first, believed in the West. Later, despite their willingness to use the Holocaust for purposes of propaganda, the American and British governments failed to attempt any rescue of the hapless victims.

Part of the Nazi strategy was to entrap Jews in various ghettos, most notoriously in Poland and especially in Warsaw. Hilberg believes the Jews reacted to the Nazi assault with an "almost complete lack of resistance." Instead of meeting gross terrorism with violence, they persisted in the long tradition of the Diaspora—a mix of appeals and compliance with state demands. "In exile the Jews had always been a minority, always in danger, but they had learned that they could avert or survive destruction by placating and appeasing their enemies. . . .

The abandonment of human dignity and decency is the most lasting impression conveyed by this disturbing street scene of ignominious death amid the passersby in the Warsaw Ghetto. A film still from *Mein Kampf*. (Columbia Pictures, 1961; Museum of Modern Art Film Stills Archive).

Armed resistance in the face of overwhelming force could end only in disaster." By the time Jewish leaders realized that the Nazi threat was different in kind from all that had gone before, the "2,000-year-old lesson could not be unlearned; the Jews could not make the switch. They were helpless . . . caught in the straitjacket of their history." This view has been disputed by some other historians, notably Yuri Suhl in *They Fought Back* (1967).

About 4 million people, Gentiles as well as Jews, died at Auschwitz-Birkenau. Millions died elsewhere. The number is based on computations made by surveying the terrain, the chambers equipped with instruments of death, camp documents, the number of surviving prisoners, and the magnitude of human artifacts and possessions of the dead victims. Apart from Jews, the victims included Gypsies, political dissidents, and those considered to be social deviants (the handicapped, homosexuals, and criminals).

At Auschwitz, the most notorious of all the camps, the first attempts at mass extermination by gas (Cyclon B) took place on September 3, 1941. Until four huge gas chambers and crematoria were built at Birkenau, gassing was done in two nearby farmhouses. Victims about to be gassed were told to undress and that they were to have a shower in the bathhouse. They were herded in great numbers in gas chambers of about 210 square meters that had showerlike devices in the ceiling. After a sortie of some 2,000 victims had been killed by Cyclon B, the chamber was opened and professional scavengers were employed to take off the victims' rings and jewelry, to extract gold from their teeth, and to cut off their hair (which would be used to make tailors' lining). Then the corpses would be taken to the ovens of the crematoria, and their personal documents destroyed. The professional scavengers were a special draft of prisoners *(Sonderkommando)* who were postponing their own execution by their terrible work, until they had learned too much and were also eliminated in turn.

The bodies were burned in crematoria, but the great number of victims also led to their being buried in common graves or burned on immense pyres. The ashes were scattered and buried in ponds. According to Auschwitz camp commandant Rudolf Höss:

Towards the end of the summer [1942] we started to burn bodies at first on wood pyres bearing some 2,000 corpses, and later in pits, together with bodies previously buried. In the early days oil refuse was poured on the bodies, but later methanol was used. Bodies were burnt in pits day and night, continuously. By the end of November 1942, all mass graves had been emptied. The number of corpses in the mass graves amounted to 107,000.

The stench of burning flesh was carried for many miles, and the population of the entire district began to talk about the burning of Jews. Höss stated that the local German air-defense service complained about the fires visible from afar at night. The numbers of victims were so great that it was quite impossible for the authorities to dispose of their property—clothes, shoes, towels, spectacles, baby carriages, valuables, and general luggage. It was, perhaps, this mountain of evidence that indicated something of the extent of the massacres when the camps were liberated by the Russian or American armies in 1945.

Auschwitz had about forty branches, or subcamps *(Nebenlager)*, situated near foundries, mines, and factories in Silesia. There the prisoners

The hapless victim of atrocity has expired and awaits burial after unceremonious transportation on a rough-hewn hearse. A film still from *Mein Kampf.* (Columbia Pictures, 1961; Museum of Modern Art Film Stills Archive).

were set to work making guns and chemicals and mining coal, sometimes for twelve hours a day. The grueling work and intimidation and beating by sadistic guards took their toll, and about 30,000 prisoners died in the IG Farben factories at Auschwitz in the period 1942–45. Some of them were producing Cyclon B used for gassing other prisoners.

As to the "survivors," the terrible, badly prepared, and unsavory food amounted to an average daily ration of three hundred to seven hundred calories, far below the calorie requirements of a body at rest. About three-quarters of the prisoners were undernourished. Continuous calorie deficiency led to protracted starvation sickness, in which the victims' bones were scarcely covered by skin and their eyes became glazed. Their complete physical decline led to mental exhaustion, listlessness, and indifference to their degraded surroundings. The medical examination of prisoners at Auschwitz, after the camp was liberated by the Red Army in the spring of 1945, showed that the prisoners weighed between 50 and 70 percent below what their normal weight should have been.

A final degredation. The pitiful victim is consigned to entombment among others, now nameless, by being slid down a wooden shaft into a pit below. A film still from *Mein Kampf*. (Columbia Pictures, 1961; Museum of Modern Art Film Stills Archive).

Some women bore children and often died of infection after delivery, while their infants were taken by SS doctors, tattooed on buttocks or thighs, and killed or allowed to die within a week or two. Epidemics of typhus and diarrhea sometimes claimed hundreds of victims. Experimental surgical operations were conducted by sadistic doctors intent on learning surgery by using living bodies. The experiments of Dr. Carl Clauberg and Josef Mengele ("the angel of death") were especially notorious as they searched for rapid ways of exterminating a whole people.

The camps were run with the most savage forms of sadism and butchery. Even tiny infringements of the rules were punished by flogging, torture, hanging from the stake, prolonged solitary confinement, starvation, and shooting. Here the oppression of the individual by society reached its most extreme forms. Auschwitz camp commandant Höss described the hopelessness of his prisoners:

302

I know from my own experience that prisoners, and especially those in concentration camps, are oppressed and tormented and brought to the verge of despair
far more by the psychological than by the physical effects and impressions of
the camp's regime and life. One must mention here the uncertainty and the
lack of hope to regain freedom—the majority of prisoners were sent to camp
for an indefinite period of time—together with the terror and the uncertainty of
tomorrow, which were always oppressing them.

Not knowing why they were arrested, the prisoners broke down, lost the will
to live, and coming to the conclusion that they would not survive anyway, as
they could be shot, for instance, in the nearest future, they decided to make an
end to their sufferings. Suicide was often the most acute phase their depression
could lead them into. . . .

Women endured the life in camp to a certain point of time. But after having
reached, both physically and mentally, their zero point of resistance, they
would rapidly deteriorate.

All of the stories associated with this incredible episode in human
barbarism carry something of the tenor and numb disbelief of the
victims. Many of the survivors can scarcely believe what they endured.
Some survivals were miraculous. In *Auschwitz* (1985), a survivor, Sara
Nomberg-Przytyk recalls how a teen-age girl escaped the gas chambers
by hiding in the chimney of a wood-burning vehicle used to carry bodies
to the crematorium.

Sara Nomberg-Przytyk was a Polish Jew active in Communist circles
before the war. She tells us in *Auschwitz* how the Nazis, astonishingly,
entrusted much routine administration of the camp to the prisoners and
that many of these administrators belonged to the mainly Communist
resistance movement. This was true of positions up to *Lagerälteste*
(camp elder). The resistance took care of its members as much as was
possible. Nomberg-Przytyk explains the complex, often contradictory
behavior of those prisoners who had a modicum of authority, such as
Orli Reichert, a German Communist who served as camp elder. At one
time, Reichert saved a prisoner from the gas chamber; at another, she
assisted Josef Mengele in sending ten to their deaths. Thus some prison
administrators surrendered to cynicism and despair, while others assumed a position of self-preservation at all costs.

Nomberg-Przytyk is most sensitive to the ways in which she was
"taking part in this deception that was helping the Germans to send
millions of people, without difficulty, to a tortuous death." Perhaps the

The utmost testimony to the bestiality of the Nazis is provided by such horrific pictures as this photograph taken for the U.S. Army Signal Corps of the unidentified victims of massacre by retreating Germans. The Library of Congress does not have exact identification of this scene, but it may be of the Stalag Tekla massacre. It was taken in April 1945. (Library of Congress).

most moving sections of her book are reports of the debates among prisoners in charge about their obligations to other inmates. Was it better for people to die with some dignity, aware of their terrible fate, or not to know until they were on the verge of oblivion? One clerk says of her failure to inform prisoners:

We didn't tell them the terrible truth, not out of fear for our own lives, but because we truly did not know what would be the least painful way for the young women to die. Now they didn't know anything, they were carefree, and death would be upon them before they knew it. If we told them what was in store for them, then a struggle for life would ensue. In their attempt to run from death they would find only loneliness, because their friends, seeking to preserve their own lives, would refuse to help them. . . . Today I know that it was fear for our own lives that . . . induced us to believe that sudden, unexpected death is preferable to a death that makes itself known to your full and open consciousness.

Those Nazis in the camps who were directly involved in the "final solution" were so obsessed with obliterating European Jewry that they never allowed the wider war with its inevitable defeat of Germany to hamper or retard the machinery of death.

France lost 25 percent of its Jewish population in the war. This was far less than the countries of central and eastern Europe. Moreover, in France, divided until 1943 between the German-controlled northern section and the supposedly autonomous Vichy regime to the south, there was something of a time lag between persecution of Jews in the two zones. In this respect, Vichy France was less collaborationist than Germans bent on the "final solution" would have preferred. This was partly because the Vichy collaborators distinguished between those Jews born in France, especially if they were veterans of World War I, and more recent working-class and merchant Jewish immigrants and partly because Vichy wanted to keep the property of French Jews out of German hands because it was, of course, French property.

In the early 1940s, there were about 150,000 Jews living in Paris and its suburbs, of whom half were French citizens but were insufficiently protected by their status. The Vichy General Commission for Jewish Affairs combined strategies with the Nazis and created a coordinating section of French Jewish leaders to prepare the ground for genocide. Misguidedly and unwittingly, the Union Générale des Israelites de France (UGIF) became something of a Nazi tool. Its refusal to accept Jewish immigrants as the equals of French Jews gave it less of a chance to protect all Jews as it dutifully carried out preliminary paper work. In his *The Jews of Paris and the Final Solution* (1987), Jacques Adler explains how cruel was the dilemma faced by Jewish community leaders. When they were instructed by the Nazis to collect blankets and shoes—presumably for the inmates of concentration camps—they pondered whether it was compliance or refusal that would most aid Germany. Compliance was undoubtedly a form of collaboration; refusal would deprive the hapless victims of their most basic needs for any form of survival. The very act of shielding Jewish children, the most innocent of victims, was hazardous for the survival of the UGIF itself. This disturbing realization led to the agency eventually yielding the children to the Germans and thereby leading to their removal to concentration camps only three weeks before Paris was liberated. There were underground heroes and heroines, often refugees fighting alongside Communists or Socialists, who acted independently or in cadres. It is their sustained resistance that, once again, illustrates how tyranny can never finally extinguish the spirit of freedom among the bravest souls.

Victims of the Holocaust

The number of Jews killed by country of origin is estimated as

Poland	2,600,000
USSR	750,000
Rumania	750,000
Hungary	200,000
Germany	180,000
Lithuania	104,000
Netherlands	104,000
Latvia	70,000
France	65,000
Austria	60,000
Czechoslovakia	60,000
Greece	60,000
Yugoslavia	58,000
Bulgaria	40,000
Belgium	28,000
Estonia	26,000
Italy	9,000
Luxemburg	3,000
Norway	1,000
Denmark	100

For many people, one book became the most significant icon of the Holocaust because it was a synopsis provided by a most vulnerable victim, a child. This was the diary of Anne Frank, the adolescent girl hiding with her Jewish family in Amsterdam almost to the end of the war. Some time on August 4, 1944, after the Allied invasion of Europe, the Nazis penetrated their secret hiding place above an office at Prin-

When the U.S. Army liberated German concentration camps in April 1945, the soldiers in the Signal Corps could scarcely believe the horrors they witnessed. Three soldiers open an oven used to cremate victims gassed to death in a pictorial composition that makes more macabre the terrible subject matter because of its symmetrical balance. (Department of Defense; Library of Congress).

sengracht 263. The Franks were sent to Westerbrook among the very last cargo designated for "special treatment" and thence to various concentration-extermination camps whence only the father, Otto Frank, returned. The mother, Edith, died in Auschwitz; Anne and her sister, Margot, died in Bergen-Belsen shortly before the camp was liberated by the British. Throughout their years in hiding, the Franks were sustained by a small group of Gentile friends such as Miep Gies who, every day, courted danger to provide them with food, gifts, and news. It was she who gave Anne her first and only pair of high-heeled shoes, and it was she who rescued the crucial diary after the Franks were arrested. She

307

and her husband, Jan, acted as confidantes to a family beset by cabin fever of the most intense kind in a terror seemingly without end. Behind them was the loyal but fractious resistance, official and unofficial, of the courageous Dutch people.

We find it difficult to credit that appeals for help went largely unheeded by Allies apparently intent upon the elimination of fascism and racism. David Wyman has shown something of the Allies' shoddy response in his *Abandonment of the Jews* (1984). In his review of Wyman's book for the *New York Times* (1984) A. J. Sherman calls that response "a complex story from which very few individuals emerge with credit, and some, notably President Franklin D. Roosevelt, stand clearly indicted for a cold indifference in practice utterly at variance with lofty humanitarian sentiments publicly proclaimed for political advantage."

David Wyman records how first reports of the genocide from Poland in 1942 produced stunned disbelief. The press was loath to carry such news; and both press and politicians soon retreated to an attitude that since nothing could be done to stop the horror or aid the victims, the most appropriate responses were to fight the war to a swift conclusion and promise retribution on the perpetrators. The churches were also reluctant to become involved in what could be considered an essentially Jewish problem. However, public awareness of the extent of what was happening inevitably spread, first among the Jewish community at large and then in Britain. Public concern led to an Anglo-American conference held in Bermuda in 1943. Described as a "preliminary two-power discussion on the refugee problem," it was intended to revive the Inter-Governmental Committee on Refugees, a somewhat discredited and totally inactive body created before the war. The conference achieved nothing. It quickly transpired that what both the State Department and the British Foreign Office feared was that any major initiative on their part, such as a feasible rescue of Jews from occupied territory, would oblige Germany to shift policies from extermination to expulsion. This would leave the United States and Britain with the headache and heartache of coping with millions of refugees and the social dislocation this would cause, at the same time as they were fighting an unlimited war. Where could any rescued Jews be placed? Both the State Department and the White House agreed they could not be admitted to the United States. The British Foreign Office refused to consider receiving them anywhere in the British Empire, including Palestine. It was the fear of a massive influx of destitute Jewish refugees as permanent immigrants that convinced American and British officials they must resist any scheme, however minimal, that might stimulate a refugee movement out of continental Europe.

However, in September 1942, at a time when Jews were being deported out of France en masse, pressure from Eleanor Roosevelt and various agencies aiding refugees resulted in the State Department reluctantly agreeing to admit 5,000 Jewish children from France. However, this minimal offer was accompanied by such bureaucratic stalling and ever more stringent tightening of immigration restrictions by the Visa Division of the State Department and by consuls in Spain and Portugal. Wyman tersely concludes: "In all, about 125 children left Spain and Portugal for the United States during 1943 under the special program. Another dozen followed before the war ended in Europe."

Officials concealed their motives for doing next to nothing behind a front of excuses, such as shipping shortages and security problems—difficulties swiftly overcome when they wanted to admit other groups. Thus, 400,000 prisoners of war and 100,000 Greek, Yugoslav, and other Gentile refugees were transported across the Atlantic in Allied ships. Moreover, vessels supplying the European theater from the United States regularly returned empty. The passenger ships of such neutral nations as Spain, Portugal, and Sweden sailed across the Atlantic throughout the war, with only small numbers of passengers.

The American Jewish community, wary of stimulating anti-Semitism and xenophobia in the United States, remained ambivalent toward the problem. The Jewish community was fearful of lobbying the government for rescue efforts and was divided internally by feuds between Zionists and non-Zionists. Jews in high office tended to minimize the dangers confronting European Jews. As Wyman writes, even "Jews who were close to the President did very little to encourage rescue action." Thus Samuel Rosenman, special counsel to FDR, "considered the rescue issue politically sensitive, so he consistently tried to insulate Roosevelt from it." He even opposed the creation of a rescue agency, deliberately weakened a declaration on war crimes to eliminate what he considered "excessive emphasis on the Jews," and argued how "government aid to European Jews might increase anti-Semitism in the United States." The honorable exception to the general "washing of hands" was provided by Secretary of the Treasury Henry Morgenthau. Eventually responding to

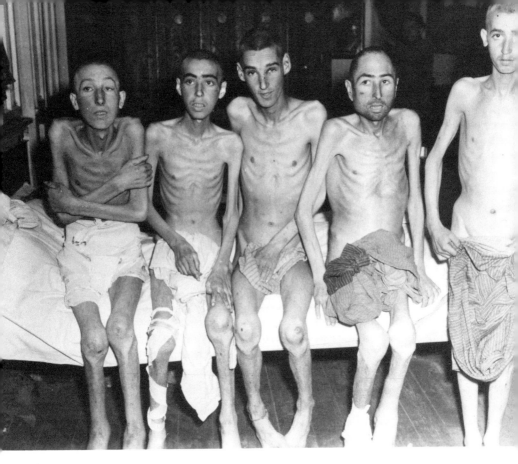

Five emaciated victims of German labor-death camps at the time of their liberation by the U.S. Army in mid-April 1945. (Department of Defense; Library of Congress).

pressure fourteen months after the first authenticated reports of genocide, FDR created the War Refugee Board. However, it had a diminutive budget and little real authority, and its missions were often sabotaged by the State and War Departments. Nevertheless, the board succeeded against considerable odds in saving 200,000 Jews and evacuating another 15,000 from territory held by Germany and Italy, thanks to the courage and energy of a small number of dedicated workers from the Treasury.

Even token gestures, such as sending food parcels from neutral Portugal to Jews in Nazi-held eastern Europe, were opposed by such officials as Assistant Secretary of State Dean Acheson. Wyman concludes, "Few in Congress, whether liberals or conservatives, showed much interest in saving European Jews. Beyond that, restrictionism,

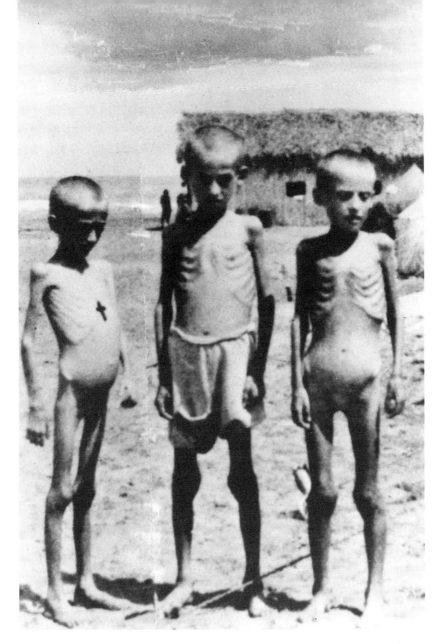

Pity the little children. During and immediately after the war some Polish refugees, like this emaciated trio of innocents, were able to escape the Nazis and were sheltered first in Iran before traveling to Western Europe or the Americas. They were supported by the Polish-American Council based in Chicago, which distributed photographs to the world at large to expose German atrocities in the way of starvation. (Library of Congress).

especially opposition to the entry of Jews, was strong on Capitol Hill." In this, Congress reflected "the indifference of much of the non-Jewish public." Some rescue attempts were made as the Allied armies closed the net first around Nazi satellite countries and then around Germany in 1944 and 1945. However, these were too little and too late. As the eastern front collapsed, the victorious Soviets could have done much more to halt the precipitate forced marches of victims and the complete breakdown of supply routes that led to the deaths of far more victims than of Nazis.

The heroic achievements of the Swedish diplomat Raoul Wallenberg in Hungary demonstrated what could be done to rescue Jews, as he provided them with technically neutral status and arranged for their safe passage out of Hungary. Yet when Hungary finally fell to the Red Army, Raoul Wallenberg was taken by Soviet authorities and disappeared. His possible survival and whereabouts remain the subject of considerable speculation to this day.

Here was a profound tragedy not only for the nations but for all human beings—the survivors, the witnesses, the villains, and those who stood by. "The perpetrators were Christians—Christianity and Western civilization failed." In *Beyond Belief* (1985), Deborah E. Lipstadt records how the American press was generally uninformed and uninforming about Adolf Hitler and the Holocaust. As critic Arnold Beichman surmises, the implication of Lipstadt's work is clear. Had syndicated press and major radio stations been less skeptical of refugee reports about what was happening in Germany, they might have published more and thereby moved an ignorant Congress and public to propose more enlightened and humane immigration policies before the war and during the war itself. The federal government would have been obliged to pursue a more aggressive military strategy against the death camps, hastening the end of the war in order to rescue the Jews.

It is, of course, easy to exaggerate the influence of the press. After all, the majority of leading newspapers backed FDR's rivals for the presidency in his four campaigns with precious little effect on public opinion. Nevertheless, it is also clear that an editor faced by a choice between exciting authentic stories about the battle of Stalingrad, D Day, or the Battle of the Bulge and an unsubstantiated refugee story would choose the military story every time. Furthermore, some of the stories and indeed the entire circumstances of the Holocaust were, as Lipstadt explains, "beyond belief" and seemed like a gross counterpoint to the discredited German cadaver and other atrocity stories of World War I. Faced with government reports about Nazi atrocities, the American press remained incredulous. Jewish witnesses told of events too horrifying to be plausible. It was one thing for barbarous acts to be committed by soldiers in the heat of battle. It was quite another to credit that a supposedly civilized country like Germany would order the burning of bodies in ovens.

Some writers recognized the terrible evil in the Hitler dictatorship from the start and believed the worst later on. They included Otto Tolischus and Anne O'Hare McCormick of the *New York Times*; George Sokolsky of the *New York Sun*; H. R. Knickerbocker of the *New York Evening Post*; Alexander Uhl of *PM*; Louis Lochner of the Associated Press; Dorothy Thompson, a syndicated columnist; and Edward R. Murrow of CBS News. Such writers found their work subject to the contrary gales of opinion as to what was good copy. Thus, sometimes the major papers and networks would ignore a major story about the Holocaust one day and then publish a similar story under a banner headline on the next.

Not only was the Holocaust momentous in itself, but it had profound consequences for world history. Collective Gentile guilt over the Holocaust led to wider support for the Zionist movement to create a Jewish state in Palestine—Israel. It united the leaders of the Grand Alliance in a determination to eliminate right-wing dictatorships among the defeated powers at the end of the war. It justified the division of Germany in 1945. Above all, the Holocaust spoke the message that this had, after all, been a righteous war.

The Allies agreed in London in August 1945 to bring German and Japanese war criminals to trial for crimes against peace, humanity, and even the laws of war. From November 20, 1945, to October 1, 1946, a military tribunal at Nuremberg, at which Associate Justice Robert H. Jackson acted as special prosecutor, tried twenty-four leading Nazi offenders. Twelve of the accused were sentenced to death by hanging: Reichsmarschall Hermann Göring (who committed suicide by poison on the eve of his execution); Martin Bormann, tried in absentia; and ten who were hanged on October 16, 1946, including Joachim Ribbentrop and Field Marshal Wilhelm Keitel. Three were acquitted, including Franz von Papen. Three escaped trial: Martin Bormann; Gustav Krupp, because of age and ill health; and Robert Ley, who committed suicide after being indicted.

The United States conducted another twelve trials in which 836,000 former Nazis were tried in the American zone in Germany. Of these, 503,360 were convicted; 430,890 were fined less than 1,000 RM *(Reichsmark)*; 27,413 were sentenced to perform community work; 7,768 were sentenced to short terms in labor camps; 18,503 were pronounced ineligible to hold public office; and 20,865 had part of their property confiscated.

Ironically, the deathly silence of Western Civilization during the war was followed decades later by the self-serving regret of later politicians and a competitive industry of plangent commemoration.

A Second Chance

American diplomats assumed that this terrible war would provide the United States with a second change to make the world safe for democracy. They believed this could be achieved by a new international community based on collective security, the United Nations. In the 17 February 1941 issue of *Life*, Henry Luce, the editor of *Time* magazine, explained that the United States must "assume the leadership of the world" and inaugurate "the American century." In a speech of May 8, 1942, Vice President Henry Wallace foretold a "people's revolution," leading to the "century of the common man."

As FDR had told the country on December 9, 1941, "we must begin the great task that is before us by abandoning once and for all the illusion that we can ever again isolate ourselves from the rest of humanity." Permanent alliances, previously banned as a means of promoting national interest, were to become a regular feature of American foreign policy, as the United States first promoted and joined the United Nations in the early 1940s and then in the late 1940s and 1950s signed a network of security treaties, affecting the Americas, the North Atlantic, Southeast Asia, and the Middle East.

Historian Richard W. Leopold (1962) observes that "seldom has past experience played so large a role in shaping foreign policy as it did in marshalling popular sentiment for membership in the United Nations." A legend developed that America's refusal to join the League of Nations

Young Jewish girls, probably in Kaunitz, liberated from a German camp at the end of the war. (Library of Congress).

in 1910 and 1920 had condemned the League to a futile existence, incapable of resisting aggression. The weakness of the League had resulted in World War II, and thus the American government was a partner to the tragedy. Therefore, to avoid another international catastrophe, the United States must take a lead in creating a new system of collective security throughout the world.

By the early 1940s, veteran foreign-affairs commentator Walter Lippmann had shed his earlier Wilsonian convictions and did not share his contemporaries' sudden idealism. In his *U.S. Foreign Policy: Shield of the Republic* (1943), he repudiated many of his earlier ideas. His conclusions had come "slowly over thirty years, and as a result of many false starts, mistaken judgments and serious disappointments. They represent what I now think I have learned, not at all what I always knew." Thus, "if there is to be peace in our time, it will have to be peace among sovereign national states." Nations could only achieve

315

security by forming combinations (or alliances) with others. The failure of European countries to unite against Hitler had led to Nazi domination of the Continent. The lesson was clear. The Allies—America, Britain, and Russia—must stay united after the defeat of Germany and Japan. "The failure to form an alliance of the victors will mean the formation of alliances between the vanquished and some of the victors," as had happened in 1919. America and Britain must remain linked by the Atlantic, while Russia must be brought into the "nuclear alliance."

Lippmann's analysis was based on the principle of American self-interest. The Russian-American alliance would be subject to strain after the war. Thus, the West should not try and rebuild the prewar *cordon sanitaire* of eastern European states with quasi-fascist governments hostile to the Soviet Union. Instead, it should realize that the Russians would never tolerate anti-Soviet regimes on their borders. Thus, eastern Europe would have to be neutral; and the settlement depended on "whether the border states will adopt a policy of neutralization, and whether Russia will respect and support it."

The book was published at a time when Americans, having rejected isolationism, were looking for a guideline. Lippmann's direct, well-phrased arguments were about cooperation among the great powers and not about international assemblies or pacts to outlaw war. Lippmann's realism is summed up in his much-quoted dictum that a workable foreign policy "consists in bringing into balance, with a comfortable surplus of power in reserve, the nation's commitment and the nation's power." Put more colloquially by Lippmann's biographer Ronald Steel, it amounted to "don't bite off more than you can chew." There was also a corollary: "don't chew more than you can swallow." *U.S. Foreign Policy* soon sold almost half a million copies. The book was condensed by *Reader's Digest*, and the *Ladies Home Journal* reduced its argument to seven pages of strip cartoons. The American armed forces distributed a paperback edition costing twenty-five cents to the troops. It seemed Lippmann's preferred solution of cooperation among the great powers was a more hopeful option than bankrupt isolationism and wishful universalism.

Nevertheless, the book had its critics. Senator Robert Taft of Ohio told the American Bar Association that "if world federalism was impractical," then "a postwar military alliance as advocated by Walter Lippmann and others was frightening." An Anglo-American agreement to police the world would produce a "profession of militarists" and lead the United States to "occupy all the strategic points in the world and try to maintain a force so preponderant that none shall dare attack us." Moreover, "potential power over other nations, however benevolent its purpose, leads inevitably to imperialism."

Whereas Woodrow Wilson's heirs wanted a new league of nations based on collective security, Lippmann, as he told Professor Quincy Wright in a letter of July 22, 1943, was most concerned that any organization "directed against everybody in general and nobody in particular, would quickly develop a pro and anti-Russian alignment," since the first bones of contention would be the states on the Russian frontiers. "The great object of international organization in the next generation is to hold together the alliance and to hold it together at almost any cost." Lippmann's interpretation seemed cynical to those Americans committed to Wilsonian liberalism who believed that it was only Europeans who had colonies, client states, and spheres of influence. Senator Henry Cabot Lodge, Jr., of Massachusetts, grandson of the man who had led the fight to stop America joining the League of Nations, declared that America must now lead the world because it alone had no imperial ambitions. In a private letter of July 1, 1943, Lippmann gave Lodge an elementary lesson in foreign policy. "You say that Britain has a very practical national aim, which is to maintain the Empire, but that we have no such practical aim. In fact, in this respect we have exactly the same definite practical aim as Britain: we too intend to maintain our pre-war position—in Alaska, Hawaii, the Philippines, in the Caribbean, and in South America. The British aim to hold what she had is so obviously our own aim too that it is universally taken for granted and outside the bounds of discussion."

Lippmann had also introduced the idea of "national security," by which he meant the protection of the United States and the preservation of its democratic institutions. Later, statesmen and diplomats would use the concept of national security as the basis for a global foreign policy that Lippmann spent the last years of his life decrying.

Americans, conveniently forgetting about their privileged position in Latin America and the Caribbean, professed outrage at the cynical idea of a Russian sphere of influence. Lippmann thought it was clear that the Russians must exercise a dominant influence in those areas they thought essential to national security. In his column of 14 December 1943, he

Judgment at Nuremberg. Among the accused perpetrators of war crimes on trial for their lives were Hermann Göring, with a sadistic smile creased into a grimace *(extreme left)*, and other leading Nazis. A still from *Mein Kampf.* (Columbia Pictures, 1961; Museum of Modern Art Film Stills Archive).

pointed out how "we must not make the error of thinking that the alternative to 'isolation' is universal 'intervention.' " Answering those who wanted to use the United Nations to contain Russia, he repeated how peace must rest on cooperation between the great powers and on respect for spheres of influence. To deny this would be to indulge in "the pretense, wholly illusory and dangerously confusing, that every state has an identical influence, interest, power and responsibility everywhere."

In order to ensure that he could bring the United States into his grand design, FDR studied Woodrow Wilson's strategy anew and determined to avoid his errors. He decided, therefore, that any new covenant must be kept separate from any peace treaty; that its terms must be publicized while they were being devised; and that he must seek its adoption before the end of the war dissipated the unity of the Grand Alliance abroad and the wartime enthusiasm and responsibility in Congress at home. He decided to obtain legislative approval for his proposals before principles were translated into specific clauses. Moreover, he knew he must anticipate the harmful and disruptive effect of party politics by having the charter drafted by delegates from both parties and from both houses. FDR disclosed his ideas slowly, partly so as not to move too far ahead of public opinion and partly to prevent diplomatic ends getting confused with military strategy. Nevertheless, he allowed a four-power declaration at the foreign ministers' conference at Moscow on November 1, 1943, to assert "the necessity of establishing at the earliest practicable date a general international organization, based on the principle of the sovereign equality of all peace-loving states, and open to membership by all such states, large and small, for the maintenance of international peace and security."

Moreover, the political climate at home encouraged hopes that the United States would not only take part but also lead the United Nations, notably when a measure proposed by Congressman J. William Fulbright of Arkansas passed the House by 360 votes to 29 on June 15, 1943. The House resolved that the United States should take the initiative in forming the United Nations with machinery to settle disputes, if necessary by the use of force. On November 5, 1943, the Senate adopted a similar resolution proposed by Thomas Terry Connally of Texas, which incorporated key portions of the Moscow declaration, by 85 votes to 6.

Thus by the summer of 1944, FDR and Secretary of State Cordell Hull had persuaded Britain and Russia, the Senate and the House, and Democrats and Republicans to learn from the mistakes of history. By May 29, Hull had concluded discussions of the draft charter with the Senate Foreign Relations Committee; Stalin then approved the text on July 9, 1944; and talks began at the Dumbarton Oaks estate in Washington, D.C., on August 21, 1944.

Experience with the League of Nations had taught delegates at Dumbarton Oaks what to keep and what to discard. Despite its numerous problems, the League had been structurally sound; and delegates soon agreed to retain a Security Council, a General Assembly, a Secretariat, and an International Court of Justice in the new United Nations. As to the League's weaknesses, delegates agreed that they should not insist on unanimity in the United Nations's Security Council or Assembly before any important move could be made; and that all member nations must pledge to accept and act upon findings of the Supreme Council in advance and place some of their armed forces at its disposal. Each of the Big Three wanted a right of veto before decisive action on any major issue, partly to protect their own interests and partly to be able to justify international use of resources and troops to their own peoples. In the United States, disputes tended to devolve on old controversies. Could the president place American forces at the disposal of the Security Council by executive agreement and thereby evade the treaty-making process? Could the American representative on the Security Council move American troops without the authority of Congress? With some fundamental principles settled, the leading nations began to ponder the problems of subsidiary agencies to the United Nations.

At the conference in Bretton Woods, New Hampshire, which opened on July 1, 1944, diplomats met and made arrangements providing for an international bank and a world fund for stabilizing currencies and providing funds to reconstruct countries ravaged by war. This was the International Monetary Fund (IMF), but it did not begin to work effectively until 1946. The primary aim of these institutions was to bring stability and order to international banking and to make possible national reconstruction schemes.

In addition, the United Nations was to fund a series of relief agencies. The first of these was the World Food and Agriculture Organization (usually, FAO), eventually established in Quebec out of a conference in October 1945 to allot surpluses of scarce foods to countries most in need. It had been planned originally at a conference in Hot Springs, Virginia, in 1943, following a suggestion from FDR. UNESCO, the agency intended "to contribute to peace and security by promoting international collaboration in the fields of education, science and culture," was first conceived at a council of ministers of education of the Allied countries held in London in 1942. The United Nations Relief and Rehabilitation Administration (UNRRA) was created in November 1943. Between 1944 and 1947, it provided massive aid to countries devastated by war, thereby saving their populations from starvation and disease.

[8]

ONE WORLD, OR TWO?

Yalta

W INSTON CHURCHILL gave the title *Triumph and Tragedy* to the last volume of his history of World War II. He was referring to the triumph of the Grand Alliance over Hitler and the Japanese, and the tragedy of the imminent dissolution of the alliance. Both were apparent at the Crimean conference of the Big Three, usually known as the Yalta conference, that met from February 4 to February 12, 1945. In all Allied meetings prior to Yalta, the discussions had centered on the strategy for defeating the Axis powers. However, by the time the Big Three met at Yalta, the defeat of Germany was imminent; the debate now turned to problems of the postwar world.

Since D Day Churchill had been trying to reach an accord with FDR on postwar Europe. The prime minister's priorities were defined by the traditional British aversion to continental dominance by one great power. By 1944, it was obvious to Churchill that the Soviet Union would gain that ascendency in continental Europe after the defeat of Germany. He was also aware that Britain alone could not contend with the threat posed by a powerful Soviet Union. If a peaceful balance of power, upon which British security was predicated, were ever to be achieved, then

This classic photograph of the Big Three at Yalta in February 1945 conveys the charged atmosphere among the Grand Alliance. FDR's visage betrays the pallor of death; Churchill's smile is professional rather than spontaneous; and Stalin is inscrutable. The convoy of high-ranking aides and uniformed officers above adds more than a touch of menace to the composition. (Library of Congress).

the United States would have to be persuaded to stand as a counterweight to Russia in Europe. However, Churchill's hopes of establishing this balance of power were jeopardized by the expected American commitment to withdraw from Europe once victory over Hitler was achieved and a settlement was reached on the future status of Germany.

Churchill had gone the year before to the second Quebec, or "Octagon," conference of September 11 to September 16, 1944, hoping to persuade FDR to keep an American presence in Europe. By raising the bogey of the Bolshevik menace, he tried to alert Roosevelt to the necessity of the American presence as a part of a new balance of power in Europe. Unfortunately for Churchill, FDR refused to be drawn into this issue. However, he did put his signature to an ill-conceived plan for the future of Germany. The plan was the brainchild of Secretary of the Treasury Henry Morgenthau. The scheme aimed at "pastoralizing" Germany—that is, reducing it to an agrarian nation devoid of industrial potential. Churchill rejected the plan. If implemented, the plan would have left Germany terminally weak and reliant upon a high level of industrial support that Britain simply could not afford to provide. Churchill argued that the vacuum in central Europe would be filled inevitably by the Soviet Union. However, Britain's own need for immediate economic support from America forced Churchill to withdraw his opposition. To gain the prime minister's approval, Morgenthau offered $3.5 billion worth of lend-lease supplies to be delivered until the defeat of Japan and a further credit of $3 billion for nonmilitary purposes.

When Churchill returned to London, his war cabinet rejected outright the Morgenthau plan. Similarly, FDR's advisers in Washington persuaded him to withdraw his support for the scheme. FDR then repudiated the plan and imposed a moratorium on all further discussions about Germany's future status.

Having failed to involve the United States in his plans for postwar Europe, Churchill had no alternative but to seek out an accord with Stalin. At the Moscow conference of October 9 to October 17, 1944, Churchill sought to gain assurance that the future government of Poland would comprise not only the Moscow-backed Lublin Committee but also representatives of the London-based government in exile. While Churchill made no progress on this issue, he and Stalin did reach agreement on future spheres of interest in eastern Europe. It was decided that Russia was to have 90 percent predominance in Rumania and 75 percent predominance in Bulgaria. Britain would have 90 percent predominance in Greece, and Anglo-Soviet influence in Hungary and Yugoslavia would be split fifty-fifty.

With the postwar balance of power taking shape, Churchill went to Yalta seeking a similar understanding upon the postwar status of Poland and Germany. Churchill was anxious to reach an agreement while the Allies were still united in the common fight against Germany and before the United States began its proposed withdrawal from Europe. He was also aware that concessions could be wrung from Stalin while Russia was still dependent upon American supplies of war materiel.

On this point, he was supported by policy planners in the State Department. In the weeks prior to Yalta, they argued that, when discussing the future of Poland, FDR should use the promise of future aid to gain leverage over Stalin. However, FDR had no intention of bargaining away the future of eastern and central Europe. He did not share Churchill's enthusiasm for a division of Europe into spheres of influence. To FDR and his close advisers, the idea of peaceful coexistence through a postwar balance of power was a dangerous fallacy. It had, in their opinion, not only failed to prevent the two world wars but had also made such conflicts inevitable.

Nor did FDR share Churchill's utter distrust of Stalin. Indeed, he believed that he shared much the same ground as "Uncle Joe." This misconception informed his views on the postwar settlement. FDR was convinced that a lasting peace could only be achieved by developing the wartime unity of purpose into a permanent feature of great-power relations. This spirit of unity was, of course, to find expression in the proposed United Nations. If the Soviets could be persuaded to commit themselves to this organization, then potentially explosive issues, such as Poland, could be settled amicably upon a basis of consensus and mutual understanding.

Thus, FDR went to Yalta seeking not to confront Stalin but to gain concessions from him. The first concession related directly to the president's plans for the postwar world.

Progress toward the establishment of the United Nations had been severely impeded at the Dumbarton Oaks conference of August and September 1944 by Soviet objections to the proposed formula for voting in the Security Council. The Soviets were adamant that no action could be recommended by the Security Council unless all five permanent members (which later included China and France) were in unanimous agreement. In effect, they defended their right to veto any course of action that might in some way redound upon their own interests.

By the time he arrived at Yalta, FDR was fearful that, unless this issue was settled, the United Nations would be stillborn. At Yalta, the debate was settled to his satisfaction. Stalin agreed that permanent members should not be allowed to vote should they be party to disputes that could be settled by peaceful means. Conversely, permanent members should be entitled to vote if they were party to disputes that required the application of economic, political, or military sanctions.

Having resolved this problem, discussions then moved on to the demand for the admission of all sixteen Soviet republics to the United Nations General Assembly. In a private aside, FDR commented that, if the Soviets were accommodated on this point, he would ask for separate membership for all forty-eight states of the Union. However, the Russians had compromised their position and were now willing to accept membership of just three republics—the Ukraine, Belorussia, and Lithuania—besides Russia itself. The British and Americans were happy to consent to this on the condition that, for the sake of parity, the United States should also have three votes in the General Assembly. Stalin promised his support for such a proposal, and the Big Three agreed to send representatives to a meeting in San Francisco on April 25, 1945, to draft the United Nations Charter. Stalin was concerned that the United States could, by its largess, influence the vote of many small nations in the General Assembly and that Britain could count on the votes of the Commonwealth nations.

FDR went to Yalta with two principal objectives: One related to his plans for postwar cooperation. The other concerned his desire for further wartime cooperation with the Russians. On this issue, what he wanted was a guarantee that the Soviets would enter the war against Japan. At Quebec in September 1944, Churchill and FDR had agreed that the target date for ending the war against Japan should be set at eighteen months after victory over Hitler. Conventional wisdom among FDR's planners held that the end of that war would come only with a full-scale invasion of Japan and the destruction by force of its military capacity. Estimates of the human cost of attaining victory were put at one million American casualties.

Destruction of the Japanese military machine would mean not only invading the homeland but also confronting the one-million-strong Japanese force in Manchuria. American military leaders regarded the prospect of invasion with deep foreboding. Throughout the war, they had looked with dread upon the self-sufficient Kwantung Army. It was well trained, well equipped, and, because of the industrial potential of the region that it controlled, it had the capacity to continue the fight long after Tokyo was taken.

FDR did not know it, but, at the time of Yalta, the Kwantung Army was a paper tiger. Allied intelligence services had failed to note that by 1945 some thirteen divisions, numerous supporting units, vast quantities of supplies, and the bulk of Japanese air strength in Manchuria had been secretly diverted from China. American military planners were unaware that they had, since February 1944, been fighting the cream of the Kwantung Army in the Pacific. Had FDR known this, it is probable that he still would have pressed for Soviet entry into the war in the east. The passing of the Kwantung threat would release Russian troops for a coordinated invasion of Japan.

At Yalta the American ambassador to the Soviet Union, Averill Harriman, and the Russian foreign minister, Vyacheslav Molotov, drew up a draft agreement on this issue and then passed it to the Big Three for ratification. As it transpired, Stalin promised that the Soviet Union would declare war on Japan two or three months after the surrender of Germany. In return, Russia would get the Kurile Islands and southern Sakhalin; an international guarantee of the autonomous status of Outer Mongolia (that is, tacit Allied acceptance of that republic as a satellite of the Soviet Union); renewed leases for Soviet use of Darien as a commercial port and Port Arthur as a naval base; and joint control, with the Chinese, over the Chinese Eastern and South Manchurian railroads. We should note that, with the exception of the Kurile Islands, these territorial concessions involved land taken from Russia by Japan in the Russo-Japanese War of 1904–5. FDR suggested that Darien should be declared an international port and that the Manchurian railways should be run jointly by Russia and China. He insisted that the Soviet Union declare its support for the Kuomintang government of Jiang Jieshi. Stalin agreed that China should retain full sovereignty over Manchuria, while FDR promised to deliver Jiang's full support for the accord.

Negotiations were carried out in secret, and, when the accord was signed, Jiang was not informed. Such secrecy was justified on grounds of security. So untrustworthy were Jiang's advisers that to tell him would have been tantamount to sending a telegram to Tokyo giving details of Russia's impending entry into the war. Nevertheless, some believe Jiang (who was not present) gained more at Yalta than anyone else.

FDR could look with satisfaction upon the Yalta conference. He had succeeded in achieving his two main objectives: Soviet commitment to the United Nations and a Soviet promise to declare war on Japan. To win Stalin's confidence and cooperation, FDR had avoided detailed discussion of issues that might threaten the unity of the alliance. As to the treatment of Germany, the Allies were in unanimous agreement on

Waves of consolidated B-24 liberator planes of the 15th Army Air Force retreat from the Concordia vegal oil refinery in Ploesti, Rumania, heedless of bursting flak, having discharged bombs upon the oil-cracking plant. Shafts of black smoke arise from damaged storage tanks and other installations. (Photo of May 31, 1944, by U.S. Army Air Force; Library of Congress).

the need to eradicate the Nazi party, its laws, institutions, and general militarism. However, when Stalin proposed dismembering Germany, Churchill voiced his distinct reservations about the plan and suggested long and detailed scrutiny of the issue before a decision was made. Aware that such scrutiny might lead to acrimony, FDR succeeded in postponing the debate until a special committee was established in London to frame an agreement on dismemberment.

The Big Three also decided to postpone agreement on the thorny issue of reparations. At Yalta Stalin demanded that Germany be stripped of $20 billion worth of industrial plants by way of reparations, of which 50 percent were to go to the Soviet Union. The British rightly recognized this as another attempt to "pastoralize" Germany and soundly rejected it. Another potentially disruptive debate was avoided by an agreement to refer the question to a three-power reparations commission that was to convene in Moscow at a later date.

While FDR was inclined to agree with Churchill on the question of reparations, he refrained from saying so for fear of antagonizing Stalin. He believed that if Stalin were to conclude that the western Allies were ganging up on him on specific issues, then he would refuse to cooperate on issues of more immediate importance, such as the United Nations and Japan. Thus, at Yalta FDR tried to assume the role of honest broker, mediating between Britain and the Soviet Union. In such circumstances, Churchill had little hope of gaining American support for a balance of power in Europe. Therefore, if the United States could not be relied upon, Churchill turned to France for support. At Yalta he gave his full backing to de Gaulle's demand for a leading role in the postwar settlement of Germany. At the conference, first FDR and then Stalin succumbed to Churchill's pleading on de Gaulle's behalf. France was duly accorded a place on the Control Council for Germany, and a French zone was carved out of the British and American zones of occupation. France was also given a sector in the capital, Berlin, in the eastern zone controlled by the Soviet Union.

Stalin was willing to compromise on this issue, but he drew the line on Poland. On this subject, the Big Three were poles apart. The Polish question proved the most time-consuming of all, and discussions extended for six days and nights. At the time of the Yalta conference, Russian troops already had crossed the whole of Poland and were driving the Nazi forces back into Germany. There was a Polish government in exile in London, composed of centrist and right-wing shades of opinion.

On April 16, 1943, BBC radio in London had reported how Germany had announced the discovery of the mass grave of many thousands of Polish officers in the Russian territory now under its control. The implication was clear. These were the corpses of Poles taken prisoner by the Red Army in 1939 and massacred. The Germans suggested that the International Red Cross should conduct an impartial investigation into the affair. The Polish government in London agreed, and the Soviet government interpreted this demand as a hostile act and broke off diplomatic relations with the Poles in London.

The situation worsened. In early January 1944, the Red Army was pushing the routed German forces back into western Europe. The German forces crossed the pre-1939 frontier of the Soviet Union and moved across Poland. Beginning on August 1, 1944, the valiant and desperate Poles staged an astonishing uprising in Warsaw—the terrible climax of years of bitter resistance. However, the Germans used all their available infantry and air power to crush the insurrection and devastate Warsaw by October 2, leaving it in ruins. Meanwhile, the Red Army waited some distance from the city and watched while Warsaw was reduced to rubble. One reason was that the Polish Home Army owed its allegiance to the London Poles, whom the Russians no longer recognized as the Polish government in exile. Another reason was that the Soviet Union wanted to be the sole liberator of Poland. (The Russians entered Warsaw on January 11, 1945.) Another, even more sinister reason, was that many able partisans, who would have resisted communism, perished in the carnage of the Warsaw uprising. Thus, Hitler was doing Stalin's work for him. The devastation wrought on Poland, and especially Warsaw, enabled the Soviets to construct far more easily the sort of Polish state they wanted.

In the summer of 1944, the Soviet government created a Polish Committee of National Liberation, which was composed almost exclusively of Communists and was based in Lublin. The committee was entrusted with the civil administration of Polish territory as it was freed by the Red Army. On January 1, 1945, Stalin recognized the Lublin committee as the legitimate provisional government of Poland. Thus, there were now two Polish governments: one in London, the ally of Britain and the United States; the other in Lublin, the ally of the Soviet Union. However, the real ruler of Poland was the Red Army; under its protection, the Polish Communist party was assured effective power.

FDR tried to be pragmatic. He wanted a new provisional government to be drawn partly from the Poles in Lublin, partly from the Polish government in exile in London, and partly from other Poles within the country. Such a government would not be hostile to the Soviet Union, and it would be representative enough to govern Poland until national elections could be held. This compromise was accepted by Churchill (who preferred the London Poles) and Molotov (who wanted the Lublin Poles). However, insisting on the London Poles was useless since that group would have had to return to and brave a country dominated by hostile Russian troops.

To appease Churchill and, to a lesser extent, FDR, Stalin agreed that the Lublin committee might be augmented by representatives from other émigré circles. Elections could then be held to establish a permanent government in Poland. However, the western Allies were loath to recognize the Lublin committee, seeing it as little more than a Soviet puppet regime that was being foisted upon the Polish people. They argued that the London-based group was the true representative of Poland's political aspirations and insisted that its members be accorded a predominant role in the provisional government. They also wanted the proposed elections to be supervised by the Allies.

Stalin held his ground, and the British and American argument collapsed. Churchill and FDR agreed to grant formal recognition to the "Provisional Government which is now functioning in Poland." They also agreed that the proposed elections were to be free of Allied supervision.

However, the Big Three agreed upon the frontiers of the new Poland. The Soviet Union was to be given the former areas of Poland east of the so-called Curzon line, and Poland would be compensated by the cession of German lands in East Prussia and in the west. Stalin wanted the western frontier of Poland to run from Stettin in the north, along the length of the Oder and western Neisse rivers down to the frontier with Czechoslovakia. This would not only restore to Poland territories taken by Hitler in 1939 but also add Pomerania and Silesia, including the ancient German city of Breslau. FDR thought these demands excessive, and he and Churchill persuaded Stalin to postpone the final decision on the exact Polish-German frontier until a peace conference. (In fact, the Potsdam conference of summer 1945 failed to resolve these differences.) The extent of the territorial compensation to which the Poles helped themselves, with Russian support, was far greater than America and Britain had intended. The western frontier of Poland was a clear violation of the principles of the Atlantic Charter. Five million Germans were never allowed an opportunity to determine their future. The final effect of Big Three negotiations was to push both the eastern and western boundaries of Poland farther west than ever before.

The future of other eastern European states received far less attention at Yalta. Here, potential differences were papered over by an agreement enshrined in the American-sponsored "Declaration on Liberated Europe," drafted partly to satisfy American public opinion. In this document, the Allies promised to cooperate in helping the people of liberated states and former Nazi satellites to "form interim governmental authorities, broadly representative of all democratic elements in the population and pledged to the earliest possible establishment through free elections of governments responsive to the will of the people." Roosevelt, Churchill, and Stalin also promised that their governments would consult each other immediately on the "measures necessary to discharge [their] joint responsibilities." In Yugoslavia, Tito was able to form a government he wanted despite British attempts to have Yugoslav exiles included. The governments of Hungary, Rumania, and Bulgaria —all countries now dominated by the Red Army—were strongly pro-Soviet. Finland had also allied itself with Hitler, but Russia did not interfere in Finnish politics, apart from taking Petsamo in the north.

German forces withdrew from Greece in early autumn 1944. The resistance there was largely Communist, or Communist inspired, and Churchill dispatched 60,000 British troops to support the king of Greece in his attempt to regain the kingdom, although his record was far from democratic. The British defeated the resistance, and Stalin sent no aid to the Communists. Churchill and Anthony Eden went to Athens on Christmas Day and imposed a provisional government under Archbishop Damaskinos, thereby demonstrating Churchill's opposition to communism and, perhaps, confirming Stalin in his belief that he must have a free hand in his own war zone. Charles E. Bohlen, a State Department official who acted as FDR's interpreter, later told the foreign relations committee of the Senate that the ensuing situation in Eastern Europe and the Balkans was essentially the product of the war and that there were really no alternatives to the decisions reached at Yalta.

At the time, the American and Allied press praised those portions of the Yalta agreement made public. Since Russia and Japan were not yet at war, plans for Russia to declare war on Japan were kept secret. Veteran foreign-affairs commentator Walter Lippmann summed up the consensus of approval in his "Today and Tomorrow" column of 15 February 1945: "There has been no more impressive international conference in our time, none in which great power was so clearly hardened to the vital, rather than the secondary, interests of nations."

Was the Yalta conference and its decisions a disaster for the West, as some conservative critics of FDR would have us believe? In reality FDR went to Yalta not to command but to sue, and he returned having achieved his two objectives — the breakdown of Soviet intransigence about the United Nations and Soviet agreement to enter the war against Japan. However, to secure these objectives, he had to make concessions in order to win Stalin's cooperation. It was FDR's willingness to make concessions that later persuaded his critics to see Yalta as a betrayal of Western interests. For three years, Stalin had been in a weaker position than either Churchill or FDR. He had had to beg them to open a second front while being unable to offer any special inducements, since the Russians would, of course, continue to fight valiantly for their independence. Now the Joint Chiefs of Staff had convinced FDR and Churchill that Russian intervention in the war against Japan was worth almost any price. Neither Churchill nor Roosevelt had much choice. They were at war with Japan; Stalin was not. Stalin's armies had moved across eastern Europe; theirs had not.

Did FDR make irresponsible concessions to Stalin in the Far East? At Yalta, FDR had no idea that a Japanese surrender could be obtained without Russian participation in the war. The specter of the Kwantung Army hovered over negotiations between FDR and Stalin on this issue. In striking his bargain with Stalin, FDR believed that he was helping to save countless thousands of American lives. Also, ever since Pearl Harbor, FDR's primary goal had been to win the war as quickly as possible. The logical route to that goal would be to involve the Red Army in the final onslaught against Japan. Thus, given the circumstances under which he was operating, FDR's bargain on Russian entry into the war in the Far East was almost wholly favorable to American interests. It was guaranteed to save American lives and shorten the war.

Did FDR betray Poland and eastern Europe to the Soviets? In fact, he was in no position to take a firm stand. The only leverage he had lay in a possible threat to stop lend-lease deliveries in the Soviet Union. Moreover, such a policy would have been counter to American interests, for it would have weakened the Soviet effort on the eastern front; slowed down their offensive in that theater; allowed Hitler to transfer men and supplies to the western front; and resulted in greater American casualties and prolonged the war.

Furthermore, the very threat of such a strategy also would have poisoned relations between the two great powers, ruined FDR's efforts to win Stalin's cooperation on other more urgent issues (the United Nations and Japan), and shattered his hopes for postwar cooperation.

FDR appeased Stalin on Poland because he wanted to avoid confrontation. For the same reason, he welcomed and encouraged the postponement of the decisions on German reparations, the dismemberment of Germany, and the future status of eastern Europe. It was his belief that such contentious issues could be settled amicably at a later date. This optimism was inspired by the success that he encountered in establishing the United Nations, intended as the institution that would resolve differences. It was FDR's hope that, once accepted into the comity of nations, the Soviet Union would abandon its traditional distrust of the West and commit itself to upholding the principles enshrined in the Atlantic Charter.

FDR's optimism was also inspired by his belief that he had the measure of Marshal Stalin. He was not so naive as to think that goodwill by itself could be the sole basis of future great-power relations. The United States had to have the means with which to persuade the Soviets to cooperate. At Yalta FDR knew that in the postwar era he could use the promise of economic aid to gain leverage over the Soviets. He knew then that he would also have another valuable bargaining counter. This asset was then under construction at a specially built physics laboratory in Los Alamos, New Mexico—the atomic bomb.

Ronald Steel, Walter Lippmann's biographer, sums up FDR's attitude thus: "With its overwhelming economic strength, its predominance in Latin America, its undisputed naval power in the Pacific, its incomparable industrial and military machine, its control over the world's raw materials, the United States would have nothing to fear from a devastated and war-impoverished Russia. This great scheme would all be codified in May, Roosevelt thought, in San Francisco with the creation of the United Nations."

However, foreign policy in the time of Roosevelt and Churchill was not simply a matter of adroit exercise of military strength, formal diplomacy, or economic pressure but also a matter of the control of such new currencies of power as aviation and oil. The way the United States and Britain sought to manipulate the politics of aviation and oil profoundly impaired their special trust and modified the unanimity of the Grand Alliance. Airpower and oil were changing the world.

Civil Aviation

Journalist Anthony Sampson (1976) notes how, as World War II drew to a close, more people began to express concern for the future of civil aviation. In particular, the London blitz, the devastating Japanese attack on Pearl Harbor, and the fire bombing of Dresden had made Americans think long and seriously about the international security of aviation. Thus, people and politicians supported a general notion of "freedom of the air" as part of the diplomatic package that the new United Nations must achieve if it were to ensure freedom and security for the future. Sampson comments that "the huge technical advances of wartime, together with the mood of global idealism, encouraged the misty visions of a world unified by the air. The Pan American emblem, of a globe divided only by latitudes, was the symbol of the new hopes of a world which ignored frontiers."

Wendell Willkie proclaimed a new universality of the air when he became the spokesman for one world. It was all very well for hardboiled men of commerce like Juan Trippe, head of Pan Am, to attack such a nebulous concept as freedom of the air as "woolly-headed internationalism," or for ambitious politicians like Clare Boothe Luce to refer to Wallace's rhetoric in the House as "globaloney," but, nevertheless, Willkie was expressing what a generation was thinking. Welch Pogue, the chairman of the Civil Aeronautics Board, later recalled how "the imagination of men's minds leaped to the view that in the postwar era the airplane would 'shrink' the world so much, both militarily and in a civil sense, as to make every civilization and its trade and commerce available to every other civilization on earth. Suddenly, civil aviation had become vitally important."

By now Trippe's domestic rivals were ready to challenge Pan Am's monopoly of overseas routes. For one thing, in their competition of domestic passengers, they had been developing bigger and faster planes. These included the Douglas DC-4, or "skymaster," a four-engined plane

The tragedies of war spurred the development of civil, as well as military, aviation. This included airport design and construction, notably the National Airport in Washington, D.C., where the first building to have a concave concourse opened in 1941. (Office of War Information; Library of Congress).

that could carry forty-two passengers at 200 miles per hour and the Boeing 307, or "Stratoliner," that could carry forty-four passengers. The old division of tasks between land planes for crossing land and flying boars for crossing sea was less relevant now that long-range planes could traverse both land and sea—unlike trains or ships.

Airchiefs of the "Big Four" airlines (American, TWA, Eastern, and United) were eager to expand, notably Cyrus Smith of Texas who led American Airlines. In 1942, American was awarded a contract for the route to Mexico City; and in 1943, a smaller airline, Braniff, gained a similar contract. Moreover, the "Big Four" were supported by government officials who had their own reasons for restricting Trippe. Trippe's most formidable opponent was General Henry ("Hap") Arnold, chief of staff of the Air Corps, who was one of the founders of Pan Am who had been dislodged when Trippe's group took the airline over. Arnold was also a personal friend of Cyrus Smith, whom he recruited to run Air Transport Command. Arnold was convinced that other airlines should be extended overseas. Accordingly, in mid-1943 Arnold invited the heads of eighteen airlines to a secret meeting in Washington, D.C., to discuss postwar air policy and invited them to form a committee to ensure effective competition. Trippe demurred and persuaded William Patterson, president of United, to refrain from attending. Those who did not come issued a joint statement that air transport overseas should not simply be left to "the withering influence of monopoly." By now several airlines already were flying overseas on military missions, notably American to Europe, United to Australia, and Eastern to Brazil. Thus, Pan Am was beginning to face some formidable competition. Moreover, Welch Pogue announced in October 1943 that in future the State Department and the Civil Aeronautics Board (CAB), and not the airlines, would negotiate overseas routes.

FDR's policies on civil aviation were largely shaped by his forceful adviser in the State Department, lawyer Adolf Berle. "I feel that aviation will have a greater influence on American foreign interests and American foreign policy than any other non-political consideration," he advised Secretary of State Cordell Hull in September 1942. Berle was determined to anticipate an expected division of spoils by a new and furtive oligarchy of the airlines and the federal government. "In the air," he declared in 1944, "there is no excuse for an attempt to revive the sixteenth- and seventeenth-century conceptions . . . for a modern air

British East India Company or Portuguese trading monopoly or 'Spanish Main conception.' " Concerned that British plans for postwar civil aviation were more advanced than those of the United States, Berle created a committee, including Robert Lovett of the War Department, that recommended an international air conference. Encouraged by Roosevelt and Churchill, the conference met in Chicago where it was easily dominated by the "ABC" powers—the United States, Britain, and Canada.

The Americans were manufacturing almost all civilian planes and thus had a considerable advantage over the others. However, although Britain was manufacturing only war planes and dreaded a glut of American planes, it still had its precious network of bases across the globe, including the islands used as refueling stations; and it could use these stations as bargaining counters to protect British interests. For its part, Canada had the advantage of controlling the airport at Gander, the principal landing point between the United States and Europe—at least until airplanes could traverse the Atlantic without stopping to refuel. Technically, Gander was in Newfoundland, a British colony until it became part of Canada in 1949. However, commercially it was part of the Canadian system and was linked with Montreal and Quebec. Hitherto, Canadian diplomats had felt their fledgling air business somewhat threatened by American continental domestic air routes. Now, encouraged by the pivotal role Canada had played ferrying planes to Britain in the war, they acted as conciliators between the Americans and the British.

In August, the Russians proposed an international air force, and Churchill regarded this as a crucial breakthrough to atone for the opportunity missed in 1919. However, the Russians proved adamantly opposed to any genuine attempt to internationalize civil aviation that would intrude on tight Soviet control of planes, pilots, and merchandise in air space over the Soviet Union. Their intransigence greatly reduced the prospects for global agreement. When the major conference on civil aviation opened in Chicago in November 1944 by FDR, the Soviet Union withdrew just before the opening session, ostensibly because such neutral states as Portugal, Spain, and Switzerland were present. To make matters even more difficult, Lord Swinton, formerly resident minister in West Africa, who headed the British delegation, took an instant dislike to Berle, whom he called "easily the most disagreeable person with whom I have ever negotiated." The dislike was mutual. Swinton conciliated his colleagues from the Commonwealth; but he was ill at east with Americans, and, for that matter, with Europeans. Furthermore, the British did not take the Chicago conference seriously. They considered aviation primarily a technical subject outside diplomacy and underrated its immense significance. Leading the American delegation, Berle spoke for "open skies," a policy as exactly attuned to American supremacy in the air as freedom of the seas had been when Britain was master of the seas. In fact, Berle compared the skies to the sea—"a highway given by nature to all men." Moreover, he warned against the repetition of the shortsighted self-interest of certain powers that had led to the denial of equal opportunity for navigation, which had "made the sea a battleground instead of a highway."

Underlying the debate at the conference was the question of whether nations would allow one another's airlines the five freedoms—that is, the technical arrangements that defined the rights of air traffic. They were the freedom to fly over a nation; the freedom to land in a nation; the freedom to transport passengers or goods from the home nation to a foreign nation; the freedom to transport passengers or goods from a foreign nation to the home nation; and the freedom to pick up and land passengers or goods belonging to a foreign nation between intermediate points. While Britain agreed to cooperate and exchange landing rights, the British delegates were acutely aware of Britain's shortage of aircraft and wanted a system to prevent airlines from flooding their routes. Instead of a free-for-all that would inevitably provide America with an overwhelming advantage, the British delegates proposed escalation, which would regulate the frequencies of planes according to the numbers of passengers. This would have allowed Australia, New Zealand, and the European countries time to organize their own aviation industries. However, the American delegation turned escalation down, and the Canadians proposed a compromise. At this point, the British got into a muddle and conceded all but the fifth freedom. This referred to regulating traffic between points en route. Berle asked FDR to intercede, and he wrote to Churchill, "Your people are now asking limitations on the number of planes between points, regardless of the traffic offering. This seems to be a form of strangulation. It has been a cardinal point in American policy throughout that the ultimate judge should be the passenger and the shipper. The limitations now proposed would, I fear, place a dead hand on the use of the great air trade-routes." In his reply, Churchill reminded FDR that Britain had already "agreed to throwing open our airfields all over the world to aircraft of other nationalities." Roosevelt said that British restrictions would be inoperable in many countries and would jeopardize round-the-world routes. He assured Churchill that American airline would not "so fill the air on long routes that nobody else could get in and survive."

At the conference, Fiorello La Guardia, the mayor of New York City, infuriated Swinton by declaring, "It was pointless to make arrangements for airfields if you had no planes which could fly into them." Other countries—Holland, Sweden, and those of Latin America—fearful of British imperialism, supported the United States. Britain was given only token support by Australia, New Zealand, and France. Berle could claim, with some justification, that Britain's policy was "simply blown out of the water" by the opposition of the smaller countries it claimed to protect. In the end, the conference delegates agreed to accept a compromise proposed by KLM, by which the first two freedoms were accepted and a decision on the others was deferred.

In essence, the Chicago convention simply extended prewar agreements at Paris and Havana. The convention firmly stipulated in ARTICLE 1: "The contracting states recognize that every state has complete and exclusive sovereignty over airspace." "The conference was outwardly a failure and essentially a great success," observed British delegate Paul Gore Booth. It created the International Civil Aviation Organization (ICAO) as an agency based in Montreal under the United Nations to coordinate and maintain rules of the air. Its first president was American aviation expert Edward Warner, a former professor of aeronautics.

FDR, stung by criticisms that Berle had made too many concessions to foreign airlines, dismissed him after the conference was over. In fact, both America and Britain miscalculated the outcome. Subsequently, the enemy countries that had been pointedly excluded became major air powers. Britain lost its major bargaining power as its empire disintegrated, and it no longer required long-range planes for its isolated bases. Canada lost its bargaining power when planes could fly direct from New York City or Chicago to Europe and bypass Gander and Montreal. The United States abandoned the fifth freedom when it realized it did not really want foreign airlines flying between American airports. The early domination of the air by the United States was

This striking photograph of Roosevelt and King Ibn Saud at an impromptu reception in February 1945, taken from above, has an interesting mix of subject, composition, and texture in which the angle of the photograph emphasizes the haphazard interplay of carpet design, Arabic headdresses, and Western furniture. (Library of Congress).

interrupted by rising rivals in Germany, Holland, and Japan. Far from representing a fundamental new agreement, the Chicago convention simply reflected the state of power politics. The worst casualty was New Zealand's hope for a genuinely international system. The Soviet Union opposed all five freedoms and maintained close supervision of the air above its vast landmass. Nevertheless, the Chicago convention, through its creation, the ICAO, encouraged the phenomenal growth of postwar civil aviation. It allowed for exchanges of landing rights and information on technology and safety systems.

Britain wanted to revive the IATA to discuss how airlines could cooperate and arrive at reasonable fares. Although American delegates at Chicago, in keeping with their antitrust laws, were sensitive to any suggested conspiracy between airlines, they agreed with a BOAC proposal to call a conference at Havana for April 1945 to discuss this very point. There, thirty-one nations duly approved a revived IATA (now the International Air Transport Association). By the time of the next major conference in Bermuda, in 1946, the association was fully operational. It was led by Canadian Herbert Symington with headquarters in Geneva and Montreal. The IATA was a trade association sanctioned by governments as part of their bilateral agreements—most effectively since most airlines were now nationalized. It proved to be an international fare fixer, something the Americans accepted in exchange for certain British concessions. Moreover, the IATA, unlike the ICAO, could provide the machinery to coordinate and synchronize the rapidly expanding network of air routes. Moreover, this victorious triumvirate could insist that their own English language should now become the international language of flight—perhaps not the least of the victories won in World War II by the Anglo-American alliance.

Oil and Diplomacy in World War II

The course of America's future foreign relations in the Middle East was being determined largely by the way the great oil companies had penetrated and were using the region for their own ends. Just how the United States, Britain, and the oil companies managed the delicate situation disclosed the biting relationship underlying the Anglo-American alliance. To the Arab world, the companies were larger than the Western nations themselves, for it was the great international oil companies, known as the "seven sisters," who by their economic penetration of one country rather than another advanced or retarded its growth and generally impressed their own character on this emerging region. In the late 1930s and early 1940s, Standard Oil of New Jersey (later Exxon) and Shell were the rival giantesses among the sisters. Their rivalry was to form a backdrop to the crucial interplay of diplomacy. The two companies were almost private governments to which some Western powers, including the United States and Britain, had abdicated some of their diplomacy.

Texaco and Standard Oil of California, or Socal, were concerned that the extravagant, spendthrift King Ibn Saud of Saudi Arabia might revoke their concession if they could not provide him with more ready cash. Rather than simply accede to his demands and hand out more money, they decided on a complex, delicate strategy of trying to persuade the American and British governments to subsidize Ibn Saud, while still retaining firm control of the precious concessions themselves. In the ensuing controversy, all the old arguments about the control of oil resurfaced.

At first, Britain bore the brunt of subsidizing Ibn Saud, to the tune of $20 million; but in time, the United States became concerned that the British might become too influential with the king. When Britain dispatched an expedition, which included geologists, to deal with locusts, the United States became even more concerned. Furthermore, the Americans feared that the old king, who had several wives and twenty sons, might soon be succeeded by a less complaisant monarch. Therefore, in February 1943, Star Rodgers, chairman of Texaco, and Harvy Collier, president of Socal, enlisted the aid of Secretary of the Interior Harold Ickes, who was also the petroleum administrator during the war. To counter undue British influence, they persuaded Ickes to secure lend-lease funds for Saudi Arabia. Accordingly, FDR sent a letter to Undersecretary of State Edward Stettinius on February 18, 1943, that declared, "I hereby find that the defense of Saudi Arabia is vital to the defense of the United States." Saud's adviser, Harry St. John Philby, described how the flow of American money led to "a further orgy of extravagance and misarrangement, accompanied by the growth of corruption on a large scale in the highest quarters."

The oil companies thought they had achieved their objective of government funds without government interference, but they were wrong. Herbert Feis, economic adviser to the State Department, put it this way, "They had gone fishing for a cod, and caught a whale." In short, Texaco and Socal had interested Ickes and the American government far more than they had intended. Once again the federal government was concerned about running short of oil. Thus William Bullitt, undersecretary of the navy, outlined the problem in a memo to FDR of June 1943 wherein he explained, "To acquire petroleum reserves outside our boundaries has become . . . a vital interest of the United States." Moreover, Texaco and Socal were concerned that the British might prevail on Ibn Saud "to diddle them out of the concession and the British into it"; thus, they wanted to get "a direct American government interest in their concession." Bullitt proposed that the federal government create a Petroleum Reserve Corporation to acquire a controlling interest in Saudi Arabian oil production and to construct a refinery on the Persian Gulf. The new joint venture was the Arabian-American Oil Company, or Aramco.

Ickes liked Bullitt's idea and knew that existing government machinery and the legacy of the New Deal would make it possible to create a new nationalized industry. Ickes quickly won over FDR; and on June 30, 1943, the president authorized the creation of a new corporation to buy 100 percent of the Arabian concession. Herbert Feis recalled the careless, impulsive way in which the crucial decision was reached: "The discussion with the President had been jovial, brief and far from thorough. A boyish note was in the President's talk and nod, as usual when it had to do with the Middle East." The new corporation, the Petroleum Reserve Corporation (PRC) was led by Ickes as president and included the secretaries of State, War, and the Navy among its directors and employed Abe Fortas as secretary. Yet this august body found its proposal for outright ownership of Aramco flatly rejected by Texaco and Socal. Instead, they offered the government a one-third interest. Ickes and the PRC were ecstatic at the prospect of limitless oil to be siphoned from Arabia and dispatched an expedition there led by oil geologist Everett De Golyer, whose final report confirmed their enthusiasm. "The center of gravity of the world of oil production is shifting from the Gulf-Caribbean areas to the Middle East, to the Persian Gulf area, and is likely to continue to shift until it is firmly established in that area."

Ickes still intended to strike a deal with Texaco and Socal; but in October 1943, negotiations with Star Rodgers of Texaco broke down after only a week. At the onset, Texaco and Socal had been concerned because it seemed German forces might overrun the entire Middle East. However, once Rommel was dislodged in North Africa, the danger of German occupation of the Middle East passed. Thus, by mid-1943 Texaco and Socal no longer required government protection in Saudi Arabia. American officials had different verdicts on the failure of the proposal. George McGhee, assistant secretary at the State Department after the war, told British investigative journalist Anthony Sampson that the idea could not have worked. "It's not the American way," he said, "only Ickes was really for it." However, Abe Fortas differed. "At least it would have given the government a seat at the poker-table."

Ickes did not abandon his grand scheme of government control. He proposed a government-constructed pipeline extending one thousand miles across Saudi Arabia to the Mediterranean. In return, the oil companies should guarantee 20 percent of the oil fields as a naval reserve, with oil to be awarded the navy at a cheap rate. This plan received the wholehearted support of America's military strategists, partly because it would reinforce the American presence in Arabia and partly because it would move oil more quickly. Moreover, Texaco and Socal were convinced because the pipeline would transport their oil more cheaply than any tanker. Thus, the two companies signed an agreement with Ickes. The diplomatic implications of Ickes's pipeline were considerable. Karl Twitchell, an American geologist and Socal adviser, remarked how it committed the government to a fixed foreign policy for the next twenty-five years.

However, the agreement and the pipeline caused an uproar. Britain recognized a naked threat to its dominance of the Middle East. Other American oil companies were disturbed that two of their competitors, Texaco and Socal, would enjoy the advantage of cheap transportation. The jealous rival companies formed a special committee on national policy that proclaimed how harmful was government interference "to this most individualistic of all economic activities, the oil industry." Senator Moore of Oklahoma (an oil-producing state) denounced the pipeline as an imperialist adventure. Eugene Holman of Exxon staunchly maintained how the United States was self-sufficient in oil and had enough reserves to supply demand at the present rate for one thousand years. Texaco and Socal kept their own counsel, prudently leaving the government to speak for them.

FDR and Ickes tried to parry British opposition by getting Churchill to recognize American interests in the Middle East. Churchill retorted that some Britons suspected the United States of trying to deprive Britain of its oil interests. FDR responded by saying some Americans were accusing the British of trying to penetrate America's right to oil in Saudi Arabia. In the end, to resolve matters, Hull and Ickes met a British delegation headed by Lord Beaverbrook and completed an agreement, signed on August 4, 1944. Although quite inocuous, the agreement provoked another storm of abuse from other American oil companies about the creation of a supercartel. This led to its defeat in the Senate, its revision and renegotiation with the new Labour administration in Britain after the war, followed by a renewed attack by American oilmen, and a second defeat in the Senate in July 1947. As a result, any chance of a joint Anglo-American policy in the Middle East collapsed.

A footnote to the cracks in the Anglo-American alliance after Yalta was provided by the way both Roosevelt and Churchill competed in courting King Ibn Saud of Saudi Arabia whose oil had helped them master Hitler. On his return from Yalta, FDR entertained King Ibn Saud of Saudi Arabia aboard the cruiser *Quincy*, along with a royal entourage of fifty, including two of the twenty sons, a prime minister, flocks of sheep for slaughter, and the royal astrologer. In return for royal gifts of jeweled daggers and swords, FDR promised Ibn Saud an airplane. Three days later Churchill received the king at the Hotel du Lac at Fayoum Oasis. In exchange for more precious swords, Churchill promised Ibn Saud an armor-plated Rolls Royce motor car. History does not relate whether the old reprobate king and his two suitors made sheep's eyes at one another or simply passed them to one another from the main dish. Nevertheless, Churchill realized that Ibn Saud, for all his royal pleasantries, was really looking to the United States both for his future income and his defense. That defense was about to pass into new hands on the tiller of America's ship of state.

Washingtonians mourn the late president as his bier passes by in the street. (Library of Congress).

The Death of FDR

FDR served less than three months of his fourth term. Already Iwo Jima had fallen, Okinawa had been invaded, and the navy was sending planes to bomb Japan from aircraft carriers only fifty miles offshore. In Europe, American troops had crossed the Rhine; and, in his bunker, Adolf Hitler faced utter destruction amid the rubble of Berlin. Even the proclamation of victory, which Harry Truman would read on May 8, had already been written.

People now began to be struck by FDR's ashen, wasted appearance. The day before his fourth inaugural he held a cabinet meeting. "We were all shocked by the President's appearance," Dean Acheson recollected in his memoirs of 1969. "Thin, gaunt, with sunken and darkly circled eyes, only the jaunty cigarette holder and his lighthearted brushing aside of difficulties recalled the FDR of former days." Of the inaugural ceremony next day, John Gunther remembered in his *Roosevelt in Retrospect* (1950), "I was terrified when I saw his face. I felt certain that he was going to die. All the light had gone out underneath the skin. It was like a parchment shade on a bulb that had been dimmed. I could not get over the ravaged expression on his face. It was gray, gaunt, and sagging, and the muscles controlling the lips seemed to have lost part of their function." There were times when, as Gunther also remarked, FDR's exhaustion was so great that "he could not answer simple questions and talked what was close to nonsense."

In these last months, FDR's doctors were in anguish. William D. Hassett said the president was just drifting to death. He had not the energy or control even to sign his name. His case was hopeless, unless he could be totally isolated from pressure. On April 11, Hassett wrote in his diary:

Shocked at his appearance—worn, weary, exhausted. He seemed all right when I saw him in the morning. He is steadily losing weight—told me he has lost twenty-five pounds—no strength, no appetite, tires easily—all too apparent whenever you see him after midday. Again observed this to Dr. Bruenn. He admits cause for alarm.

Walter Lippmann's feelings toward FDR had always been ambivalent, but he recognized the president's unique qualities and achievements. Fearing that Roosevelt might not live much longer, Lippmann wrote a tribute to him—a premature obituary that FDR could read. "His estimate of the vital interests of the United States has been accurate and far-sighted," he wrote for his column on 7 April 1945. "He has served these interests with audacity and patience, shrewdly and with calculation, and he has led this country out of the greatest peril in which it has ever been to the highest point of security, influence, and respect which it has ever attained."

In Warm Springs, Georgia, on April 12, 1945, Roosevelt was having his portrait painted by Elizabeth Shoumatoff. It was to be a gift for the daughter of Lucy Mercer Rutherford, the woman with whom FDR had had a longterm affair. The artist despaired of getting him to keep a pose as he habitually became engrossed in his papers or laughed together with Lucy after he had made some amusing remark. At one o'clock he told the artist, "We've got just fifteen minutes more." A little later, he put his left hand to his temple and pressed his forehead. "I have a terrific headache," he said as his arm fell and his head slumped forward. It was 1:15 P.M. Lucy Rutherfurd and Elizabeth Shoumatoff scuttled away together. Dr. Bruenn came to his patient's aid and discovered that an artery in the brain had been punctured, and blood was seeping into cavities around the brain. FDR's eyes were dilated to the point of distortion and he had acute vertigo. He was having a massive cerebral haemorrhage. The only sounds were great gasping snores of anguish. Just as Dr. James E. Paulin, a distinguished Atlanta specialist, arrived at Warm Springs, at about 3:35 P.M., the president died.

In Washington, D.C., Eleanor Roosevelt heard the news from aide Steve Early, and she sent for Harry Truman. "Harry, the President is dead," she said. He was dazed and confused and asked what he could do for her. "Is there anything *we* can do for you?" she said. "You are the one in trouble now." Churchill was told while entering his study at 10 Downing Street and said he "felt as if I had been struck a physical blow."

Anne O'Hare McCormick wrote in the *New York Times* how FDR had "occupied a role so fused with his own personality after twelve years that people in other countries spoke of him simply as 'The President,' as if he were President of the World. He did not stoop and he did not climb. He was one of those completely poised persons who felt no need to play up or play down to anybody. In his death this is the element of his greatness that comes out most clearly." The writer of the official obituary in the *New York Times* declared, "Men will thank God on their knees a hundred years from now that Franklin Roosevelt was in the White House when a powerful and ruthless barbarism threatened to overrun the civilization of the Western World." Robert A. Taft of Ohio commented, "He dies a hero of the war, for he literally worked himself to death in the service of the American people." Congressman Lyndon Baines Johnson of Texas maintained, "He was just like a daddy to me always. He was the one person I ever knew, anywhere, who was never afraid. God, God—how he could take it for us all!"

The four hundredth and final journey of FDR's special train carried his body and the chief mourners from Atlanta to Washington, D.C. Citizens and soldiers met the train at every grade-crossing to show their respect and grieve with the president's wife and closest advisers. In the capital, the casket was borne from Union Station to the White House on a small, black-draped caisson led by six white horses and a seventh outrider. The horses' stirrups were reserved, with a sword and boots turned upside down and hanging from the stirrups—an ancient mark of a fallen warrior. "It was so sudden," wrote Bernard Asbell in *When FDR Died* (1961). "It came so quietly. It seemed so peculiarly small. Just a big-wheeled wagon, dragged slowly, bearing the flag-covered oblong box. It was not a huge thing at all, as somehow everyone expected it to be. It was small, as though it might be any man's." At the service in the East Room of the White House FDR's empty wheelchair stood by the side of the makeshift altar. The mourners sang the navy hymn "Eternal Father, Strong to Save."

The cortege then left by train, first for New York City before arriving at Hyde Park early Sunday morning. A cannon was fired. FDR was buried on the family estate behind a ten-foot hedge in the rose garden. A squad of West Point cadets fired three rounds in the air.

In New York City, Eleanor Roosevelt dismissed a group of reporters who wanted her version of events with the cryptic words, "The story is over." This was dramatic and succinct but not literally true. From now on all presidents who followed Franklin Delano Roosevelt would be in the shadow of FDR. Besides, FDR had been one of the titans who had ensured that America was already entering an atomic age.

The death of FDR was certainly a turning point in world history, followed closely as it was that very month by the summary and horrendous execution of Mussolini, first shot and then hanged upside down by partisans on April 28, and the subterranean suicide of Adolf Hitler on April 30. These awesome events were followed by the temporary eclipse of Winston Churchill from British politics and world affairs in the midst of the Potsdam negotiations. Churchill, faced with increasing demands from his war colleagues in the Labour party for a return to the traditional two-party system in Britain, in place of the wartime coalition, had to accept the prospect of a general election before the war against Japan

was over. While his election campaign had marks of a triumphal procession, he chose to make exaggerated claims of what a Labour victory
would entail for Britain and failed to sense a shift in party allegiance in
a nation ready for profound social reform. Labour's careful program of
economic and social reform suited the country better than jingoism and
Tory flamboyance. In the election on July 5, 1945, Churchill suffered
the indignity of seeing his Conservative party reduced to only 213 seats
in a House of Commons of 640. Thus a tidal wave of 393 Labour MPs
swept Clement Attlee and the Labour party to power, eventually for six
years of the most profound reforms, including socialized medicine and
the semipermanent nationalizing of major industries.

Jiang Jieshi was to survive as leader of China for four years. Only
Joseph Stalin survived in total control as leader of the Soviet Union
until his death in 1953.

The San Francisco Conference

All nations who had signed the United Nations Declaration by February
8, 1945, or had entered the war by March 1 could attend the San
Francisco conference that opened on April 25 to organize the United
Nations. The American delegation was bipartisan. Led by Secretary of
State Edward Stettinius, it included from the Senate Tom Connally and
Arthur Vandenberg of Michigan; from the House Foreign Affairs Committee Sol Bloom, Democrat of New York, and Charles A. Eaton,
Republican of New Jersey; Harold E. Stassen, former governor of Minnesota and ally of the late Wendell Willkie; and Virginia C. Gilder-
sleeve, dean of Barnard College. The fifty nations discussed and revised
the Dumbarton Oaks proposals and the Yalta protocol. They added an
idealistic preamble to the charter; they devised a series of trusteeships
for various dependent territories; and they accepted the jurisdiction of
the International Court of Justice. A committee of jurists meeting in
Washington, D.C. from April 9 to April 20, 1945, already had drafted
a statute that enlarged the role of the General Assembly, which could
now make recommendations to member states or to the Security Council. The idea was to expand the forum of unrestricted freedom of debate.

The United States and the Soviet Union agreed to differ on the rights
of the Security Council. The Dumbarton Oaks agreement had forbidden

Field Marshal Wilhelm Keitel was one of many leading German officers who took part in surrender formalities in Berlin at the end of the war in Europe. He is signing documents of surrender for the Soviets. His face conveys all the hauteur of the old Prussian aristocracy tempered by the determination to mask his bitter resentment of how events have come to pass. (Library of Congress).

members to enforce peace under regional arrangements, thereby nullifying the Soviet Union's recent mutual-aid pacts with Poland, Czechoslovakia, and Yugoslavia and the United States's plan for hemispheric defense, as proposed by the Act of Chapultepec of March 6, 1945. Nevertheless, a Military Staff Committee, consisting of the chiefs of staff, was to advise and assist the Security Council. Until the Security Council acted, each member had the right to defend itself either individually or collectively by "regional agreements" (ARTICLE 51).

The obligations of the United States in the charter somewhat resembled the Lodge reservations of 1919–20 to the League of Nations. Whereas Woodrow Wilson had intended the league to be a coercive body, in which members pledged to apply sanctions automatically and come to the rescue of one another, Henry Cabot Lodge had tried to transform the league into a noncoercive organization in which the absolute promise to aid a victim of aggression was subordinated to less demanding processes.

For minor breaches of the peace, the United Nations might mobilize its great collective force by resolution, sanction, or military intervention. However, in any major case affecting the interests of the great powers, a great power could use its veto to block any attempt to see if there had been an act of aggression, to designate the guilty party, and to decide the use of economic sanctions or military intervention. Richard W. Leopold (1962) concludes that "the veto represented the antithesis of Wilson's ideal; its insertion in the Charter meant that the new organization should not and could not be drawn into efforts to implement the principle of collective security in opposition to a permanent member. Indeed, the existence of ARTICLE 51, proclaiming the inherent right of individual and collective self-defense, is a virtual invitation to return to the old balance of power concept to deal with threats to attack by nations possessing the veto."

This time there was no doubt that the Senate would approve the charter. President Harry S. Truman told the upper house on July 2, 1945, that the choice "is not between this Charter and something else. It is between this Charter and no Charter at all." It embodied the bitter experience of recent history, "of a world where one generation has failed twice to keep the peace." The historical arguments for American isolationism and neutrality did not meet the needs of the mid-twentieth century. This time there must be no compromises or half measures. In comparison with 1919, when the Senate had debated the League of Nations for six weeks and divided itself into three camps, opposition was minimal. The hearings began on July 9, 1945, and lasted five days. When the Senate Foreign Relations Committee published its findings, it was in one report not three. The report recommended consent without modification. When the issue came to a single vote on July 28, 1945, it was approved by 89 votes to 2. The two Republican dissenters were William Langer of North Dakota and Henrik Shipstead of Minnesota. Of the five abstaining, the sole opponent was the unreconciled Hiram W. Johnson of California, now on his deathbed.

However, there were still a few outstanding, disturbing questions.

Jubilant Londoners crowd around Nelson's column in Trafalgar Square in celebration of V-E Day. (Library of Congress).

Did the American delegate to the Security Council have the right to commit American troops without authority from Congress? Was ARTICLE 43, by which members placed military resources at the disposal of the Security Council, to be ratified by treaty, joint resolution, or executive action? Although Connally and Vandenberg would have preferred this second question to be settled by Congress at a later stage, their desire to avoid any revision to the charter was in marked contrast to the bitter partisan attitudes of Wilson and Lodge. Moreover, Truman swept this problem aside when he cabled from Potsdam on July 27, 1945, that he would obtain congressional approval for all future military arrangements.

The United Nations Participation Act of December 20, 1945, passed the Senate by 65 votes to 7 and the House by 344 votes to 15. The only revision by the Senate was to require its consent to the appointment of delegates to the General Assembly and the various commissions, as

353

well as to the Security Council. Various amendments that would have required the president to seek permission of Congress each and every time American troops or materiel were used by the United Nations were decisively rejected. On August 2, 1946, the Senate by 60 votes to 2 accepted the optional clause of the Statute of the International Court of Justice. By joining the United Nations, the federal government automatically became a member of the new tribunal whose jurisdiction extended to all matters provided for in the charter and in other treaties. However, the Senate exempted those disputes that specific treaties required to be settled elsewhere, those arising from a multilateral pact, and those pertaining to the domestic matters of the United States, "as determined by the United States." This last phrase, sometimes known as the Connally Reservation (after its author), marked one limit upon the overwhelming, newfound support for ending isolationism so obvious in the Senate's reception of, and verdict upon, the United Nations Charter.

Recalling how the Treaty of Versailles had perpetuated wartime hatreds and how the Covenant of the League of Nations had frozen an incomplete peace, the American delegates at the Potsdam conference of July 17 to August 2, 1945, succeeded in deferring a formal conference. Instead, they created the Council of Foreign Ministers from the United States, Britain, Russia, France, and China to undertake necessary preparatory work. In the meantime, the protocol of August 1, 1945, provided that the Big Three should determine the principles behind the settlements with Hungary, Bulgaria, and Rumania; that France should take part with them in settling peace with Italy; that Britain and the Soviet Union would deal with Finland; and that the Security Council might be used later for treaties with Germany and Japan. Truman hoped that, once the treaties had been drafted, they would be submitted to a general conference at the United Nations for adoption. It took three sessions of the Council of Foreign Ministers between September 1945 and December 1946 to reach a peace settlement with Italy and the lesser enemy powers. The texts were drafted by the Big Three and were signed in New York City on February 10, 1947.

After considerable discussion and dispute as to the most suitable city and site for the headquarters of the United Nations, John D. Rockefeller, Jr., offered $8.5 billion to purchase an area extending for six blocks along the East River in Manhattan at 42d Street. This was the location to which the United Nations moved in 1951.

The Atomic Bomb

In December 1938, German chemists Otto Hahn and Fritz Strassmann discovered that the nucleus of the uranium atom could be split; thus, they discovered nuclear fission. Their discovery was the climax of work over thirty years by eminent scientists such as Enrico Fermi of Italy, Frederic Joliot and Irene Curie in France, James Chadwick in England, and Ernest Lawrence in Berkeley, California. Fermi had shown that almost every element would undergo nuclear transformation when bombarded by neutrons. When so bombarded, uranium produced what seemed entirely new substances, radioactive elements heavier than uranium that Fermi called "transuranic." Hahn and Strassmann used barium as the carrier in their experiment to split uranium. Barium is element 56 in the table of elements and is heavier than uranium, which is element 92. When three radioactive isotopes came down with the barium, Hahn and Strassmann discovered they had split the atomic nucleus since the artificial radium produced was itself barium.

Their discovery posed new challenges for science, marking an adventure in nuclear physics. Scientists realized that it might be possible to loosen the colossal energy inside the atom. In 1940 in England, two refugee scientists from Germany, Otto Frisch and Rudolf Peierls, demonstrated that an explosion of considerable power would result if small amounts of pure metallic light uranium (U^{235}) could be brought quickly together to make a sphere of critical size. Their theoretical demonstration was written up in a memorandum that Britain shared with the United States in 1941.

FDR had been alerted already to the possibility of building an atomic bomb by Albert Einstein, who wrote to the president in 1939, informing him that "a single bomb of this type, carried by a boat and exploded in a port, might very well destroy the whole port together with some of the surrounding territory." At that time, British and French scientists were working toward the construction of such a bomb. However, in the United States, work in this field was still oriented toward nonmilitary uses of atomic power.

In the fall of 1940, Sir Henry Tizard, the British scientist with overall responsibility for investigating the use of nuclear energy as a weapon, arrived in America to give his hosts "all the assistance I can on behalf of the British government to enable the armed forces of the USA to reach the highest level of technical efficiency." In July 1941, the British Maud Committee, which had been established to study the feasibility of producing atomic bombs during the war and analyzing their possible military impact, sent its report to Washington. In this document, the committee concluded that "it will be possible to make an effective uranium bomb which, containing some 25 pounds of active material, would be equivalent as regards destructive effect to 1,800 tons of TNT and would also release large quantities of radioactive substances, which would make places near where the bomb exploded dangerous to human life for a long period." In August 1941, Churchill authorized the production of such bombs. Two months later, FDR wrote to Churchill, suggesting "that any extended efforts on this important matter might be usefully co-ordinated or even jointly conducted."

On December 6, the day before Pearl Harbor, Dr. Vannevar Bush, director of the United States Office of Scientific Research and Development, decided to divert the agency's energies into the construction of a nuclear weapon and created a special committee comprising America's foremost physicists to work on the task.

Time was now of the essence, for the Allies believed that the Germans were working on a similar project. Given the United States's industrial, academic, and financial resources, FDR and Churchill decided in June 1942 that the United States should take the lead in the construction of the bomb. Thus throughout 1942, the British nuclear effort diminished while the American work on the Manhattan Project continued apace. The large-scale production plants were at Oak Ridge, Tennessee; Richland, Washington; and Santa Fe, New Mexico, where Robert Oppenheimer was in charge of the Los Alamos project. Everything was done in top secret. Workers who cleared a hillside in Oak Ridge, Tennessee, eighteen miles northwest of Knoxville, had not the slightest idea what they were preparing the ground for. Asked what he was making, a worker answered, "A dollar thirty-five an hour."

America's technological elite of professors from the Massachusetts Institute of Technology and the California Institute of Technology, and industrial scientists and executives also met in Chicago at Eckhert Hall as part of the Chicago Metallurgical Project. They were asked to produce material they had never seen for a purpose unknown to them, except that it was absolutely essential to the war effort. The federal

The devastation of aerial bombing, one of the crucial factors that prompted the Japanese surrender, is suggested in this bombing attack in 1945 upon the Nakajima Aircraft Engine Plant, part of the Mitsubishi industrial empire that extended 5 million square feet in an area near Tokyo. (Library of Congress).

government pledged $400 million immediately and, in the end, paid $2 billion. The ultimate secret was confined to a few scientists, a major general, and a handful of civilians selected by FDR.

What the scientists most dreaded was that German scientists would invent the bomb first and reward Hitler with an arsenal of atomic weapons. The Hitler the Americans and British feared in 1941 was not simply an autocrat totally reliant on existing armaments and facilities. He was, rather, the brilliant strategist of military surprise not yet halted in his war on two fronts. Hence, both Roosevelt and Churchill were concerned that Hitler's scientists would produce a bomb ahead of America and Britain. Ironically, Germany never tried resolutely to do so. McGeorge Bundy explains why in his *Danger and Survival: Choices About the Bomb in the First Fifty Years* (1988). For one thing, Hitler never made a decision to build a bomb. Moreover, German physicists, who were well aware of the dramatic possibilities of the conquest of fission, resisted all attempts to develop a coordinated research program. This was partly because they were opposed to centralizing research in Berlin. Moving separately, they retained individual control of the direction their work on uranium would take. German scientists discovered the significance of separated U^{235} and the potential of plutonium (identified by others), but they did not think it would be possible to create a nuclear explosion given the exigency of the war.

The most preeminent German physicist was Werner Heisenberg. At the age of twenty-five he had formulated the principle of uncertainty— of what could and could not be discovered about physical phenomena. He was also the winner of a Nobel Prize. During the war, Heisenberg was still in his early forties. Heisenberg realized exactly how crucial were the earlier experiments by Otto Hahn and Fritz Strassman. Moreover, at the start of the war he was ordered to work on uranium. However, he preferred to concentrate on the peaceful uses of atomic energy. His pioneer theorizing foreshadowed the postwar development of nuclear reactors.

Nevertheless, Heisenberg was concerned that the Allies might develop a nuclear bomb and use it against Germany. Hence, in October 1941 he went to Copenhagen to interview his former teacher, the distinguished Danish physicist Niels Bohr. McGeorge Bundy concludes that Heisenberg wanted to persuade Bohr to see if, between them, they could ascertain whether physicists across the world might agree to refrain from producing a bomb during the war. He perhaps wanted to give assurances that German scientists would refrain if only they could be sure that American and British scientists would also do so. Whatever Heisenberg's intention, he failed to persuade Bohr. Bohr was aghast that Heisenberg had condoned the German invasion of Poland. He was in no frame of mind to trust any of Heisenberg's timid attempts at wheedling endearments. Their conversation, stifled by formalities and Heisenberg's understandable caution that his remarks could be interpreted as dealing openly with Germany's enemies, led to a cruel misunderstanding. Bohr believed that Heisenberg's message was unequi-

The devastating mushroom of the atomic bomb as it explodes upon Nagasaki, the second and last atomic attack of the war. (U.S. Army Air Force photo; Library of Congress).

vocal: there was no call for international scientific restraint; Germany was trying to make a nuclear bomb. This was the opposite of what Heisenberg intended to convey. Yet, it was what Bohr reported in Britain in 1943.

A prime reason why German scientists did not press a case for all-out research into nuclear weapons was their political prudence. They realized that the war effort in Germany was almost entirely bound up with the personality of Adolf Hitler. If the führer had agreed to commit himself and Germany's precious resources to research into a decisive weapon, then they would be compelled to produce results that equaled his enthusiasm and urgency. Clearly, they were more prudent about arousing his attention. Hitler was innately distrustful of experts in fields he could not understand and was highly suspicious of academics. Moreover, his limited understanding of nuclear physics was clouded by his pathological anti-Semitism; he called it Jewish physics.

Among those closest to Hitler only Albert Speer, his former architect and now minister of supply, raised the subject of nuclear fission and, then, only once in numerous meetings. When in 1942 Speer proposed to allow the scientists a small sum of money so that they could continue uranium research, he deliberately presented the request in a low-key way that aroused little interest. It was in this way that Albert Speer moved nuclear projects along. He wanted the development of a uranium pile producing energy; for his part, Werner Heisenberg moved toward general, nonapplied research.

Moreover, Germany could not field as many qualified scientists and engineers as the United States; nor could it afford sufficient large research instruments. Nor could it shift gears in its industrial organization, which was committed to conventional war supplies, in order to make a bomb that would require special allocation of personnel and materials. The building of an atomic bomb also would have required huge plants that could not have been easily camouflaged and disguised and thus would be vulnerable to air attack. This vulnerability was a decisive factor among the many that explain why Germany could not take on an atomic project.

This was to remain an American and British preoccupation. The principal problem for their research scientists was to find a way of making an atomic bomb. In theory, it should have been possible for them to develop a chain reaction when neutrons were introduced into a pile of U^{235}. The neutrons were supposed to split the U^{235} atoms, each of which would liberate another one, two, or three neutrons that would split more atoms in their turn, and so on in the cycle until the critical mass was reached. Of course, the scientists could not allow this to happen in a laboratory. Therefore, they used graphite to slow the neutrons down but found that some went astray. It would only be possible to get a chain reaction if successive generations of neutrons got larger and longer. This was called the K factor. It could be achieved only if 100 neutrons that had caused fission in 100 U^{235} atoms gave birth to a generation of new neutrons, 105 of which were left to cause fission, of which the ratio would be 105 to 100. The K factor would then have a value of 1.05, and so on, until the mass was formed. If the K factor fell below 1.05, it would be inadequate. Early experiments yielded a birthrate of only .87 per 100 neutrons.

The main problem was the impurity of the uranium. Only by stepping up production of Westinghouse uranium from 8 ounces a day to over 500 pounds a day could the necessary 3 tons be achieved by November 1942. At the same time, two carbon companies produced a graphite resistant to neutrons, while Professor Frank H. Spedding of Iowa State College and his team improved the Westinghouse uranium, transforming it into lumps called "Spedding's eggs."

The precious pile of uranium was delivered and deposited in a former squash court on Ellis Avenue at the University of Chicago. To prevent a nuclear accident of a spontaneous chain reaction, seven strips of cadmium and three rods of boron steel (both metals being avid consumers of neutrons) were passed in and out of the pile. Layer after layer of uranium was added to the pile until the twelfth layer was in place on the night of December 1–2, 1942. The mass of uranium, graphite, cadmium, boron, and other materials weighed 12,400 pounds. All the control materials were gradually removed, and the K factor climbed to 0.99 and then to 1.05 and up to 1.10. The chain was now self-perpetuating.

Its transformation was a separate, technological problem to be managed by a different team of scientists. FDR wanted the two teams kept apart and unaware of each other's presence in Chicago. Roosevelt's attitude toward the Manhattan Project was ambivalent. He trusted people, wanted to pool common knowledge, and wanted the United States to share its learning with the world; at the same time, he was secretive.

By the end of 1943, the majority of British scientists had been absorbed into American research teams. However, there was no Soviet participation in the project. Indeed, from the outset, FDR and Churchill were determined to keep Stalin in the dark. At the first Quebec meeting, the Quadrant conference of August 1943, the two leaders promised that neither nation would use the weapon against the enemy without the consent of the other. Of even greater significance to great-power relations, they also promised that neither nation would give information relating to the weapon to another power without the consent of the other. A veil of secrecy was thrown over the Manhattan Project, and Stalin was not even informed of its existence.

FDR certainly did not intend to use the bomb as a direct threat to Stalin. Rather than coerce Stalin, he meant to coax him to enter into amicable discussion. Along with the promise of economic aid, he intended to offer the expertise and technology necessary for the creation of atomic weaponry as a means of winning Stalin's confidence and cooperation. Thus, at Yalta, FDR was willing to postpone decisions on issues pregnant with disruptive possibilities. He was sure that time and technology were on the American side.

During this period leading physicist J. Robert Oppenheimer was under surveillance by army agent Boris Pash, partly because he was known to have contributed to liberal causes in the 1930s and in the 1940s and had come close to marrying Dr. Jean Tatlock, a psychiatrist from San Francisco who was also a Communist. Indeed, Communists were anxious to infiltrate the project, and Soviet consular official Anatoli A. Yakovlev wove a spider's web through various agents. His people included Harry Gold of Philadelphia, Julius and Ethel Rosenberg of New York City, and Ethel's brother, Sergeant David Greenglass, who worked on top-secret material at Los Alamos. The most crucial member was noted atomic scientist and member of the Los Alamos elite Klaus Emil Fuchs. Originally a native of Germany, he had come to England as a refugee from Nazi persecution and had become a naturalized British citizen whose loyalty to the war effort went without question. Thus he enjoyed top security clearance, and, apparently, no one wondered why the Nazis were after a Gentile physicist whose specialty was theoretical physics. Fuchs was a committed Communist.

Harry Gold's contact with David Greenglass came when he arrived at Greenglass's apartment at 209 North High Street, Albuquerque, New

Mexico, with the torn half of the top of a raspberry Jell-O box. The other half was kept by Julius Rosenberg, and all Gold had to say to Greenglass was "Julius sent me." David Greenglass was recruited and copied various schematic drawings of flat-top lens-mold experiments for detonating an atomic bomb. The experiments consisted of a mix of high explosives that would focus detonation waves, and Russian knowledge about them would enable Soviet scientists to omit expensive and time-consuming experiments of their own. Whereas all concerned made out that their business was sharing information for the good of mankind, David Greenglass's wife, Ruth, was somewhat antagonized by her husband's acceptance of $500 in cash from Harry Gold. "It's just like C.O.D.!" she is supposed to have exclaimed. Fuchs received no money. He betrayed what he knew on principle and in Santa Fe provided Gold with typed notes on the application of theoretical fission to the building of a bomb. Further information was supplied by two more spies, Morton Sobell and Alan Nunn May.

The Russians already had both the theoretical knowledge and skilled technologists to develop the bomb. Moreover, Edward Teller had described the most intimate mechanism of the bomb at a Los Alamos seminar. This was two hemispheres brought into contact until the mass reached the critical point and detonated itself. What was unknown was the amount of U^{235} needed, the size of the two halves, the speed with which they must collide, the scattering angle, and the range of the neutrons to be projected by the chain reaction.

Harry Dagnian, one of the scientists working on this part of the project, accidentally set off a chain reaction while he was holding a small amount of fissionable material. Although it lasted only a fraction of a second, his right hand was saturated with radiation. In hospital, he became delirious, his hair fell out, the white corpuscles in his blood multiplied, and he died in great agony.

Another scientist who perished was Louis Slotkin, a Canadian adventurer who had fought with the Loyalists in Spain during the civil war and with the Royal Air Force during the battle of Britain. He came into the Manhattan Project because he was too shortsighted to remain a pilot and had the right sort of scientific training. He would tinker with two live hemispheres, using screwdrivers to slide them toward one another on a rod while he watched. On one occasion a screwdriver slipped, and the two halves came too close together. There was a blinding blue flash.

Slotkin tore the hemispheres apart and saved the community at the price of his own life. Ironically, Klaus Fuchs was the scientist assigned to study the terrible incident and to ascertain what could be deduced from it.

It is important to keep in mind the sheer hatred, terror, and utter fear that Adolf Hitler aroused, and that partly explains the dedication of the Los Alamos scientists to their terrifying project. They believed either that Hitler already had such a weapon or that he would soon have one. In the fall of 1943, Britain and the United States had a special intelligence unit formed under the code name Alsos. It was to be landed in Normandy on D Day, and its task was to collect data about the extent of Hitler's atomic research. The documents were to be translated and appraised by Dr. Samuel A. Goudsmit of Holland, a distinguished experimental physicist who also dabbled in criminal investigation.

In fact, Germany had no atomic weapons. Anti-Semitism had driven outstanding Jewish physicists abroad. German chiefs of staff were indifferent to long-term research. Indeed, what atomic research there was, was being carried out independently by three separate ministries without any coordination. Nevertheless, Germany had three of the most brilliant physicists (Carl von Weizsäcker, Max von Laue, and Werner Heisenberg), whose interest in building a uranium pile and acquiring atomic energy from it had been halted by Hitler in June 1942. Confident of victory, Hitler ordered Albert Speer, his minister of supply, to put an end to all research on new weapons except those that could be produced and used within six weeks. Thereafter, Hitler discouraged Speer from nuclear research and production, even though the Germany navy was interested in an energy-producing uranium motor for propelling machinery.

While Germany's initial research was known outside the Reich, Hitler's countermanding of nuclear physics was not known until the Allies took Strasbourg on November 23, 1944. Goudsmit, senior member of the Alsos intelligence team, found that Carl von Weizsäcker had already escaped and the remaining German scientists refused to discuss the subject with him. However, Weizsäcker's private papers, which Goudsmit read by candlelight as GIs played cards nearby, disclosed the extent of the Reich's U project and the Uranium Verein (Uranium Society). It was clear that the Germans were at least two years behind

Tangled, jagged remnants of buildings in Hiroshima in September 1946—one year after the atomic blast that brought the war to an abrupt end and changed the nature of the world that followed. (Library of Congress).

the Los Alamos research and lacked plants for the manufacture of PU^{239} (plutonium) and U^{235}.

However, Werner Heisenberg had been continuing research, first in the Dahlen Institute, then in a warehouse owned by a Stuttgart brewery in the foothills of the Swabian Alps, and finally in a great cave hollowed out of a rock near Tübingen. In February 1945, Heisenberg and his team had begun to construct a large pile—rather like the Americans' pile in the squash court under Stagg Field. The American military commander of Alsos sent a unit of rangers to destroy the German apparatus, to recover precious cubes of uranium that the Germans were trying to smuggle out in a load of hay on an ox cart, and to capture the German physicists.

From then on, officers and physicists who had worked on the Manhattan Project were divided between those who wanted to use the bomb and those who did not. Some of those who simply wanted the United States to share its knowledge urged Niels Bohr to try and persuade FDR and then Churchill of their point of view. Although well-meaning, Bohr was verbose and simply confused both leaders. Bohr wrote to FDR how "the fact of immediate preponderance is . . . that a weapon of unparalleled power is being created which will completely change all future conditions of warfare. . . . Any temporary advantage, however great, may be outweighed by a perpetual menace to human security."

In Washington, D.C., in April 1945, another letter from Albert Einstein awaited the president. Alongside it was a memorandum from the American physicist Leo Szilard. They earnestly advised the president to have all work on the atomic bomb suspended. They argued how a changing world situation had made the bomb militarily unnecessary and politically damaging. They explained how any strategic advantage the United States would gain from its use would be offset by political losses and psychological damage to American prestige. Moreover, the use of a nuclear bomb might encourage a nuclear armaments race.

To confront Hitler, who was supposed to have been working toward an atomic bomb, with an American bomb was one thing; but to use it against Japan was something else. Japan was not advanced in physics or technology. Thus, because the Japanese could not build such weapons, ran the argument, it was unthinkable to use an atomic bomb against them. There were no precedents for the mix of politics and physics that this huge but intricate subject required. Clearly a major war did not provide the right sort of environment for a disinterested display of scientific statesmanship. This was especially so in a war that America had finally entered following a devastating attack by air.

Another envoy of the scientists who favored nuclear research for peaceful purposes was Alexander Sachs, who was also a friend of Roosevelt's. He discussed the subject with FDR at the White House in December 1944 and, after the president's death, said that Roosevelt agreed that any successful atomic test should be followed by a second to be attended by Allied and neutral scientists. They then should circulate a detailed report on the atomic bomb and the implications of using it to other scientists. Finally, the Allies should persuade the enemy to evacuate a specified territory and be given a demonstration of the bomb's power. After the demonstration, the enemy should be given

The Japanese surrender party arrives on the USS *Missouri* to sign the official documents, marking the formal end to World War II. (Library of Congress).

an ultimatum to surrender or face untold devastation. Of course, the Roosevelt-Sachs interview was not attended by any other witnesses. Moreover, FDR did not mention it to Stimson, his secretary of war. In fact, FDR was good at giving all his guests the impression that he agreed with their advice. We also know that he rarely made up his mind until he had to. Stimson recorded the last conversation on the Manhattan Project he had with FDR in his diary entry of March 15, 1945: "I went over with him the two schools of thought that exist in respect to the future control after the war of this project, in case it is useful, one of them being the secret close-in attempted control of the project by those who control it now, and the other being international control based upon freedom of science. I told him that those things must be settled before the project is used and that he must be ready with a statement to come out to the people on it just as soon as that is done. He agreed to that."

The first test of an atomic bomb was carried out at Almagordo in the New Mexico desert at 5:30 A.M. on July 16, 1945. The steel tower on which the bomb had been placed was vaporized. The blast knocked down men standing 10,000 yards away; and, for the first time, the mushroom cloud rose, carrying the dust of the earth that it was to make radioactive.

When Truman heard of the successful test he was at the Potsdam conference. Here it seemed was a bargaining counter he could use in dealing with Stalin, whom he now accused of reneging on the Yalta agreements, in particular about the governments in Rumania and Bulgaria. Truman wanted free elections in these Balkan states, which were to be organized by provisional governments composed of "representatives of all significant democratic elements."

In the Franck Report of June 11, 1945, scientists warned the federal government that the West did not have a monopoly on the atomic bomb. The materials were available across the world, and the basic scientific facts were widely known. The Franck Report warned that a nuclear arms race would develop if the bomb were used. Thus, it proposed that the bomb should be used in a demonstration to ally and enemy alike. "If the United States were to be the first to release this new weapon of indiscriminate destruction upon mankind, she would sacrifice public support throughout the world, precipitate the race for armaments, and prejudice the possibility of reaching an international agreement on the future control of such weapons." At about the same time, a report for the federal government argued against a public demonstration on the grounds that it would be impractical and might prolong, rather than shorten, the war. Instead, it report recommended that the bomb be dropped on a dual target, a military installation or industrial plant near houses. It seemed that of all American statesmen, only Secretary of War Stimson was trying to grasp what the scientists were saying.

The decision to drop the atomic bomb on Japan was perhaps the most controversial military and political decision of the twentieth century. Truman stated most forcefully that the bomb was dropped in order to save the lives of American soldiers, who otherwise would have had to invade the home islands. Nevertheless, military leaders did challenge such assumptions. Thus Eisenhower, informed at Potsdam about the dropping of the bomb expressed his misgivings, "first on the basis of my belief that Japan was already defeated and that dropping the bomb was entirely unnecessary, and secondly because I thought that our country should avoid shocking world opinion by the use of a weapon whose employment was, I thought, no longer mandatory as a measure to save American lives."

MacArthur frequently said that the dropping of the bomb was militarily unnecessary. Although he was commander in the Pacific, he was not consulted about it but simply informed shortly before its use. Other military leaders, such as Admirals Leahy and King and Air Force Generals Arnold and LeMay, also considered its use unnecessary. Even the Joint Chiefs of Staff thought that Japan could be reduced to unconditional surrender without the use of the bomb and without invasion.

With the passing of time, many historians have concluded that the bomb was used as much for political reasons and because it had been made as it was for military reasons. At the United States Atomic Energy Commission Oppenheimer Hearings, Vannevar Bush stated that the bomb "was also delivered on time, so that there was no necessity for any concessions to Russia at the end of the war." Secretary of State James F. Byrnes (1945–47) never denied a statement attributed to him that the bomb had been used to demonstrate American power to the Soviet Union in order to make it more manageable in Europe.

The Japanese were staggered by the devastation of the first atomic bomb dropped on Hiroshima on August 6; the formal entry of Russia into the war against them on the previously agreed date of August 8; and a second atomic bomb dropped on Nagasaki on August 9.

The official American report noted of the first bomb dropped on Hiroshima that "what had been a city going about its business on a sunny morning went up in a mountain of dust-filled smoke, black at the base and towering into a plume of white to 40,000 feet." The bomb had more power than 20,000 tons of TNT. When it was dropped, the explosion was so great that it was forty-eight hours before photographs of the devastation could be taken from the air. Then it became clear that four of the seven square miles of Hiroshima had been obliterated. Of the 90,000 buildings in the city, 65,000 had either collapsed or been badly damaged. Official estimates of the number of people killed was 100,000 or more. Later statistics of February 2, 1946, declared that 78,150 people had been killed, and another 13,983 were missing. (This was fewer than the 83,000 victims claimed by the fire raids on

Tokyo of March 9 and 10, 1945.) The explosion produced a ground temperature of 3,000° C (5,400° F), causing intense and widespread thermal radiation that killed people three-quarters of a mile away. About 60 percent of the deaths were due to heat flash and fire burns. Thus, over 50,000 of the people who had died had been burned to death.

The second atomic bomb dropped on Nagasaki, the port and armaments center on the west coast of Kyushu, at noon on August 9, resulted in a black cloud that rose ten miles into the air and could be seen 250 miles away. Unlike Hiroshima, Nagasaki lay in a series of ridges and valleys; thus, parts of the city escaped destruction. Nevertheless, one-third of the city was obliterated. There were fewer casualties. In its 1950 report on the effects of atomic weapons, the Los Alamos Scientific Laboratory emphasized that in Tokyo the mortality rate per square mile of city destroyed by high-explosive bombing was 5,200 per square mile. In Nagasaki, it was 20,000 per square mile and in Hiroshima 15,000 per square mile.

This was not simply another new development in military technology. It was a revelation of man's power and propensity to destroy himself. Truman used triumphant imagery: "The force from which the sun draws its power has been loosed against those who brought war to the Far East." A British prisoner of war in Nagasaki told a BBC correspondent, "I cannot make you understand how bright that flash was. . . . It went through you first like the shock you get from an electric battery. . . . It was terribly hot as well—just like solid heat coming at you. It was like the sunlight coming from half a dozen suns instead of one." Man had found the light—a light so bright that the shadows remained etched on the pavements of Hiroshima long after the bodies that cast them had been blasted out of existence. A writer in the *New York Herald Tribune* of 7 August 1945 described the force as "weird, incredible and somehow disturbing; one forgets the effect on Japan or on the course of the war as one senses the foundations of one's own universe trembling."

The mood of the American public bordered on febrile hysteria as people pondered the effect the bomb would have on the course of the war. Truman's behavior aboard the *Augusta* reflected the public mood. His famous declaration was delivered with deep satisfaction: "This is the greatest thing in history." In Japan, the calamities gave the prime minister, Shigemitsu Mamoru, the foreign minister, Togo, and the doves in the cabinet the opportunity to persuade the emperor first to overrule the war ministers and military leaders and then to insist on surrender. It is possible that it was neither the atomic bomb nor Russia's entry that determined the decision to surrender, but rather the submarine blockade of the Japanese Islands, which had prevented the exploitation of Japan's newly won colonies and had led to the sinking of merchant ships. This was the way Japan's leaders looked at the hopeless situation. As for the people, it was the earlier, devastating bombing that had made them fully aware that defeat was imminent. Destruction of the navy and air force had jeopardized the security of the home islands. However, Japan's principal armies never had been defeated. Therefore, army commanders wanted to continue the struggle. Yet Japan's cities were destroyed; its resources were extinct; its government was bankrupt of respect. The atmosphere—political as well as military—was pregnant with people's desire for change. The message of unconditional surrender was passed to the Allies on August 14, 1945, through Japanese ministers in Sweden and Switzerland. It is clear that without the intervention of the emperor, the military leaders would have remained determined to continue the senseless struggle whatever the odds. In all, Japan's war dead amounted to 2.5 million, whereas about 10 million soldiers and civilians died at Japanese hands in the Co-Prosperity Sphere.

The formal surrender of Japan took place aboard the battleship *Missouri* on September 2, 1945, when the prime minister signed the document, along with MacArthur and various representatives of Britain, the Soviet Union, France, China, the Netherlands, Australia, New Zealand, and Canada. This was V-J Day (Victory over Japan). World War II was at an end.

Whereas the city of Nuremberg has become synonymous with the international trial of criminal Nazis, its complementary trial in Tokyo, while no less sensational and far longer and more elaborate, received far less press scrutiny at the time and later. Journalist Arnold C. Brackman, who covered the trial for the United Press, is among the few historians to redress this neglect. His *The Other Nuremberg* (1987), published posthumously, is the first complete account of the trial from first day to last.

There were, altogether, 28 "Class-A" defendants, of whom the most notorious was Japan's wartime prime minister, Tojo Hideki, 11 judges

Japanese prisoners of war on the island of Guam hear the broadcast news of the Japanese surrender in mortified silence. (Library of Congress).

from as many countries led by Sir William Webb of Australia as chief judge, 419 witnesses, and 779 affidavits. Thus the trial that ran from June 3, 1946, to November 12, 1948, was probably the most complex major proceeding in all legal history. The case for the prosecution, led by an American attorney, produced irrefutable proof of Japanese conspiracy to wage war, first on China and then on the United States and its allies. The methods of war included not only armed aggression but the wanton torture, rape, and murder of thousands of defenseless civilians and prisoners of war. While the defendants were undoubtedly guilty, the conduct of the trial showed they were assumed to be so from the start. Here the behind-the-scenes influence of the supreme Allied commander, General Douglas MacArthur, was decisive.

Tojo and Generals Seishiro Itagaki, Kenji Doihara, Heitaro Kimura, Iwane Matsui, and Akira Muto were all sentenced to death and hanged in Tokyo on December 23, 1948. Admiral Shigetaro Shimada and army chief of staff Yoshijiro Umezu and 14 others were given life sentences. Former foreign ministers Togo Shigenori and Shigemitsu Mamoru were given prison sentences. By October 1949, 4,200 Japanese had been convicted; 720 of them were executed.

The question of how far the emperor, Hirohito, was also responsible for Japanese war crimes remains unanswered. Hirohito (Michinomiya Hirohito) (1901–89), emperor of Japan (1926–89) and supposedly a direct descendant of Japan's first emperor of legend, Jimmu, was, supposedly, absolute ruler of Japan until 1945. His reign was designated *Showa* (bright peace), and in his early years he ratified policies formulated by his various ministers. Subsequently, Japan became a totalitarian state dominated by the emperor. Until 1945 he was not only head of state but also was regarded among his people as divine. He personally ordered the Japanese surrender after Hiroshima and Nagasaki had been devastated by atomic bombs. However, his exact role in the increasing drift to brutalism in the Japanese state after his accession in 1926, most particularly the political swing to totalitarianism and the military conquests of the 1930s and 1940s, has remained obscure. "Was he," asks historian Gaddis Smith (1987), "merely a symbolic presence with no more political power or responsibility than a statue in a shrine? . . . Or was he the hidden intellectual and political force behind a grandiose, immoral scheme of conquest?" During the war Hirohito seemed as evil to the American people as Hitler. Thereafter, the Allies debated his future. Should Hirohito be put on trial and the imperial monarchy brought to an end? Or should he be transformed into a constitutional monarch, who would represent a stabilizing force and, perhaps, help prevent destabilization, anarchy, and the rise of communism in Japan? This was the argument of Britain's foreign secretary, Ernest Bevin, who reminded his colleagues at home and abroad of a historical parallel: by driving the German kaiser, Wilhelm II, into exile in 1918 and by even threatening him with trial and execution, Woodrow Wilson and the Allies had summarily deprived Germany of the political option of constitutional monarchy, unintentionally paving the way for the rise of Hitler and the Nazis. Bevin's analogy was convincing. The emperor was divested of direct political power and all pretence of divinity. However, he was spared indictment and trial and from being forced to give evidence against others. Although much of the testimony at the Tokyo war-crimes trial pointed to the emperor, such leads were

German refugees, displaced by the turmoil of the war, await decisions on their future movements in Berlin's Anhalter Station after the end of the war. (Library of Congress).

never pursued. It seemed, concludes Gaddis Smith, that "the prospect of trying and convicting the embodiment of the Japanese nation was psychologically and politically too disruptive to contemplate."

Nevertheless, the general credit given to the emperor for ending the disastrous war by insisting upon the surrender of Japan after the dropping of the two atomic bombs suggests he, too, must share in the blame for starting the war and gives the lie to the postwar historical resuscitation of the emperor, implying he was the unwilling victim of militarists who had usurped power. Throughout the war he signed all war orders and directed several key campaigns. Some continued to believe in the emperor's culpability including the Japanese Communist party, committed to the abolition of the monarchy, who continued to declare his responsibility. Historian Professors Jiro Yamaguchi and Naoko Sakai wrote to the *New York Times* in 1988, "It is clear from the recorded accounts of his entourage and other published sources that Emperor Hirohito positively supported the activities of the military's adventurism from 1930 on. It would be logically absurd if he could end the war yet could not have decided against starting war in the first place."

Amid the revival of the controversy of the emperor's putative war guilt following his death in January 1989 some commentators detected a feeling of relief in Japan. Freed at last from the stigma of its defeat by the death of the last of the leaders of World War II, Japan, the world's second economic power, would now have the chance to move to the fore of the world's political stage. Hirohito had been enthroned under the 1889 Meiji Constitution that awarded "sacred and inviolable" sovereign powers to the emperor. The postwar Constitution of May 3, 1947, eliminated his supremacy and awarded him only the status of a constitutional monarch. Conservative author Hideaki Kase said in the late 1980s, "A majority of our people believe the emperor is sacred and divine, not in the Christian or pagan sense of the word, but in hogyo (reverential) sense."

The Cost

American fighting in World War II had lasted three years and eight months. During the war, the armed forces of the United States suffered approximately one million casualties, including 600,000 wounded, 250,000 dead, and 60,000 missing. Altogether, 75,000 servicemen were taken prisoners of war. Of the 250,000 dead, 200,000 were buried on foreign soil (122,000 in northwest Europe; 41,000 on the Mediterranean coasts; 29,000 in the southwest Pacific; and 11,000 on the Pacific islands). The Russians lost between 6 and 7 million soldiers and between 10 and 12 million civilians. The Germans lost over 3 million soldiers, sailors, and pilots; the Japanese some 1.2 million. Many now wondered if another war might not mean the end of mankind.

The total monetary cost of the war (excluding interest on loans given to government, pensions, and postwar aid programs) was, approximately, $350 billion—that is, ten times the cost of World War I. About 40 percent of this cost was met by taxation; the rest was borrowed. The

United States Treasury went into the red by $40 billion annually, borrowing freely from banks at between 1 and 1.5 percent interest. By the end of hostilities, the national debt amounted to $250 billion. Federal spending during the years of combat exceeded the United States's combined budgets for the years 1789 through 1940. The American gross national product had increased from $90 billion in 1940 to $213 billion by the end of the war.

The Onset of the Cold War

The elimination of Germany and Japan as first-class military and economic powers in 1945 shifted the political balance of the world just as surely as did the widespread devastation of World War II. Only four powers could now truly claim the status of first-class powers. Of these, China could make only a tentative claim. Despite its huge population and considerable industrial and agricultural potential, the disruption of war and the continuing and adverse legacy of the Japanese invasion and the civil war between Nationalists and Communists were still crippling the sleeping giant. The decline of Britain as an empire, an industrial power, and a commercial center was well advanced. Nevertheless, Britain's reputation as the sole European power to withstand Hitler in the crucial months during 1940 and 1941 had done much to enhance its prestige as a bastion of democracy, despite its truculent resistance to national movements for independence in its various colonies in Africa and Asia.

Of the other two great powers, the United States was the stronger. World War II had made it richer than ever, partly because of its greatly expanded industry and agriculture, partly because of its favorable position as a creditor nation, and partly because of the general devastation across the world that the United States had been spared. Its territory was inviolate. Unlike the other protagonists in the war, the United States had lost approximately one million servicemen. Moreover, it alone possessed atomic weapons.

As to the Soviet Union, by entering the war against Japan after the defeat of Hitler, it had been able to recover the territorial position in the Far East it had held before the disastrous Russo-Japanese War of 1904–5. However, Russia's principal gains were in central and eastern

Europe, where it had not only broken Germany's shattered grasp but had also consolidated and advanced its frontiers. Nevertheless, the Soviet Union itself had lost about 18 million people in the war, servicemen and civilians alike. It had also suffered considerable material damage.

Among the countries of western Europe, France and Italy were somewhat vulnerable to communism, having large, well-organized Communist parties. Nevertheless, the countries of eastern Europe had no considerable radical tradition. With the exception of Czechoslovakia, their governments before 1939 as well as during the war itself were essentially fascist in complexion. The first oratorical shot in the Cold War was delivered by Winston Churchill, former British prime minister, in a speech at Fulton, Missouri, on March 5, 1946—a speech that was delivered in the presence of President Harry S. Truman, who was also a speaker on the platform.

Churchill used Goebbel's earlier phrase about the "iron curtain" to describe the way Soviet influence had descended "from Stettin in the Baltic to Trieste in the Adriatic." Thus Europe was in a state of armed truce. "There is nothing they admire so much as strength," observed Churchill of the Russians, "and there is nothing for which they have less respect than weakness." Churchill's criticisms of Soviet foreign policy were poorly received in America, and the odium attached itself to Truman. In fact, Churchill was ahead of his time. The upheaval of the Cold War occurred over a brief period—thirteen months in 1945–46—after which public opinion in the United States and Western Europe came to accept renewed mutual hostility between the superpowers as inevitable.

As far as the Cold War is concerned, the later 1940s can be divided into two periods: a transitional period in 1945–47 and an intense period of hostility from 1947 to 1949. Thereafter, in the 1950s, the focus of attention shifted somewhat to Asia, notably to Korea and Indochina; to the Middle East, especially Israel, Egypt, and Iran; and to technological competition in the space race.

The transitional period of 1945–47 was largely determined by four distinct features of Russian policy: First, Russia rolled its western frontiers farther into northern and central Europe—even farther than in the early period of 1939–41 when Russia was Hitler's nominal ally and had acquired certain sections of Finland in the Russo-Finnish War of

1939–40. The process of acquiring additional territory for the Soviet Union added an additional 21 million people to the population.

Second, the Soviet Union showed its determination to achieve complete security on its western frontiers by taking control in several countries of central and eastern Europe—countries with an aggregate population of about 100 million people. These satellite countries were to act as buffers against a third invasion from western Europe that might follow the paths trodden by the armies of Napoleon and Hitler. Not only had such countries as Poland and Hungary been easy victims for Hitler, but they had also tried (as had Russia) to act as his greedy, if junior, accomplices in the 1930s. Given the political complexion of their governments, they could be relied upon to support only ultraconservative foreign policies utterly hostile to the Soviet Union.

The method by which the Soviet Union acquired its European satellites was sometimes known as "progressive communization," or more accurately, piecemeal communization, popularly known as "salami tactics"—that is, the successive pairing away of eastern European countries in a series of not-so-thin slices. This was much the same as Hitler's strategy of conquest in the 1930s in the reverse direction. By the end of 1945, Rumania, Bulgaria, Yugoslavia, and Albania had, with Soviet assistance, acquired Communist governments; by the end of 1947, Poland and Hungary also had done so. The only exception in central Europe was Czechoslovakia.

A third feature of Soviet policy was the exaction of maximum reparations from Germany to compensate for the considerable devastation of the war. Fourth, there was a return to what we might call orthodox, or traditional, communism within the Soviet Union. Thus, instead of government propaganda about cooperation with the West against the threat of fascism, the Soviet Union harped back to the old doctrine of capitalist encirclement. Moreover, the government returned to its discredited prewar policies of five-year economic plans to reconstruct the country's agriculture, industry, and general military might. In consequence, virtually all contacts with the West were severed—except the bare necessities of diplomatic relations. Of all the shifts in policy, this proved the most disturbing to Western hopes that the wartime spirit of cooperation would continue in peacetime.

American policy in the same initial phase of the Cold War had two principal features. First, there was a profound desire to return to peace-

Waiting in the wings. War heroes Churchill and Eisenhower arrive in London at Victoria Station in December 1946. Churchill would return to power as prime minister (1951–55), and Eisenhower would become the thirty-fourth president (1953–61). (Library of Congress).

time normality as soon as possible. At Yalta, Roosevelt had observed that he did not think he could maintain American troops in Europe for more than two years from the end of the war. Although this was not an entirely accurate prediction, demobilization was somewhat precipitate. In June 1945, for example, there were 12.1 million Americans in the services. A year later, the number was 3 million; and in June 1947, the number was only 1.6 million. There was a widespread American belief that it would be possible to return to some kind of normality although the three decades preceding World War II had witnessed successive waves of abnormal economics—preparedness and prosperity in World War I, the tawdry affluence and social dislocation of the 1920s, and the treacherous waters of the Great Depression in between. Another generally held belief concerned the need to sign peace treaties. Indeed, treaties were signed with the minor allies of Germany—Italy, Hungary, Bulgaria, and Rumania—but never with Germany itself.

The second feature of American policy was the establishment of a mechanism to preserve peace, of which the principal expression was the United Nations. The United States mistakenly believed that the United Nations would continue and preserve the Grand Alliance. However, the United Nations was riven with bitter disagreements. The Soviet Union made repeated, ugly use of its veto on the Security Council to block decisive actions. Tensions between the superpowers charged the atmosphere of conferences in Moscow in 1945 and Paris in 1946. The universal jubilation at the end of World War II was being transformed into febrile suspicion as the world—East and West, capitalist and Communist—moved inexorably into the Cold War.

BIBLIOGRAPHY

Acheson, Dean. *Present at the Creation: My Years in the State Department*. New York, 1969.

Adamic, Louis. *A Nation of Nations*. New York, 1945.

Adler, Jacques. *The Jews of Paris and the Final Solution*. New York, 1987.

Alperovitz, Gar. *Atomic Diplomacy: Hiroshima and Potsdam, The Use of the Atomic Bomb and the American Confrontation with Soviet Power*. New York, 1965. Rev. ed. 1985.

Ambrose, Stephen E. *Eisenhower*. Vol. 1, *Soldier, General of the Army, President-Elect 1890–1952*. New York, 1983.

———. *Rise to Globalism: American Foreign Policy Since 1938*. London, 1971.

———. *The Supreme Commander: The War Years of Dwight D. Eisenhower*. Garden City, N.Y., 1970.

Andesser, K. T. "Last Hired, First Fired: Black Women Workers During World War II." *Journal of American History* 69 (1982): 82–97.

Archibald, Katherine. *Wartime Shipyard: A Study in Social Disunity*. Berkeley, 1947.

Asbell, Bernard. *When FDR Died*. New York, 1961.

Biddle, Francis. *In Brief Authority*. Garden City, N.Y., 1962.

Blum, John M. *V Was for Victory: Politics and American Culture During World War II*. New York, 1976.

Brackman, Arnold C. *The Other Nuremberg. The Untold Story of the Tokyo War Crimes*. New York, 1987.

Brogan, Dennis. *The American Character*. New York, 1944.

Brown, Francis, and Joseph S. Roucek. *One America: The History, Contributions, and Present Problems of Our Racial and National Minorities*. New York, 1945.

Buchanan, A. Russell. *Black Americans in World War II*. Santa Barbara, Calif., 1977.

Bundy, McGeorge. *Danger and Survival: Choices About the Bomb in the First Fifty Years*. New York, 1988.

Burns, James MacGregor. *Roosevelt, Soldier of Freedom*. New York, 1970.

Cable, John L. *Loss of Citizenship: Denaturalization; The Alien in Wartime*. Washington, D.C., 1943.

Cargas, Harry J. *The Holocaust: An Annotated Bibliography*. Chicago, 1985.

Carr, E. H. *A History of Soviet Russia*. New York, 1950.

———. *The Soviet Impact on the Western World*. New York, 1947.

Carr, Lowell J., and James E. Stermer. *Willow Run: A Study of Industrialization and Cultural Inadequacy*. New York, 1952.

Cashman, Sean Dennis. *America in the Twenties and Thirties: The Olympian Age of Franklin Delano Roosevelt*. New York and London, 1989.

Clinard, Marshall B. *The Black Market: A Study of White Collar Crime*. New York, 1952.

Cohen, Warren I. *The American Revisionists: The Lessons of Intervention in World War I*. Chicago, 1967.

Cole, Wayne S. "American Entry in World War II: A Historiographical Appraisal." *Mississippi Valley Historical Review* 43 (March 1957): 575–617.

———. *Roosevelt and the Isolationists, 1932–1945*. Lincoln, Neb., 1983.

Conn, Stetson. *Guarding the United States and Its Outposts*. Washington, 1964.

Dallek, Robert. *Franklin D. Roosevelt and American Foreign Policy, 1932–1945*. New York and Oxford, 1979.

Dalfiume, Richard M. "The Forgotten Years of the Negro Revolution." *Journal of American History* 55 (1968): 90–106.

Daniels, Roger. *Concentration Camps USA: Japanese and World War II*. New York, 1971.

de Bedts, Ralph F. *Recent American History*. Vol. 1, *1933 Through World War II*. Homewood, Ill., London and Georgetown, Ontario, 1973.

D'Este, Carlo. *Bitter Victory: The Battle for Sicily, 1943*. New York, 1988.

Diamond, Sander A. *The Nazi Movement in the United States, 1924–1941*. Ithaca, N.Y., 1974.

Dinnerstein, Leonard. *America and the Survivors of the Holocaust*. New York, 1982.

Divine, Robert A. *The Illusion of Neutrality*. Chicago, 1962.

———. *The Reluctant Belligerent: American Entry into World War II*. New York, 1976.

———. *Roosevelt and World War II*. Baltimore, 1969.

Edey, Maitland A., ed. *This Fabulous Century: Sixty Years of American Life*. vol. 5, *1940–1950*. New York, 1969.

Ellis, John. *The Social History of the Machine-Gun*. New York, 1975.

Fehrenbach, T. R. *F.D.R.'s Undeclared War, 1939–1941*. New York, 1967.

Feis, Herbert. *Churchill, Roosevelt, Stalin: The War They Waged and the Peace They Sought*. Princeton, 1957; 1967.

Fine, Sidney. "Mr. Justice Murphy and the Hirabayashi Case." *Pacific Historical Review* 33 (May 1964): 195–209.

Finkle, Lee. "The Conservative Aims of Militant Rhetoric: Black Protest During World War II." *Journal of American History* 60 (1973): 692–713.

Flynn, George Q. *The Mess in Washington: Manpower Mobilization in World War II.* Westport, Conn., 1979.

Foner, Philip S. *American Socialism and Black Americans.* Westport, Conn., 1977.

Gilbert, Martin. *The Holocaust: A History of the Jews in Europe During the Second World War.* New York, 1985.

Girdner, Audrie, and Anne Loftis. *The Great Betrayal: The Evacuation of the Japanese-Americans During World War II.* New York, 1969.

Gluck, Sherna Berger. *Rosie the Riveter Revisited: Women, the War, and Social Change.* Boston, 1987.

Green, James R. *The World of the Worker: Labor in Twentieth Century America.* New York, 1980.

Greenfield, Kent Robert. *American Strategy in World War II: A Reconsideration.* Baltimore, 1963; Westport, Conn., 1979.

Grodzius, Martin. *Americans Betrayed: Policies and the Japanese Evacuation.* Chicago, 1949.

Gunther, John. *Roosevelt in Retrospect: A Profile in History.* New York, 1950.

Harris, Seymour E. *Price and Related Controls in the United States.* New York, 1945.

Hart, B. H. Liddell, *History of the Second World War.* New York and London, 1971.

Havighurst, Robert J., and H. Gerthon Morgan. *The Social History of a War-Boom Community.* New York, 1951.

Hilberg, Raul. *The Destruction of the European Jews.* Chicago, 1961; New York, 1985.

Holbrook, David. *Flesh Wounds.* London, 1987.

Hosokawa, Bill. *Nisei: The Quiet Americans.* New York, 1969.

Irons, Peter H. "The Test is Poland: Polish Americans and the Origins of the Cold War." *Polish American Studies* 30 (Autumn 1973).

Isaacs, Harold R. *Scratches on Our Minds: American Images of China and India.* New York, 1958.

Keegan, John. *Six Armies in Normandy: From D-Day to the Liberation of Paris.* New York, 1944.

———, ed. *The Rand McNally Encyclopedia of World War II.* Chicago, 1977.

Kimball, Warren F. *Franklin D. Roosevelt and the World Crisis 1937–45.* Lexington, Mass., 1974.

———. *The Most Unsordid Act: Lend-Lease 1939–1941.* Baltimore, 1969.

———, ed. *Churchill and Roosevelt, the Complete Correspondence.* 3 vols. Princeton, 1984.

Kitano, Harry H. L. *Japanese Americans: The Evolution of a Subculture.* Englewood Cliffs, N.J., 1969; 1976.

Kolko, Gabriel. *The Politics of War: The World and United States Foreign Policy, 1943–45.* New York, 1968.

Koppes, Clayton R., and Gregory D. Black. *Hollywood Goes to War: How Politics, Profits, and Propaganda Shaped World War II Movies.* New York, 1987.

———. "What to Show the World: The Office of War Information and Hollywood, 1942–45." *Journal of American History* 64 (June 1977): 87–105.

Korvitz, Milton. *The Alien and the Asiatic in American Law.* Ithaca, N.Y., 1950.

Lamb, Richard. *Montgomery in Europe, 1943–45: Success or Failure?* New York, 1984.

Larabee, Eric. *Commander in Chief: Franklin Delano Roosevelt, His Lieutenants, and Their War.* New York, 1987.

Lash, Joseph P., ed. *From the Diaries of Felix Frankfurter.* New York, 1975.

Leopold, Richard W. *The Growth of American Foreign Policy.* New York, 1962.

Levin, Nora. *The Holocaust: The Destruction of European Jewry 1933–1945.* New York, 1968.

Lichtenstein, Nelson. *Labor's War at Home: The CIO in World War II.* Cambridge and New York, 1982.

Lippmann, Walter. *U.S. Foreign Policy: Shield of the Republic.* Boston, 1943.

Lipstadt, Deborah E. *Beyond Belief: The American Press and the Coming of the Holocaust, 1933–1945.* New York, 1985.

McGuire, Philip. *Taps for a Jim Crow Army: Letters from Black Soldiers in World War II.* Santa Barbara, Calif., 1983.

Manchester, William. *American Caesar: Douglas MacArthur, 1880–1964.* New York, 1978.

———. *The Glory and the Dream: A Narrative History of America, 1932–1972.* Boston, 1973; London, 1975.

———. *Goodbye Darkness: A Memoir of the Pacific.* Boston, 1980.

Mansfield, Harvey C. *A Short History of OPA.* Washington, D.C., 1948.

Mason, Alpheus T. *Harlan Fiske Stone: Pillar of the Law.* New York, 1956.

Medoff, Rafael. *The Deafening Silence: American Jewish Leaders and the Holocaust 1933–1945.* New York, 1986.

Merton, Robert K. *Mass Persuasion: The Social Psychology of a War Bond Drive.* New York and London, 1946.

Millis, Walter. *The Road to War.* Boston, Mass., 1935.

Montgomery, Brian. *A Field-Marshall in the Family.* London, 1987.

Mumford, Lewis. *Faith for Living.* New York, 1940.

Nomberg-Przytyk, Sara. *Auschwitz.* New York, 1985.

Perrett, Geoffrey. *Days of Sadness, Years of Triumph: The American People 1939–1945.* New York, 1973.

Pogue, Forrest C. *George C. Marshall.* Vol. 3, *Organizer of Victory: 1943–1945.* New York, 1973.

Polenberg, Richard. *One Nation Divisible: Class, Race, and Ethnicity in the United States Since 1938.* Harmondsworth, Middlesex, and New York, 1980.

———. *War and Society: The United States, 1941–1945.* New York, 1972.

Prange, Gordon W. *At Dawn We Slept: The Untold Story of Pearl Harbor.* New York, 1981.

Pratt, Julius W. *Cordell Hull.* Totowa, N.J., 1964.

Puttkammer, Ernest W., ed. *War and the Law.* Chicago, 1944.

Pyle, Ernie. *Brave Men.* New York, 1944.

———. *Here Is Your War.* New York, 1943.

Rauch, Basil. *Roosevelt: From Munich to Pearl Harbor.* New York, 1950.

Rhode, Eric. *History of the Cinema: From Its Origins to 1970.* New York, 1985.

Riggs, Fred W. *Pressure on Congress*. New York, 1950.

Roucek, Joseph S. "Foreign Language Press in World War II." *Sociology and Social Research* 27 (July–August 1943).

Ruchames, Louis. *Race, Jobs and Politics: The Story of FEPC*. Chapel Hill, N.C., 1948; New York, 1953.

Sampson, Anthony. *Empires of the Sky: The Politics, Contests, and Cartels of World Airlines*. London and New York, 1985.

———. *The Seven Sisters: The Great Oil Companies and the World They Shaped*. New York and London, 1976.

Sherwood, Robert E. *Roosevelt and Hopkins: An Intimate History*. New York, 1948.

Shryock, Jr., Henry S. "Redistribution of Population, 1940–1950." *Journal of the American Statistical Association* 46 (December 1951).

———. "Wartime Shifts of the Civilian Population." *Milbank Memorial Fund Quarterly* 25 (July 1947).

Seton Watson, Christopher. "The Cold War: Its Origins." In *Since 1945: Aspects of Contemporary America*, edited by James L. Henderson. London, 1966.

Sitkoff, Harvard. "Racial Militancy and Interracial Violence in the Second World War." *Journal of American History* 58 (1971): 661–68.

Smith, Gaddis. *American Diplomacy During the Second World War, 1941–1945*. New York, 1965.

Smith, Jeanette Sayre. "Broadcasting for Marginal Americans." *Public Opinion Quarterly* 6 (Winter 1942).

Snell, John L. *Illusion and Necessity: The Diplomacy of Global War*. Boston, 1963.

Snowman, Daniel. *America Since 1920*. London, 1968. Rev. ed. 1978.

Spengler, Oswald. *The Decline of the West*. Translated by Charles Francis Adams. 2 vols. New York, 1926–28.

Sperber, A. M. *Murrow*. New York, 1986.

Steel, Ronald. *Walter Lippmann and the American Century*. New York, 1980.

Strong, Samuel M. "Observations on the Possibility of Attitude Modification: A Case of Nationality and Racial Group Inter-Relationships in Wartime." *Social Forces* 3 (March 1944): 323–31.

Suhl, Yuri. *They Fought Back: The Story of Jewish Resistance in Nazi Europe*. New York, 1967.

Taylor, A. J. P. *English History, 1914–1945*. Oxford and New York, 1965.

Terraine, John. *A Time for Courage: The Royal Air Force in the European War, 1939–1945*. London and New York, 1985.

Thomas, Dorothy S. *The Salvage*. Berkeley, 1952.

Tucker, Robert C., and Stephen F. Cohen, eds. *The Great Purge Trial*. New York, 1965.

Warner, W. Lloyd. *Democracy in Jonesville*. New York, 1949. Rev. ed. 1964.

Willkie, Wendell. *One World*. New York, 1943.

Wiltz, John E. *From Isolation to War, 1931–1941*. Arlington Heights, Ill., 1968.

Winkler, Allan M. *The Politics of Propaganda: The Office of War Information, 1942–1945*. New Haven, 1978.

Wohlstetter, Roberta. *Pearl Harbor: Warning and Decision*. Stanford, 1962.

Wyman, David S. *The Abandonment of the Jews: America and the Holocaust, 1941–45.* New York, 1984.

Wynn, Neil A. *The Afro-American and the Second World War.* London, 1976.

———. "Black Attitudes Toward Participation in the American War Effort, 1941–1945." *Afro-American Studies* 3 (1972): 13–19.

INDEX